DIVESTING NATURE'S CAPITAL

DIVESTING NATURE'S CAPITAL

The Political Economy of Environmental
Abuse in the Third World

edited by
H. Jeffrey Leonard

HM

HOLMES & MEIER
New York   London

First published in the United States of America 1985 by
Holmes & Meier Publishers, Inc.
30 Irving Place
New York, N.Y. 10003
Great Britain:
Holmes & Meier Publishers, Ltd.
Unit 5   Greenwich Industrial Estate
345 Woolwich Road   Charlton, London SE7

Book design by Rachael Bickhardt

Library of Congress Cataloging in Publication Data
Main entry under title:

Divesting nature's capital.

   Includes bibliographical references.
   Contents: Resource limitations, environmental deterioration,
and economic progress / H. Jeffrey Leonard—Environment,
economic growth, and income distribution in the Third World /
Henry Bienen and H. Jeffrey Leonard—Political and economic
causes of the Third World environmental degradation /
H. Jeffrey Leonard—Rhetoric and reality / David Morell, with
Joanna Poznanski—[etc]
   1. Environmental policy—Developing countries—Addresses,
essays, lectures.   2. Developing countries—Economic
policy—Addresses, essays, lectures.   3. Conservation of
natural resources—Developing countries—Addresses, essays,
lectures.   I. Leonard, H. Jeffrey.
HC79.E5D58   1985   363.7'009172'4   83-18534
ISBN 0-8419-0897-4

Manufactured in the United States of America

CONTENTS

FOREWORD

Research for this study was supported by the Agency for International Development's Civic Participation Division, Bureau for Program and Policy Coordination under contract #OTR-G-1844.

We are very grateful for the interest and advice of Jonathan Silverstone, Gary Hansen, and Bert Printz of USAID.

At Princeton University, Gautham Dutt of the Center of Energy and Environmental Studies was a participant in our early discussions. The CEES also supported some of Jeffrey Leonard's work, and we are grateful for the help of the center and its director, Professor Robert Socolow.

The Woodrow Wilson School's Research Program in Development Studies provided a physical, intellectual, and administrative home for our work. We are happy to acknowledge our thanks to Dean Donald Stokes. The administrative staff of RPDS was invaluable to our work. Thanks go out to Jerri Kavanagh, Office Coordinator, and to Shirley Canty and Natalie Johnson. Michelle Krichten was extremely helpful in all our endeavors and we express our special appreciation to her.

My own personal thanks go to the editor and chief contributor, H. Jeffrey Leonard, who cheerfully took on a writing and coordinating task he did not anticipate.

Henry Bienen
William Stewart Tod Professor
of Politics and International Affairs
Princeton University

DIVESTING
NATURE'S CAPITAL

INTRODUCTION

H. Jeffrey Leonard

The possible limitations placed upon man's economic aspirations by the availability of the so-called renewable natural resources and the absorptive capacity of the natural environment have emerged as important issues for worldwide inquiry. Resource scarcities and environmental pollution have required far-reaching adaptations by governments, enterprises, and individuals in most parts of the world during the last two decades. Mounting concern about the pollution of air and water, particularly in the advanced industrial nations, prompted outcries from ordinary citizens and became a significant force shaping domestic political processes. The economics of public and private enterprise were substantially altered by increased demands that expenditures be made to reduce the amount of wastes released into the environment. Although fewer remedial actions have been initiated, attention has also been drawn to the possible long-term threats that man's activities may pose to the world's endowment of forests, agricultural land, fresh water and living species.

Our intention in this book is to examine how various natural resource and environmental constraints affect contemporary economic development strategies and prospects of the so-called developing nations in the world. We outline some of the key resource and environmental problems in the developing world and assess the possible implications these problems hold for long-term economic development. We also examine some of the responses being made in individual nations to such problems or, alternatively, some of the political-economic factors that make effective remedial actions very difficult in many countries.

Development specialists have paid considerable attention to the role that the exploitation of natural resources plays in economic development, but they have devoted much less attention to the relationship between long-term management of renewable natural resources and economic development. Generally, a country's endowment of soil, water, and trees has been taken as a given, just like its endowment of iron ore or crude oil. But renewable natural resources are not infinitely resilient. They can be destroyed or seriously depleted with resulting adverse effects for economic development, particularly in countries where the vast majority of people still depend directly on the land for their existence. Conversely, not enough emphasis has been placed on the positive role that man's managing and augmenting the resources he finds on (rather than beneath) the earth's surface have played in the development of the now advanced countries.

In the past several years, there has been increased international recognition of the possible long-term economic development implications associated with natural resource degradation in the third world. The OECD's 1979 report, *Interfutures: Facing the Future*, noted that needed increases in agricultural production in much of the world will depend on adequate soil conservation. However, the report said, "Loss of productive soil is one of the most pressing and difficult problems facing the future of mankind."[1]

Although it failed to elaborate or study these problems in any depth, the Brandt Commission's report at least acknowledged the seriousness of the problem, describing the "increasing threats to the environment and the international commons through deforestation and desertification, overfishing and overgrazing, the pollution of air and water."[2] As a consequence, the report noted, "A number of poor countries are threatened with the irreversible destruction of their ecological systems. . . . "[3]

Echoing the Brandt Commission, a special *Scientific American* issue on economic development also referred to what continued resource degradation could mean for the poorest people in the poorest countries of the world:

Slim margins hedge the bare subsistence of these 1.2 billion people from disaster. Their increasing numbers endanger the fragile tropical environments in which they live. They have cut down their forests. Lacking any water management infrastructure and so lacking adequate irrigation, they are afflicted alternately by flood and drought and suffer persistent loss of the long-term fertility of their soil to erosion and creeping deserts. . . . These countries have had to begin to face the grim possibility that their ecosystems may not be capable of feeding their people unless measures to reverse the deterioration are taken now.[4]

In fact, recent years have witnessed an outpouring of numerous other reports from the U.S. government, United Nations agencies, other international organizations, and private groups such as the Worldwatch Institute, all pointing out serious environmental problems in developing countries.[5]

Even such explicit descriptions of the problems, however, tend not to be articulated as an integral part of the overall economic development outlook for developing countries. On the whole, the international development community has not given priority to the concerns being raised about the environment in developing countries. It continues to view most natural resources and environmental quality issues as secondary to the primary mission of stimulating economic development and, in particular, as antithetical to the immediate needs and interests of the lowest-income countries and the poorest people in all countries.

The World Bank's annual *World Development Report*, for example, has never addressed problems of resource management or environmental pollution in any detail; nor does it include any natural resource or environmental data in its lengthy statistical annex of development indicators in 125 countries.[6] Certainly, there have been no comprehensive efforts by development experts to examine resource abuse and environmental degradation as among the most formidable hurdles for particular developing countries in their efforts to cope with their myriad economic problems and to achieve sustained economic development.

Yet, in many third world countries—and particularly in low-income countries—there are numerous examples of renewable resource mismanagement that may directly affect the ability of developing countries to satisfy their future economic development aspirations. Forests are being cut down far faster than they can be replaced, creating shortages of wood for construction and for cooking and heating. Deforestation also contributes to increased soil erosion and downstream problems with silt that builds up in river channels, in irrigation systems, and at the base of dams. Although in many cases forest land is being cleared for agricultural purposes, forest soils often lose their fertility after a very short period because they tend to be shallow and subject to hardening and the leaching of nutrients. In many arid countries, the pressures of wood gathering, backward farming techniques, and grazing of goats and other animals is contributing to desert incursions that only decrease further the productive capacity of marginal lands.

Although they are often considered to be problems that arise in tandem with rapid economic growth, serious industrial pollution problems, as well as urban congestion and squalor, are also evident where significant economic growth has not yet taken place or where it has not benefitted the masses. Most large third world cities have service delivery problems that are far worse than those of New York, London, or Tokyo. Water supplies, sewer systems, and solid waste disposal facilities, if they exist at all, are severely strained and erratic. New growth takes place in areas of natural hazards (e.g. floodplains or hillsides) and in patterns that increase congestion and further overload existing services. Serious air and water pollution also plagues many third world cities—pollution generated both by industrial facilities and numerous stationary and mobile sources associated with the industrial economy (automobiles, electricity generators, domestic heating sources, etc). In addition to causing serious diseconomies in urban areas, these pollution problems may impinge upon production outside of the urban sector, since pollution can ruin downstream fishing grounds, reduce crop yields in adjacent agricultural areas, or despoil profitable tourist attractions.

These are the primary problems which this volume seeks to study. In particular, our focus is on how, as a result of both development and underdevelopment, man-induced changes in the productive capacity of renewable natural resources (especially soil, water, and trees) as well as certain pollution problems, may have adverse effects on present and future prospects for economic development.

It is important to point out from the outset that we are not primarily concerned with evaluating the global implications and limitations of natural resource degradation and environmental pollution. Many recent studies have looked at the potential threats posed to mankind by, among other things: pollution (loss of ozone in the atmosphere, transfrontier pollutants, spoilation of global commons), and tropical forest loss (rise of carbon dioxide in the atmosphere, global climate change, melting of polar icecaps).[7] Without disregarding the potential implications of these predictions (and without making any effort to assess their likelihood), our focus is on how resource and environmental problems affect individual nation-states trying to achieve rapid and sustained economic development.

Although it may be true, as economist Kenneth Boulding has facetiously suggested, that economic development represents "the process by which the evil day is brought closer when everything will be gone,"[8] our perspective is one of decades and human generations, not the theoretical time when the earth's limits are reached. Hence, we also do not consider the implications of the entropy law that all resources, whether so-called renewable or non-renewable, are subject to gradual (if not rapid) diminishment.[9] These views may or may not prove to be true; our concern is not with such millenial questions about the fate of mankind or the limits inherent in the earth's total supply of resources.

For the purposes of this volume we assume, therefore, that with prudent use of non-renewable resources, proper management of renewable resources and precautionary measures to reduce "bottlenecks" created by environmental pollution, economic development sustainable in the long term is a viable goal for poor countries. We are concerned with the prospects for attaining such economic development and with how degradation of the land's productive capabilities and proliferation of pollution and congestion in strategic instances may have pernicious effects on these prospects if unattended by individual governments.

NATURAL RESOURCES AND ENVIRONMENT IN ECONOMIC DEVELOPMENT

In Section 1 the links between economic prosperity and environmental management are considered from both historical and contemporary perspectives. Chapter 1 emphasizes that natural resource and environmental restraints on economic progress are not unique to the late twentieth century. Large areas of the earth's surface, particularly around the rim of the Mediterranean basin and in the Middle East, were once fertile and forested lands but today bear the scars of past abuse at the hands of man. Great Britain and the Western European countries, spared from the deforestation and aridification that defaced much of the Mediterranean area in the Greek and Roman ages, themselves faced serious forest depletions during the early stages of the industrial revolution when wood fuel was used for heating, cooking, and as the primary source of industrial energy. Serious pollution problems were experienced in and around the great industrial cities of Europe that grew up with the advent of coal as a source of energy in the nineteenth century. And in the United States, helter-skelter settlement of the midwestern plains in the late nineteenth and early twentieth centuries brought problems of soil erosion and dustbowls on a scale never before known in human history.

Indeed, the progress of civilizations and nations through recorded history can in part be measured by the responses engineered to one or another of these impending resource scarcities or environmental limitations. Enduring economic and political advancement have invariably required finding ways to maintain or enlarge the effective yield from the resource base upon which a civilization or nation draws. Such alterations have come about through some combination of: remedial steps to offset environmental degradation; more efficient management and use of an available resource pool; technological innovation or substitution with some more abundant resource; the discovery of new resource reserves; and the importation of resources from abroad—either through fiat or trade.

One of the most striking lessons Chapter 1 notes from history is that the most predominant response to local ecological decline has been some form of flight from the problem. Populations have dispersed, or food and resource production have been moved to other places. Although flight is more frequently resorted to, some societies have been able to respond to inherent natural resource limitations or severe ecological problems through adaptation. Most successful adaptations in history resulted from technological innovations or resource substitutions which enabled an economy to attain an even higher level of economic prosperity than had been previously possible. On the other hand, adjustments of land and resource management techniques to avert impending natural resource scarcities or degradation have been far rarer in history. Such adaptations often require large-scale social, economic, and political changes. The historical examples have generally been those societies which have had a cohesive social structure and a very strong state with a highly centralized system of controlling and mobilizing resources.

Another lesson is that present gains in agricultural production may be illusory if they are purchased at the price of long-term sustainability. In the case of medieval Europe, for example, the thirteenth and fifteenth centuries brought rapid growth in agricultural productivity, investment, urbanization, and trade that increased prosperity. However, in both cases, such progress turned out not to be self-sustaining, since it induced offsetting increases in population, and the high levels of agricultural productivity upon which it depended could not be maintained. The children of the fourteenth and sixteenth centuries paid the delayed costs of the previous centuries' prosperity, as agricultural yields declined markedly and much land that had provided ample food had to be abandoned to recuperate. Sustained economic progress in preindustrial Europe was not possible until this cycle could be broken and current food needs could be met by means other than through agricultural practices that induced permanent or periodic fertility declines.

One interesting and underexplored aspect of the European experience in transcending the limits of the local environment under then prevailing agricultural techniques is the role played by individual response to economic incentives. If those countless individuals who daily tilled the soil and sought to harvest its fruits had not simultaneously responded to new economic opportunities and felt that they would directly benefit from their initiatives, European agriculture might not have so easily broken out of its perpetual cycle of periodic soil exhaustion and land abandonment.

But history is replete with losers as well as winners—nations and civilizations which could not adapt to their resource and environmental constraints. Increasingly, as Chapter 1 indicates, historians, anthropologists, and archeologists have found evidence that shortages of vital resources, declines in the productive capabilities of the soil, or the degradation of water and other resources have been important contributing factors in the decline of past civilizations and empires. Rarely have the immediate catastrophes precipitating economic decline or political disintegration been directly attributable to resource shortages or environmental degradation. But societies which have failed to respond to scarcity or degradation of their natural resources through better management, substitution, or importation have left themselves more vulnerable in the long run to economic stagnation, slow disintegration, military conquest, or internal political turmoil.

What parallels can be drawn to the third world today? In many respects, countries which still are underindustrialized and whose economies are heavily dependent upon their local environment to yield food and raw materials face ecological predicaments which are similar to those of societies prior to the age of industrialization. As in many ancient civilizations, the pressures of rapid population growth, increased demand for wood, and the spread of cultivators onto marginal or sloping lands is causing very severe problems of soil erosion, deforestation, and water availability that threaten to undermine the productivity of the local environment.

Yet, much has changed that makes it less likely that twentieth century nation-states will decline or perish if they fail to recover and maintain the productivity of their lands. In times past, only imperial powers (Greece, Rome) or seafaring peoples (the Phoenicians, the Italians), conquering or trading for food and raw materials from far-flung places, could long sustain themselves beyond the carrying capacity of their lands. In modern times, with the continued spread of industrial development, increasingly global networks of trade and capital flows, and a safety net of food and fiscal assistance provided by the advanced nations and international organizations, even a very poor nation's survival may not be as directly linked to the productivity of the lands within its borders as was that of non-imperial ancient civilizations. In short, the parallel between the ecological predicaments faced by ancient civilizations and those of present-day developing nations should not be overdrawn.

Nevertheless, it is clear that the environmental abuse and poor natural resource management prevalent throughout the third world may directly affect the present and future economic development prospects of countries and the welfare of the masses still heavily dependent on the land for food and as a way of life. Consequently, Chapter 2 considers how overall national economic growth, future levels of affluence and the present and future distribution of income in developing countries are linked with environmental problems.

Natural resource endowments, and long-term changes in these endowments induced by man, may influence the choice and chances for success of the economic development strategy pursued by a country. A number of the major steps necessary for initiating the process of sustained development—increased agricultural productivity, population stabilization, reduction of absolute poverty, industrial expansion, diversification of exports, and reduced fiscal fluctuation—are integrally linked to resource productivity and hence management, since land and human labor are the primary factors of production available to the masses of people in most poor countries.

Most poor countries have well over 50 percent of the population living in rural areas and dependent upon the land for their well-being, and many countries are without adequate export revenues to pay for huge food and raw material imports. For the foreseeable future, economic development, not to mention human welfare, in these poor countries is going to continue to be heavily dependent upon improved productive utilization of basic renewable resources: forests for pulp and paper, home construction, fuel, foreign exchange revenues, and a host of watershed functions; a soil base conducive to increased agricultural productivity to enable people to produce a surplus and feed an industrializing and urbanizing nation; and stable water resources for generating power, irrigation, food production, human consumption, and industrial use. Productive use of these resources is already marginal and continuing to decline in very poor countries such as Haiti, Nepal, Bangladesh, the Sahel countries, and many more local areas in Africa, Latin America, the Middle East, and Southeast Asia. If economic development prospects appear bleak today in these places, they will be even bleaker in the future as renewable natural resources continue to be degraded.

Environmental degradation also goes right to the heart of one of the most vexing and potentially explosive issues in many developing countries—the distribution of national wealth (and political power) between different ethnic or religious groups, economic classes, or political constituencies. Noting that in the study of economic development there has often been a complete separation between analyses of income distribution and analyses of environmental problems in developing countries, Chapter 2 argues that these issues are conceptually and empirically related. Distributional issues often determine who benefits from environmental exploitation, who must pay the costs, and whether these two sets of actors are overlapping.

If academic and policy analysts have failed to examine systematically relationships between distribution and environment, it is not surprising that policy makers have also failed to look at these relationships. In the absence of sweeping political and economic changes it is exceedingly difficult to alter or redistribute income profiles, much less to deal with problems of environmental degradation as part of a distributional strategy or to redistribute in order to preserve the environment and renewable resources. Even in reformist-minded developing countries, failures to stop poor people from cutting trees, migrating to cities, and invading new lands for farms and pastures are partly a consequence of the fact that the alternative may be to permit more equitable access to already available natural resources, an issue governments are reluctant to tackle. Conversely, privileged access to natural resources may result in wealthy people or large corporations enriching themselves at the expense of the long-term public weal—carrying out massive crash logging operations, converting fragile lands to large cattle ranches, mining and despoiling adjacent land, or overdrawing available ground and surface water resources.

Governmental attempts to reduce income distribution disparities can also lead to environmental degradation. Many third world governments try to achieve both growth and better distribution through spatial redistribution strategies associated with growth pole strategies and movement of peoples from densely settled to less densely settled rural areas. Mexico and Indonesia are examples. However, careful environmental planning has not been associated with these attempts; rarely have growth objectives been achieved and often serious environmental consequences have been entailed. Also, commitments to new capital cities, such as Abuja in Nigeria and Brasilia in Brazil, may have serious and unplanned environmental consequences as spatial redistributions are undertaken. Once again, short-run political and economic goals are maximized at the expense of longer-run economic and environmental welfare.

In spite of a growing voice among some environmentalists and the political left that government strategies to redistribute land and decentralize political power will lead to better environmental management at the local level, Chapter 2 argues that these assumptions cannot be taken for granted. There is no assurance that dividing land up among peasants or turning resource management responsibilities over to the poor will reduce degradation or lead to more careful and sustained exploitation of natural resources. These may only come about when the state, whether reformist or authoritarian, asserts its role as steward of the national patrimony and ceases to depend on unsustainable exploitation of renewable resources *either* as a means to avoid confronting the income distribution question *or* in an effort to enlarge the current pool of exploitable resources at the expense of the future.

POLITICS, PUBLIC POLICY, AND ENVIRONMENT

The key question addressed by the chapters in Section 2 is why environmental abuses and natural resource degradation remain so widespread in the third world even when the resulting problems are clearly harmful to present economic well-being and long-term economic development. Chapter 3 identifies a host of political and economic factors that make it rational, profitable, expedient, or necessary for people and national governments to take or permit actions in the short term that may well undermine their long-term prosperity. Some of the administrative barriers and difficulties that may render new regulations or other remedial steps taken by developing country governments ineffective are delineated in Chapter 4.

In many poor countries, where people depend on local soil conditions and wood and water supplies for their welfare, continuing deterioration in the productivity of these resources poses serious problems for present and future economic development. Yet the question of how these countries are going to stabilize and then adequately manage their renewable resource bases is complicated by numerous political and economic factors that are often overlooked or underplayed by development assistance providers and conservationists.

Responding both to their broadened perspectives of development needs and to growing pressures from international conservation groups, the United Nations, the World Bank, the USAID, other development assistance organizations, and many nongovernmental organizations have sought to help developing countries deal with their resource problems. They are furnishing more expertise and more training in resource management, assessing the environmental impacts of their development projects, providing for more infrastructure and projects designed to protect and restore the productivity of already overextended or depleted forests and soils, and working to instruct poor countryfolk and villagers how to keep themselves fed and warm without injuring their future economic well-being.

A nagging question that Chapter 3 raises is whether all these actions—important though they are—will fundamentally alter the behavior of enough individuals to reduce the worst environmental problems. Any attempt to design strategies to reduce environmental abuse in developing countries must begin by examining how intricately the various forms of resource and environmental mismanagement are interwoven into the fabric of individual societies. After all, as Chapter 3 points out, it is the internal distributions of political and economic power in developing countries that often perpetuate inequalities, control access to certain resources, and structure economic incentives and administrative interventions in manners which hold people in situations where abuse of local natural resources is an important aspect of their daily living.

Money and expertise from numerous international sources, while beneficial, cannot overcome the basic fact that environmental abuse is rampant in the developing world because of much larger and more complex failings of individual political and economic systems. Environmental degradation at the local level, or national strategies for depleting forest and fishery reserves, may well represent the most expedient responses by individuals and countries to situations which would otherwise require fundamental political and economic reforms. Or power and authority may be exercised to shift the cost of environmental externalities from one group to another.

Paradoxically, it may be the rural poor who, because of their lack of political power and economic resources, cause the most serious land management related ecological problems in developing countries and at the same time suffer the most from these problems. The fact that the vast majority of people in poor countries still must work the land for their fuel supplies and sustenance implies enormous, if disguised, unemployment or underemployment. This is a waste of labor, but it also leads people to crop marginal lands, overtax soils, or cut trees far beyond a sustainable yield. Chapter 3 points out that building large dams, teaching people more "ecologically sound" agricultural techniques, helping them set up village woodlots, training experts in conservation and environmental impact assessments, and numerous other large-scale natural resource management programs being carried out in developing countries today may be difficult to sustain in the long term if the masses of rural people remain marginally employed on the land and squeezed by numerous political and economic incentives to damage future natural resource productivity. Consequently, it is imperative that developing country governments and international development assistance agencies make more concerted efforts to integrate environmental rehabilitation and resource management programs into their overall strategies for achieving economic development.

Over the past decade, a confluence of domestic and international political forces have led nearly all of the world's developing countries to pass new environmental laws and to establish new executive-branch agencies or boards responsible for the administration of environmental programs. Today, more than 100 countries have identifiable environmental agencies—a vast increase from the eleven countries which had reported the presence of such agencies less than a decade earlier, at the time of the Stockholm Conference. This statutory and institutional response to worsening environmental problems has been impressive, but Chapter 4 points out that it has not been sufficient to meet the challenge. Indeed, enforcement of environmental laws has been weak or nonexistent, and many (even most) of the new agencies are small, ineffectual, and politically impotent in the face of their powerful competitors for bureaucratic power.

This immense gap between rhetoric and reality in the administration of environmental programs in developing countries is the central focus of Chapter 4. Initially the chapter explores the emergence of environmental concern—the political pressures which have led to the impressive set of statutory and institutional responses. Although the attitudes toward environmental protection prevalent in less developed countries (LDC's) in the early 1970s were largely negative, the rise of environmental policies in developing countries was directly influenced by the exportation of the environmental movement that emerged in the developed countries—emulation, information, education, aid program requirements. At the same time, domestic political pressures for greater environmental action were evident in many countries, forcing governments to respond with new laws, new institutions, and new control mechanisms. Mass protest has normally only occurred when environmental problems have arisen because of a lack of vital public services, or when industrial pollution threatened the economic livelihood of a particular group of fishermen or farmers. There are few examples of poor people in rural areas coming together to protest deforestation, soil erosion, or similar problems where the groups most affected are also the ones who, out of economic necessity, actually promote the environmental destruction.

Based on this analysis of growing political pressures for environmental action, Chapter 4 explores the institutionalization of environmental concern, both legislative and organizational. But more important than the rhetoric of laws and programs and agencies is the reality of their effectiveness. One conclusion emerges clearly: that the growing concern over environmental problems in developing countries has not led to the creation of rigorous systems to prevent pollution, nor of procedures to control the excesses of deforestation, soil erosion, and other environmental impacts. Mass pressures have been sufficient to engender an initial (and superficial) institutional and statutory response, but have not been sufficient to induce strict enforcement and effective implementation of environmental programs.

In light of the enormous difficulties developing countries have in enforcing existing regulations and administering new environmental programs, Chapter 4 sets forth several recommendations designed to reduce the present imbalance between rhetoric and reality in environmental management in developing countries. Effective long-term action will only occur when environmental issues gain greater sustained political salience and more technical skills are acquired in these countries. Some crude but flexible measures for enforcement are suggested as an appropriate interim measure. These include: the development of priorities for attention to the major sources of environmental harm; the selective use of effluent taxes and other fiscal measures instead of regulatory ambient standards and emissions permits; greater use of easy-to-verify technology-based minimum standards for pollution abatement; and decentralized pollution control by industrial or area-wide zones that require less detailed source-by-source regulation.

Of course, these policy and administrative suggestions will have the greatest impact on coping with problems of industrial pollution. The problems associated with poor land management in rural areas are likely to be much more difficult to address from an administrative perspective; emergence of strong public advocacy for environmental action seems an essential prerequisite to achieving changes in rural public administration or in the approach to environmental management. Because of the deeply rooted political problems noted in Chapters 2 and 3, effective administration of rural resource management programs may await the time when government elites—generally urban dominated—decide that concerted attention to the problems of the rural poor is an absolute political necessity.

DEFORESTATION, DESERTIFICATION, POLLUTION

Section 3 examines the political and economic themes raised in previous chapters within three specific issue areas: deforestation, desertification, urban and industrial pollution. The chapters in this section draw on recent case study research conducted by the respective authors. In all three chapters, an effort is made to identify the environmental resource problems, their immediate causes, the groups which profit and which lose the most from the perpetuation of the problems and some remedial actions which might be possible both in light of the short-term political context and in terms of long-term systemic changes.

Tropical moist forests are disappearing at a rate unequaled in the earth's history. The problem of tropical deforestation has received a great deal of international attention in recent years, in part because of the potentially profound consequences for all mankind: extinction of economically valuable or genetically distinct species; possible global climate changes due to an increase in atmospheric CO_2. Chapter 5 argues that the consequences of tropical deforestation at the local and national level are also significant.

As Chapter 1 emphasizes, deforestation has occurred in virtually every forested region of the world as population and economic activity in these areas have expanded during the last 2,000 years. Today, it is occurring in most of the developing countries that lie within the thick green belt of tropical forests girdling the earth in the equatorial zones. Yet, as satellite monitoring by the United Nations' Environment Program indicates, many recent studies appear to have exaggerated the rate of such deforestation on a global basis; the most critical problems seem to be in specified areas where deforestation means little in terms of global figures but a great deal in terms of local economic and social circumstances. The study, by the Global Environment Monitoring Systems (GEMS) suggests that:

. . . . while popular concern for the Amazon and the great forests of the world is not entirely unfounded, it may be somewhat misdirected. Urgent concern, the summaries reveal, perhaps ought to be directed towards nine countries which will lose their forest entirely within twenty-five years if present trends continue, and towards another eleven countries which risk losing half their forest in the same time. Together these twenty countries possess but 1.5% of the world's total closed tropical forest; the loss may seem insignificant, but it could have important implications, both nationally and globally. [10]

This point was emphasized by Edouard Saouma, director general of the UN Food and Agricultural Organization, who said recently that destruction of forest in developing countries "is unacceptable, not so much as a percentage of forest total but because of where and why it is happening." [11]

The specific causes of tropical deforestation are varied, but they are deeply rooted in the economic, social, and political problems of tropical developing countries. Probably the most universal cause of tropical deforestation is slash-and-burn agriculture, which is still practiced in many tropical areas of Africa, Latin America, and Asia. The dominant practitioners of slash-and-burn agriculture in many of these countries are no longer tribes of shifting cultivators. Increasingly, tropical forests are being invaded and cleared by groups of peasants and even former urban dwellers who lack other employment opportunities. Often they are abetted by new government roads built deep into tropical forests, and sometimes forest migrations are even encouraged by governments hard-pressed to find employment or better lands for cultivation. Because of the fragility of forest soils, many of these migration projects have failed, leaving behind a legacy of devastation.

But tropical forest losses are also caused by large commercial timber exploitation, especially in Southeast Asian countries, and grand schemes for creating cattle pens for beef production or various commercial agriculture ventures, especially in Latin America. In these cases, often with large funding from international sources, tropical country governments rarely have considered the serious ecological consequences that may result. However, as Chapter 5 clearly illustrates, these ecological problems have frequently undermined the economic viability of the projects in the longer term.

In the cases of both the micro and the macro causes of deforestation, governments continue to follow the path of short-term expedience—initiating or permitting the deforestation in lieu of more difficult (but in the long term, necessary) adjustments. Population pressure leads to increased colonization of forest areas but since population will, in many countries, grow markedly, policy measures must sooner or later be taken to lessen pressures on forest lands. These include land reform and labor-intensive manufacturing. Yet, the continued tolerance of forest incursions by governments is often a sign that this is seen as a cheaper and politically easier strategy than generating other more gainful and in the long term, productive means of employment. Furthermore, it is politically and administratively risky to enforce laws against deforestation when there are many violators, and where those responsible for deforestation are few in number they usually wield enormous political and economic clout.

Ultimately, a major calculation made by many governments is that the majority of persons harmed most in the short run by deforestation are rural, poor, and not sufficiently organized to threaten political retribution. These include tribal people dependent on the forest for their livelihood; peasants living in or near forested areas who require fuel or forest foods and other forest products; farmers who suffer from soil erosion at forest sites, and from floods and impaired irrigation works downstream.

In addition, a major portion of the costs of tropical deforestation are being passed along to be borne by future generations. For example, "one shot" deforestation of a relatively few species of internationally coveted hardwoods probably has a high future opportunity cost. Many economic uses for the presently unknown species may be found if they are not driven to extinction by habitat loss. The irony, of course, may be that the chief losers as a result of these delayed costs will be the very groups that are benefitting most from deforestation in the short term and who continue to inhibit governmental steps to slow the careless destruction of forests: the wealthy, the politically powerful, and a small number of international groups interested most in short-term profits.

Most observers of the economic development process agree that adverse ecological circumstances—harsh weather, arid climate, poor soils, shortages of other resources—are not fundamental barriers to economic development. In fact, economic development has proceded in a number of countries which started with poor fragile natural resource bases.[12] However, it remains true that a large number of the world's poor countries are located in zones which are classified as primarily consisting of marginal lands.

The problem is that many poor countries which encompass large areas of marginal lands have been unable to move their economies beyond heavy dependence on local land-based production. At the same time, population pressures, coupled with numerous geopolitical circumstances, often contribute to further marginalization of the land as local soil, water, and vegetative resources are consumed or destroyed far faster than they can be protected or replenished.

The economic and environmental problems facing poor people on marginal lands may be the most intractable of all environment and development dilemmas. Perhaps nowhere else on earth are the economic problems and the human suffering related to continuing destruction of already miserly ecosystems more vividly illustrated than in the countries which fall in the Sahel zone of Africa. Yet even in the Sahel, where natural and human forces have encouraged not only the southern extension of the Sahara Desert, but also desert-like conditions that "leapfrog" well ahead of the actual sand dunes, some groups prosper and remain unscathed while others are fully exposed to hunger and severe hardship.

Thus picking up on themes raised in previous chapters, the treatment of the Sahel in Chapter 6 presents an ideal case study of how political, geographical, social, administrative, and economic factors can combine to marginalize further already ecologically fragile regions in poor countries. The confluence of all these factors leads to desertification in the Sahel because it creates the need or the incentive (depending on the level of poverty) for individuals to mine the soil and desiccate trees, grass, and other vegetation.

A major argument of Chapter 6 is that little is likely to change in the Sahelian countries until groups take collective responsibility for common property resources—pasture, timber, agricultural lands, and water rights—or individuals receive assurance that they will be able to capture the benefits for managing some small chunk of these resources. In either case, the "system" is not likely to change easily.

Drawing on examples from Niger, Chapter 6 argues that peasants have only passive vetoes on government programs and bureaucrats' activities because administrative and political systems remain highly centralized. Consequently, they remain unlikely to undertake the environmental management efforts upon which their own long-run salvation rests. Effective environmental activities depend on localization of anti-desertification efforts, which will require changes in land and tree tenure and legal systems.

Many systemic factors work against localization. There is national distrust of certain ethnic groups. There is administrators' ingrained perception of their "duty" to exert control over all problems in any way related to the public good as they define it, and a correlative distrust of autonomous local organization, both bequeathed from French colonial traditions. Other barriers include: a distaste by administrators for "inconveniences" associated with popular input to policy making, and a lack of strong incentives to launch new, i.e., environmentally relevant, projects at the sub-national levels. These impediments severely hamper local level initiative to address local environmental problems.

Balanced against these are a few emergent incentives for elites to change their administrative policies or to take up the reform banner. In particular, concern to achieve food self-sufficiency and foreign donor insistance that environmental problems be faced may, when coupled with observation of environmental degradation, provoke new elite initiatives. But it is likely that progress toward stabilizing the deteriorating environment in the Sahelian countries will be slow and subject to severe setbacks when nature brings another drought cycle as occurred in the 1970s.

Despite the obvious prevalence of many serious urban and industrial pollution problems in the third world, many observers have argued that problems relating to environmental pollution are only of secondary importance to countries still struggling to achieve rapid economic growth. Not only can developing countries supposedly not afford to deal with these problems, it is pointed out that the masses are unlikely even to perceive such problems until they share in the economic growth which presumably results from urban and industrial expansion.

There is some logic, of course, to this sequence. Pollution and squalor are difficult problems to prevent in countries were people are very poor and industrial enterprises are in the fledgling stage. In the early phases of industrial development, as most development economists point out, countries (and private companies) depend heavily on maintaining high rates of savings for capital accumulation and on keeping the costs of labor, raw material, and other aspects of production as low as possible. Pollution—the disposing of wastes or by-products from industrial processes into air, water, or adjacent land—is another important means of minimizing costs for industries and governments.

The argument is often made by economists that from nature's point of view, too, it is not as necessary for a country at an early stage of industrial development to be seriously concerned about controlling pollution. All natural systems have a certain "assimilative capacity" to absorb, dilute, and degrade most industrial pollutants and urban wastes. In underindustrialized countries the limits of this capacity generally have not been reached. Pollution control technology for factories or elaborate municipal waste treatment facilities would only duplicate at great waste of scarce capital resources what nature can accomplish. As a country reaches a stage of industrial development where nature's assimilative capacity is being taxed (implying that substantial economic growth is taking place) pollution control steps can be implemented incrementally.

In spite of these general suppositions, there are a number of factors in many rapidly industrializing nations that make mounting urban and industrial pollution a matter of concern now and are making ordinary people more aware of some of these problems than might intuitively be predicted. Chapter 7 examines the magnitude and principal causes of urban and industrial pollution in developing countries, arguing that the problems are both more severe and more complex than they were for cities in the advanced developed countries during their stages of rapid expansion and industrialization.

The total costs of these pollution problems—in terms of direct economic damage, future clean-up, and public health—cannot even be roughly estimated. Yet, it is clear from the numerous examples cited in this chapter that pollution related to urban and industrial growth is causing major economic disruption and severe public health problems throughout the third world. These costs, though, are not at all distributed evenly; they are only rarely paid by those who create the problems and are instead generally borne disproportionately by poorer urban dwellers and by certain economic groups in the rural economy.

In the extreme, such environmental pollution problems may put a brake on economic development in major urban areas, choking off certain growth possibilities; draining capital for large public works or infrastructure just to keep the urban economy functional; forcing expensive and often unwieldy industrial decentralization plans for outlying areas where transportation, energy, infrastructure, building costs, and wage rates (for skilled and managerial personnel) are often higher; adversely affecting the health of the urban workforce; and leaving haphazard or poorly planned development subject to a demolition in periodic natural disasters such as floods, mudslides, earthquakes, and monsoons.

Externalities caused by the urban and industrial sectors also frequently spill over and impinge on other sectors of the economy. Air and water pollution from all the sources described above have caused numerous problems for rural residents, notably farmers and fishermen, throughout the third world. Crops have been killed or their yields substantially lowered, and fishing in rivers and bays below major third world urban areas has almost invariably declined substantially in recent decades. The consequences of these developments are enormous for countries where a major percentage of the population still earns its livelihood from these pursuits and most of these people already subsist close to the margin.

Notes

1. Organization for Economic Cooperation and Development, *Interfutures: Facing the Future* (Paris: OECD, 1979), p. 23.

2. *North-South: A Program for Survival*, The Report of the Independent Commission on International Development Issues Under the Chairmanship of Willy Brandt (Cambridge, Mass.: MIT Press, 1980), p. 47 (hereafter cited as Brandt Commission Report).

3. Ibid.

4. K. K. S. Dadzie, "Economic Development." In *Economic Development*, reprint of *Scientific American*, September 1980 (San Francisco: W. H. Freeman and Co., 1980), pp. 6–7.

5. Many of these are listed in the footnotes for Chapters 2, 3, and 4.

6. World Bank, *World Development Report*, published annually.

7. All these potential problems are described in, among many others, *The Global 2000 Report to the President: Entering the Twenty-First Century* (Washington, D.C.: Government Printing Office, 1980) volume 1: The Summary Report.

8. As quoted in Theodore Morgan, *Economic Development: Concept and Strategy* (New York: Harper and Row, 1975), p. 7.

9. Nicholas Georgescu-Roegen, *The Entropy Law and the Economic Process* (Cambridge, Mass.: Harvard University Press, 1971).

10. United Nations Environment Program, *GEMS: Global Environmental Monitoring System* (Kent, England: Penhurst Press, 1982), p. 25.

11. Edward Saouma, "Statement by the Director General of FAO," at 8th Annual World Forestry Conference, Jakarta, October 16–18, 1978.

12. See Chapters 1 and 2.

Natural Resources
and Environment
in Economic Development

CHAPTER 1

RESOURCE LIMITATIONS, ENVIRONMENTAL DETERIORATION, AND ECONOMIC PROGRESS: A HISTORICAL PERSPECTIVE

H. Jeffrey Leonard

How a civilization (tribe, city-state, nation, or empire) manages the renewable resources at its disposal—whether in the long term it improves or degrades them—has often had a fundamental impact on the fate of that civilization through history. In fact, for preindustrial civilizations, the degree to which production of food and raw materials from the local environment could be maintained and expanded (as population and economic activity increased) was often the difference between prosperity and decline. This chapter explores the links that have existed between environmental management and economic prosperity and, conversely, how natural resource shortages or degradation have constrained economic progress in history. Following an examination of historical examples, the chapter outlines key lessons and speculates on their relevance to developing nations today.

NATURAL RESOURCES AND ENVIRONMENT IN HISTORY

Ancient Babylon and the other large cities of Mesopotamia prospered in large measure because extensive networks of irrigation ditches and canals made it possible to produce enough food to support large, concentrated populations. At its peak, it is estimated that the population of Mesopotamia was about 25 million, far more people than could have been fed prior to the building of the irrigation systems.[1] With irrigation, the Mesopotamian cities were able to cultivate intensively large areas of fertile soil in the lowland areas between the Tigris and Euphrates Rivers.

Even with their advanced knowledge of cultivation and irrigation techniques, the Mesopotamian civilizations could not maintain the productive capacity of the "fertile crescent" over the centuries. Although the decline of ancient Mesopotamia occurred during repeated periods of nomadic invasion, archaeologists have found a great deal of evidence that the economy of the area was undermined prior to the invasions. Most observers now agree that declining food production—precipitated by soil erosion, sedimentation in irrigation canals, and reduced soil fertility due to growing soil salinity—was a major factor in the downfall of Mesopotamia's ancient civilization.[2]

The original Mayan empire, which flourished in pre-Columbian Central America, supported its large, dense populations on a sophisticated *milpa* (shifting cultivation) system of agriculture until sometime between the sixth and seventh centuries. The decline has frequently been attributed to catastrophes such as earthquakes, disease, or invasion. However, since the Mayans appear to have dispersed and migrated gradually and established new villages in the Yucatan (where the later Mayan civilization discovered by the Spanish was located) and in present-day Guatemala, these explanations have been suspect.[3] Twentieth-century students of Mayan culture have increasingly accepted the notion that the exhaustion of tropical soils cleared of their forest cover was the most probable cause of the Mayan migration.[4] The essential factor to continued soil fertility in any shifting cultivation system of agriculture is an adequate period of fallow to enable the soil to replenish its nutrients. However, population pressures led the Mayans, like many other tropical civilizations past and present, to shorten the fallow period gradually (and perhaps imperceptibly) until this led to exhaustion of the land.

The Incas and the Aztecs, too, depended upon similar systems of shifting cultivation of maize. However, circumstances they faced better enabled them to avoid soil exhaustion problems. The Incas, for example, cultivated an area with lower rainfall (so fewer soil nutrients were lost through leaching) and eventually developed extensive irrigation and drainage systems and elaborate terracing procedures which permitted high yields, reduced erosion, and preserved soil fertility.[5] The Aztecs, although inhabiting areas more similar to those of the Mayas, built their largest city on a lake, which enabled them to use water transport to tap a wider area of land for shifting cultivation.[6]

Many preindustrial civilizations appear to have eventually reached a point where they had increasing difficulty feeding and equiping themselves as a result of either declining productivity owing to resource degradation or increasing population beyond the carrying capacity of the local resource base. In many places lands that were fertile and supported large human populations in ancient time today are barren and barely produce enough for small populations. Jacks and Whyte concluded more than forty years ago that:

Erosion has, indeed, been one of the most potent factors causing the downfall of former civilizations and empires whose ruined cities now lie amid barren wastes that once were the world's most fertile lands. The deserts of North China, Persia, Mesopotamia and North Africa tell the same story of the gradual exhaustion of the soil as the increasing demands made upon it by expanding civilization exceeded its recuperative powers. Soil erosion, then as now, followed soil exhaustion.[7]

Deterioration of the Mediterranean Basin

Environmental deterioration in the forms of deforestation, soil erosion, and aridification was significant in the Mediterranean basin during Greek and Roman times. Although not responsible for the declines of these two classical civilizations, the lowering of land-based productive capacity certainly had important influences upon the economics and politics of the Greek and Roman empires.

As population increased in ancient Greece, for example, food demands necessitated the cutting of forests and cultivation in hilly terrains and less productive soils. Under Southern European climatic and soil conditions, the fertility of the land was reduced in time and the forests were replaced with scrub vegetation or barren surfaces. These trends were exacerbated by the growing demand for timber for buildings and ships, and by the widespread proliferation of the goat in the Greek countryside.[8] Plato, writing in the fifth century B.C., noted that Attica, once a much forested and fertile region, was by then a naked upland:

What now remains compared with what then existed is like the skeleton of a sick man, all the fat and the soft earth having been wasted away, and only the base framework of the land being left.[9]

Under these conditions of soil depletion and degradation, the Greek city-states found it necessary to meet their expanding food demands through the importation of grains from other areas. Only by the conquest and maintenance of agricultural colonies for grain production was ancient Greece able to transcend the shrinking limits of the environmental carrying capacity on the Greek peninsula. Nevertheless, even today much land in Greece remains barren or marginally productive as a result of the environmental deterioration process initiated by ancient Greek civilization.[10] Ironically, most of the very areas that once served as the breadbaskets for Greece also are far less fertile and forested than they were in antiquity as a result of abuse at the hands of previous civilizations.

Similar problems of environmental deterioration were later encountered in Italy during the Roman empire. Although overcropping for export to Greece led quickly to deterioration in some Greek colonies, Italy still was able to produce abundant supplies of food locally at the time of Rome's independence. Farming was a noble profession in Rome, and Roman farmers, in part because the climate of much of Italy was dry and the terrain hilly, are reputed to have been astute and cautious stewards of the land. Not only did Roman farmers adhere to careful fallowing procedures and make extensive use of crops such as alfalfa that improve soil fertility, but they also took great pains to terrace and contour sloping lands to reduce the threat of erosion.[11]

But careful husbandry was not in itself sufficient to prevent ecological deterioration in many parts of Italy. As in many other agricultural-based civilizations, past and present, the dynamics of economic and population expansion put greater and greater cultivation pressures on marginal and hilly lands, and continuously drove up demand for timber for ships, fuel, and construction.[12] Consequently, like Greece before it, Rome faced "deteriorating soils, growing populations, and smaller yields," and eventually "came to depend on imported grains from other countries, particularly Carthage, Libya, and Egypt."[13]

Even prior to the industrial age, civilizations which were experiencing serious reductions in their local environmental carrying capacity could compensate if they had the political and military power to draw food and raw materials from afar. Both the Greek and Roman civilizations were able to prosper well beyond the level of subsistence even though the countrysides of Greece and Italy were less capable over time of producing enough food and raw materials to meet their expanding economic needs. The real economic implications of declining carrying capacity of the local natural resource base were not felt until the political-military prowess of the Greek and Roman empires declined and neither civilization could any longer exact food as tribute from far-off colonies. The consequences then were more severe for Greece than for Italy, because Roman agricultural methods and the more durable Italian soils meant that overtaxed soils recuperated more quickly in Italy after being abandoned.[14]

The Medieval Agricultural Trap

The depletion of trees and degradation of the soil in Southern Europe was slowed and even reversed to some extent during the Dark Ages that accompanied the decline of Rome, since vast areas of land which had been cultivated previously were abandoned.[15] Even so, the center of Italian culture and economy shifted toward the northern third of the peninsula, in part because this was the only place where food production was maintained at high levels of prosperity. The great Italian trading city-states which flourished during the Renaissance period depended as much on the fertility of their soils as they did on their commerce—itself supported by the ships built from the forests of northern Italy.[16]

But by the twelfth and thirteenth centuries the Mediterranean basin along the Italian and Iberian peninsulas was once again facing severe problems from forest depletion and soil degradation. The forest depletion came as the city-states of the Mediterranean—Italian, French, and Spanish—built larger and larger commercial fleets of wooden ships. Fernand Braudel contends that various parts of Italy suffered from "wood famine" and notes that the "Mediterranean navies became accustomed, little by little, to go looking further for what they couldn't find in their own forests."[17] Deforestation was compounded in the hills of northern Italy, Mediterranean France, and Castilian Spain by herds of sheep and goats, which took out quantities of the smaller trees and other vegetation that had been left because it was too small for shipbuilding.

The deforestation problems of southern Europe posed some economic hardships and increased erosion problems in hilly areas during the mercantilist era. However, lumber supplies for further boatbuilding could be procured from the Baltic and Nordic countries, so the shortages were not crucial. But, even more importantly, these activities altered permanently the look and productivity of the landscape along much of the Mediterranean and Adriatic littorals. Says H. C. Darby: "The result of this interference, human and animal, coupled with the dry climate and the poor soil, is that much of the Mediterranean lands are covered by semi-natural bushwood communities,"[18] an ecologist's euphemistic way of saying that today the land is arid and covered primarily with scrub vegetation where majestic forests once stood.

The maintenance of soil fertility proved to be a significant problem in much of Europe following the great land reclamations that occurred as Europe emerged from the Dark Ages in the eleventh and twelfth centuries. Indeed, while historians disagree in their explanations of the causes and meaning of the great cyclical waves of economic growth and depression that swept over much of Europe between about 1150 and 1750, most agree that the waxing and waning of soil fertility was at least one of the factors that had a strong influence on medieval and early capitalist European economies.[19]

From about 1150 to 1300, much of Europe enjoyed an increasing prosperity under a feudal economy. Nearly everywhere, from the Mediterranean to the North Atlantic, but especially in west central Europe, lands were reclaimed and forested areas were cleared for agricultural production. Whereas most of the continent north of the Mediterranean rim had been densely and continuously forested, villages and agricultural lands spread across the continent by 1300. New aspects of agriculture—areal specialization and a feudal economy—increased productivity per unit of labor, permitting further urbanization and freeing up labor to clear more forests, drain swamps, build dikes, and perform other tasks to increase further agricultural production. Some of the virgin soils brought into production proved to be extraordinarily fertile, adding still further to agricultural surpluses.

During this great wave of reclamation and internal colonization, new towns sprang up across the continent and key urban areas, fed by the agricultural surpluses from the hinterlands, grew to sizes not previously sustained in Europe—from upper limits of about 10,000 inhabitants to more than 100,000 in some instances. This urban growth reflected colossal overall population expansion; most experts believe European population at least doubled and perhaps tripled in the two centuries leading up to 1300.

As a result of these trends, the face of much of Europe had been fundamentally changed by 1300, in economic, demographic, social, and ecological terms. Yet, despite all the changes and the expansion of inter-European trade, prosperity on the continent was still dependent primarily on the continuance of local soil fertility and the availability of timber.

In sharp contrast to the previous century and a half of huge land reclamations and population increases, the fourteenth century was a period of sharp economic downturn and abandonment of many of the lands that had recently been colonized. There were many political, social, and economic causes for the *Wüstungen*—the recession of villages from marginal land—during these years. Not least, in addition to the general effects of economic recession, was the search for physical security once internecine wars overtook much of the European countryside and the onset of profound changes in European agrarian social structure—the "enclosure" of land by an emerging landlord class.

However, students of medieval Europe are in general agreement that in many areas land was abandoned in the fourteenth century because soil productivity declined as a result of the intense cultivation it had been subjected to in the thirteenth century.[20] Throughout Europe, the forests, swamps, marshes, moors, and fens—"the wasteland which Europe's peasants settled and largely put into cultivation between the years 1000 and 1250"[21] could not sustain their fertility under the feudal system which held thousands of serfs to the land and forced them to "squeeze" as much immediate production as possible from the soil. One recent study notes that two centuries of expansion and prosperity "had been purchased on credit using as collateral Europe's natural resources, which were being rapidly depleted." The result was that, in the fourteenth century, "nature foreclosed."[22]

Under the conditions of the social system of feudalism, a growing population and the prevailing agricultural techniques, agricultural productivity from the European resource base could not be sustained at a high enough level. Summing up the crisis of the fourteenth century, Perry Anderson says that "the basic motor of rural reclamation, which had driven the whole feudal economy forwards for three centuries, eventually overreached the objective limits of both terrain and social structure."[23]

Varying Responses to Europe's Ecological Problems

As a result of the prolonged recession, many areas of Europe were in dire need of more food in the fourteenth and fifteenth centuries. In addition, deforestation as a result of agricultural clearings, fuel needs, and shipbuilding had left many areas short of wood for fuel and construction. Since the limits of the lands already in cultivation had been reached (and in many cases were declining because of soil exhaustion), this food could only be procured through some combination of possible adaptive responses. The territorial base upon which Europe drew for food production could be expanded, new agricultural techniques could raise or at least preserve productivity, or new forms of land management could be adopted to ensure the maintenance of productivity and permit more intensive cultivation of existing lands. The range of responses to this dilemma by various emergent European nation-states during the following two to three centuries is not only fascinating in its own right; it also has a great deal of relevance to the present day situation in developing countries.

Expansion of the lands providing food and fuel for the European states was a universal response in the fifteenth and sixteenth centuries. Cultivation and silviculture for the European market thus spread successively into the Mediterranean and Atlantic islands, North and West Africa, eastern Europe, the Americas, Russia, and even central Asia. Western Europe, in essence, sought to overcome the limits of its own resource base by drawing on resources from other areas. Historian G. B. Masefield notes that without the new crops imported from the Americas, "Europe might not have been able to carry such heavy populations as she later did. . . ."[24]

This movement of food production from the center of Europe helped to relieve the ecological pressures on these lands and to ensure that the fertility of good lands could be regained and marginal lands could be used for different purposes than bulk production of food staples. But, in many cases, the soil fertility problems of Europe were simply transferred to other areas. This is especially true with regard to the production of sugar, tobacco, potatoes, and other monocultures imposed upon the Mediterranean and Atlantic Islands and later the Americas. These crops, produced for consumption in Europe, "murdered the soil" in many places and created a situation where production was moved steadily eastward because of continuous soil exhaustion.[25] Europe, as had Greece and Rome before it, relieved some of the strain on its own natural resource base and attained adequate food supplies by importing food and, in the process, exporting ecological problems.

The southern flank of Europe, notably Italy and Spain, did not, for a variety of reasons, export food production to the degree that the western and northern European countries did.[26] Instead, the Mediterranean countries concentrated on "internal colonization," to bring additional lands under cultivation in order to increase food supplies. Historians disagree on the reasons why Spain and Italy were "occupied with the conquest at home of the entire area that could be cultivated by the technology then available from the flooded plains to the tops of the mountains," instead of conquering and securing production from far-off lands.[27] What is clear, however, is that this extracted a heavy ecological toll—resulting in serious problems of soil exhaustion and aridification in both countries and further intensifying the pressures to bring new lands under cultivation and to push existing lands to their limits.[28]

Thus, European nation-states between the fifteenth and eighteenth centuries responded to the natural resource limitations they faced in ways similar to the ancient civilizations already noted: they expanded the area within their territories under cultivation and they shifted food production beyond their territories to draw on a wider natural resource base. But neither solution dealt directly with the problem of resource degradation. Invariably, new internal agricultural settlements tended to be on inferior soils or in marginal areas because of terrain. The movement of certain types of food production to peripheral countries only transferred problems of soil exhaustion from one place to another. Indeed, in spite of this movement, many areas of western Europe continued to experience periodic declines in agricultural productivity as a result of overtaxing of the soil that invariably followed prosperous times and high demand for grains.[29]

But some European nations responded to the natural resource limitations by adapting their technologies and agricultural management practices in addition to simply exporting or accepting them. There remains a great debate among economists and historians as to "whether relative hardship stimulates people's wits, or exhausts their mental energies."[30] In general, most observers of history believes that prosperous and successful societies are those which encounter obstacles or natural ceilings to their economic and political aspirations, devise creative solutions to these barriers, and are consequently propeled forward to higher than ever levels of prosperity. Arnold Toynbee, for example, in *A Study of History*, offers such a theory of challenge and response as a primary cause for the will to progress that enables some societies to advance under conditions that are similar to those that have brought stagnation to others.[31] The responses of the Dutch and later the British to the resource limitations and ecological stresses they faced can be viewed in this context.

An important example of adaptation to overcome difficult ecological circumstances is found in the Dutch, who became the first hegemonic power of the European economic system which arose as feudalism declined in the fourteenth and fifteenth centuries. Of all countries in Europe, Holland—dubbed by one historian a "sand and mud dump left over from the ice age"[32]—was probably the least well endowed with a natural resource base and climate suitable to the production of an agricultural surplus.[33]

As a result of its poor native agricultural conditions, the Dutch economy was at first oriented toward the sea. With the development of large factory ships in the fifteenth century, the Dutch became the most efficient producers of fish in the world, supplying much of the rest of Europe. But what is most remarkable for many historians is that by the early seventeenth century, Holland had also become the pre-eminent agricultural nation of Europe as well.[34] With the invention of the windmill, the Dutch engaged in massive poldering efforts—pumping shallow waters off lowlands to create agricultural land. Even with this expansion, however, land shortages forced the Dutch to develop elaborate techniques for highly intensive agriculture. Just as significantly, the Dutch came to concentrate on horticulture, dairy products, and industrial crops (flax, hemp, hops, etc.) since grain and other food crops were more difficult to sustain under prevailing soil and terrain conditions. The surplus from trade in fish and these agricultural goods then was used to import grain for Holland's expanding and increasingly affluent population. All these trends were both fostered by and creative of greater opportunity for urbanization and industrialization. As a consequence, Holland came also to be the leading and most efficient producer of industrial goods during much of the seventeenth century.[35]

This process of rapid economic development, during which Holland became the "first country to achieve self-sustained growth,"[36] was possible only because Holland was able to exceed and expand the limits of its local natural resource base. The initial spark, of course, was the ability to create a surplus by tapping the abundant resources of the sea. But the Dutch used this surplus to improve the productive capacity of their land and to move into the production of industrial goods.

The waves of famine, disease, and depopulation that afflicted Europe periodically prior to the seventeenth century had marked influence on the great classical economists of the eighteenth and nineteenth centuries, who still viewed the agricultural economy as the lifeblood of economic civilization. For all the attention devoted by Smith, Malthus, Ricardo, and others to the increasing practices of urban crafts, industrial production, and commercial trade, land-based production remained for these economists the fundamental means of creating the capital necessary to engage in industrial pursuits.

Looking out on a continent where population had exploded with the renewed agricultural productivity increases of the seventeenth century, a prime concern for these economists was how western European countries could continue to feed an accelerating population. Although they gave markedly different assessments as to the possibilities of perpetuating economic prosperity under conditions of continued population expansion, the key limiting factor for all the classical economists was the amount of food production that could be wrought from the available supply of cultivable land without pushing Europe once again into the "medieval trap" of stagnant or declining agricultural production per capita.

Malthus believed that food production could not keep abreast with the natural rate of human reproduction and formulated his pessimistic views of an economy which, in spite of increased agricultural production, would always be brought back to equilibrium at a subsistence level per capita.[37] Ricardo, believing that all the best lands were already in production, formulated his law of diminishing returns on the assumption that future expansions of agriculture would require the use of more and more marginal lands.[38] For Ricardo, the way out of the diminishing returns trap was through increased specialization and trade, not increased efforts to bring more land into production.[39]

Malthus and Ricardo were both realists; they looked at the debilitating forces that had been set in motion by economic progress in previous centuries. Adam Smith, on the other hand, saw the opportunity for an economy to spin out of this cycle where equilibrium would always tend back toward the subsistence level. Much of the secondary literature on Smith emphasizes his views that growing industrial production would enable unbounded prosperity if unimpeded by the regressive interventions of government. Yet, even while stressing the profound importance of the division of labor and capital accumulation for industry in the *Wealth of Nations*, Smith pointed out that these economic activities were possible because land "produces a greater quantity of food than what is sufficient to maintain all the labour necessary for bringing it to the market."[40] Consequently, Smith emphasized that "the most opulent nations, indeed, generally excel all their neighbors in agriculture as well as manufactures."[41]

Like Ricardo after him, Smith saw that much of the land beyond that closest to the villages and the farmers' houses appeared marginal and scraggly. But he took a very different view of the productive potential of this land than that which prompted Ricardo to formulate the law of diminishing returns. In essence, Smith saw the way out of the diminishing returns and low-level equilibrium trap in the application of better husbandry and more capital investment on lands that were only marginally productive.

Drawing primarily on observations in his native Scotland, Smith saw that many formerly unproductive lands had been improved in his lifetime by two key developments. First, the building of good roads and canals, "by diminishing the expense of carriage, put remote parts of the country more nearly upon a level with those in the neighborhood of the town."[42] Second, farmers throughout Scotland had taken major new steps to introduce a system of husbandry that increased and perpetuated the productivity of vast areas of the lowlands. Key to the new husbandry techniques, Smith noted, was the extension of manuring practices which previously had only been intensively undertaken on lands closest to villages. The increased manuring resulted because of the availability of transport into the hinterlands and, even more importantly, because Scotland's entrance into a customs union with England had increased the price of cattle and thereby indirectly vastly increased the available supply of manure.[43]

Prior to these developments, Smith described a general system of land management prevailing over the low country of Scotland in which present production consistently induced future diminishing returns. Seldom he said, could more than one-third or one-fourth and often as little as one-fifth or one-sixth of the arable lands be kept manured and managed and thus "kept constantly in good condition and fit for tillage."

The rest will, the greater part of them, be allowed to lie waste, producing scarce anything but some miserable pasture, just sufficient to keep alive a few straggling, half-starved cattle; the farm though much understocked in proportion to what would be necessary for its complete cultivation, being very frequently overstocked in proportion to its actual product. A portion of this waste land, however, after having been pastured in this wretched manner for six or seven years together, may be ploughed up, when it will yield, perhaps, a poor crop or two of bad oats, or of some other coarse grain, and then, being entirely exhausted, it must be rested and pastured again as before and another portion ploughed up to be in the same manner exhausted and rested again in its turn. . . . The rest were never manured, but a certain portion of them was in its turn, notwithstanding, regularly cultivated and exhausted. Under this system of management, it is evident, even that part of the land of Scotland which is capable of good cultivation could produce but little in comparison of what it may be capable of producing.[44]

Although much of western Europe was able simultaneously to reduce ecological stress and increase food availability as a result of increased trading and specialization that arose with the worldwide European economic system, problems of deforestation continued to increase during the seventeenth and eighteenth centuries. During the period between the emergence from the Dark Ages and the replacement of wood as the predominant fuel and material in shipbuilding, the once heavily forested European countryside was radically altered. Impending wood shortages, particularly in England, threatened by the seventeenth century serious economic consequences, since wood was used not only for domestic heating and cooking purposes, but for construction, shipbuilding, and industrial purposes.[45]

Many students of economic history see the challenge of this wood shortage as a major reason why the industrial revolution began in England. L. J. Zimmerman notes:

The wood shortage that already had become manifest in the United Kingdom during the reign of Queen Elizabeth was the challenge which had to be answered. From 1540 to 1640 the price of wood increased three times as much as the general price level. Wood was needed mainly for construction, for shipbuilding, for fuel and industrial purposes. Shipbuilding was assigned top priority, and by decree all persons were forbidden to cut wood for other purposes within fourteen miles of the coast. This shortage of wood stimulated the tendency to substitute coal for wood in industrial production, and this practice finally led (although it was completely unforeseen at the time) to the great Industrial Revolution.[46]

Even with the transition to coal as the major industrial fuel, England and the rest of Europe continued to be plagued by the problem of timber shortages for the shipbuilding industry. The answer to this problem, and the eventual reduction of pressure on Europe's dwindling forests, did not come until 1862, when the U.S. Civil War battle between the Monitor and the Merrimac at Hampton Roads, Virginia, symbolically ended the era of the great wooden sailing vessels.[47]

Ultimately, it took European civilization almost 1,000 years, from the end of the Dark Ages to almost 1900, to transcend fully the limits that the natural environment placed on population and economic progress. To some extent, it can be argued that the need to adapt only grew acute with time; that it took a thousand years because only then did the pressures of soil exhaustion and timber shortage make adaptation necessary. Yet, as a glance over European history shows, medieval and mercantile Europe were faced with periodic crises during this period because existing levels of population and economic prosperity could not be sustained on the productivity from the local environment. These problems were reduced (often after famine and economic recession) through the reclamation of internal lands, the movement of food production to other places, and increased specialization facilitated by growing world trade. Relief from the cyclical grip of the Malthusian population-food-natural resource trap only really came with industrial development and the transition of European economies to dependence on fossil fuels and fossil minerals.

Reactions by Other Societies

It is worth noting that the initial reaction to the problems of soil exhaustion and deforestation by European societies was not the institution of better agricultural and silvicultural management practices. Even the Dutch, who developed intensive agricultural techniques and instituted elaborate public works efforts to reclaim land, did so after they had generated a surplus from their fishing which relieved some of the pressure to produce food grains at home. The countryside management techniques for both forests and agricultural lands which are practiced today in Europe, and are renowned worldwide, only came into widespread use *after* the European populations did not have to depend on their lands for every meal and on their forests for fuel and construction.

   Although not in Europe, there are examples of civilizations which were able to muster the will to change their methods for securing production from their lands even while they continued to depend directly on products harvested from these lands. For example, while shifting cultivation continues to be the predominant form of agriculture even today in much of tropical Africa, a few tribes were forced by their circumstances to develop sophisticated soil management and conservation practices long ago. The Bakara, living on the island of Ukara in Lake Victoria, faced population density higher than could normally be sustained on the basis of shifting cultivation. Gradually, then, the Bakara evolved a system of agriculture very different from the typical African cultivator, including crop rotations, green manuring, stall feeding of stock, use of manure for fertilizer, pit cultivation, and contour ridging.[48] As noted earlier in this chapter, the Incas also developed elaborate management practices in response to the prospects of erosion and soil exhaustion in their mountainous environs.[49]

   Perhaps the best large-scale examples of environmental adaptation without flight of people or production and in the absence of fundamental technological changes are found in Oriental history. Lester Bilsky argues, for example, that this was the case in ancient China.[50] Bilsky describes the period from the eighth century B.C. to the third century B.C. as one in which cyclical "population growth, economic development, and the need for military preparedness in (rival) states . . . all put increasing pressures on the states' natural resources."[51] He shows how periodic famines and plagues, while exacerbated by frequent natural disasters, correlate with periods after war or severe repression and taxation of farmers by local rulers. Both of these events caused more rapid exploitation of the resource base, and thus Bilsky claims the next generation suffered the delayed effects of deforestation, soil exhaustion, and soil erosion.[52] Bilsky shows how reductions in taxation and truces, as well as increased use of fallowing, manuring, and labor-saving metal tools, were able to head off such crises, but not until they had exacted large human and ecological tolls.[53]

It wasn't until the third century B.C., however, when China was unified into one empire by the state of Ch'in that the problem of periodic ecological crises was eased. Bilsky attributes this to the reductions of land pressures formerly caused by local exploitation of small farmers and wars, the development of one bureaucracy to control the use of natural resources, the setting up of transportation and food storage systems to augment hard-pressed areas, and the institution of massive public works programs that improved the land (terracing, irrigation systems, etc.).[54] A strong-willed government in control of all China used its political and bureaucratic powers to re-orient agricultural practices and institute new land management programs.

Of course, all of the adaptations either to reduce pressures on local resources (flight, importation, substitution, population decline) or to increase the long-term productivity of these resources (better management, technological advancement), only offer a society the *chance* to reduce its long-term ecological problems. The substitution of fossil fuels for biological resources does not ensure that forests will not be in short supply. The importation of large amounts of food may not be enough to reverse local soil degradation if farmers continue to abuse the soil. Even the use of modern agricultural machinery and large doses of chemical fertilizers does not prevent soil exhaustion and soil erosion.

The development of the United States, more than perhaps that of any civilization in history, indicates that so long as land, forests, and water are abundant, the tendency is to utilize them extensively rather than intensively. In spite of the fact that the era of American industrialization set in almost entirely after wood was no longer the predominant source of industrial fuel and shipbuilding never was a serious drain, American forests were dissipated at rates unprecedented in human history. By the early nineteenth century, New England, almost completely forested a century before, had been cleared and extensively cultivated. As in parts of Europe, the rich initial agricultural yields of early years declined thereafter, as shallow soils lost their nutrients. Later, much of this land was converted to pasture and today a large amount of it has returned to forests with low commercial yields.[55] The economic consequences, for New England, were quite dissimilar than for Europe because the region became the first in America to industrialize (owing to both low farm productivity and available water power), because population densities in America were only a fraction of those in Europe, and because people could move westward into the frontier at will.

Ohio and much of the American Midwest, once more than 90 percent forested, were permanently converted to highly productive agriculture with greater reward, owing to climate, soil characteristics, and terrain.[56] Yet, it remains true that millions of acres of what would today be enormously valuable hardwoods were burned in place by westward moving pioneers who felt no pressures of scarcity or sense of economic value for the timber resources. Transportation to the East or to foreign ports was simply not economical.[57]

As well, millions of acres of highly productive soils were squandered during the nineteenth and into the twentieth centuries, as pioneer farmers practiced a linear form of shifting cultivation by moving on to new farms upon wearing out the soil of their present ones.[58] That the ritual of exhaustion and migration is not such a distant custom as some may think is captured by the apocryphal story of the New Deal agricultural extension worker who went to a midwestern farm to teach the owner the latest soil conservation techniques. The old farmer is supposed to have rejected the young man's advice, replying: "Son, what can you tell me about soil conservation that I don't already know from experience? Why, I wore out three farms before you were even born."[59]

The United States has never reached the point where economic needs and population density could not be sustained with available natural resources, as occurred in medieval Europe at periodic intervals. However, this is due to the immensity and lushness of the North American resource base, relatively low population density, and the coincidence of U.S. development with the advances of the industrial revolution. It is not attributable to any superior sense of land management or stewardship instilled in American pioneers and farmers. It took the great dust storms of the depression era and serious flooding in the major river catchments exacerbated by soil erosion for the U.S. government to take steps to encourage farmers to preserve the long-term productivity of American farmlands.[60] Even today, there are serious questions about whether soil erosion and degradation are continuing at levels that will reduce the productive potential of large areas of land in the future.[61]

SOME LESSONS FROM HISTORY

One of the striking lessons to note from history is that the most predominant response to ecological decline at the local level has been some form of flight from the problem. Populations have dispersed, migrated, or declined; food and resource production have been moved to other places. In either case, lands were abandoned or used less intensively than they had previously been used. Sometimes, as in Europe, the ecological decline has been temporary. In other places, as in southern Europe and the Middle East, the productivity of the land left behind has never been restored.

Certain instances of flight are actually calculated and economical rationally under existing circumstances. For some civilizations, especially relatively small and primitive ones, a cyclical pattern of flight (shifting cultivation) is part of an integral strategy for perpetuating an adequate yield of food and raw materials without causing widespread soil exhaustion and deforestation. In nations or on continents which still have an open frontier of rich soil, lush forests, and abundant water, continuous flight from reckless land clearing and careless agricultural practices may not only be possible but may be far easier and more economical than making investments to protect the resource base or regulate production over the long term.

The problem with these strategies of calculated flight is that they tend to be limited in duration. So long as shifting cultivation economies need not return to previously exhausted land before nature's recovery is complete, they can be perpetuated. Once they cross this threshold—whether because of population and economic expansion or geopolitical restrictions on territory—productivity will decline and population must either decline or disperse. The limits of the frontier are spatial: sooner or later the frontier must start to close and land becomes a scarcer commodity. The future opportunity costs of squandering soil fertility and "strip mining" forests for immediate gain mount up, as new land and trees are no longer endlessly available. In both instances, the dynamics of time sooner or later make flight a strategy of diminishing returns.

In many other cases, flight is much more of an immediate response to an impending crisis than it is a calculated strategy. Population dispersals or famines in history are frequently associated with rather sudden declines in agricultural productivity that were facilitated by previous overextensions of the land. Lacking external means of securing adequate food supplies in the face of such productivity declines, the people of the Mesopotamian and Mayan civilizations dispersed, and the people of fourteenth-century Europe abandoned large areas of land and were thinned by famine.

A different form of flight has been possible by societies that have secured access to external supplies of food and raw materials in the face of declining resource productivity at home. Politically powerful empires or colonial nations have been able to impose the ecological costs of food production on other areas in the face of deterioration of their soils at home. This was the case with ancient Greece, Rome, and early colonial Europe.

Although it is more common for people to flee or to import supplies from other locations, some societies have responded to their own inherent natural resource limitations or to ecological declines which threaten their resource base. Most examples of successful adaptations are of countries which overcame the limits of their natural resources to attain a higher level of economic prosperity. Invariably, such a response has involved trade and specialization. Often the most dynamic trading and manufacturing peoples of a particular epoch have been ones who have found that their soils were not fertile enough or their populations were too large to produce the agricultural surplus necessary to meet their economic aspirations.

Sometimes, a gradual series of social and economic forces has encouraged the institution of better husbandry and enabled a society to attain new levels of agrarian-based affluence. This is what Adam Smith witnessed in Scotland: a perpetual cycle of agricultural methods that led to great inefficiency in land use, broken by two significant developments that revolutionized land management practices. One involved the provision of public goods. But the other development was the simultaneous and unplanned response of countless individuals throughout the countryside to changing economic incentives that made available large quantities of manure and rewarded improved husbandry of the land. This is an important lesson. All of the public infrastructure that permitted better access to peripheral lands and better transport to urban markets could not by themselves have brought the changes Smith observed in the Scottish countryside. They could not have occurred if the day in, day out techniques of the masses who actually worked the land had not also changed to ensure continued productivity from the land. It was, more than anything, the individual response to new economic incentives that broke the erratic cultivation and exhaustion cycle which for centuries had left a high percentage of the land at any given time unproductive.

Nonetheless, all pitfalls of diminishing returns on cultivated lands cannot be erased everywhere as simply as this. It is important to remember that Smith was observing lowland Scotland, an area where soils are generally good, rainfall adequate, and terrain gentle. Here, good husbandry clearly was the missing link to perpetual agricultural productivity. In many developing countries today, the problem is that additional lands available for cultivation truly are more marginal than those already under cultivation.

Indeed, one of the reasons Ricardo presented a more pessimistic view on this matter than Smith was probably that by his time new husbandry techniques of the sort Smith lauded were being maximally applied on the base lands of the United Kingdom and the rest of Europe. Given equal doses of capital and labor (even labor employing careful husbandry techniques), Ricardo saw that lands in marshy areas, having poor soils, in sloping terrain, or with decreased water availability would yield less than the flat, fertile lands of Europe's valley floors which were already in use. In essence, Ricardo saw that the medieval trap had entailed more than just the inability to care for good farmlands; it had also included the tendency of population pressures to push cultivation beyond these good lands to more and more marginal lands.

The views of both Smith and Ricardo provide important lessons, even for countries today. Each identified an essential component of the problem of diminishing returns over time that had plagued Europe through the medieval ages. Smith noted that even good lands not properly managed will lose productivity with time. Such waves of diminishing returns on any given piece of land can only be averted if the individual cultivators who work the land adopt techniques that maintain or enhance soil fertility rather than degrade it on an annual basis. Ricardo pointed out that agricultural productivity secured on good lands cannot be sustained with equal amounts of capital and labor when cultivation extends to more marginal lands. Ricardo's dimension of diminishing returns cannot be changed. Where all good arable land is presently in production, expansions of land in agriculture will yield decreased productivity per units of labor and capital applied.

Of course, Ricardo did not even deal with the fact that marginal lands are also much more susceptible to ecological deterioration than are good lands. In Scotland, the lowlands could recuperate fairly quickly once abandoned because of reduced soil fertility. In due course, agricultural production could be renewed until the next fertility decline. But marginal lands often suffer much worse deterioration because erosion, soil hardening, or aridification may be induced by harsher ecological and geographical circumstances. Thus, as the historical examples of southern Europe indicate, marginal lands may never recuperate once they suffer the sort of diminishing returns that Smith identified in Scotland.

Successful adaptations to a declining natural environment which threatens to undermine the entire prosperity upon which a civilization is built are not numerous in history. Adaptation to these circumstances require either the institution of better resource management techniques—to reverse declining productivity— or substitution of more abundant resources for those in decline or scarce supply. Many societies in history have been able to accomplish neither, instead "blindly trying to continue their modes of living until they could not manage any further."[62]

Adjustment of land and resource management techniques to avert economic problems requires large-scale social, economic, and political changes. The historical examples—the Incas and the Chinese offering perhaps the best— have been those societies which have had a cohesive social structure and a very strong state with a highly centralized system of controlling and mobilizing resources. Two things are involved. First, the day-to-day relationship of people to the land must be altered so that resources are used on a sustainable basis. This may require redefining land tenure, forcing people to account for social and long-term costs of their actions, changing the techniques and implements they use on the land, and reorienting local educational and social patterns. Second, large supplies of labor and capital must be mobilized to institute terracing, irrigation, ditch digging, planting, or other public works projects. The difficulties inherent in making the necessary changes to reverse the trend of ecological decline or break out of the cycle of periodic productivity decline can be measured by the few civilizations in history which have successfully responded in this manner.

The most fundamental adaption to the problems of local resource productivity in modern history was the shift from wood to fossil fuels for industrial and domestic purposes, which originated in Europe and quickly spread to North America. This shift, coupled with the subsequent substitution of other raw materials for shipbuilding, was imperative. Even at early industrial production rates, which are dwarfed by today's standards, Europe's available supply of wood was heavily constrained.

However, the industrial revolution—originally fueled by wood but only reaching present levels because of the use of fossil fuels—intensified problems of environmental pollution previously experienced in European and North American cities and brought on some new ones. While many of these problems were not addressed until relatively recently, the numerous steps taken to prevent pollution problems from imposing prohibitive economic costs during the nineteenth and twentieth centuries should not be ignored.

In a millennial sense, of course, the exchange of coal and oil for wood as an industrial fuel, and the increased use of subsurface minerals, is only an interim solution to the problem of providing energy for industry, transportation, and domestic use. Fossil resource scarcity on a global basis must sooner or later require another more permanent energy and raw material transition.

But, even more germane to our concerns, is the fact that the move to substitute fossil resources for biological resources as implements of production—and the subsequent mechanization of cultivation and resources procurement—also has not ended the threats of soil exhaustion, soil erosion, and deforestation. Petroleum-based, mechanized economies, while better able to feed themselves through intensive cultivation and to mediate their consumption of forests, must take steps to ensure that their soils and their forests are sustained for productivity in the long run.

Even with all of these responses to problems of perpetuating the productivity of living and creative resources, there is a certain tendency for societies to push toward the limits of the land. Prior to widespread world trade and specialization, population growth or decline of existing resources caused societies to spread cultivation activities to new lands. In a world of trade and commerce, the impact of rising agricultural prices may have the same effect. Such "internal colonizations" have historically created more problems than they have solved. Uncultivated lands lying within already settled territories are usually not cultivated for a good reason. They may have poor soils, rugged terrain, poor drainage, or numerous other characteristics that may lead to serious ecological and economic problems. Societies which have followed this path out of greed or in an effort to increase production because they could not import food or generate enough of a surplus on existing lands have not fared well in history—witness the continuing ecological and economic decline of Spain and Italy in the late Middle Ages and mercantilist era. Technical advances are, of course, possible as a means of improving productivity, but history tells us that more intensive cultivation, more careful management of existing lands, or large-scale entry into world commerce are often better solutions than a gradual spread of agriculture over increasingly marginal lands.

Of course, new technologies, transportation systems, public works projects, or changing political circumstances may make vast areas of previously unconquered land available and attractive. Some virgin land schemes have been notably successful. It is easy to remember the experiences of the Netherlands, the U.S. prairies, or the Argentine pampas.[63] But many other land rushes into virgin territory have brought only ephemeral results or induced major ecological disasters: the thirteenth-century sweep across Europe, the wholesale cultivation of New England, the homesteading of the arid American Southwest, and the gigantic efforts in the late 1950s to cultivate vast Russian grasslands all ran up against serious ecological obstacles.

The clearest lesson from history, then, is that every civilization must be cognizant of the limits of its soil, forest, and hydrological resources. These limits may vary tremendously depending upon climate; the original endowment of trees, water, and forests; social, economic, and political structures; and technological factors. There are, nevertheless, types of cultivation that reduce future cultivatability and a level at which the cutting of trees brings scarcity. Soil erosion, caused by careless agricultural practices and wanton destruction of trees and watersheds, may also lead to serious long-term difficulties in water availability and reduced capacity in the management of water resources for irrigated agriculture. Some societies have exceeded these thresholds for quite some time without responding, because of the richness of their resources. Others have paid the price on a cyclical basis, retrenching and allowing nature to replenish itself. Still others have only lasted long enough to pay the price of soil exhaustion and deforestation once.

ENVIRONMENTAL DETERIORATION IN CONTEMPORARY DEVELOPING COUNTRIES

Management of natural resource systems to increase and maintain the production of food and raw materials was the pillar upon which most of the great human civilizations prior to the industrial revolution rested. For some societies, the challenge of management was more easily met than for others. The early Egyptians, for example, were passive managers, maintaining soil fertility by utilizing the annually renewed alluvial fan of the Nile River. The Babylonians, on the other hand, used their elaborate engineering and hydraulic skills to manipulate the waters of the Tigris and the Euphrates Rivers and thereby produce an abundant surplus to sustain life in their densely populated city-states.

Some civilizations, such as the Greek and Roman empires, never did establish management practices that could maintain their local land productivity in perpetuity—eventually they were compelled to draw on surplus food and raw materials from other geographical areas. Others, such as the Babylonians, could not maintain in perpetuity the elaborate resource management networks upon which their economies depended.

As the brief historical review in this chapter emphasizes, many past civilizations faced severe economic problems and food shortages because they could neither foresee the long-term implications of their day-to-day land management practices nor react quickly enough to alter their productive methods when their lands could no longer yield the food and raw materials necessary to maintain their economies. In the twentieth century, even accounting for the new possibilities opened up by industrialization and world trade, some observers of history have insisted that the historical precedents will be repeated: that modern nation-states may decline and disintegrate as did ancient societies which could not manage their natural resources over the long term. Writing during the depression, G. V. Jacks and R. O. Whyte issued an ominous prediction:

That the ultimate consequence of unchecked soil erosion, when it sweeps over whole countries as it is doing today, must be national extinction is obvious, for whatever other essential raw material a nation may dispense with, it cannot exist without fertile soil. Nor is extinction of a nation by erosion merely a hypothetical occurrence that may occur at some future date; it has occurred several times in the past.[64]

Other more recent observers have sought to make this point as well. J. E. Becht and L. D. Belzung contend that many nations today are evidencing the same propensities to mismanage the land as did ancient societies. Unless dramatic action is taken to alter man's abuse of the land, they say, "current incapacitating blights will overwhelm civilizations of today, as well as those of tomorrow."[65]

Lester Brown sees environmental and natural resource deterioration as a threat to national security that rivals and may even surpass the danger of military conquest. He warns:

The numerous new threats derive directly or indirectly from the rapidly changing relationship between humanity and the earth's natural systems and resources. The unfolding stresses in the relationship initially manifest themselves as ecological stresses and resource scarcities. Later they translate into economic stresses—inflation, unemployment, capital scarcity and monetary instability. Ultimately, these stresses convert into social unrest and political instability.[66]

Indeed, Brown says in his recent book, *Building a Sustainable Society*, that history is likely to repeat itself once again on a global level; that environmental stresses affecting food supply "threaten to undermine our contemporary global civilization as they did earlier, local ones."[67]

Many studies and reports in recent years have warned of the potential threats to worldwide creative and biological resources. Yet, most scientific experts do not see the likelihood that the major food producing areas of the modern world will collapse under environmental stress. Soil erosion, the loss of prime agricultural lands to urban development, water availability, and the escalation of the price of energy and petroleum-based fertilizers without question pose very significant future ecological challenges in the advanced industrial countries which presently produce the vast majority of the world's food.[68] Even so, it does not appear likely that the food production capabilities of North America, Europe, and several other strategic places on the earth will undergo continuous long-term declines such as those that occurred in the ancient civilizations noted in the first chapter.[69]

On the other hand, countries which still are underindustrialized and whose economies are heavily dependent upon their local environment to yield food and raw materials may face ecological predicaments which more closely parallel those of ancient civilizations prior to industrialization. In most of the world outside of North America, Europe, and a few other advanced industrial economies, economic activities and social systems for a high percentage of the population continue to center on land-based modes of production. Even in many third world countries where urbanization has proceeded at extremely rapid rates in recent years, much of the population continues to depend on food grown on small plots adjacent to urban areas and on wood and other fuels scavenged or purchased from the surrounding countryside. And, as in many ancient civilizations, the pressures of rapid population growth, increased demand for wood, and the spread of cultivators onto marginal or sloping lands are causing very severe problems of soil erosion, deforestation, and water availability that threaten to undermine the productivity of the local environment.[70]

In spite of striking similarities in the environmental predicaments faced by current underindustrialized nations and many ancient civilizations, much has changed that makes it less likely that twentieth-century nation-states will perish if they fail to recover and maintain the productivity of their lands. Now, with the wide spread of industrial development, global networks of trade and capital flows, and a safety net of food and fiscal assistance provided by the advanced nations and international organizations, even a very poor nation's survival may not be as directly linked to the productivity of the lands within its borders as was that of non-imperial ancient civilizations.

Thus, the parallel between the ecological predicaments faced by ancient civilizations and those of present-day developing nations, while useful, must also not be exaggerated. The main issue may not be whether or not developing countries undergoing extreme environmental deterioration will suffer the precise fate of past civilizations. It may instead be how these problems will affect the aspirations and efforts of these developing countries to reach the stage where economic development is self-sustaining and the mass of the population labors each day to increase its affluence and prosperity rather than to secure the minimum amount of sustenance to subsist. In other words, a vital if underexplored question is: How do the ecological problems facing many developing countries today interfere with the long-term potential for economic development? This is a major concern of Chapter 2.

Notes

1. The estimate is from W. C. Lowdermilk, "Conquest of the Land Through Seven Thousand Years," U.S. Department of Agriculture, *Agriculture Information Bulletin*, no. 99, August 1953.

2. One recent study suggests:

Demand for food forced cultivation ever higher up the steep slopes in the hilly and mountainous watershed to the north, sheep and goats overgrazed the hill pastures, and trees were felled indiscriminately for lumber and fuel. These practices denuded the watershed, causing severe erosion and erratic river flow. Large sediment loads were carried by the rivers in sloping areas where flow was rapid, but the sediment was dropped where flow rate decreased on the level areas. Sediment was deposited in the river bed and, more importantly, in the irrigation canals and ditches. This sediment had to be removed for irrigation to continue. In time, human labor was insufficient to cope with removal, so sections of irrigated land were abandoned. No plant cover grew on the abandoned land because the area was arid. Without vegetative cover, wind eroded the fields, and drifting soil filled the remaining irrigation structures. Eventually the whole irrigated area was abandoned. The large population, much of it in the larger cities, could not be supported. Cities were abandoned, and the area became a desert of shifting sand.

G. V. Jacks and R. O. Whyte, *Vanishing Lands: A World Survey of Soil Erosion* (New York: Doubleday, Doran and Co., 1939), pp. 6–7. Another study adds "that growing soil salinity played an important part in the breakup of Sumerian civilization seems beyond question." Thorkild Jacobsen and Robert M. Adams, "Salt and Silt in Ancient Mesopotamian Agriculture, *Science* 128, no. 3334, pp. 1251–8 (November 21, 1958). See also, John H. Davis, "Influences of Man upon Coast Lines," in *Man's Role in Changing Earth*, edited by William L. Thomas, Jr. (Chicago: University of Chicago Press, 1955), pp. 509–511. Frederick R. Troeh, J. Arthur Hobbs, and Roy L. Donahue, *Soil and Water Conservation for Productivity and Environmental Protection* (Englewood Cliffs, N.J.: Prentice Hall, 1980), pp. 26–27, and J. Oates, "Prehistoric Settlement Patterns in Mesopotamia," in *Man, Settlement and Urbanism*, edited by P. J. Ucko, R. Tringham, and G. W. Dimbleby (London: Duckworth, 1973), pp. 299–310.)

3. The various explanations are offered in Pierre Gourou, *The Tropical World: Its Social and Economic Conditions and Its Future Status*. Translated by E. D. Laborde (London: Longmans, Green, & Co., 1953), pp. 47–49. For a general description of the Mayan agricultural economy, see D. E. Dumond, "Swidden Agriculture and the Rise of Maya Civilization," in *Environment and Cultural Behavior: Ecological Studies in Cultural Anthropology*, edited by Andrew P. Vayda (Garden City, N.J.: Natural History Press, 1969).

4. Gourou, *Tropical World*, pp. 49–50. This explanation was first offered by O. F. Cook in 1909.

5. Edward Hyams and George Ordish, *The Last of the Incas* (New York: Simon and Schuster, 1963), pp. 8–9.

6. Colin Clark and Margaret Haswell, *The Economics of Subsistence Agriculture*, 3rd ed. (London: Macmillan, 1967), p. 52.

7. Jacks and Whyte, *Vanishing Lands*, p. 6. See also George P. Marsh, *The Earth as Modified by Human Action* (New York: Charles Scribner's Sons, 1898), pp. 2–4.

8. See Troeh, Hobbs, and Donahue, *Soil and Water*, pp. 29–30; Edward Hyams, *Soil and Civilization* (London: Thames and Hudson, 1952), pp. 91–114; and Tom Dale and Vernon Gill Carter, *Topsoil and Civilization* (Norman, Okla.: Oklahoma University Press, 1955), pp. 88–108.

9. Plato, *Critias*, as cited in H. C. Darby, "The Clearing of the Woodland in Europe," in *Man's Role in Changing the Face of the Earth*, edited by William L. Thomas Jr. (Chicago: University of Chicago Press, 1956), p. 185. See also Clarence J. Glacken, "Changing Ideas of the Habitable World," and Fritz M. Heichelheim, "Effects of Classical Antiquity on the Land," in the same volume.

10. Ibid. See also, Troeh, Hobbs, and Donahue, *Soil and Water;* and Hyams, *Soil and Civilization*.

11. Troeh, Hobbs, and Donahue, *Soil and Water*, pp. 30–32.

12. See Hyams, *Soil and Civilization*, pp. 244–247; and Dale and Carter, *Topsoil and Civilization*, pp. 121–147.

13. Troeh, Hobbs and Donahue, *Soil and Water*, p. 31.

14. A. Harry Walters, *Ecology, Food and Civilisation* (London: Charles Knight and Co., 1973), pp. 52–89.

15. "The inherent fertility of the soil deteriorated little, if any, between the fifth and eleventh centuries. . . . (T)he abandonment of considerable areas by the cultivators served more to increase than diminish the productivity of the soil" (Dale and Carter, *Topsoil and Civilization*, p. 151).

16. "Flanders and north Italy are by far the most interesting areas because the fertility of their soil and the ease with which they could import extra food from nearby 'breadbasket' regions had favoured high density of population. This gave them not only a large reservoir of part-time peasant labor free for country industrial work but enabled them also to urbanize a greater proportion of their population" (Sylvia Thrupp, "Medieval Industry, 1000–1500," *Fontana Economic History of Europe*, I [1971] p. 47).

17. Fernand Braudel, cited in Immanuel Wallerstein, *The Modern World System I: Capitalist Agriculture and the Origins of the European World. Economy in the Sixteenth Century* (New York: Academic Press, 1974), p. 43.

18. H. C. Darby, "The Clearing of the Woodland in Europe," in *Man's Role in Changing the Face of the Earth*, edited by William L. Thomas, Jr. (Chicago: University of Chicago Press, 1955), p. 188.

19. The period 1150–1750 is generally divided into four distinct economic phases: 1150–1300 (economic expansion); 1300–1450 (economic contraction); 1450–1650 (economic expansion); and 1600–1750 (economic contraction). Debates among historians tend to center on what caused the economic crises of the fourteenth and seventeenth centuries. The question, particularly concerning the latter crisis, is of enormous ideological importance because of disagreement about when and how capitalism came to pre-

dominate in the European world economic system. To some, the crisis of the fourteenth century was a "crisis of feudalism" and the seventeenth century the first "crisis" of the emerging world capitalist system. To others, the seventeenth century marks the final gasp of an Ancient Regime in Europe and the birth of a new capitalist economy. The debates are eloquently summarized, albeit not necessarily impartially, by Wallerstein in *Modern World System I*, pp. 15–38; and Wallerstein, *The Modern World System II: Mercantilism and the Consolidation of the European World Economy, 1600–1750* (New York: Academic Press, 1980), pp. 3–34. In spite of the ideological disagreement, most scholars of European preindustrial revolution economic history, as Wallerstein makes clear, agree that soil fertility was an important influencing factor.

20. Wallerstein argues that there are three main explanations of the crisis of the fourteenth century: cyclical economic trends; the fact that the limits of agricultural production had been reached (and subsequently declined) under the feudal system; and a shift in European climatological conditions. In this view, soil productivity was reduced both as a result of exhaustion under peasants forced to extract larger and larger surpluses from their lands and by the bad seasonal growing conditions resulting from the weather. Wallerstein, *Modern World System I*, p. 37.

21. Archibald R. Lewis, "The Closing of the European Frontier," *Spectrum* 33, no. 4 (October 1958), p. 476.

22. Charles R. Bowlers, "Ecological Crisis in Fourteenth Century Europe," in *Historical Ecology: Essays on Environment and Social Change*, edited by Lester J. Bilsky (Port Washington, N.Y.: Kennikat Press, 1980), p. 94.

It will not be too fanciful . . . to see in the falling production of the later centuries a natural punishment for earlier overexpansion. As long as the colonization movement went forward and new lands were taken up, the crops from virgin lands encouraged man to establish new families and settlments. But after a time the marginal character of marginal lands was bound to assert itself, and the honeymoon of high yields was succeeded by long periods of reckoning, when the poorer lands, no longer new, punished the men who tilled them with failing crops and with murrain of sheep and cattle (M. M. Postan, *Essays on Medieval Agriculture and General Problems of the Medieval Economy* [Cambridge, England: Cambridge University Press, 1973], p. 14).

23. Perry Anderson, *Passages from Antiquity to Feudalism* (London: New Left Books, 1974), p. 197.

24. G. B. Masefield, "Crops and Livestock," in *The Economy of Expanding Europe in the Sixteenth and Seventeenth Centuries*, edited by E. E. Rich and C. H. Wilson, Vol. IV of *Cambridge Economic History of Europe*, (Cambridge: Cambridge University Press, 1967), p. 276.

25. The phrase is quoted from Richard Pares, *Merchants and Planters, Economic History Review Supplement* No. 4 (Cambridge: Cambridge University Press, 1960), p. 20. Also p. 40. See also, Richard S. Dunn, *Sugar and Slaves* (Chapel Hill: University of North Carolina Press, 1972), pp. 26–30; Masefield, *"Crops and Livestock,"* Wallerstein, *Modern World System I*, pp. 88–89; and Wallerstein, *Modern World System II*, pp. 161–165.

26. ". . . the Mediterranean lived essentially from the products of its own agriculture. Nothing occurs comparable to what develops in [Western and Northern Europe]. The urban universes did not give over to anyone else the task of supplying them with provisions." Braudel, quoted in Wallerstein, *Modern World System I*, p. 217.

27. *Ibid.*

28. See Orazio Cancilo and Jose-Gentil da Silva, as cited by Wallerstein, *Modern World System II*, p. 146.

29. See Wallerstein, *Modern World System II*, pp. 13–34, for a description of the prolonged economic contraction that swept over Europe between about 1600 to 1750.

30. The quote is borrowed from W. Arthur Lewis, *Theory of Economic Growth* (New York: Harper and Row, 1965), p. 53.

31. Arnold Toynbee, *A Study of History*, 6 vols. (New York: Oxford University Press, 1948). Ester Boserup, in *The Condition of Agricultural Growth* (London: Allen & Unwin, 1965), proposes that demographic expansion (and consequent pressures on production systems) induces technical change and more intense cultivation in agriculture. L. J. Zimmerman, in *Poor Lands, Rich Lands: The Widening Gap* (New York: Random House, 1965), sees economic development as fundamentally linked to a nation's recognizing the necessity and possibility of adapting to some challenge which threatens or limits its economic welfare (p. 131).

32. Joh Van Veen, *Dredge, Drain, Reclaim* (The Hague: Martinus Nijhoff, 1950), p. 11.

33. See Ivo Schoffer, *A Short History of the Netherlands*, 2nd ed. (Amsterdam: Allert de Lange bv, 1973), pp. 9–13.

34. See Wallerstein, *Modern World System II*, pp. 40–42. Ruggiero Romano, according to Wallerstein, calls the period from 1590 to 1679 the "Dutch Agricultural Century," pp. 41–42. Aldo de Maddalena, in "Rural Europe, 1500–1750," in *The Fontana Economic History of Europe, II: The Sixteenth and Seventeenth Centuries*, edited by C. M. Cipolla (Glasgow: Collins, 1974), p. 313, says: "How can we ignore the relationship between the remarkable development of Dutch agriculture and the pre-eminence of the Low Countries in the seventeenth century economic scene?"

35. See Wallerstein, *Modern World System II* pp. 41–45.

36. Douglas C. North and Robert Paul Thomas, *The Rise of the Western World*, (Cambridge: Cambridge University Press, 1973), p. 145.

37. See D. V. Glass, ed., *Introduction to Malthus* (London: Watts, 1953).

38. See David Ricardo, *The Principles of Political Economy and Taxation*, Everyman's Library 1911 Edition (London: Dent and Sons, 1969) pp. 34–45.

39. *Ibid.*, pp. 71–82.

40. Adam Smith, *The Wealth of Nations*, Pelican Classics Edition (London: Penguin Books, 1970), note 21, pp. 250–480.

41. *Ibid.*, pp. 111.

42. *Ibid.*, p. 251.

43. *Ibid.*, pp. 324–334.

44. *Ibid.*, pp. 326–327.

45. See Darby, "Clearing of the Woodland," pp. 199–203.

46. L. J. Zimmerman, *Poor Lands, Rich Lands: The Widening Gap* (New York: Random House, 1965), pp. 108–109. Zimmerman contends that the supply of wood was more stable and the clash between the shipbuilding and industrial sectors not so acute in continental western Europe as in England. Hence, he says, on the continent, "the availability of the traditional factors of production impeded technological progress" (*Ibid.*, p. 109). Nevertheless, continental industries did follow British industries and switch en masse to coal fuel by the nineteenth century.

47. Darby, "Clearing of the Woodland," pp. 201–202.

48. Jacks and Whyte, *Vanishing Lands*, pp. 272–273.

49. Hyams and Ordish, *Last of the Incas*, pp. 8–9. For an elaboration, see R. A. Donkin, *Agricultural Terracing in the Aboriginal New World* (Tucson: University of Arizona Press, 1979).

50. Lester J. Bilsky, "Ecological Crisis and Response in Ancient China," in Bilsky, *Historical Ecology*, pp. 60–73.

51. Ibid., p. 6.

52. Ibid., p. 65.

53. Ibid., pp. 66–68.

54. Ibid., p. 69–70. Bilsky does point out that China eventually outgrew the limits of these improvements as well. Still, one could argue that the Chinese focus on increasing agricultural productivity through labor-intensive improvements of the land is a similar response in modern times.

55. See Troeh, Hobbs, and Donahue, *Soil and Water*.

56. Ibid.

57. See J. Edwin Becht and L. D. Belzang, *World Resource Management: Key to Civilizations and Social Achievement* (Englewood Cliffs, N.J.: Prentice Hall, 1975) pp. 160–161.

58. Adam Smith, *The Wealth of Nations*, pp. 328–329, quoted a Swedish traveler to the North American colonies as reporting in 1749 that the settlers were forsaking many of the careful conservation techniques then beginning to become widespread in Europe:

> They make scarce any manure for their corn fields, he says; but when one piece of ground has been exhausted by continual cropping, they clear and cultivate another piece of fresh land; and when that is exhausted, proceed to a third. Their cattle are allowed to wander through the woods and other uncultivated grounds, where they are half-starved; having long ago extirpated almost all the annual grasses by cropping them too early in the spring, before they had time to form their flowers, or to shed their seeds. The annual grasses were, it seems, the best natural grasses in that part of North America; and when the Europeans first settled there, they used to grow very thick, and to rise three or four feet high. A piece of ground which, when he wrote, could not maintain one cow, would in former times, he was assured, have maintained four, each of which would have given four times the quantity of milk which that one was capable of giving. The poorness of the pasture had, in his opinion, occasioned the degradation of their cattle, which degenerated sensibly from one generation to another.

59. Charles M. Hardin, *The Politics of Agriculture: Soil Conservation and the Struggle for Power in Rural America* (Glencoe, Ill.: The Free Press, 1952).

60. Ibid.

61. For a balanced perspective, see Sandra Batie, *Soil Erosion: Crisis in America's Cropland?* (Washington, D.C.: The Conservation Foundation, 1983).

62. Erich Fromm, as quoted in Zimmerman, *Poor Lands, Rich Lands*, p. iv.

63. The late Rene Dubos, in fact, noted that: "Contrary to popular belief, farmland is not a 'natural' resource. It had to be created out of some wilderness, at sometime in the past, and once created it had to be maintained in a fertile condition." See "Creating Farmland Through Science," *The New York Times*, October 14, 1981.

64. Jacks and Whyte, p. 6.

65. J. Edwin Becht and L. D. Belzang, *World Resource Management: Key to Civilizations and Social Achievement* (Englewood Cliffs, N.J.: Prentice Hall, 1975), p. x.

66. Lester Brown, *Human Needs and the Security of Nations*, Headline Series No. 238 (New York: Foreign Policy Association, February 1978), p. 55.

67. Lester Brown, *Building a Sustainable Society* (New York: Norton, 1981), p. 6.

68. The litany of problems is enumerated in Brown, *Building a Sustainable Society*, among many others.

69. For a balanced perspective on many of these problems in the United States, see Sandra S. Batie and Robert G. Healy, eds., *The Future of American Agriculture as a Strategic Resource* (Washington, D.C.: The Conservation Foundation, 1981); and Sandra S. Batie, *Soil Erosion: Crisis in America's Farmlands?* (Washington, D.C.: The Conservation Foundation, 1982).

70. See, for example, Erik P. Echkholm, *Losing Ground: Environmental Stress and World Food Prospects* (New York: Norton, 1976).

CHAPTER 2

ENVIRONMENT, ECONOMIC GROWTH, AND DISTRIBUTION IN THE THIRD WORLD

Henry Bienen and H. Jeffrey Leonard

Since the end of World War II, the development of the world's underdeveloped or backward countries has become a major international concern. Although development is generally also acknowledged to involve a long-term process reshaping people's social, political, and cultural attitudes and institutions, it is the quest for economic improvement and eventual prosperity that has, for obvious reasons, been the central focus. To a degree unprecedented in history, the rich countries and the poor countries themselves have been preoccupied with the question: How can the poor countries of the world be made richer?

As universally endorsed as the quest for economic development has been, there has been far less agreement on what it means to make the poor countries richer. The notion of national wealth or income, as Pigou emphasized, must be broken down into at least three components: *average size*, which is a function of total national income and population; *stability over time*, which is related to the amount of current income that goes to adding or maintaining productive capacity and the degree to which current consumption patterns are sustainable; and *equality of distribution*, which is related to numerous sociopolitical factors. Prevailing differences in ideologies, fertility rates, political systems, cultures, and numerous other factors have prompted different countries, or at least their strategic political elites, to attach greater or lesser importance to each of these criteria in their quest to get richer.

In this chapter, we explore some of the possible ways in which careful environmental management or, conversely, environmental degradation, can affect an underindustrialized country's economic development—its current wealth, its future economic potential, and its pattern of income distribution. It is striking that despite large and growing literatures covering both developmental and environmental economics, few theorists have treated the myriad relationships between environment and development in more than cursory fashion.[1]

NATURAL RESOURCES AND ECONOMIC GROWTH

The fundamental requisite for economic growth is, of course, the availability of surplus capital for investment. In a closed economy, this surplus must be created by domestic savings. People must produce more than they consume and allocate the remainder for investment in the future. Participation in the international economy opens numerous other avenues for capital raising in addition to domestic savings. Raw materials and, later, finished products may be sold to other nations to generate revenues for investment. Private entrepreneurs and investors from abroad may be encouraged to transfer loans and investments, or international organizations may offer specialized loan programs or outright assistance to countries in need of capital.

In practice, most developing nations rely on all of these sources to meet their capital needs. However, some countries have been able to generate much more capital internally—domestic savings plus export earnings—than others. In the early stages of the economic development process, the choice to emphasize domestic savings, export revenues, or some combination of external assistance may be significantly influenced by a country's overall natural resource endowment.

Resource Endowments and Development Strategy

In the early post–World War II period, an important theoretical question was whether there was a link between resource endowments and national economic development and, conversely, whether underdevelopment in many countries might be associated with such factors as adverse climate, poor soil conditions, or lack of mineral deposits and petroleum. Much of the debate about "geographic determinism"[2] centered on the question of whether tropical climate was responsible for the relative lack of economic growth in the "backward areas."[3] In addition, some analysts pointed out the problems of infertile soils, erratic water availability, and inhospitable natural environments in many of these areas and speculated how these resource limitations might help explain low agricultural productivity and the general lack of economic development.[4]

Most observers have eventually concluded that although natural resources are an important basis for economic development, limitations in the natural environment do not satisfactorily explain economic underdevelopment.[5] In addition, abundant resources, most observers agree, are not sufficient in themselves to assure economic prosperity. In an era of rapidly shifting comparative advantage in industrial production, a worldwide network for transporting both raw materials and finished goods, and the huge export-oriented successes of resource-poor manufacturing countries, few now make the case that natural resource endowments are fundamental determinants of underdevelopment and development. Indeed, in his recent book, *The Nature of Mass Poverty*, John Kenneth Galbraith says bluntly that the "relation of resources to well-being is so erratic as to be flatly worthless."[6] At the same time, one need not ignore the fact that many developing countries lie in areas of the world where in the absence of technological improvements—e.g., in dryland agriculture, new disease resistant crops, etc.—nature's limitations on land-based production are still formidable.[7]

Most students of economic development today do emphasize that natural resources are an important factor for a developing country to take into consideration in charting the best economic development strategy. Clearly, mineral and petroleum wealth can contribute significant revenues which may better enable a country to implement ambitious development plans and give a country a comparative advantage in procuring raw materials for downstream industrial development—mineral processing, iron, steel, and petrochemicals, for example. A country with large supplies of fertile soils and fresh water has significantly more chance over the long term of increasing domestic savings by improved agricultural productivity than a country with a fragile ecosystem and limited quantities of key renewable resources.[8]

As a consequence, a growing body of development planning literature is concerned with the development and controlled exploitation of natural resources. The most important questions are those of optimal uses and rates of exploitation for developing countries, with the focus on pricing, terms of trade, timing, and the strategic use of proceeds for investment in future economic production.[9]

Depletion: A Path to Development or Underdevelopment?

In line with the concern about strategies for exploiting nonrenewable natural resources, the economic implications of global or national depletion of fossil fuel and mineral supply has been a matter of periodic debate for over a century. The eminent nineteenth-century British economist, W. Stanley Jevons, for example, warned that the impending exhaustion of Britain's coal reserves would have catastrophic economic effects, since he rightly assessed that Britain's burgeoning industrial prosperity was based on her abundant and cheap supply of coal.[10] In reality, however, individual countries whose economies depend upon certain resources need not face economic disaster if they deplete their own fossil fuel and mineral resources, so long as world supplies remain and the country can secure access to them through political or economic means.

Barring global shortages, the dangers of domestic fossil resource depletion may be more critical for countries which export such resources than for those which import them. Even though most third world mineral exporting countries only consume small quantities of nonrenewable resources (in comparison to the industrialized countries), many depend heavily on receipts from sales of these commodities to the advanced industrial economies. Exhaustion of indigenous supplies, especially fuel supplies, could have disastrous impacts on developing economies dependent upon such revenues. As well, depletion for the sake of monetary gain now might have significant future deleterious effects for a country as it reaches the stage of industrial development when its internal demand for fuel and minerals has grown to higher levels than at present. Finally reaching the stage when it has the technological capability and capital resources to reap the higher value-added benefits from domestic processing and manufacturing of raw materials, a developing country may find that domestic supplies have already dwindled.

On the other hand, resource depletion may actually be an important element of development strategy for some developing countries. Countries may find it advantageous to maximize income from mineral exports in the short run, even if it means depleting their existing reserves, on the grounds that they can utilize the funds to create productive capital for the future.[11] If sale of a natural resource is used to create new productive capital resources—instead of squandered on present consumption—the country may be better off in the long run even after supplies of the natural resource are depleted.

Sometimes, a strategy of depletion of biological resources may also be followed to a certain point in order to maximize present income and/or to create another natural resource. The best example of both may be found in the treatment of forest resources. Timber exports, just like mineral exports, may provide important revenues for financing development plans in other sectors. And, as we saw in Chapter 1, the plunder of forest resources has sometimes culminated in the creation of valuable agricultural lands.

In either case, however, several ecological complications make the depletion of renewable resources somewhat trickier than depletion of nonrenewable resources. First is the question of how far depletion of forests can go before soil erosion, soil laterization, species extinction, hydrological problems, climate changes, and other adverse consequences of deforestation become too costly. Second is the problem of actually reversing behavioral patterns and economic incentives from a depletion to a sustainable yield strategy at some point in the future. Third, the depletion of forests as a means of creating productive agricultural land is a very risky business because of the nature of forest soils.

We will return to these and other pitfalls of treating renewable resources as nonrenewable resources in later chapters. The points to emphasize here are that a) although renewable resources can be strategically depleted, at some point in time it becomes necessary to manage such resources at a level of sustainable yield production; and, b) depletion of one renewable resource can also bring about undesirable and possibly irreversible degradation of renewable resources—biological or soil and water resources.

To sum up, although natural resource endowments do not determine whether development does take place, they can clearly influence the best course to follow for accomplishing development. A country with fertile soil, abundant land, good climate, and available water is most likely to develop an agricultural surplus that supports growing urbanization and industrialization. Countries rich in mineral, fossil fuel, or marketable renewable resources may generate capital for economic development through the sale of these raw materials in international markets. By contrast, one that is resource-poor in relation to its population may depend more on manufacturing or commerce as its motor of economic expansion. These countries may be most dependent upon external sources of capital investment to provide the initial "priming" of the economic development pump.

The long-term treatment of natural resources may be very important to the success of any of these capital-raising strategies over time. This is obvious in the case of countries relying upon increased agricultural production or the sales of natural resources abroad. Degradation of soil or depletion of valuable natural resource supplies prior to the time that the economy has diversified and reached a level of self-sustaining economic growth may have serious consequences. Long-term natural resource management is also important for resource-poor nations relying on external capital. The more food these countries can produce for themselves through improving the productivity of their lands, the less it will be necessary to spend large amounts of potential investment capital on food imports.

Some of the possible influences that resource endowments and long-term resource management may have upon economic development strategy are summarized in Table 1.

SECTORAL IMPACTS OF ENVIRONMENTAL DEGRADATION

Prevailing views on what constitutes economic development and what steps are necessary to accomplish economic development have evolved significantly in recent decades. The metaphor of a vicious circle of poverty, in which poverty is both a result of poverty and a cause of further poverty, is still as widely used today as it was in the 1950s. But the notion that this circle can be broken by a single, concentrated takeoff into sustained growth has been superseded by much more complicated models of how economic growth can best be stimulated and perpetuated in developing countries. Furthermore, no matter what the aggregate economic growth rates may be, it is now clear that poverty among the

TABLE 1: Natural Resource Endowments, Resource Management, and Economic Development Strategy

A. Resource Endowment	B. Development Strategy	C. Possible Outcomes	D. Implications for Development
I. Abundant fertile soil and water for cultivation	*Classical Model* Agricultural surplus frees labor, provides capital for gradual urbanization and industrialization	1) Improved management of renewable resources yields increasing agricultural surplus for overall economic development	1) Sustained and simultaneous productivity increases in agricultural and industrial sectors fuel rapid economic development
		2) Surplus agricultural product generated and invested for development, but at a cost of long-run degradation of renewable resources	2) Increased costs to reduce ecological problems or to import food may offset gains being made in other sectors
		3) Poor management of soil and water resources results in diminished agricultural production before surplus fuels growth of other sectors	3) In extreme, continuous abuse of soil may result in permanent environmental degradation that leaves country in same position as III

Resource category	Model	Outcomes	Consequences
II. Abundant minerals, fossil fuels, or renewable resources, such as forests	*Bonanza Model* Depletion of resources, to generate development capital and create future productive potential	1) Depletion of fossil resources with positive investments in other economic activities 2) Depletion of renewable resources with positive investments and switch to sustainable yield prior to irreversible degradation 3) Depletion of renewable resources with positive investments but not sustainable yield, inducing long-term irreversible degradation 4) Depletion of fossil or renewable resources without positive investments	1) Conversion of natural resource into productive capital resources enhances long-term development prospects 2) Long-term ecological and economic costs of Renewable Resource exhaustion may offset benefits from conversion of natural resources to productive resources 3) May result in gradual evolution of resource endowment to category III
III. Shortages of resources in relation to population	*Labor Surplus Model* Rapid industrial or commercial expansion to transcend resource limits	1) Rapid industrial growth spurs overall economic development 2) Failure to generate or wisely invest initial capital in dynamic industries and sectors of trade, leaving country in debt, but also unable to feed itself adequately on its poor natural resource base	1) Industrial exports pay for food imports; industrialization removes pressures of surplus labor on scarce land resources, paving way for gradual upgrading of agricultural productivity 2) Continued circle of poverty in which resource limitations may be continually exacerbated by large population trying to eke out a living and exceeding carrying capacity of the land

masses of people in poor countries and even in most middle income countries is chronic and only likely to change over an extended period of decades or even generations.

The poverty of the masses in many developing countries is chronic and self-perpetuating in part because people who are uneducated, continually under-nourished, and highly susceptible to disease and even small food shortfalls generally find it difficult to muster the energy, skills, or knowledge to take steps that might bring significant and enduring changes in their welfare. The great majority of people who live at the margin are tradition-bound and conservative. They do not or cannot make investments today that will improve their lot tomorrow. They are this way out of necessity; a mistake, a bad investment, or even a delayed payoff may mean the difference between subsistence and famine, between relative and absolute deprivation.

Poverty in both the low- and middle-income countries is also chronic in that it does not result only from the inability of individuals, families, villages, or even whole tribes to motivate and organize themselves to make better use of the available factors of production. Underutilization of labor, misuse of resources, and unavailability of capital for investment—whether endemic to an entire society or a function of dualistic development—must be viewed within the context of the political and economic circumstances prevailing in nation-states and the terms under which these nation-states participate in the international system as a whole. Poor people must struggle within political systems that may allocate power or economic resources in ways that frustrate this struggle. Moreover, the degree to which the entire nation secures advantageous terms of trade and competes successfully in world markets for capital and manufactured goods may have a fundamental bearing on the fortunes of the poorest of the poor even when they participate little in their own economies.

Clearly, these and numerous other external and structural obstacles to economic development are little affected by an individual country's ability to manage, maintain, and improve productivity from its natural resource base. Still, overexploitation of natural resources, leading to depletion and degradation, may be one way that developing country governments or their populations respond in the short term to international economic constraints that limit their prospects for aid and trade. International circumstances beyond the control of an individual developing nation may significantly increase the strains already imposed on natural resource systems. This, in turn, causes or complicates other obstacles within particular sectors that can be more directly related to poor resource management and environmental deterioration. These obstacles, explored below, include: energy availability and affordability; agricultural productivity; primary export dependence; population growth and international migrations; and urban and industrial pollution. Nevertheless, specialists in these areas—energy, agriculture, demography, urban planning—have often failed to examine the debilitating sectoral effects that environmental degradation has in many developing countries.

Energy and Environment

Energy and environmental concerns, for example, are inextricably linked in the developing world. The non-petroleum producing developing countries were the hardest hit of all by the energy shockwaves of the 1970s. Most low-income countries experienced much more difficulty in adjusting to the oil price increases than the developed countries. In conjunction with (and exacerbated by) the world fossil fuel crunch, another energy crisis has been equally as debilitating in many poor countries. Most people in the low-income countries depend almost entirely on traditional fuels—especially wood, agricultural wastes, and animal excretion—for their household needs. In many areas of the developing world, serious shortages of such fuels have arisen.

Many developing countries today confront a dilemma similar to the one faced in Europe during the seafaring and early industrialization era. The growing demand of their populations and enterprises for fuels derived directly from local biological resources has not only depleted timber supplies but brought also many serious ecological consequences associated with deforestation: soil erosion, disrupted hydrological cycles, depletion of other flora and fauna dependent upon forest cover. In parts of India and other countries which long ago depleted most available forests, people rely heavily on other biological resources, particularly animal dung, as their chief domestic fuel. Although this may prevent further wood-clearing, it too has serious consequences as dung is often the only source of fertilizer for people to apply to their crops.[12]

Many factors have inhibited developing countries from following the path of the West and making the transition from biological fuels to fossil fuels in the face of increasing scarcity and growing ecological consequences. What has happened, instead, is that most developing countries have made a partial transition, with the segment of their industrial enterprises and urban economy which deals with the outside world developing a healthy appetite for fossil fuels for industry and transportation. Thus, many developing countries have high oil (and coal) import bills at the same time that the masses of people and small-scale enterprises continue to depend on local biological resources for fuel. Now, with the world price of fossil fuels so high, and availability itself an uncertain question, the transition is stalled if at all possible. It is highly unlikely that rapid progress can be made to provide the masses of people in the third world substitute fuels so that the pressures on local forest resources can be diminished and dung can be used as fertilizer rather than for cooking.

In response to the dilemma posed by these three converging problems— fossil fuel affordability, biological fuel scarcity, and ecological deterioration associated with depletion of biological resources—developing country governments and international benefactors have in recent years begun to mount large-scale efforts to increase the supply of available biological resources for fuel, especially wood, and to make available alternative sources of energy through projects to tap solar, wind, and water power.[13]

Reforestation projects designed to build up huge industrial forests or village woodlots with fast-growing species such as eucalyptus trees have been introduced in a large number of third world countries experiencing the pains of two energy shortages simultaneously.[14] These projects could be of major significance for many developing countries in the future, and Chapter 6 illustrates the severity of economic and ecological consequences of fuel scarcities in poor countries such as those in the Sahel region of Africa. On the other hand, as later chapters indicate, there are many political, administrative, and economic factors that frequently work against the success of large schemes to create abundant and sustainable supplies of wood for energy.[15]

The energy situation in most developing countries poses several very significant threats to their economic future. Their continued dependence on traditional biological fuels is in many cases seriously undermining their forest, agricultural, and water resources. The transition to fossil fuels is either blocked or greatly slowed by world price and scarcity. Some of the ecological and economic pressures may be removed by management schemes to "mass produce" forests for energy. But it is unlikely that such schemes can support all the energy needs of an industrializing and urbanizing nation in the future. The most obvious strategic answer from an economic and ecological standpoint is for the poor developing nations to skip directly into the post-fossil fuel energy transition by relying on solar, wind, water, and other power-generating schemes that directly tap the undepletable rhythms of the earth. This, however, is no easily accomplished or short-term task. For now, the answers to the developing countries' energy problems are going to remain heavily dependent upon the institution of far-reaching programs to cultivate and manage biological fuel sources and small-scale technological innovations that help households and local enterprises use the energy supplies they have more efficiently. The extent to which progress can be made in these two directions may have major development implications for many developing nations in upcoming decades.

Agricultural Productivity

Following World War II, development planners for third world countries were preoccupied with stimulating rapid industrial development. Not only did few governments place significant emphasis on the development of the agricultural sector, many (no doubt influenced by the rapid industrialization experience of the Soviet Union) pursued policies designed to squeeze surplus capital out of agriculture and into the industrial sector. By the 1960s, however, an increasing number of development specialists had begun to emphasize that during the early stages of development, increases in agricultural productivity were crucial to the whole development process.[16] The neglect of the agricultural sector in many parts of the developing world is seen today as one of clearest obstacles to long-term economic development. Agriculture has therefore been given much greater emphasis in development plans and within international development assistance circles.

Some notable success in increasing agricultural production has been achieved in key developing countries which have come to realize that a necessary condition of economic growth is sustained increases in agricultural production. In Taiwan and South Korea, for example, agrarian reform policies, improved incentives for farmers, and development of irrigation and infrastructure have gone hand in hand with large-scale industrial development.[17] India and several other countries, assisted by large inputs of new "Green Revolution" technologies, while not rid of their agricultural problems, have at least managed to increase production faster than population in recent decades.[18] And China, primarily through the mobilization of its massive human labor potential for farming and the provision of local infrastructure (irrigation, terracing, etc.) has also developed a more stable agricultural base with which to feed its people, and contribute to industrial development.[19]

In addition, some countries in recent decades have actually managed quite well by nearly forgoing land-based productivity altogether and concentrating instead on selling manufactures or essential raw materials to the world and purchasing sustenance from these revenues. The best examples from the post–World War II era are city-state sized nations such as Hong Kong and Singapore and the oil-rich states of the Middle East. Still, these countries have achieved such economic growth under very special circumstances which cannot be duplicated by all underindustrialized nations. Hong Kong and Singapore, for example, have benefited from their small sizes, and the availability of large, skilled, and highly disciplined work forces living in close proximity. The Middle Eastern nations have large sparsely populated territories, rich in a commodity with an enormous and highly inelastic demand.

Except for the very few nations which fit these special circumstances, no nation has achieved sustained economic progress and increased industrial development without making significant, simultaneous increases in productivity from the land.[20] To initiate the capital formation process that must underlie economic growth and development, a nation must produce a surplus above the subsistence level. Lacking minerals, oil, or other resources to sell to external bidders, the primary source of growth capital at the early stages of a country's development must be improved agricultural production.

It is clear, as Arthur Lewis has recently pointed out, that across-the-board increases in agricultural productivity in many parts of the third world may not come until better dryland farming techniques are introduced.[21] Thus, for countries lying in predominantly dry areas, agricultural development may take more than merely better stewardship of the land. What is alarming is the fact that in many such countries, agricultural production has actually been declining in recent years. The Brandt Commission stated:

The first priority of food policy in developing countries, particularly in those of sub-Saharan Africa and South Asia which face the most serious deficits, is greater domestic production. Self-sufficiency is not necessarily sensible for all countries. . . .But if a country has two-thirds of its labor force engaged in agriculture and still cannot provide food of its own, and if it has ceased to be self-sufficient in the last two decades without any corresponding increase in cash crops or other exports to pay for imports, there is obvious cause for concern.[22]

This is precisely the situation in many developing countries, particularly in sub-Saharan Africa. Indeed, data from the UN Food and Agricultural Organization (FAO) indicate that between 1970 and 1978 food production grew more slowly than population in 58 out of 106 developing countries.[23] In countries where industrial employment is still very low, improved agricultural production is not only the main determinant of growth for the whole economy, it is the only means of improved welfare for poor people living in rural areas. People and nations who cannot afford to buy food at the market place—by providing manufactured or other products for trade—must at least manage to grow their own if they are to avoid serious food shortfalls and economic stagnation.

The stagnation or decline in agricultural productivity occurring in many poor countries is circularly linked to endemic natural resource management failures. Rapid population growth places great pressures on poor people throughout the developing world to crop marginal areas, such as poor or dry soils, hillsides, and cleared, but fragile forest soils. Although not necessarily unfarmable, many of these soils require special care and elaborate investments of labor (or capital) to construct irrigation channels, terraces, dikes, drainage ditches, and other infrastructure. Yet, with an entire family's labor necessary in some parts of the developing world just to create enough agricultural surplus for an extra child, there is little opportunity to leave available land uncropped or make significant improvements to the land.[24] Under such circumstances, the likelihood of production increases taking place—already made difficult by population growth and various ecological constraints—is even further diminished by declining soil productivity, nonexistent water management, and misapplication of agricultural techniques.

Of course, many observers have seen the answer to the agricultural problems of developing countries as coming from more sophisticated agricultural technologies in the form of both machines and scientific advancements. This is a debate which we need not enter here, though other observers have pointed out the energy costs and possible ecological consequences of the Green Revolution and other similar experiments in the third world.[25]

The important point to note is that in many developing countries where national income is still heavily skewed in favor of the agricultural sector, soil erosion, soil exhaustion, aridification, and desertification are leading to a situation where increasing amounts of arable lands are slipping into the problem category. Larger doses of capital and greater portions of remedial labor are going to be necessary to maintain or increase agricultural production on these lands than would otherwise be necessary. Thus, whether a poor country tries to improve its agricultural production by capital-intensive technological innovation or by mobilizing its rural population in a labor intensive approach, continued deterioration of the land is going to make the process lengthier and more costly.

Population Growth and Rural-Urban Migration

The environmental deterioration that is occurring in many rural areas of poor countries may have significant bearing on the demographic problems these countries face, too. Although encouraging declines in birth rates appear to be occurring in some of the most populous developing countries (India, China, for example), rapid population growth remains a serious problem in many of the poorest countries. Moreover, even in countries where population growth rates are declining, decades of very high growth rates have altered the age structure so that a high percentage of the population is at or below peak childrearing years—meaning that populations will inevitably continue to expand rapidly for at least several more decades. And the population problems in developing countries are not only a matter of aggregate numbers; migrations from the countryside to urban areas are swelling third world cities at even more rapid rates than overall population growth.

There is, of course, a great deal of debate among economists about the influence of rapid population growth and rural-to-urban migrations on economic growth. Some of the most rapidly developing countries in the world today have population densities far higher than those that prevail in most countries of Africa and Latin America; in fact many countries on these two continents remain underpopulated in terms of their long-term industrial development needs. The problem is not overpopulation, per se. It is that in countries which are not experiencing significant economic growth, rapid population growth only increases all the other strains faced by poor people in poor countries.

Similarly, most students of economic development believe that the migration of surplus labor from the countryside is a fundamental aspect of economic development—both for increasing agricultural productivity and for providing a pool of labor for industrial expansion. The problem in many developing countries is that high rural fertility rates mean that population in the countryside is not shrinking as it did as a result of rural-urban migration in Europe. And, since industrial growth is not taking place fast enough in most developing countries, the vast majority of urban migrants participate in the economy in submarginal service-providing capacities rather than in industry—a trend which does not parallel the Western development experience, where urban migrants moved overwhelmingly into industrial employment. Thus, internal migrations are creating huge social and economic distortions in developing countries but they do not appear to be "paying off" in the same way as they did in Europe and the U.S. development experience.

Most demographers agree that fertility rates tend to decline when wealth flows from an older generation to the younger generation rather than, as in traditional societies, from the young to the elders, that is, when children become an economic burden for parents rather than a source of increased production. This transition is likely to be slowed in areas where environmental deterioration is making marginal agricultural production even more difficult. In response to stagnant or declining production on available lands, labor is often the only factor of production whose supply poor people have the capacity to increase, which they can do by having more children. Thus, to the extent that increased numbers of children are needed by families to work deteriorating or already deteriorated soils, rural population growth rates are that much less likely to slow or even level off.[26]

Paradoxically, the degradation of the rural environment also can contribute to migration into urban areas of third world countries. A number of observers have taken note in recent years of the numbers of "ecological" refugees fleeing eroded, deforested mountainous, or arid areas where they simply can no longer manage to maintain enough production for subsistence.[27] While there are a great many other reasons for rural to urban migration, the push off the land from the ravages of deforestation, soil erosion, aridification, and declining soil fertility cannot be dismissed.

Of course, many thousands of marginal agricultural peasants were also pushed off the land during the preindustrial and early industrial periods in western Europe, though the push came more from political forces than from ecological ones. In Europe, though, this movement contributed to increased agricultural production, since landholdings were consolidated and capital and labor more efficiently allocated. The problem in many third world areas undergoing depopulation pressures is that much of the land left behind is already so marginal that reclamation is going to take extended periods of time and large amounts of remedial care.

Thus, the migration of people from barren, deteriorated lands does not open up easy opportunities to increase agricultural productivity in many developing countries. This only widens the rift between rural and urban economies and increases a country's food import needs. Already, the prosperity and food needs of most large third world cities are not organically linked with their countrysides. In very few third world countries is it true, as William Jennings Bryan said of the United States, that if the country's farms are destroyed, "grass will grow in the streets of every city in the country."[28] Migrants from the countryside whose exit does not create the supply of surplus food necessary to feed them in the city (because the lands they leave are so marginal or deteriorated), only further divorce the countrysides from the cities in developing countries.

Export Specialization

A large number of the low-income developing countries still depend heavily upon the revenues from one or two primary commodities to support the rest of their economy.[29] Outside of the petroleum exporting countries, countries which still depend mainly on a small number of agricultural products, industrial raw materials, or mineral commodities have not fared well on international markets in recent years. The lack of diversification that this concentration implies has left these economies highly vulnerable to fluctuating world demand and market prices.

The dangers of overspecialization, of course, vary with the elasticity of world demand for the product; oil-exporting countries have obviously not suffered the same fate as zinc or sugar exporters. In addition, the tremendous revenues being reaped by advanced countries (especially the United States, Canada, and Australia) for exports of agrarian products belie the once sacred notion that terms of trade would always work in favor of industrial exports. Despite these factors, overspecialization in primary commodities in world markets is a source of economic instability for many developing countries.[30] Moreover, in the agricultural sector in particular, a country's vulnerability as a result of narrow specialization can be significantly increased by the difficult natural resource management demands that accompany monocropping.

The potential ecological dangers associated with monocropping of certain agricultural commodities without adequate crop rotation and care for the soil were illustrated in Chapter 1. Many islands in the Atlantic and Caribbean, as well as areas on the American continents, faced severe soil degradation problems in the eighteenth and nineteenth centuries as a result of the introduction of large-scale sugar, potato, and tobacco production by European colonists. This same problem can be observed in many developing countries today where farmers are producing mainly cash crops such as ground nuts and sugar.[31]

Although many observers are critical, there is nothing intrinsically wrong with concentrating on one or two particular agricultural commodities, nor with cash cropping for export instead of providing a diversity of food crops for local consumption. As in the production of industrial goods, specialization in agricultural production is the secret of success in international trade. And, cash cropping can provide a country with valuable foreign exchange earnings to import both food and capital goods.[32]

The problem in many developing countries is that in addition to leaving countries subject to external terms of trade fluctuations, specialization in one or a few cash crops also leaves countries highly susceptible to natural disasters that affect certain crops—a particular blight or insect—or to lapses in soil and water resource management that affect productivity over the years.[33] In other words, the fact that many developing countries depend so heavily on a few agricultural crops for export earnings only magnifies the consequences of poor land management practices that frequently exist in the developing countries.

Urban and Industrial Pollution

For a number of reasons, industrial pollution problems in developing countries tend to be highly concentrated both in location and type. This problem is further exacerbated by the fact that industrial concentrations in developing countries tend also to be located in close proximity to the major urban concentrations. The combination of industrial pollutants, untreated sewage, garbage, vehicle emissions, and soot from wood, charcoal, or coal fires means that air and water pollution in large third world cities are much worse than in many developed country cities by several orders of magnitude.

Moreover, many large third world cities are plagued by increasing congestion problems because of their size, the rapidity of their growth, and the inability to adapt street configurations and traffic flows to the exploding numbers of automobiles. Even in the best planned developing country urban areas, huge haphazardous squatter settlements, often on the most marginal, hilly, or polluted fringes of the city, only complicate the general problems of pollution, squalor, and congestion.

In the extreme, such environmental pollution problems may put a brake on economic development in major urban areas: choking off certain growth possibilities; draining capital for large public works or infrastructure just to keep the urban economy functional; forcing expensive and often unwieldy industrial decentralization plans for outlying areas where transportation, energy, infrastructure, building costs, and wage rates (for skilled and managerial personnel) are often higher; adversely affecting the health of the urban workforce; and leaving haphazard or poorly planned development subject to demolition in periodic natural disasters such as floods, mudslides, earthquakes, and monsoons.

Externalities caused by the urban and industrial sectors also spill over and impinge on other sectors of the economy frequently. Air and water pollution from all the sources described above have caused numerous problems for rural residents, notably farmers and fishermen, throughout the third world. Crops have been killed or their yields substantially lowered, and fishing in rivers and bays below major third world urban areas has almost invariably declined substantially in recent decades.[34] The consequences of these developments are enormous for countries where a major percentage of the population still earns its livelihood from these pursuits and most of these people already subsist close to the margin.

THE POLITICS OF DISTRIBUTION AND ENVIRONMENT

Distributional issues are frequently at the heart of discussions concerning the environment and are especially central to discussions that involve natural resources, both renewable and nonrenewable. Distributional issues are also invariably present when environmental degradation is analyzed in terms of costs of pollution and/or the affect of exploitation of one set of resources on the continued viability of other resources, e.g. the relationship between cutting trees and the maintenance of downstream soil resources. The most common forms in which explicit discussion of environment and its link to distributional concerns takes place are around the idea of common property or the problems of the "commons," externalities, and the distribution of income.[35]

The idea of the commons and exploitation of resources focuses on the charges levied on resource use, or the lack of charges, and the exploitation of the resource by those who have access to the resource. Especially important is the idea of access to a resource at a given time where exploitation by many at one time may make the resource unavailable or unusable later. While the idea of the commons is frequently discussed in terms of a resource that is of finite supply and likely to be overused if available free or at low cost, equally important is the idea that future generations may not have access to depleted or ruined resources. Another concern, one sometimes implicit rather than explicit, is that the commons are more easily available to some rather than to others. Those far away from the area of resource may not, in practice, have access to it even if, in principle, they might. Or, the "commons" may exclude people from different jurisdictions, local, regional, ethnic, or national (as in fishing rights) or resources and amenities reserved for people of a particular race or ethnicity. When the resource involved is regenerative but potentially depletable as in pasture land, fisheries, or clean water, the issue of generational use or access at a given time is posed very sharply because the resource may be unavailable at a future time. The political and moral issues may be somewhat different than those involving access to resources that are exploited once and for all, for example, mineral deposits or the consumption of particular products, e.g. foodstuffs.

Of course, distributional issues arise over any valued good and the arguments for providing basic needs—health, education, a certain caloric intake, some specified minimum standard of housing—suggest to some people that there is a close relationship between exploitation of renewable but potentially depletable resources and consumption of products or resources that are exhaustible. The argument that all minerals or land should be held in common by the state for all the people can be traced to an idea of common access to resources. Some individuals who would not agree that all private property should be abolished might well agree to socialization of the critical means of production, agriculture, health services, or some other specified service, commodity, or resource. They may think that equal access or roughly equal consumption of certain valued goods is essential whether those goods have a finite time horizon for consumption or whether they might be extended indefinitely with prudent management.

Thus people divide within and between societies and the issues: which groups shall have access to what resources or use resources in certain ways; who pays costs and who gets benefits? How are costs passed on to other groups or other generations? How are demands for resources modified or curtailed? What are the control mechanisms and the gains and risks for certain controllers and consumers in the use of different mechanisms—those of price, direct rationing, prohibition through repression?

Societies also differ over the institutional mechanisms that are developed for handling the regulation of resource use and the regulation of pollution. Private-public mixes vary with respect to regulation. There is *devolution,* in which the public authorities transfer control to private hands; *regulation,* in which the state or public authority leaves control in private hands but regulates private operation through various direct and indirect means; and *operation,* in which the state takes over and performs activities.[36] We must try to assess whether and in what ways these forms make a difference and to whom and for what.

We cannot assume that the state is a purposive actor maximizing some defined objective, be it that of an institution, class, ethnic group, or the public interest or social welfare.[37] We must examine the divisions within bureaucracies and constituencies inside the state itself. As Young puts it:

Some groups gain the upper hand in conjunction with certain collective choices, while other interests and functions triumph when it is necessary to arrive at social choices in different areas.[38]

While this view may seem appropriate to pluralistic societies, and may be thought of itself as a pluralistic vision, empirical work on the Soviet Union shows that this view may apply to control over resource allocation decisions there as well. For example, even in a system in which Soviet cities possess formidable legal powers to control development and preserve greenbelt areas, and where local Communist party officials may be committed to limiting expansion so that urban services are not overwhelmed, decisions to locate industry are usually made by industrial managers. And these decisions are designed to maximize production rather than to optimize the quality of urban life. But the usually dominant value of production may not prevail in every case, much less over every major issue in the Soviet Union any more than in the United States. Underlying priorities will be elaborated within various structural arrangements, group and individual competition, and coalitions.[39]

General consumption of goods produced by particular persons, agencies, or corporations (the free-rider problem) has political consequences, as does specific consumption of or access to goods that are ostensibly held in common, e.g., leasing or concessional use of national forests, private use of underground water, pollution of air and seas. A whole range of actions by some agents that affect use of resources by others, where the latter do not control the former, refer to externalities. The political implications of irreversible outcomes, or outcomes which can only be altered at great costs and/or over extended time, e.g., the pollution of lakes, are very salient political phenomena. The generational shifting of costs may provide entirely different consequences for political outcomes; may, indeed, provide a completely different environment which structures political and economic competition. An example is the politics and economics of a deforested area or one where soil erosion has made agriculture impossible. Migration of peoples and the disappearance of occupational and social groups mean that the very building blocks of politics have changed. That decisions about allocation of resources may have to be made under new conditions of extreme scarcity and constraint means that the politics of distribution may have shifted onto a very different plane from one period to another. This has occurred for parts of the Sahel, Haiti, and many other areas.

How we get from one situation to another when confronted with difficult choices and under conditions of uncertainty and high risk is an issue area that engages us very much.[40] We are especially interested in the unintended consequences of past policies, or the masked consequences of them, or deflection of the goals of policies as their implementation is structured by agencies or interests that capture agencies. Thus we get economic protectionism in the name of conservation; mining profits and the abandonment of environmental protection in the name of secure supply of minerals or fuels; and for that matter the preservation of elite access to specified areas and resources in the name of preservation and conservation.

Income Distribution and Environment

Distributional issues are at the core of environmental concerns in that the way resources are depleted affects who gets what and who pays costs in the present and future. Still, conventionally there has been a separation of analysis of income distribution in developing countries and analysis of environmental issues especially when these issues are posed in terms of exploitation of renewable resources and the degeneration of those resources. Case studies or general works devoted to the study of income distribution and redistribution in developing countries do deal with problems of poverty, and often they examine growth versus equity trade-offs. An examination of growth versus equity trade-offs involves us in analyses of present and future levels of the economy and present and future distributions of assets and income. But depletion of resources and degradation of the environment may affect future streams of income in the not so long run and may be thought to be partial causes of present maldistribution of income. Interestingly, despite this belief, the growing number of studies dealing with income distribution usually have not analyzed directly the impact of environmental change or income on the ways that income distribution patterns are correlated with environmental degradation or natural resource exploration.[41] There have been some general discussions of environmental protection and income distribution which have examined the costs of protection and whether these costs are shared proportionately or not among income classes. Baumol finds that environmental measures may, in the short run, reduce job opportunities and thus the costs may fall most heavily on those who can least afford them. The supply of public goods is often excessive in the eyes of the poor and inadequate in the opinion of the wealthy. Whereas public goods may be regressive in their distributions, there are special reasons, Baumol argues, why this may be the case for environmental programs where tangible real income of individuals and groups is forgone.[42]

The World Bank insists that project analyses which it funds consider distributional and environmental issues. And, specific cost benefit analyses often consider the problem of intergenerational equity through the social rate of discount. Many economists have a propensity to want us to consume more in the present because they believe that people in the future will be better off. There is a presumption in favor of future growth. Environmentalists, on the other hand, raise questions as to whether or not environmental degradation will lead to conditions of lower growth either through deterioration in quality of life or through the destruction of renewable resources.

Neglecting Environmental Concerns

Thus distributional issues get taken up in various literatures on cost benefit and project analyses, regulation, and the economics of environment. But it is nonetheless striking that direct attempts to account for specific country income distribution profiles and to model the future do neglect problems of resource degradation.[43] While studies that deal with income distribution do look at factor endowments, and some look at investments in human capital, there is an obvious lack of concern with trying to include environmental issues in the analysis. While the argument is made that natural resource–scarce countries have had to rely on human resource development as a substitute for their poor natural resource base, we do not get to see the process of environmental degradation affecting strategies for development. (As we shall see, the literature on migration and urbanization does relate environmental degradation to social processes, although less so to economic distributions.)

The impact of tariff policies, land reform measures, and budget policies on distribution have been examined; the decision to adopt export-oriented rather than import substitution strategies has been analyzed for consequences for distribution. Decisions to invest in one sector rather than another or to adopt capital rather than labor-intensive techniques are salient in discussions of income distribution. But the affects of pollution or loss of resources are not systematically modeled for their distributional consequences.

We have reasons to be surprised at the lack of concern with environmental issues in the literature on income distribution. We can hypothesize that environmental degradation is a factor in producing certain income inequality profiles, or that groups and governments will respond to income inequality with various natural resource exploitation strategies, or that environmental degradation will provoke certain kinds of groups or governments into actions either in the name of equality or to deal with the environment in ways that will affect distributional profiles.

Certainly, observers want to look at the relationship between income and the kinds of goods that are consumed as a share of income. But aside from the assumption that more wealthy countries will be willing to spend a greater share of income on their environment—an assumption made in the literature on the economics of environment—there are few empirical attempts to show in the literature on income distribution in developing countries that this assumption holds between groups within a country.

Even the literature on basic needs has usually not analyzed the impact of environmental degradation on distributions of income that accrue to sectors and groups. True, this literature has been sensitive to human capital issues and has made arguments about the impact of nutrition, housing, and sanitation on productivity. This literature has also been at pains to argue that there is no contradiction, or need be no contradiction, between economic growth and basic needs. Environmentalists have been making the same argument between growth and preserving renewable resources and between growth and environmental degradation. Of course, it would be no simple matter to cost out the distributional effects for Nigeria of rapid oil development that also produces oil spills in river delta areas. It would not be an easy task to calculate the impact of air pollution in Mexico City on life expectancies of different income categories and also to calculate the distributional effects to mitigate air pollution or to alter the siting of industries, although in principle these could all be modeled. A large dam on the Senegal River may increase the incidence of schistosomiasis. Does the incidence of the disease fall equally on farmers who work different-sized plots? What does the disease do to labor costs and to supply of labor? Many variables would have to be considered in analyzing the distributional effects of a large dam project.

Those who have stressed the need to develop strategies for overcoming poverty through human development and basic needs approaches have paid more attention to environmental concerns than those who have stressed growth strategies per se. But aside from suggesting that human development will reduce fertility and thus affect urban blight and soil degradation and deforestation through lessened population pressures, the basic needs literature has not closely tied its concerns, analytically speaking, to environmental issues. Writers who stress basic needs have not tried to develop strategies for rates of exploitation of natural resources or to systematically deal with problems of the commons, externalities, and transition costs or types of regulation to be invoked in exploitation of resources. The World Bank's *Poverty and Human Development*[44] never deals with environmental issues. The ILO's *Employment, Growth and Basic Needs: A One-World Problem* does not either and when it comes to "Major Issues for Discussion," natural resources are nowhere to be found.[45] The ILO's case studies of Kenya and the Philippines, two countries that have severe problems of deforestation and soil erosion, among others, do not discuss environmental problems.[46]

The development of a physical quality of life index (PQLI) did not include environmental indicators, though obviously environment affects life expectancy and infant mortality. No attempt was made to include natural resource issues per se in any model of disparity reduction rates in social indicators in terms of the affect of natural resource degradation on PQLI.[47]

Environment and Distribution: Debating the Issue

Perhaps the most direct analysis of relationships between distribution and environment have been undertaken by environmentalists, by certain analysts of integrated rural development, and by those who have studied the impact of fertility rates on resource depletion and the affects of rapid urbanization on urban life. In these literatures, rural-urban balances are examined; urban blight is described; the impact of unregulated exploitation of resources and the impact of unregulated markets and property rights is described. However, while spatial patterns are often analyzed through studies of migration to cities or the opening of forest lands to farmers in order to relieve pressures on already built-up farming areas, there is relatively little systematic analysis of intersectoral income distribution and its relationship to environmental issues. This is true both for the literatures on urbanization and for those on hunger and rural poverty.

Those who have been concerned with massive rural to urban migration in developing countries have described the pressures of urban growth on sanitation systems, scarce housing stock, and urban greenbelts.[48] They have also noted the high rates of unemployment in urban areas and the growth of a large urban informal sector as manufacturing sector expansion did not lead to absorption into the formal sector of the growing urban labor force. But these facts, and they are facts, must be weighed against the many studies we have which show that household incomes improved through rural to urban migration and that, in survey after survey, migrants respond that they are better off in urban areas.[49]

Overall income distribution may worsen with rural to urban migration because productivity is higher in urban than rural areas, but levels of poverty may decline. Moreover, without large migration from rural areas, rural degradation may proceed through soil erosion, river and underground water pollution, and deforestation.

Those who have been concerned with rural poverty have been at pains to describe maldistribution of landholdings. There has been an implicit assumption that land reform is environmentally preserving. It may be quite true, as George Ledec argues,[50] that deforestation proceeds in Latin America through commercial timbering and cattle ranching schemes on fragile soils. But it also has been the case that breaking up large holdings often has meant more intensive cultivation with serious consequences. Land resettlements to marginal soils in forest areas have occurred in Indonesia and elsewhere and have had environmentally severe consequences.

Rene Dumont and Nicholas Cohen have argued that much land could show increased returns, or even be brought into production, by radical political reforms such as change in the system of ownership, more equal land values, and fairer prices paid for its produce.[51] Dumont and Cohen point to a variety of political, social, and technical factors working against effective employment of land resources and leading to extension of desert, deterioration of soils, and loss of land for agriculture owing to growing urban populations. Their argument is explicitly political and is that the politics of agriculture overrides the physical constraints on land and is responsible for inequalities in production and distribution.[52] The argument is one deeply suspicious of the Green Revolution and indeed suspicious that technical breakthroughs can solve food and environmental problems.

Dumont and Cohen have a framework for analysis and a set of policy conclusions which include land reform, setting fairer exchanges of values between products, and taking out of market exchange certain commodities such as staple foods. They also want to put "the peasant in command." Whether small peasant producers could produce enough to feed themselves and growing urban populations, even urban populations postulated to grow at slower rates, is a critical question, of course. Dumont and Cohen point again and again to China as a model. Recent discussion by Chinese of their own experiments (as well as a growing secondary literature) raise many doubts about the Chinese model. We do not, in any case, want to argue the merits or the empirical base of Dumont and Cohen's arguments. They represent a thrust of analysis which does try to link distributional concerns to environmental issues, although there is no demonstration that putting the peasant in command or suspending or altering exchange values will alter the structure or exploitation of renewable resources under the conditions of growing populations.

It is, however, an environmentalist, Lester Brown, who has most explicitly argued that inequitable distributions, especially of land, lead to large-scale migration to urban areas and to the deterioration of urban environments; to encroachments on grasslands, which spreads deserts; to deforestation of mountain and forest areas with attendant consequences for soil erosion. The argument is taken another step when the consequences of environmental degradation are said to accentuate income inequalities. Offshore pollution or overfishing force fishermen into towns or to become rural wage earners with a loss of income. Brown puts it sharply when he says: "Of all the sources of growing income disparity, ecological deterioration may be one of the most difficult to remedy."[53] The arguments are extended to income disparities between, as well as within, nations when Brown and others argue that rich countries consume large shares of processed natural resources.[54]

These propositions—that unequitable distributions cause environmental degradation and that more egalitarian distribution will be environmentally enhancing—are highly contentious. Certainly there is room for some skepticism that redistribution, by itself, will lend automatically to better environmental management or to more concern for the welfare of future generations.

Strategies for Distribution and Environmental Risk

Given the uncertainty about the relationships between distribution and natural resource and renewable resource depletion, it is perhaps not very surprising that policy makers have been reluctant to frame policies for dealing with equity issues which also have an environmental component. Indeed, even in reformist-minded developing countries, it has been hard enough to exert centralized or decentralized controls to stop relatively poor people from cutting trees, migrating to cities, invading new and often fragile ecological areas in search of pastures or farm land, and to stop rich people or large corporations from massive logging, conversion of fragile land to large cattle ranches, mining and at the same time despoiling the land, or overusing water resources. Moreover, in the absence of sweeping political and economic changes accompanying revolutions or civil wars, it has been exceedingly difficult to alter or redistribute income profiles, much less to deal with problems of environmental degradation as part of a distributional strategy or to redistribute in order to preserve the environment and renewable resources.

Controversies abound over which countries have been successful at redistribution, with the Korea and Taiwan cases often cited as successful "deviant" cases—deviant in that unfavorable levels of inequality appear to have been altered during two decades of rapid growth.[55] Other countries which are sometimes cited as having less inequitable distributions of income such as Cuba, Tanzania, and Sri Lanka, either raise severe problems of equity with low growth, that is, a leveling downwards (Cuba and Tanzania), or had a large measure of rural equality to begin with (Sri Lanka).[56] The constraints and limits of nonrevolutionary income distribution have been examined at length and it is not our intention to once again do this[57] nor to debate reform versus revolution. Those who have argued that socialist developing countries have followed a more equitable path have asserted that socialist countries have altered money income flows and made basic services—housing, health, and education—accessible to a wider population. The argument has also been made that China, Cuba, and other socialist countries have preserved the environment better through land reform and government controls over resource use, and have managed renewable resources better. There is considerable evidence to the contrary.

Highly centralized countries may be better able to control population movements and to control behaviors of the population than countries with weaker political centers. But highly centralized polities also give decision makers vast power to exploit resources or to degrade the environment without constraint as has occurred in China, Eastern Europe, and the Soviet Union. Highly centralized systems also allow mistakes to be centralized and to ramify throughout the systems. Moreover, not all countries that call themselves socialist and have set out on development paths which are ostensibly aimed at more equitable outcomes are effective in exerting controls over resource exploitation. Tanzania is not more effective at forest management than Kenya. Angola and Mozambique have had their waters overfished by the Soviet Union, which extracts protein from their seas in payment for military assistance and political support.

A number of countries have tried, however, to achieve growth while raising the income levels of poor people through spatial distributions by arguing that there are diminishing returns from further exploitation of already densely settled lands or from overindustrialization and overurbanization in built-up cities. Indeed, defining distributional problems in spatial terms often recommends itself to policy makers precisely because they hope to avoid the political problems attendant on decomposing populations in other ways. It may be more politically loaded to divide populations for distributional purposes into rural and urban sectors and into income deciles in order to ask what shares of total income the groups get. We also could ask what shares of income accrue to capital and to labor in a country. Or we could examine inter-industry wage differentials, farm and off-farm income in rural areas, the formal and informal urban sector shares, the income shares that accrue to farmers with different-size holdings, the income that accrues to people with various levels of education or length of stay in a city, or to families of various sizes, or to inhabitants of cities of different size, data permitting, of course.

Policy makers frequently want to avoid treating distributional problems in terms of class or of social groups. True, if the politics of a country have been defined in terms of communal struggle, then a policy aimed at spatial distributions, say a strategy based on new growth poles which has been discussed in Kenya, or the movement of people from central Java to Indonesia's outer islands, or the creation of a new Federal capital city in Nigeria, away from the Yoruba heartland, will immediately raise communal problems. But even in

these situations, policy makers can and will argue that both growth and environmental goals can be maximized at the same time. Thus Nigeria's leaders, in
deciding to press ahead with a new capital at Abuja, argued that Lagos was
unsanitary, congested, and that both diminishing economic returns and degradation of the environment would occur with the further growth of Lagos. The
movement of people from central Java to Sumatra was defended in terms of
relaxing pressures on agricultural resources and urban areas in congested Java,
and accommodating new growth in the undespoiled environments of the outer
islands. At the same time, this policy appeals to Javanese decision makers who
hope to change ethnic balances on the outer islands.

In Mexico, there has been a growing awareness that there are important and
perhaps increasing income inequalities.[58] But Mexican decision makers have
been extremely reluctant to express these inequalities in terms of classes or to
develop strategies that will risk political struggle over redistribution of income
understood in terms of population deciles or rural-urban terms. Thus the Mexican leaders have stressed the maldistribution of persons and production as a set
of spatial imbalances, rather than emphasized the maldistribution of incomes.
At the same time, they can argue that Mexico City is overdeveloped and that
this is expressed in terms of water and air pollution, traffic congestion which
raises transport costs, and pressure on housing stock. The argument is one of
diseconomies to scale. Thus, it is argued, deconcentration makes sense in
environmental, equity, and efficiency terms.[59]

These arguments are not based on a careful analysis of the optimal size of
Mexico City or of other cities.[60] It is not at all clear that equalizing incomes in
Mexico City would relax pressures on renewable resources. More cars and
greater consumption of goods leads to pollution and solid waste disposal problems. On the other hand, greater income may lead to more effective demand for
dealing with the environment. And this is not just a matter, as economists tell
us, of people with higher incomes being inclined to spend more on their environment. It is frequently a matter of people with higher incomes having more
power to enforce regulations in their neighborhoods or to get government to deal
with squatters and to provide better services to themselves. Nor is it clear that
investment and development in relatively smaller cities or even in backward
rural areas will lead to a better distribution of personal income overall. The
outcome will depend on migration patterns and on who benefits in specific
areas. But the efficiency rationale is appealing when it can be made in terms of
market failure and the discrepancy between market and social costs.[61] Thus the
Mexican *Plan Nacional de Desarrollo Urbano* called for slowing the growth of
the Mexico City metropolitan areas, Guadalajara, and Monterrey by regulating
new industries and obliging the beneficiaries of public services to pay full costs
and by promoting the location of public higher educational facilities and public
sector entities outside the Federal District. Fiscal incentives and financial
mechanisms were to be used to encourage siting also, as well as credit facilities

and housing, construction, and transportation programs, so that Tampico, Salina Cruz, and Las Truchas would develop.[62] And, indeed, urban growth as measured by population increases is much greater in these smaller cities than in the larger ones.

However, just as development of a natural resource such as oil can be threatening to a fragile river delta ecology in the Bendel or River States of Nigeria, so the construction of oil facilities and oil-linked industries in Chiapas or the Yucutan in Mexico can be threatening to the ecology, especially when rapid expansion of construction and transportation takes place under boom conditions with little planning. And the smaller towns may be ill suited to absorb a large influx of new people.

The governments of Tanzania and Nigeria argued that new capitals sited in the center of their countries and away from built-up areas, as Brasilia has been sited away from Rio de Janeiro, would open up new regions for development and would spread economic benefits to areas where people had been relatively poor and where their access to services, jobs, and educational facilities left them in relatively poor positions to compete for shares of national income. However, when the Nigerians decided to build Abuja rapidly, the site choice was not based on careful planning with regard to water resources or the carrying capacity of the surrounding areas. The construction of Abuja has meant the development of shanty towns around the site.[63] Nor is it clear that construction labor is being recruited largely from the people who have lived near the site. Most of the expended funds will go, in the short run, to suppliers and contractors from outside the area.

Dodoma is attractive as a new capital to Tanzania's leaders because it is away from the coast and it is hoped that it will become a new center for inland development. But Dodoma is a small town that has not been a major center in contemporary times because it is removed from trade routes and major resources. Moreover, its surrounding grasslands ecology is easy to harm with overgrazing of cattle or intensive farming to supply the city's new needs. Water is scarce. Will the new capital have the resources and will its construction and transport grids be planned well enough to preserve the environment?

The construction of Brasilia was designed as part of the opening up of the Amazon Basin in Brazil with the aim of developing the basin for growth purposes and for creating new opportunities for people in the northeast of Brazil. There is no evidence that either Brasilia or the opening up of the Amazon has worked to lessen income inequalities in Brazil. Large, informal-sector, satellite towns have grown up around the new capital. Brasilia, like Abuja in Nigeria, accentuated problems of inflation in the country.[64]

Governments try to handle distributional issues through spatial strategies because they hope to avoid the head on politics of class and redistribution of income and they hope to achieve growth and also to achieve equity goals. Historically, it has been easier for people to move or to be moved as a response to environmental degradation than to induce or require people to adapt in place.[65] Governments often can respond to demands from the poor for access to services because they can expand services incrementally and on a limited territorial basis (especially in cities). Such demands are much easier for governments than are class-based demands for income redistribution or land redistribution.[66] Some environmental demands are also difficult to handle incrementally because the only course of action is to intervene directly to stop people from behaving in a certain way. This is especially true with regard to abuse of renewable resources. Moreover, when new capitals are being built or new areas opened up for rural or industrial development, central controls over the process are often weak precisely because the area is removed from developed administrative and policy controls. Thus, it is hard to police the development process, and there are severe political costs in getting individuals and groups to behave in ways such that renewable resources are not threatened.

Unless the government is extremely authoritarian and willing to override either legal rights or land customs, it is difficult to alter land use patterns through incremental government policies. Land rights are deeply embedded in legal and social structures in most political and economic systems.[67] Land problems are highly complex in theory and practice due to interdependencies, the specificity of locational advantages, transfer costs, and market imperfections, including corruption. Moreover, policies must be tailored to the specifics of given tenure, legal, and social structures.[68] Space and equity issues are difficult to resolve because the market value of land rises faster than the general price level. Growth in real incomes and in population create higher land values. Service shortages—even when services are fully covered by costs to users—and the imposition of land use regulations and monopolistic practices raise costs.[69] But service shortages themselves and the absence of standards lead to harmful environmental outcomes.

Governments are always facing trade-offs between the ability of relatively poor people to find shelter and obtain access to services, the costs of providing housing and services, and the need for flexibility in land use for productive purposes. As areas get built up and land becomes scarcer, and as rights get vested in residential, small business, and large business enterprises, and as waste disposal practices become established, governments find it very difficult to alter land use patterns without incurring severe economic or political costs. Moreover, the goals that governments want to maximize not only may conflict, but they are often difficult to make precise.[70] The desire to preserve amenities, ensure adequate supply of land for the future, foster growth, foster equity, and mobilize resources must all be translated into concrete objectives within specific contexts. The policy measures taken may produce unanticipated consequences in the environmental realm as they have elsewhere. Thus just as rent controls, which are established ostensibly to protect the urban poor, may wind up providing subsidies to the middle classes, so measures put forth to protect the environment may retard private investment in land or force poor people off areas where they have been established. Macroenvironmental policies may cause local hardships. And as Dunkerly and others have argued, the acquisition of land for public use does not ensure efficient, equitable, or harmonious urban land development patterns, nor does detailed public control of land allocation,[71] as the Soviet examples attest.[72]

Conscious policies which aim at containment of urban size, either through direct imposition of controls over population inflows or construction, have not been notably successful. Nor have slum clearance, the creation of new towns, industrial parks, nor the deconcentration of new industry to presumed growth poles or resiting of old or new administrative agencies to new capitals. Not only have a number of political analysts raised strong doubts about the idea that migrants to large cities are worse off than they were in smaller cities or in rural areas, but studies have also cast doubt that migrants are a destabilizing force in national and urban politics in large urban areas.[73] Not only are urban incomes larger than rural ones but urban incomes are per capita usually about twice those of rural areas.[74] We have already raised doubts concerning the belief in diseconomies of scale. Mohan notes that evidence for the United States indicates that there may be economies of scale for at least part of social overhead cost expenditures;[75] that per capita expenditures decline precipitously for cities over one million. While per capita incomes in developing countries may rise faster than per capita local government expenditures, access to urban services and public investment is greater in larger cities.[76]

While development has meant spatial redistribution of human activities and has also meant industrial concentration, urbanization and concentration of wastes and pollution in environmental terms, it is not clear that large cities are more environmentally degrading than holding populations in smaller towns or in rural areas. Indeed, if the arguments of some environmentalists are accepted that income inequality is the prime cause of environmental degradation, and if we factor in access to services as part of our income distribution profile, then we would have to argue that the long run movement of peoples to cities creates more egalitarian distributions overall. The trade-offs in specific contexts are likely to be between those of certain natural resource degradation of soils, water, and forests[77] as against concentration of wastes and pollution in cities, with the long run capability of governments to be effective environmentally much greater in cities than in spread out rural areas with dispersed populations where policing and administrative controls are weak.

Just as economists have been skeptical about deconcentration as a growth plus equity strategy in part because economies of scale are lost and these policies run against basic dynamics of economic forces, so we might be skeptical that political decentralization and local self-reliance and management will always be functional for renewable resource management. As Landau and Eagle have pointed out, a large body of literature, both theoretical and applied, is devoted to arguing that decentralization is a solution to a large number of problems.[78] Decentralization it is claimed, promotes geographical equity, increases popular capacity to ensure responsibility and accountability, enables easier access to decision points, and reduces conflict.[79] It is said that decentralization is more efficient and more effective.

As Landau and Eagle note, these are claims, not hard facts. As students of environmental regulations in the United States know, deconcentrating authority may produce a fragmentation which reduces effectiveness of administration and policing. In developing countries, local government officials and politicians may simply be captured by constituencies who do not want to manage renewable resources in an environmentally protective fashion. And, the exigencies of life may make it necessary for poor people on marginal land or who are harvesting scarce forest or marine resources to deplete these resources at a rate which is beneficial to them in the medium run. Thus neither long run growth, equity, nor environmental preservation will necessarily be served by decentralization policies any more than they will be served by policies of constraint on growth of already built up areas or by spatial redistributions.

CONCLUSIONS

We have argued that environmental issues are inextricably linked conceptually and empirically, with national economic development at all levels. The issue of how a nation's environmental management practices affect its overall development strategy, its success over time, the pace of development in specific sectors, and the distribution of economic gains deserves more attention from specialists concerned with various aspects of economic development. Yet, on the whole, the starting places for various analysts have led them to emphasize "their thing." Most economists have stressed markets; most Marxists have emphasized classes; most ecologists have looked at ecosystems.

It is, nonetheless, clear that continued mismanagement of natural resources threatens profound fiscal impacts in the future for many poor countries. At the very least, problems such as deteriorating soil capability, silted and clogged irrigation systems, or widespread loss of forest cover will, sooner or later, require large infusions of manpower and money to prevent further deterioration or to repair past damage—diverting scarce development funds from production-creating investments into remedial or production-preserving purposes. The failure of developing countries to pay more attention to the gradual erosion of their natural resource base today may thus vastly increase the capital costs of economic development in the future.

Poor land management practices may also affect the longevity of a number of large capital projects being undertaken today: dams, irrigation systems, roads, agricultural terracing, housing projects, all may become increasingly expensive to maintain as a result of deforestation, soil erosion, and flooding resulting from rapid water runoff and the filling up of river channels. Harbors and navigable waters may also be plagued by excessive siltation from upstream land abuse. While the costs of maintenance for capital projects affected by careless land management may be paid incrementally, they may be quite large and drain increasing amounts of development funds from other purposes with time. Worse yet, the costs or sheer logistics of maintenance may become so prohibitive in time that the entire project must be abandoned. As we shall see in later chapters, this is not a hypothetical outcome; abandonment of large capital projects has occurred in a number of instances in recent years as a result of long-term environmental abuse that made maintenance too difficult to sustain.

Ultimately, many of the environmental problems in developing countries harken back to the fundamental issue of income distribution—the allocation of wealth within a society and over time. Increasingly, environmentalists, especially those unhappy with distributions of power and resources as they exist in most developing countries, have argued that inequality is the root cause of environmental degradation and that power to the poor will lead to environmentally sound practices. The latter assertion has certainly not been demonstrated. Inequitable distributions of land may indeed force many poor peasants to cultivate hillsides or marginal lands, with predictable ecological deterioration a result. But redistribution of prime agricultural lands to marginal, small-scale peasants may be no guarantee of either sound environmental management or increased overall agricultural productivity.

Economists, of course, have been conscious of the problems of generational transfers, the commons, and externalities, and a number of them have tried to address environmental issues with the theoretical tools of their trade in order to analyze welfare of populations over time and to order policies in terms of management of renewable resources. But few, if any, empirical studies of income distribution have related the many ways that income can be divided (private/public; rural/urban; capital/labor; interpersonal; interregional; interindustry; intercity) to environmental outcomes. Nor have studies shown the impact of environmental degradation on distributions over time, although we have the sense that the poor can least protect themselves, for example, from soil erosion and that flimsy homes in urban areas are more susceptible to damage from flooding or earth slides. Insofar as the poor are said to benefit from environmentally degrading growth policies, it is said that they do so through employment generation. But again, rather little empirical work has been done to demonstrate the trade-offs.

Policy makers in developing countries, especially those in reformist-type regimes where there is increasing consciousness of equity problems but an unwillingness to confront equity issues head on and move toward rapid and far-reaching redistribution, often look to policies of deconcentration or to those that further growth poles. They also hope to deal with environmental degradation by moving populations to new areas and by imposing constraints on growth of already built-up areas either through construction of new capitals or new industrial centers or through financial and credit incentives or through physical and administrative restraints. However, it is hard to make these policies work, and they are no guarantees that either equity or sound management of renewable resources will be the outcome.

Notes

1. Economists have tended to pay more attention to natural resource supplies than to natural resource management or environmental degradation. However, a number of recent reports on the economic development prospects of the developing world have paid more attention to the latter. See OECD *Interfutures;* Brandt Commission Report; and K.K.S. Dodgie, "Economic Development." In *Economic Development* (San Francisco: W. H. Freeman and Co., 1980). Many environmentalists—at varying levels of economic sophistication—have considered the importance of environmental issues in economic development. See Erik P. Eckholm, *Losing Ground: Environmental Stress and World Food Prospects*(New York: Norton, 1976); Lester Brown, *Human Needs and the Security of Nations*, Headline Series No. 238 (New York: Foreign Policy Association, February 1978); Lester Brown, *Building a Sustainable Society* (New York: Norton, 1980). In addition, general surveys documenting widespread environmental abuse and natural resource degradation in developing countries include: *Environmental and Natural Resource Management in Developing Countries: A Report to Congress* (Washington, D.C.: United States Agency for International Development, February 1979); Daniel M. Dworkin, ed., *Environment and Development* (Indianapolis: SCOPE, 1974); M. Taghi Farvar and John P. Milton, eds., *The Careless Technology: Ecology and International Development* (Garden City, New York: Natural History Press, 1972); *The Global 2000 Report to the President: Entering the Twenty-First Century* (Washington, D.C.: Council on Environmental Quality and the Department of State, 1980); International Union for Conservation of Nature and Natural Resources (IUCN), World Wildlife Fund, and United Nations Environment Programme, *World Conservation Strategy* (Morges, Switzerland: IUCN, 1980). One notable attempt to integrate environmental management and economic development thinking is J. Edwin Becht and L. D. Belzang, *World Resource Management: Key to Civilizations and Social Achievement* (Englewood Cliffs, N. J.: Prentice Hall, 1979).

2. The appellation is borrowed from a chapter heading in Benjamin Higgins, *Economic Development: Principles, Problems and Policies* (New York: Norton, 1959). For a sweeping argument about how geographical conditions determined which societies and civilizations in history have prospered, see James Fairgrieve, *Geography and World Power*, 7th ed., (London: University of London Press, 1932).

3. See, for example, Ellsworth Huntington, *Mainsprings of Civilization* (New York: John P. Wiley, 1943); Clarence A. Mills, *Climate Makes the Man* (New York: Harper & Bros., 1942); Clarence A. Mills, *World Power and Shifting Climates* (Boston: Chris-

topher Publishing House, 1963); and, Sydney F. Markham, *Climate and the Energy of Nations* (London: Oxford University Press, 1944).

4. Many of the different views expressed on how the low productive potential of renewable resources could affect economic development are reviewed in Higgins, *Economic Development*, pp. 267–273. See also Pierre Gourou, *The Tropical World: Its Social and Economic Conditions and Its Future Status* (London: Longmans, Green and Co., 1953). Robert Heilbroner, in *The Great Ascent: The Struggle for Economic Development in our Time* (New York: Harper and Row, 1963) p. 34, surveyed the situation:

Much of Africa is held back by its poor soil. The North of course, suffers from totally infertile sand, and the tropical regions from earths that compact to the hardness of concrete or that tear away in the violent rainstorms. . . . It is not only Africa which suffers from this basic handicap. A great deal of the rain-forest soil of the South American Continent is also much less suitable for raising crops than its luxuriant forest cover would suggest. Across large areas of Asia, as well, the soil is also wanting: vast tracts of India are arid, while in China the land has long since been deforested and much of it overworked.

Much of the post-war cultural anthropology literature also dealt with the relationship between economic potential and environment. B. J. Meggers, for example, postulated that "the level to which a culture can develop is dependent upon the agricultural potential of the environment it occupies." See her article, "Environmental Limitation on the Development of Culture," *American Anthropologist* 56 (1954), 801–824.

5. Eugene Staley, *The Future of Underdeveloped Countries: Political Implications of Economic Development*, revised ed. (New York: Praeger, 1961) pp. 204–205, pointed out:

Natural resources are, of course, essential as a basic for any economic development. Yet a comparison of the basic resources in soil, water, minerals, forests, and so on in the economically advanced parts of the world with those in the underdeveloped areas, where people live in poverty, suggests that the difference in economic level must depend to a considerable degree on other things than differences in these resources. It would be hard to maintain that the soil, water, minerals, etc. of England, Australia, Denmark, and Switzerland are so superior to the corresponding resources of the Philippine Islands, Indonesia, Burma, Iran, and Bolivia as to account for the tremendous differences in their economic levels. Many an underdeveloped country, though not every one, seems well enough endowed by nature to be described as "a rich land inhabited by poor people."

Heilbroner, *The Great Ascent*, pp. 35–36, decided that: "viewing the problem as a whole, there is no reason to consign the great bulk of the underdeveloped world to permanent poverty because of a tragic and uncorrectable degree of nature."
P. T. Bauer, *Dissent on Development*, revised edition, (Cambridge, Mass.: Harvard University Press, 1967) p. 297, concurs:

Physical natural resources, notably fertile soil or rich minerals, are not the only or even major determinants of material progress, though differences in the bounty of nature may well account for differences in levels and ease of living in different parts of the underdeveloped world. It has always been known that physical resources are useless without capital and skills to develop them, or without access to markets. And the diminishing importance of land and other natural resources in production is also familiar. But the recent rapid development of some underdeveloped countries poorly endowed with natural resources has come as a surprise, though perhaps it should not have done so, in view of the Japanese experience. A recent but already classic case is that of Hong Kong, which has practically no raw materials, very little fertile soil, no fuel, no hydroelectric power, and only a very restricted domestic market, but which in spite of these limitations has progressed phenomenally.

6. John Kenneth Galbraith, *The Nature of Mass Poverty* (Cambridge, Mass.: Harvard University Press, 1981) p. 5.

7. W. Arthur Lewis makes this point in a recent, unpublished paper presented to the World Bank, "Development Economics in the 1950s," March 1983.

8. See especially, W. Arthur Lewis, *Theory of Economic Growth* (London: Allen and Unwin, 1965) pp. 304–340.

9. One of the classic articles on the economics of resource use is H. Hotelling, "The Economics of Exhaustible Resources," *Journal of Political Economy* 39 (April 1931), 137–175. Two systematic examinations of the economics of natural resources sponsored by Resources for the Future continue to withstand the tests of time: Harold J. Barnett and Chandler Morse, *Scarcity and Growth: The Economics of Resource Availability* (Baltimore: Johns Hopkins University Press, 1963); and Marion Clawson, ed., *Natural Resources and International Development* (Baltimore: Johns Hopkins University Press, 1964). More recent examinations include: P. Dasgupta and G. M. Heal, "The Optimum Depletion of Exhaustible Resources," *Review of Economic Studies* (Symposium) 1974; Ferdinand E. Banks, *The Economics of Natural Resources* (New York: Plenum Press, 1976); Vernon L. Smith, ed., *Economics of Natural and Environmental Resources* (New York: Gordon and Breach, 1977); and P. Dasgupta and G. M. Heal, *Economic Theory and Exhaustible Resources* (England: James Nesbit, 1979). The volume by Smith, in particular, deals with the economics of exploiting renewable as well as nonrenewable resources.

10. W. Stanley Jevons, *The Coal Question*, 3rd ed. (London: A. W. Flux, 1906).

11. W. Arthur Lewis, *Theory of Economic Growth*, p. 321, notes that the dilemma between depletion as a means of earning export funds for development capital or conservation for use by local industry in the future is particularly difficult for developing countries possessing coal or iron ore reserves.

12. The fuel wood crisis for many developing countries is described in detail in, among others: J. E. M. Arnold and Jules Jongima, "Fuelwood and Charcoal in Developing Countries," *Unasylva* 29, no. 2 (1978), Erik P. Eckholm, "The Other Energy Crisis: Firewood," *Worldwatch Paper 1* (Washington, D.C.: Worldwatch Institute, 1975); and Erik P. Eckholm and Lester R. Brown, "Spreading Deserts: The Hand of Man," *Worldwatch Paper 13* (Washington, D.C.: Worldwatch Institute, 1979).

13. See Robert E. Stein and Brian Johnson, *Banking on the Biosphere? Environmental Procedures and Practices of Nine Multilateral Development Agencies* (Lexington, Mass.: D.C. Heath, 1979); Robert O. Blake et al., *Aiding the Environment: A Study of the Environmental Policies, Procedures, and Performance of the U.S. Agency for International Development* (Washington, D.C.: Natural Resources Defense Council, February 1970); and Brian Johnson and Robert O. Blake, *The Environmental Policies, Programs and Performances of the Development Assistance Agencies of Canada, the Federal Republic of Germany, the Netherlands, Sweden, the United Kingdom and the United States* (Washington, D.C.: International Institute for Environment and Development, 1979).

14. See World Bank, "Forestry Sector Policy Paper," (Washington, D.C.: World

Bank, 1978); *The World's Tropical Forests: A Policy Strategy and Program for the United States,* Report to the President by a U.S. Interagency Task Force on Tropical Forests (Washington, D.C.: U.S. Department of State, May 1980); US AID, *Development Assistance in Forestry* (Washington, D.C.: US AID, July 1980).

15. Some of these factors are discussed generally in H. Jeffrey Leonard and David Morell, "The Emergence of Environmental Concern in Developing Countries: A Political Perspective," *Stanford Journal of International Law* 17, no. 2, (Summer 1981). See also, Chapters 3, 4, 5, and 6 of this volume.

16. See W. Arthur Lewis, *Development Planning: The Essentials of Economic Policy* (New York: Harper and Row, 1966) pp. 270–271.

17. See Raymond F. Hopkins, Donald J. Puchala, and Ross B. Talbot, eds., *Food, Politics and Agricultural Development: Case Studies in the Public and Policy of Rural Modernization* (Boulder, Colo.: Westview Press, 1979).

18. For a balanced view of progress and pitfalls in Indian agriculture, see John W. Mellor, *The Economics of Growth: A Strategy for India and the Developing World* (Ithaca, N.Y.: Cornell University Press, 1976).

19. China's massive commitment to rural development and food self-sufficiency remains the largest experiment in increasing rural agricultural productivity. See Alexander Eckstein, *China's Economic Revolution* (Cambridge, England: Cambridge University Press, 1977).

20. Lewis, *Development Planning,* p. 154.

21. Lewis, "Development Economics in the 1950s."

22. Brandt Commission Report, pp. 91–92.

23. *Ibid.,* pp. 92–93.

24. For example, productivity in some parts of Africa has changed little since George Kimball wrote: "The productivity is still so low that it takes anywhere from two to ten people—men, women and children—to raise enough food to supply their own needs and those of one additional—non-food-growing—adult." George Kimball, *Tropical Africa* (New York: Twentieth Century Fund, 1960), vol. 1, p. 572.

25. See, especially, Frances Moore Lappé and Joseph Collins, *Food First: Beyond the Myth of Scarcity* (New York: Ballantine Books) pp. 124–165.

26. See William W. Murdoch, *The Poverty of Nations: The Political Economy of Hunger and Population* (Baltimore: Johns Hopkins University Press, 1980) p. 305.

27. See especially, Eckholm, *Losing Ground.*

28. William Jennings Bryan, "Cross of Gold Speech." See also Adam Smith, *The Wealth of Nations,* Pelican Classics edition (London: Penguin Books, 1970) pp. 479–480.

29. See World Bank, *World Development Report, 1982* (Washington, D.C.: World Bank, 1982) Table 9, p. 126.

30. See World Bank, *World Development Report, 1981* (Washington, D.C.: World Bank, 1981) p. 22.

31. Richard W. Franke and Barbara H. Chasin, *Seeds of Famine: Ecological Destruction and the Development Dilemma in the West African Sahel* (Montclair, N.J.: Allenheld Osmun, 1980) argue that the overuse of land for peanut production in the Sahelian countries has disastrous effects on the soils of that region.

32. See *World Development Report, 1981* pp. 25–28.

33. See the chapter on "Agricultural Development Projects," in Raymond F. Das-

mann, John P. Milton, and Peter H. Freeman, *Ecological Principles for Economic Development* (London: John Wiley and Sons, 1973) pp. 140–181. Also Jack R. Harlan, "Crop Monoculture and the Future of American Agriculture." In *The Future of American Agriculture as a Strategic Resource*, edited by Sandra S. Batie and Robert G. Healy (Washington, D.C.: The Conservation Foundation, 1981).

34. These issues are elaborated in Chapters 3, 4, and 7 of this volume and in Leonard and Morell, "Emergence of Environmental Concern."

35. We gratefully acknowledge our debts to Professor Pratha Dasgupta of the London School of Economics. We have benefited from reading in manuscript form P. Dasgupta and Marian Radetzki, *The Environmental Component in the Social Evaluation and Pricing of Natural Resources*, May, 1980. This is a summary of the findings of the series of studies comprising UNCTAD/UNEP Project 055/006. We have also benefited from our prepublication review of Professor Dasgupta's manuscript, *The Control of Natural Resources* (Cambridge, Mass.: Howard University Press, 1983) especially Chapter 2, "Common Property, Externalities and the Distribution of Income."

36. Oran R. Young, *Natural Resources and the State: The Political Economy of Resource Management* (Berkeley: University of California Press, 1981).

37. *Ibid.*, pp. 181–182.

38. *Ibid.*

39. See William Taubman, *Governing Soviet Cities: Bureaucratic Politics and Urban Development in the USSR* (New York: Praeger, 1973); Henry Bienen and Michael Danielson, "Urban Political Development," *World Politics* 30, no. 2 (January 1978), 272.

40. See William Baumol and Wallace E. Oates, *Economics, Environmental Policy and the Quality of Life* (Englewood Cliffs, N.J.: Prentice Hall, 1979) p. 176.

41. In more than three thousand pages of case study work on income distribution in developing countries, there were almost no entries for environment among the following studies:

Juan Diaz-Canedo and Gabriel Vera, *Distribucion del Ingreso en Mexico, 1977*, Cuaderno 1 (Mexico City: Banco de Mexico, 1981); Joel Bergsman, *Income Distribution and Poverty in Mexico*, World Bank Staff Working Paper No. 395 (Washington, D.C.: World Bank, June 1980); Richard Charles Webb, *Government Policy and the Distribution of Income in Peru, 1963–1973* (Cambridge: Harvard University Press, 1977); Irma Adelman and Sherman Robinson, *Income Distribution in Developing Countries: A Case Study of Korea* (Stanford: Stanford University Press, 1978); John C. H. Fei, Gustav Ranis, Shirley W. Y. Kuo, *Growth with Equity: The Taiwan Case* (New York: Oxford University Press, 1979); Syamaprasad Gupta, *A Model for Income Distribution, Employment and Growth*, World Bank Staff Occasional Papers, No. 24 (Baltimore: Johns Hopkins University Press, 1977); Wouter van Ginnekan, *Rural and Urban Income Inequalities in Indonesia, Mexico, Pakistan, Tanzania and Tunisia* (Geneva: ILO, 1976).

Even when access to services are highlighted as an important part of income distribution analysis, there has been a neglect of the impact of environmental change on distributional profiles. See: Ergun Özbudun and Aydin Ulusan, *The Political Economy of Income Distribution in Turkey* (New York: Holmes & Meier, 1980); Henry Bienen and V. P. Diejomaoh, *The Political Economy of Income Distribution in Nigeria* (New York: Holmes & Meier, 1981); Gouda Abdel Khalek and Robert Tignor, *The Political Economy of Income Distribution in Egypt* (New York: Holmes & Meier, 1982).

An exception is: Luis A. Serron, *Scarcity, Exploitation and Poverty: Malthus and Marx in Mexico* (Norman, Okla.: University of Oklahoma Press, 1980) pp. 235–237.

42. William Baumol, "Environmental Protection and Income Distribution," in *Redistribution Through Public Choice*, edited by Hochman and Peterson, (New York: Columbia University Press, 1974) pp. 93–114. Works that deal with public choice are, of course, relevant, as are works that deal with the incidence of taxes on income groups.

43. Even the more general studies of income distribution do not deal explicitly with environmental issues. This is perhaps surprising too since the general and/or cross-national studies try to examine the relationship between stages or levels of development and concentration of income inequality. Gary S. Fields, *Poverty, Inequality and Development* (New York: Cambridge University Press, 1980); Charles R. Frank and Richard C. Webb, eds., *Income Distribution and Growth in Less Developed Countries* (Washington, D.C.: Brookings Institution, 1977); Robert Repetto, *Economic Equality and Fertility in Developing Countries* (Baltimore: Johns Hopkins University Press, 1979); Hollis Chenery et al., *Redistribution with Growth* (London: Oxford University Press, 1974); Irma Adelman and Cynthia Taft Morris, *Economic Growth and Social Equity in Developing Countries* (Stanford: Stanford University Press, 1973).

44. New York: Oxford University Press, 1980.

45. New York: Praeger, 1977 pp. 171–180. Also see Paul Streeten, et. al., *First Things First: Meeting Basic Needs in Developing Countries* (New York: Oxford University Press, 1981).

46. International Labour Office, *Employment, Incomes, and Equity: A Strategy for Increasing Employment in Kenya* (Geneva: ILO, 1972). ILO, *Sharing in Development: A Programme of Employment, Equity and Growth for the Philippines* (Geneva, ILO, 1974).

47. James P. Grant, *Disparity Reduction Rates as Social Indicators*, Monograph No. 11 (Washington, D.C.: Overseas Development Council, 1978). Paul Streeten, et. al, *First Things First*, does, like other basic needs studies, include sanitation and water supply needs, but this has to do with their impact on indicators of infant mortality. Much of the basic needs literature argues that meeting basic needs can be a powerful method of improving the quality of human resources and that this is positive for growth. However, the literature does not look at impacts on the resource base of environmental degradation or the "overexploitation" of renewable resources.

48. The literature which emerged from Habitat, the United Nations Conference on Human Settlements, is often very powerful, especially Barbara Ward, *The Home of Man* (New York: Norton, 1976). The literature is concerned with equality, with decay, and with growth that has produced blight and not mitigated poverty. But again, the analysis does not, except in a highly general way, link environment and distribution, although it goes further than the income distribution case studies we have noted above.

49. Joan Nelson, *Access to Power: Politics and the Urban Poor in Developing Countries* (Princeton: Princeton University Press, 1979); Wayne Cornelius, *Politics and the Migrant Poor in Mexico City* (Stanford: Stanford University Press, 1975).

50. George Ledec, "The Political Economy of Tropical Deforestation," this volume.

51. Rene Dumont and Nicholas Cohen, *The Growth of Hunger: A New Politics of Agriculture* (London: Marion Boyars, 1980).

52. *Ibid.*, p. 112.

53. Lester R. Brown, *The Twenty-Ninth Day* (New York: Norton, 1978), pp. 235–241.

54. *Ibid.*, p. 240.

55. For Taiwan see Fei, Ranis and Kuo, *Growth and Equity*. For Korea see Adelman and Robinson, *Case Study of Korea*. Korea and Taiwan did, of course, have bloody

foreign and civil wars and both had extensive land reforms after World War II.

56. For Cuba see Carmela Mesa-Lago, *The Economy of Socialist Cuba* (Albuquerque, N.M.: University of New Mexico Press, 1981). For Tanzania see Joel Barkan and John Okumu, eds., *Politics and Public Policy in Tanzania* (New York: Praeger, 1979); Chenery et al., *Redistribution with Growth*, pp. 268–272; Joel Samoff, "Crises and Socialism in Tanzania," *The Journal of Modern African Studies* 19, no. 20, (1981), 279–306. For Sri Lanka see Chenery, *ibid.*, pp. 273–280.

57. See Bienen and Diejomaoh, *Income Distribution in Nigeria;* Özbudun and Ulusan, *Income Distribution in Turkey;* Frank and Webb, *Income Distribution and Growth;* and Joel Bergsman, *Growth and Equity in Semi-Industrialized Countries,* World Bank Staff Working Paper No. 351, August, 1979.

58. See Pedro Aspe and Paul Sigmund, eds., *The Political Economy of Income Distribution in Mexico* (New York: Holmes & Meier, 1984).

59. Alfonso Renteria Corona, *La Economica Urbana: Ciudades y Regiones Urbanas* (Mexico: Instituto Mexicano de Investigaciones Economicas, 1974) p. 433.

60. Some have argued that even the largest is likely to be less than optimal-sized. See Koichi Mera, "On Urban Agglomeration and Economic Efficiency," *Economic Development and Cultural Change* 21, no. 2 (January 1973), 309.

61. See Secretaria de Asentaminetos Humanos y Obras Publicas, *Plan Nacional de Desarrollo Urbano,* Version Abreviada (Mexico, 1978). Also, see Secretaria de Patrimonio y Fomento Industrial, *Plan Nacional de Desarrollo Industrial, 1979–1983* (Mexico, 1979).

62. For an excellent discussion of the *Plan Nacional Desarrollo Urbano* see Kevin Henry, "Human Settlements and Industrial Location Policy in Mexico: Efficiency Considerations and Equity Implications," January 1981, Princeton, N.J. Unpublished paper. Also see, "Mexico Spends Billions to Foster Growth Outside Bursting Capital," *The Wall Street Journal,* January 20, 1981.

63. For a discussion of Abuja see Jon Moore, "Planning Abuja: The Politics of New Capital Construction." Senior thesis, Woodrow Wilson School of Public and International Affairs, Princeton University, April, 1982.

64. Norman Evenson, "Brasilia: Yesterday's City of Tomorrow," in *World Capitals: Toward Guided Urbanization,* edited by H. W. Eldredge (New York: Doubleday, 1975), p. 424.

65. See Chapter 1 of this volume.

66. See Henry Bienen, "The Politics of Distribution: Institutions, Class and Ethnicity," in Bienen and Diejomaoh, *Income Distribution in Nigeria,* pp. 127–172; Wayne Cornelius, *Politics and the Migrant Poor in Mexico City* (Stanford: Stanford University Press, 1975).

67. For one of the most thorough discussions of urban land use see Harold B. Dunkerly et al., *Urban Land Policy Issues and Opportunities,* vols. 1 and 2, World Bank Staff Working Paper No. 283, May 1978.

68. *Ibid.,* p. 15.

69. *Ibid.,* p. 6.

70. *Ibid.,* p. 13.

71. *Ibid.,* p. 14.

72. Taubman, *Governing Soviet Cities.*

73. See, among others, Nelson, *Access to Power;* and Cornelius, *Migrant Poor in Mexico City.*

74. Rakesh Mohan, "Urban Land Policy, Income Distribution and the Urban Poor," in Frank and Webb, *Income Distribution and Growth*, p. 436, citing figures from Shail Jain and Arthur Teimann, *Size Distribution of Income: Compilation of Data*, World Bank Development Research Center, Discussion Paper 4, August, 1973.

75. Mohan, *ibid.*, p. 439, citing, John M. Carson, et. al., *Community Growth and Water Resources Policy* (New York: Praeger, 1975).

76. See Michael Danielson and Rusen Keles, "Urbanization and Income Distribution in Turkey," and "Allocating Public Resources in Turkey," in Özbudun and Ulusan, *Income Distribution in Turkey*, pp. 269–348; John Waterbury, "Patterns of Urban Growth and Income Distribution in Egypt," in Abdel-Khalek and Tignor, *Income Distribution in Egypt*, pp. 307–350; Bola Ayeni, "Spatial Aspects of Urbanization and Effects on Income Distribution in Nigeria," in Bienen and Diejomaoh, *Income Distribution in Nigeria*, pp. 237–298; Richard J. Moore, "Urbanization and Housing Policy in Mexico," in Aspe and Sigmund, *Income Distribution in Mexico*.

77. For a discussion of the relationship between environment and land use see Anthony Young, "The Appraisal of Land Resources." In *Spatial Aspects of Development*, by B. S. Hoyle, pp. 29–50. (New York: John Wiley and Sons, 1974).

78. Martin Landau and Eva Eagle, "On the Concept of Decentralization," University of California, unpublished paper, May 1981, p. 10. I am grateful to Professor Landau for access to this paper, the research for which was done pursuant to Cooperative Agreement #AID/DSAN-CA-0199 between the University of California and USAID on the study of decentralization in LDC's.

79. *Ibid.*

Politics, Public Policy,
and Environment
in Developing Countries

CHAPTER 3

POLITICAL AND ECONOMIC CAUSES OF THIRD WORLD ENVIRONMENTAL DEGRADATION

H. Jeffrey Leonard

To one degree or another, all of the problems discussed in this volume are occurring on all continents and in all geographical regions of the earth. Yet, the severity, and hence the economic and human consequences, vary widely at the local level. This variation results not only from the intensity with which man undertakes his environment-altering activities, but as well from the resiliency and absorptive capacity of the local environment. Moreover, while the various problems frequently are overlapping, each local environment is more or less susceptible to or plagued by different types of natural resource and environmental problems.

Thus, while they may occur wherever people settle and work, problems such as deforestation, desertification, erosion, declining soil fertility, and environmental pollution tend to reach economically disruptive proportions in certain concentrated areas that can be identified both on a global and a regional level.

In spite of wide variations by geographical region, local habitat and type of problem, there is nothing particularly mysterious from a technical standpoint about why certain kinds of environmental problems are worse in some local environs than others under similar man-imposed stresses. The ecological equation is relatively straightforward even if imprecise: every natural environment has a certain carrying capacity beyond which its productivity cannot be sustained and its physical state cannot remain intact.

Far more than was the case with preindustrial societies, or even the first industrializing nations of the previous two centuries, scientists working in developing areas have a sophisticated understanding of the various cause-and-effect relationships that exist in the processes of environmental degradation and destruction. Soil scientists know which soils are most vulnerable and can predict with reasonable accuracy the outcomes under varying agricultural techniques, and applications of labor and capital. Foresters know, by and large, the adverse local conditions to expect if forests are clearcut or subjected to other less intensive methods of harvest. Biologists, chemists, or public health officials can assess generally the tolerances of various bodies of water to absorb and degrade pollutants and can measure the decline of that capacity under changing natural circumstances and growing levels of pollution.

A key question then is: Why do people take, and governments permit, actions that undermine the productive potential of the natural environment even when the consequences are often quite predictable in advance or, at worst, easily discernible at some intermediate point in time? If, as Chapter 2 argued, the effects of poor natural resource management in developing countries may effect so many aspects of the development process, why do not, or why cannot, governments control at least the most reckless activities? Perhaps of even greater importance, why do those individuals who suffer the most or who pay disproportionate amounts of the economic costs of environmental degradation continue to tolerate this state of affairs?

Obviously, the problems do not result entirely from poor technical knowledge about ecological concepts. The average peasant may not know that the incremental daily loss of soil from his plot may undermine his long-term productivity and (when added to the increments from other plots around his) may have deleterious effects further downstream. Still, even when local people do not have sophisticated scientific knowledge with which to judge whether they are exceeding the carrying capacity of their lands, the adverse effects become obvious enough sooner or later. While these people would most certainly be helped by improved scientific knowledge and data in making their decisions about how they utilize the natural environment around them, it is unlikely that the shortages of these "tools" are the fundamental causes of most of the widespread environmental problems in developing countries. Even primitive peoples in very underdeveloped areas of the world exhibit a vague awareness of the long-term ecological implications of their actions and, as well, how they could reduce the consequences under optimal conditions.[1]

Very serious gaps in technical expertise and knowledge about the natural environment do, of course, remain in all developing nations. But, the most serious resource and environmental probems are probably more motivated by political and economic circumstances than naivety. In fact, although the actions—overconsumption of local trees and fisheries, failure to invest in and maintain infrastructure to preserve the productivity of the land, reckless dumping of wastes into water sources, etc.—and the consequences may vary, the same set of economic incentives and political realities may be responsible for a wide range of ill-advised environmental actions in a particular country.

This chapter delineates some of these causal factors and illustrates that the natural resource and environmental problems we discuss in this volume are often not isolated phenomena but instead deeply imbedded in the social fabric of developing nations. It points out just how difficult (and sometimes unfruitful) it is to enhance technical and institutional capabilities to address the various ecological problems in developing countries when these may be overwhelmed by the weight of political and economic imbalances within individual political systems.

This is important to consider because many development assistance agencies and developing country governments have in recent years begun to put large amounts of money toward the alleviation of natural resource problems and environmental pollution. We begin this chapter, therefore, by assessing how various international interests have tended to view the problems and solutions and by considering some of the shortcomings of these views. Next we outline the range of political-economic factors that appear to underlie the different ecological problems apparent in developing countries and the forces which tend to determine whether or not these various problems are in fact reduced or relieved to any significant degree. Finally, we suggest some ways that development assistance agencies and individual governments can help to reduce the worst problems in spite of their deep-seated political and economic nature.

INTERNATIONAL CONCERN FOR RESOURCE AND ENVIRONMENTAL MANAGEMENT

Prior to the 1970s, third world governments and international aid organizations paid little heed to the potential ecological consequences of development projects or the barriers to economic development that certain environmental problems might cause. New projects such as dams, industrial facilities, and highways were planned and built with little or no attention paid to their potential impacts on the ecosystem, to the pollution they might generate, or to the long-term problems associated with the failure to manage natural resources adequately.

Today concern about natural resource management and environmental quality has become much more important in the planning and execution of most major development projects, and in overall development planning efforts in the third world. This has occurred in spite of the general lack of attention to the subjects of renewable resource management and environmental pollution in economic development and development planning literature. In many cases, the increased concern has arisen from the gradually widening perception among international and national development planners that a wide range of secondary activities is necessary to ensure successful and sustainable development projects. The stimulus for incorporating natural resource management concerns into development planning has also come partly from the concerted efforts of international conservationists to heighten awareness of such problems as deforestation, desertification, erosion, and siltation.

Development Assistance and Resource Management

Since the 1950s, there has been a gradual broadening of the missions perceived by key groups of international development assistance providers—the capital mobilizing efforts of the World Bank and regional multilateral banks, the international networks and backup assistance of the United Nations agencies and other international organizations, and the foreign aid and technical assistance programs of the bilateral agencies from Western nations. Accumulating experience in the development assistance business, and increasing evidence that the problems of the developing countries were far more complicated and deeply imbedded than originally thought, convinced development assistance agencies that more was needed than simply large infusions of in-kind grants, long-term loans, and technical assistance to stimulate growth in the industrial and the agricultural sectors. This was heightened by the concern in the early 1970s that developing nations themselves were ignoring the basic human needs of large segments of their populations and that the benefits of the economic growth that was taking place were not "trickling down" to the masses in many countries.[2]

In recent years, then, more development monies and technical assistance than in the past have gone toward making sure that supporting institutions and circumstances are conducive to the success of specific projects and general development programs. Development assistance providers now stress the importance of such secondary tasks as: orienting fiscal and monetary policies; improving the basic health, education, nutrition, and living situation for people; training technicians and workers to operate projects and participate in a changing economy; providing adequate infrastructure; building effective administrative and service delivery networks. In addition, an increasing amount of development assistance is targeted toward ensuring that projects that produce certain results today continue to produce these results in the long term. More attention is being paid to long-term policy implementation, the maintenance of capital equipment, and numerous other factors that are likely to make development projects more enduring.[3]

In these vital areas—the preparation of the overall social, political, and physical milieus, and followup planning to ensure the long-run viability of development projects—natural resource management and the minimization of certain types of pollution or congestion have necessarily, if inadvertently, assumed much greater importance than in the past. In the agricultural sector, for example, many internationally supported development projects designed to increase overall food production have been forced to include programs for alleviating or preventing soil erosion and soil exhaustion as a result of intensified agricultural techniques. More awareness is now demonstrated that projects should provide for some upstream watershed management so as to ensure even flows of water and prevent siltation of fields and irrigation systems. These are recognized as important prerequisites for development projects in the agricultural sector and, as a result of past failures and present ongoing problems in many areas that should be rich in food production, development assistance agencies have had to devote larger amounts of project resources to maintain a basic level of soil and water stability. Similarly, development assistance agencies have discovered that many large dams built to control flooding, provide water for irrigation, and generate hydroelectricity will have shortened life spans as a result of deforestation and erosion upstream. Improved watershed management has consequently become an investment-preserving component of dams built in the third world today that might be endangered by siltation from upstream erosion.[4]

Inevitably, development assistance agencies have discovered that there may be economic advantages to incorporating environmental planning and pollution controls into development projects and integrating certain environmental projects into development strategies for meeting the "basic human needs" of the world's poorest people. After all, just as much as inadequate infrastructure, wasteful fiscal policies, or political corruption, natural resource mismanagement or extreme environmental pollution can sometimes slow the completion of development projects or undermine their sustainability in the long term. In addition, especially in the rural sector, attention to such basic environmental problems as soil erosion, water quality, pesticide abuse, and deforestation often has direct and immediate implications on the quality of life and standard of living for poor people who frequently do not benefit from traditional development projects.[5]

Attention to resource management has also grown in the last decade with worldwide concern about pollution and environmental quality. Many development assistance organizations have responded by forming new agencies and departments. Thus following the 1972 Stockholm Conference on the Human Environment, the United Nations Environment Program (UNEP) assumed the function of serving as a catalyst and clearinghouse for worldwide concern about the environment. As part of its role, UNEP has worked with other UN agencies to coordinate their environmental and resource management activities. Such organizations as UNESCO, WHO, and FAO have thus launched environmental programs which address a variety of needs: the establishment of a global monitoring system for air and water quality, action programs to clean up the seas, international meetings on water, arid lands, ozone, toxic substances, and eventually, training programs in developing countries on environmental management.[6]

The World Bank, and to a lesser extent the regional economic development banks, have instituted procedures to evaluate the environmental impacts of all development projects.[7] These institutions have also been called upon to direct an increasing amount of their finances to projects to rectify undesirable side effects of past development. Projects to reduce schistosomiasis, which was increased by poorly planned dam and irrigation projects, to slow siltation problems through watershed and forestry planning, to find alternative fuel sources for populations which have exhausted their available supply of wood, and to improve polluted water supplies and inadequate waste removal systems account for growing shares of the bank's overall development financing.[8] In several instances, sectoral lending policies have been changed to accommodate these new emphases. For example, in 1978, the bank altered its policy concerning forestry loans to support environmentally protective forestry as well as industrial forestry. Since then, forestry projects, especially village woodlots for fuel wood and watershed management for flood and erosion control, have become integral to the bank's rural development programs.[9]

The USAID has placed an increasing emphasis on resource management in its sectoral programs in forestry, agriculture, energy, pest management, and water resources. In 1977, the U.S. Congress added a section to the Foreign Assistance Act authorizing USAID to furnish assistance for developing countries "to protect and manage their environment and natural resources," and "to maintain and where possible restore the land, vegetation, water, wildlife, and other resources upon which depend economic growth and human well-being, especially that of the poor."[10] Since that time USAID has expanded its programs to help developing countries deal with their environmental problems, train professionals in resource management, provide expertise and institutional assistance that further sustainable resource management, and build environmental safeguards into all development projects.[11]

Ironically, USAID's concern for environmental and natural resource management continued to expand during the same period that the Reagan Administration was drastically curtailing U.S. domestic spending for antipollution and resource management efforts. USAID administrator M. Peter McPherson, in fact, actively sought to enlist U.S. private environmental organizations to support and assist USAID's efforts to raise awareness of environmental considerations among its field mission staffs and within developing country planning bureaucracies.[12]

When asked to explain USAID's emphasis on environment, McPherson offered two reasons. First, he said, a major task he faced was to build a constituency in Congress and among the general public in support of continuing U.S. foreign assistance. U.S. environmental groups provided, according to McPherson, some of the strongest and most active supporters for increased foreign aid. Second, McPherson, an expert on population, said he had become increasingly convinced that many of USAID's development projects would fail in the long term unless resource management and basic antipollution measures were included in project design and implementation.[13]

Developing country governments themselves are also expressing a great deal more concern for natural resource management than in the past. In 1971, for example, USAID canvassed its overseas missions in an effort to identify key environmental problems and governmental responses in thirty-five nations. Overall, the report summarizing the results said, there was

. . . little evidence of awareness of environmental problems among their government administrators . . . Many countries are preoccupied with the development of their natural resources, and, to the extent that concern does exist for the environment, there appears to be apprehension that social and economic costs of environmental protection may very well outweigh the benefits.[14]

But since then many developing countries have devoted more attention to their environmental problems and sought to examine more carefully the environmental implications of development projects. A 1979 USAID report based again on mission reports from countries in Latin America, Africa, Asia, and the Near East, began on a very different note than the one of eight years earlier, contending that

. . . the governments of many developing nations have begun to recognize the importance of these issues. The consequences of inadequate resource management are no longer subtle. The continuing loss of tropical forest cover, the exhaustion of croplands, the depletion of fisheries, the advance of desert frontiers, the adverse consequences of indiscriminate pesticide use, epidemic levels of environmentally related diseases—these and other problems are steadily intensifying, and the need for a more effective response is increasingly felt. There is growing evidence that a number of developing country governments are beginning to treat these issues as matters of high priority.[15]

Focusing on Global Conservation

In addition to the internal recognition process occurring within many international development assistance organizations that preventive environmental planning can sometimes be integral to the success of economic development schemes, international conservationists have also focused more attention on the links between environment and development. A series of global reports dealing with world resource problems emerged in recent years, forecasting serious consequences for mankind if significant steps were not taken worldwide to reduce the overconsumption and misuse of resources. Unlike the neo-Malthusian *Limits to Growth* and other earlier reports, the focus of these reports was not as much on pollution and impending fossil fuel and mineral shortages (though these were considered), as it was on the assumed depletion of the earth's stock of renewable resources: soils, forests, fresh water, fisheries, wildlife, and genetic resources. Most prominent among these were the *World Conservation Strategy*, published in March 1980 by the United Nations Environment Program (UNEP) and a consortium of private environmental organizations; and two reports issued by the U.S. government under the Carter Administration, *The Global 2000 Report* (July 1980) and *Global Future: Time to Act* (January 1981).[16]

The *World Conservation Strategy* called for concerted action to halt worldwide destruction of arable land, forests, fishery resources, and plant and animal species. It asserted that these trends have potentially serious implications for the welfare of mankind:

In brief, a worldwide program to maintain, preserve and sustain the earth's renewable resources is needed to ensure the earth's capacity to support its growing population. The world already contains some four billion people, including five-hundred million who are malnourished and eight-hundred million who live at or below subsistence levels. World population is expected to rise to about six billion by the end of this century. Without a worldwide conservation program, millions more will face starvation and poverty.[17]

The *Global 2000 Report* conclusions—derived from an elaborate effort to integrate U.S. governmental data and models covering population, GNP, climate, resource, and technology trends—were even more direct. The Letter of Transmittal to President Carter warned of:

. . . the potential for global problems of alarming proportions by the year 2000. Environmental, resource, and population stresses are intensifying and will increasingly determine the quality of human life on our planet. These stresses are already severe enough to deny many millions of people basic needs for food, shelter, health, and jobs, or any hope for betterment. At the same time, the earth's carrying capacity—the ability of biological systems to provide resources for human needs—is eroding. The trends reflected in the Global 2000 Study suggest strongly a progressive degradation and impoverishment of the earth's natural resource base.[18]

Both the *World Conservation Strategy* and the *Global 2000 Report* sought to emphasize that these trends are threatening to all nations even though the physical distribution of the problems themselves may not be equal. Even if major disasters are averted, the deterioration of the carrying capacity of the world's natural systems, the reports contended, will affect: the availability and prices of resources for both developed and developing countries; international migratory patterns; international disputes and competition over access to strategic natural resources, especially energy sources; trade patterns between nations; global climatic changes; the world's stock of genetic resources; and global commons such as the oceans, the atmosphere, and Antarctica.

The key point of these reports was that unless something is done to reduce worldwide pressures on croplands, pastures, forests, and mineral and water resources, the world will become even "more crowded, more polluted, less ecologically stable, and more vulnerable to disruption than the world we live in now."[19]

These reports, particularly the *Global 2000* study, have been the focus of an intense debate among both natural scientists and social scientists concerning global environmental trends: Is the global environment being irreversibly damaged? Is the global climate being altered by burning of fossil fuels, industrial emissions, and the cutting of tropical forests? Is there an ultimate carrying capacity of the earth, beyond which population growth cannot be supported? Is pollution worldwide increasing or decreasing?

The models, assumptions, and data utilized by the U.S. government agencies that cooperated in putting together the *Global 2000* study have drawn heavy criticism not only from economists but also from natural scientists, ecologists, and social scientists.[20] To one degree or another, most of these critics have complained that the dire predictions of global resource shortages, population growth, climate changes, and international instability were based on: incomplete or outdated figures; the false assumption that current trends will continue indefinitely; and a disregard for the potential of technological change, innovation, and substitution.

Our concern, however, is not with the debate over whether the limits of the earth's carrying capacity are being reached. Insofar as economic development in certain developing countries is concerned, the more crucial question is whether mismanagement of resources and environmental degradation may undermine future prospects, both nationally and in certain local areas. To their credit, both the *World Conservation Strategy* and the *Global 2000 Report* sought to identify the potential links between economic development prospects and better management of living resources and the environment in many third world countries.

Indeed, these reports differ from the earlier *Limits to Growth* report in a fundamental and little acknowledged way. They see mismanagement of the earth's resources rather than overconsumption in any absolute sense. They stress the relationship between future economic development and the protection of resources, pointing out that economic development of a sustainable nature, far from being antagonistic to protection of global resources and the environment, is absolutely necessary to its success.

In particular, both reports see world poverty as one of the primary causes for continued resource abuse in rural areas. The *World Conservation Strategy* says:

That conservation and sustainable development are mutually dependent can be illustrated by the plight of the rural poor. The dependence of rural communities on living resources is direct and immediate. . . .

Unhappily, people on the margins of survival are compelled by their poverty—and their consequent vulnerability to inflation—to destroy the few resources available to them. . . .

It would be wrong, however, to conclude that conservation is a sufficient response to such problems. People whose very survival is precarious and whose prospects of even temporary prosperity are bleak cannot be expected to respond sympathetically to calls to subordinate their acute short term economic needs. The vicious circle by which poverty causes ecological degradation which in turn leads to more poverty can be broken only by development. But if it is not to be self-defeating, it must be development that is sustainable—and conservation helps to make it so. The development efforts of many developing countries are being slowed or compromised by lack of conservation.[21]

Thus, the reports note an urgent need for international cooperation to interrupt the cycle of poverty, population growth, and environmental degradation that is forcing people to put unsustainable pressures on the environment in much of the less developed world. Only a concerted attack on the socioeconomic roots of extreme poverty will provide people with the opportunity to earn a decent livelihood in a nondestructive manner and permit protection of the world's natural system, they conclude.

A POLITICAL-ECONOMIC PERSPECTIVE ON ENVIRONMENTAL PROBLEMS

As a result of evolutionary changes in the focus of international development assistance organizations and the efforts of international conservationists, programs to assist developing countries to better manage their renewable natural resources have expanded greatly in recent years. A growing number of environmental management demonstration projects have been implemented, and some have even shown signs of success in helping people design local watershed management conservation systems, village woodlots, soil stabilization and reclamation programs, and pollution control programs.

Nevertheless, in many poor countries where people depend on local soil conditions, wood, and water supplies for their welfare, significant deterioration in the productivity of these resources continues. The question of how these countries are going to stabilize and then adequately manage their resource base is complicated by numerous political and economic factors that are too often overlooked.

In spite of their expressed concern for highlighting the serious environmental problems that are rampant in developing countries, development assistance providers and conservationists have sometimes failed to examine the underlying political dynamics of resource and environmental abuse in the third world. Environmental abuse and mismanagement are often a result of complex political and economic circumstances and incentives prevailing in individual countries. The results may be similar in similar ecosystems all over the world— deforestation, desertification, etc.—but the causes of such environmental degradation may vary widely from place to place, region to region, country to country. This variation has significant implications for the natural resource management and environmental protection efforts of international development assistance agencies, developing country governments, and private voluntary organizations.

The macro focus on universal environmental problems by international development assistance organizations can lead to an oversimplification of solutions proposed at the local level. Project assessments, environmental guidelines, technology transfer, technical knowledge and training, while all beneficial, cannot overcome the basic fact that environmental abuse is rampant in the developing world because of much larger and more complex failings of individual political and economic systems. In such a context, resource abuse at the local level or national strategies for depleting forest and fishery resources may well represent the most expedient responses by countries and individuals to situations which would otherwise require fundamental political and economic reforms. Or, power and authority may be exercised to shift the costs of environmental externalities from one group in society to another.

In many cases, the poor, especially the rural poor, suffer great costs, while those with political power may actually gain from a strategy of environmental exploitation. At the same time, there is a tendency to overemphasize the extent to which the poverty-population conundrum is the predominant reason for environmental abuse in the poorest countries. While the link between poverty, population, and serious degradation of renewable natural resources in many countries is certainly important, such a viewpoint understates the complex factors that make environmental abuse the most logical short-term strategy for people to pursue. Overpopulation or absolute poverty are not necessarily the primary causes.

For some poor people, the cutting of saplings in arid areas or the farming of steep and eroded hillsides may well be the only alternative to starving or freezing. But, examined as cumulative regional phenomena, deforestation in Haiti, desertification in the Sahel, and urban squalor in Calcutta are much more than the result of poverty-stricken people trying to eke out a living. Invariably, deeply rooted political and administrative structures and economic incentives induce the poor and not-so-poor to cut trees, abuse the earth's soil or cram into unhealthy living quarters. Corrupt officials, overly centralized bureaucracies, inequitable land tenure patterns, or pressures for short-term successes and projects may make reckless use of the land quite rational and often lucrative.

Moreover, the image of millions of poor people abusing the land, day in day out, year after year, thereby diminishing a widening area to a barren, eroded zone or dustbowl in a continuous sequence is probably only a partially accurate portrayal of much environmental abuse that takes place in the third world. People the world over react to a continuous series of short-term circumstances that significantly affect at any given time the degree to which they abuse or care for their local environment—weather, general economic outlook, prices, political pressures, etc. As a result of these changing external factors, degeneration of renewable resources often takes place in short, intensive periods rather than at one constant rate. Often after a surge of degradation—caused by one-shot deforestation, migratory agriculturalists or pastoralists, or a confluence of poor economic return and bad weather (which, for example, may lead to rapid soil erosion)—the natural or human abuse is slowed and the lands attain a new, if diminished, threshold for their carrying capacity. While nature does not itself change by leaps and bounds, it is often diminished at a rapid and erratic pace with, perhaps, periods of relative stability in between. This fact may call for different approaches to the problem of encouraging better land management and conservation practices among the millions who live off the land in developing countries.

As well, environmental degradation in developing nations is often portrayed as a "tragedy of the commons"—no single individual has an interest in taking positive steps and collective action does not take place, so in the long term everyone suffers as lands are degraded. This, clearly, is the way that the international community has viewed the desertification problem in the countries in the Sahel region of Africa. But this image of a tragedy of the commons fails to illustrate that some benefit more than others from the short-term abuse of the land *and* that they might not benefit at all if collective actions were taken to implement sustainable land management practices.

From a social science perspective, then, there is still a great need to delineate more clearly: a) the diverse causes of resource and environmental degradation in developing countries; b) why human pursuits lead to degradation of some ecosystems and enhancement of others; and c) how a strategy of environmental exploitation—whether implicit or explicit—may be quite integral for various nations, groups, or individuals pursuing disparate goals under a wide variety of political and economic circumstances. The rest of this section examines these concerns, outlining how manipulation of political power by certain groups, lack of personal and territorial security, numerous economic incentives and disincentives, and the development planning and administration process itself often motivate environmental abuse even when the adverse consequences are obvious. This, of course, raises the question of whether development planners and development assistance agencies should try to treat the symptom or the cause.

Manipulation of Political Power

Strategic resources—especially financial capital and valuable natural resources—are scarce everywhere; there is not enough for everyone to enjoy unlimited benefits from these resources. As a result, a basic function of any political system is to allocate access to scarce resources—either by setting out priorities for their use or by protecting the "property rights" of institutions and individuals who have already secured access not available to everyone.

In addition to absolute scarcities, natural resources can be limited in their ability to contribute to the economic welfare of different groups when access to those resources is restricted. But differential access to basic natural resources in one place also can contribute to environmental degradation in other places. Within specified geographical areas, access to land for agriculture and to other land-based resources is rarely equally distributed among the inhabitants. Groups and individuals with privileged positions within the state, or whose access is protected by the prevailing political system, frequently secure the most fertile lands, the best forests, and the rights to scarce water delivered through large infrastructure. In some places, the monopolization of potentially lucrative resources by the few leaves the many dependent on land which is marginal and ill-endowed with additional resources. As was noted in Chapters 1 and 2, the carrying capacity of such marginal lands is easily exceeded when large numbers of people have no other means of securing a living except to work the land around them. Environmental degradation in many areas, then, is one more outcome of lopsided distribution of land, water, and other potentially productive natural resources.

Perhaps the most blatant example of systematic differential access to land resources according to their productive potential can be seen in South Africa. There 4.5 million whites enjoy 87 percent of the territory (including all key cities, towns, major water resources, and lush farm land), while 22 million blacks are allocated 13 percent of the country (called homelands or Bantustans), almost all of which is barren, dry, and subject to drought and erosion. Moreover, since the majority of the able-bodied men from the Bantustans work as migrant laborers in white urban areas, traditional farming has been abandoned and the large labor investments necessary to improve agricultural productivity in the Bantustans are not being made. Under these conditions, the productive capacity of what marginally arable lands there are in the Bantustans is declining.[22]

In the case of South Africa, the disparity is so marked and the land in the Bantustans so marginal that it hardly makes sense to talk about large-scale rural development projects to improve agricultural productivity for South African blacks. Under virtually any other political system imaginable, much of the land would simply be abandoned or left to a small number of nomads and ranchers. In other instances, the differential may not be so wide and the marginal lands which are allocated to the masses may not be so barren.

The hilly zones of the American tropics—southern Mexico, Central America, and the Andean countries—are also examples of marginal areas subject to intensive and often destructive use by poor people who do not have access to limited lands in flatter, more fertile terrain. A recent study has estimated that from one-fourth to one-third of the 200 million people living in the American tropics farm in high mountainous zones. About 80 percent of the area under cultivation in these zones is judged to be susceptible to serious erosion and erratic water availability if not carefully managed. Many of these people are among the poorest and least educated farmers on the continent and population growth rates continue to be high among them. The result, the report said, is that "the hillside zones are more densely populated than before, and the people continue to eke out a living on soils that are fast becoming more impoverished."[23]

In contrast to South Africa, however, there is room for many actions which could help improve and sustain agricultural productivity in many hilly areas of tropical America even in the absence of fundamental political change or widespread land reform. The problem remains that people who of necessity toil in marginal areas also generally cannot lay equal claim to other resources to help improve their lands—they are remote from key urban centers, they participate only marginally in politics, and have relatively low social status. As a result, large development projects or financing available from governments and external aid programs also tend to be focused in other areas.[24]

Access to key environmental amenities may vary widely within urban areas as well. Obviously this is the case in the large number of slums in third world cities which do not have access to piped, potable water. But it is even sometimes true when a government offers its ostensible commitment to provide services for all. In Manila there is often not enough water for all who are serviced by the city's water system. Many pipes only have enough pressure to provide water at night. Yet, short-falls are not at all distributed equitably. Through bribes to local officials and the use of illegal taps on trunk lines, wealthy households in Manila generally manage to get all the potable water they desire.[25]

Those with political power also frequently take actions that are politically expedient or enhance their own political or economic status even while leading to environmental degradation. The major expansion program for the fishing industry undertaken in Peru during the 1970s, which had widespread adverse ecological and economic repercussions, is illustrative. Much has been written in recent years about the rise and fall of the Peruvian fishing industry. Often the shift in "El Niño," a warm Pacific Ocean current which pushed the colder water of the Humboldt Current away from Peru's coast, is blamed for the disasters of the 1970s. Yet, many experts believe that massive depredations of coastal anchovy schools in the late 1960s and early 1970s also were a factor in the industry's collapse.

During the 1960s and early 1970s, overfishing resulted when investors flocked into fishing and fish processing to make quick profits. After the military took power in 1968, many of these investors continued to catch far more fish than scientists recommended to ensure stock renewal, on the assumption that the military government was planning to expropriate the industry anyway. By the time expropriation did come in 1973, the anchovy catch had dropped from 12.3 million metric tons in 1970 to 1.8 million metric tons per year.[26]

Instead of regulating the catch of the newly created state firm (Pescaperu) in order to rebuild fishing stocks, the military government embarked on an ambitious scheme to expand the fishing fleet and the industry's processing capacity. One major reason appears to have been that the military government felt enormous short-term pressure to show that the state industry could earn just as much profit as the private fishing companies had. In addition, one of the most ambitious members of General Juan Velasco's military regime, General Javier Tantalean, pushed the expansion of the industry in an effort to mold the large fishing related labor force into a powerful political base for himself.[27] Under these circumstances, the long-term sustainability of the industry was not a consideration that received much priority.

Also in Peru, the military government embarked on major efforts early in its reign to institute agrarian reform and expropriate the fertile lands monopolized by large, wealthy landowners. However, in the late 1970s under the military regime and subsequently under the civilian regime of President Fernando Belaunde Terry, the government showed a marked predilection to satisfy the land demands of various groups through jungle colonization projects rather than further redistributions of existing arable land.[28] Many of these projects were hastily undertaken with little preparatory analysis of soils, terrain, drainage, etc., and few infrastructural investments to provide adequate transportation, water management, and soil stabilization. Erosion and depletion of forest soils have thus reduced the success of some of these projects and many settlers have abandoned their newly awarded lands.

Similarly, as noted in Chapter 6, political expedience has been a major motivating factor in the Indonesian government's efforts to move large numbers of people from the densely populated areas of Java to outer areas such as Sumatra. The Transmigration Project, though justified as a means of relaxing population pressures and overcrowding of the land in Java, appears to be as much an attempt by the Indonesian government to reduce the potential of urban violence and to alter the ethnic balance and secure control of the outer islands.

As it turns out, environmental degradation of newly conquered, less densely populated areas in the outer islands is in some cases worse than on Java, where inhabitants have traditionally adopted agricultural techniques which permit highly intensive farming on a continuous basis.[29] By contrast, in the outer islands the seeming abundance of land, coupled with heavy pressure to produce quick results, has prompted the government to encourage, and colonists to follow, extensive agricultural techniques with little regard for hydrological management or long-term soil fertility. These problems are compounded by the fact that large numbers of the so-called colonist farmers who were resettled were actually unemployed urban workers with little or no previous agricultural experience. As a result, much land in northern, central, and southern Sulawesi and in northern Sumatra has been degraded and abandoned. After repeated burnings, the land has become infested by alang-alang *(Imperata cylindrica)*, followed by rapid soil erosion and finally outmigration to new areas.[30]

The logging of a proposed national park, Endau-Rompin, in Malaysia during the late 1970s provides another example where political expedience prompted officials to overlook ecological and economic considerations. The area, the last major virgin forested zone in southern peninsular Malaysia, covers about 500,000 acres astride the border between two Malaysian states, Pahang and Johore. After agreement with the states, the federal government's Third Malaysia Plan (1972) proposed the establishment of the Endau-Rompin National Park, with a core area of 224,000 acres to be left undeveloped and unharvested. Of the many reasons for maintaining the core area in pristine condition, the most important were that: a) this highland region contained the headwaters of five major rivers that form the lifeblood of virtually the entire economy of southern peninsular Malaysia and b) the core area was the principal habitat for many precious species, including about 14 Sumatran rhinoceroses, the last rhinos in Malaysia.[31]

In 1977, the Pahang state government decided to renounce its agreement and to grant logging concessions on 30,000 of the 90,000 acres it controlled in the core area. Because the Malaysian Federal Constitution leaves state governments with final say on all land management and resource development matters, the federal government could not prevent the state's action.[32]

Pahang officials said the decision was an essential one for the economic welfare of the state, contending that everyone would benefit from the income generated by the timber concessions and that the park could be forever preserved after valuable timber was harvested. Pahang State Secretary Datuk Wan Sidek bin Wan Abdul Rahman, defended the state government decision:

The Pahang State Government would not object to the setting up of the National Park, but it will only be done after the State had fully exploited its economic potential. When it comes to choosing between human welfare and animal survival, the State had to opt for the former.[33]

However, for all the pious rhetoric, the actual sum of money accruing to the state treasury from the timber concessions turned out to be very small. Under the terms of the concessions, the state was receiving a premium of between $M20 and $M80 per acre, or a total revenue which would range between $M600,000 and $M2,400,000. In reality, the concession amounted to a vast transfer of potential state revenue to a privileged few local companies and local businessmen. Local newspapers pointed out the close connections between state government officials and these business interests and stressed the importance of timber concessions to the state government as a source of political power and patronage.[34]

The logging was finally halted in Endau-Rompin after a nationwide campaign supported by the Consumers' Union of Penang, many local groups, and federal government officials. However, by that time 13,000 acres had been clear cut and heavy soil erosion and downstream sedimentation and flooding had already occurred.[35]

Frequently, those who are responsible for and benefit from major environmental problems are not the same people as those who are hurt by the damage or who must pay the remedial costs. If these groups were the ones to suffer the economic and health consequences created by their activities or had to pay the costs of repairing environmental damage, they might take serious steps to remedy the situation. But so long as they can shift the costs to other economic sectors or to other less powerful, organized, or fortunate groups, there are strong disincentives against unilateral action.

In virtually every developing country, for example, development within the modern sector (particularly industry), has created pollution problems which have impinged on traditional economic sectors, particularly farming and fishing. Chapter 7 describes in more detail some of the serious problems resulting from this transfer of costs throughout Southeast Asian countries. One country which also seems headed for inevitable difficulties is Nigeria, where the government has pushed forward a concerted industrial expansion campaign.

Despite great strides in increasing industrial output in recent years, Nigeria's Fourth National Development Plan stresses the economy's vital dependence on traditional industries—agriculture, fishing, and "cottage" manufacturing. Without rapid and sustained expansion in these traditional industries, mass unemployment and extreme poverty will grow in Nigeria no matter how successful the modern industrial sector's development proves to be. As a result, the major thrust of the fourth plan is on agriculture and rural development.[36]

Yet, continued wanton expansion of the modern industrial sector is already imposing serious costs on farmers and fishermen in rural areas.[37] The industrialization plans of Nigeria continue to concentrate on basic industries: oil refineries and petrochemicals, steel production, quarrying and related building materials, and food processing.[38] As noted in Chapter 7, these are all among the industries that are creating the worst industrial pollution problems in developing countries. Although Nigeria has a growing Environmental Protection Agency, there is little attention paid within the development planning process to how the targets set for industrial development may lead to excessive pollution and thereby undermine goals set for agricultural and rural development.[39] If the ongoing experience in most developing countries is any guide, it is likely that the traditional economy will continue to bear the costs of problems generated by the modern sector.

In the Philippines, major natural resource development projects are contributing to economic growth and greater prosperity for some, but the environmental alterations have undermined the ability of less powerful and affluent groups to survive economically. The USAID field mission's country development strategy paper for 1982 pointed out that while accelerated exploitation of natural resources in the Philippines had assisted industrialization and boosted exports, it had also caused increased environmental decline. The paper went on to point out who was paying the costs: "The irony is that in generating the benefits of growth, they also deplete the very resources required for sustained growth and undercut the poor's ability to survive."[40]

Also in the Philippines, the government has pursued an ambitious plan to dam the Chico River to generate hydroelectric power for the modern sector of Luzon. But the series of four dams threatens to submerge vast acres of carefully terraced agricultural land which has for centuries been the backbone of the closely knit economic, social, and cultural systems of the Kabinga and Bantoc tribes. Ironically, much of the land was permitted to deteriorate ecologically even before construction of the dams, when violence and guerilla warfare grew as opposition to the dam intensified. During the fighting, nearly 800,000 square meters of lush agricultural land for coffee, fruits, and rice were neglected or abandoned.[41]

Obviously, costs of environmental side effects from economic activities are shifted from one class of people to another within sectors as well as between them. Workers and the urban poor can rarely insulate themselves from industrial pollution or workplace health hazards while those who benefit from the industrial production often have ample means of insulating themselves from paying the costs. In Cubatao, Brazil, one of the most polluted industrial cities on earth, few plant managers or local politicians (including the mayor) even live in the city.[42] The serious health consequences suffered by the poor in Cubato who cannot escape the pollution are discussed in Chapter 7.

Personal and Territorial Insecurity

Security from physical violence and usurpation is a fundamental requisite for long-term land stewardship. Unless people feel that the proceeds of investments to protect and improve future land productivity will accrue to them, they will not make the effort. In many parts of the developing world, villages, tribes, and whole ethnic groups live without this security, making even well-designed rural development projects to increase the productivity of local environments extremely difficult to carry out.

In Kenya's Turkana District, for example, a harsh desert-like area between the Uganda and Sudan borders, the United States and a group of European nations have backed a $1.5 million scheme to help 40,000 of the 170,000 member nomadic Turkana tribe to switch from cattle, goat, and camel herding to stable agriculture. Kenyan government officials, missionaries, and aid workers have been teaching Turkana families to plant drought-resistant crops, to channel scarce rainfall by building walls, and to build small-scale irrigation systems to utilize underground water. To date, administrators of the scheme say they are pleased at how quickly the Turkana involved in the pilot schemes have adopted to the new lifestyle.[43]

Yet, the task of inducing the Turkana to settle and grow crops as well as tend cattle is complicated by political as well as natural and cultural factors. Like most nomadic tribes in the area, the Turkana have survived for centuries by herding their animals and staging periodic raids on the stock of other tribes. Several years ago, the Turkana were well endowed with animals and considered themselves rich. Most of this livestock was stolen by Karamajong tribesmen from Uganda using sophisticated weapons left behind by Idi Amin's army. Shortly thereafter, drought decimated the Turkana's stock even further, leaving many people destitute and starving.[44] As the Turkana slowly rebuild their herds, the sedentarization and long-term environmental rehabilitation advocated by the Kenyan government will only succeed if the government can secure the border with Uganda or find other means of protecting Turkana wealth from tribal predators. Otherwise, the will and rationality to take what the land yields and move on will remain compelling.

But security is more than simply freedom from personal violence or expropriation of property: people who work the land will not or cannot make investments to maintain long-term productivity if this entails too much sacrifice from present consumption. For millions of landless or near-landless small tenant farmers producing only slightly above subsistence level in the developing world, a key variable is the amount of tribute, tax, or rent they must pay to the nominal owners of the land. Chapter 1 illustrated how feudal systems in both medieval Europe and ancient China exacted so much excess tribute from peasants that they often could only meet their personal needs and external obligations by pushing the land beyond its long-term carrying capacity. Usurpation above reasonable market rent can thus be a powerful force in the long-term degradation of agricultural land.

In northern Ghana, many hard-working farmers of the Konkomba tribe permitted their lands to deteriorate and overextended the soil in the short term for this reason. In recent years, after violence and conflict broke out between the Konkomba and their host tribes and landlords—the Nanumba and the Gonja—persecution of the Konkomba increased. All settler farmers on Gonja tribal land were ordered several years ago to give 50 yam tubers per acre and one bag of cassava, millet, and maize per acre of farm land to the nearest Gonja chief.[45] Such exactions forced farmers to rob from the future by reducing land in fallow and farming more intensively just to maintain previous levels of consumable production for themselves.

As was illustrated in Chapter 1, flight has always been a key response by groups confronting environmental decline at the local level. In fact, many societies have based their entire economic and social systems on productive methods that depend on the exit option—notably nomadic herding and shifting cultivation. In lieu of using resources intensively through elaborate water management schemes, terracing lands or other soil enhancing measures, pastoral and swidden agriculture economies consume the accumulated natural fertility of the land and then move on to another location. Under conditions of scattered and relatively stable populations and abundant land, such economies have been able to maintain an ecological equilibrium within the broad spatial confines in which they maneuver.

But rapid population growth or changing values about mobility may significantly upset the balance between nature and groups that practice these highly extensive forms of production. Some societies have proven incapable of adopting to such long-term pressures. On the other hand, sedentarization of nomads and the switch to permanent agriculture by shifting cultivators have often been quite natural and successful responses to new environmental, social, economic, technological, or cultural constraints and opportunities.[46] Adaptions to these new circumstances seem most likely when they can be introduced gradually in response to ongoing changes. They appear least likely when the changes are imposed externally and place artificial restrictions on spatial mobility. Thus, when traditional patterns of migration are constrained by new political considerations—e.g., territorial boundaries, coerced government sedentarization programs, new land use designations—degradation of agricultural and grazing lands has quite often followed.

The ecological problems created by forced sedentarization and new political constraints on previously mobile peoples have been most clearly witnessed in Africa. What Jacks and Whyte said of African soil fertility and soil erosion problems in the 1930s is still true in many places: "The African reserves are eroding because a confined people is still continuing the practices of nomadism."[47] Traditionally, stockbreeders and farmers in the Sahelian areas of Africa, for example, survived quite well off the land as a result of complex interrelationships and movements between the northern and southern Sahel. The pastoralists, who dominated the region politically, moved their livestock from pasture to pasture according to season, years, types of livestock, and elaborate agreements with sedentary people in savanna areas to the south. During the dry season and in times of serious prolonged droughts, southward movements into the savanna areas were essential aspects of the nomadic strategy for minimizing human and livestock losses and for reducing ecological damage in the dry area.

During the past eighty years, new territorial constraints have increasingly reduced the mobility of the nomadic tribes. Under colonial rule by the French, nomadic political domination of the area was ended and the symbiotic arrangements providing the nomads territorial access to the savanna zones were altered. With independence, arbitrarily drawn political boundaries between nations also reduced mobility of nomadic groups. Since then, the expansion northward of cash cropping into former dry season grazing lands, and increasingly coercive government programs to integrate the nomads into the national economy and promote sedentarization have cut off even more lands within which nomadic tribes can make a living. In times of adequate rainfall, these nomadic groups, as always, may still survive quite well and indeed expand their livestock herds rapidly. But, with the onset of drought, as in the last decade, the movement southward to avoid serious economic loss and starvation is increasingly difficult.[48]

The Sahelian drought hit those people hardest who were unable to migrate as a result of political restrictions. Indeed, mobility appears to have been a major reason why many people in the western Sudan did not suffer nearly as tragically as did those people whose countries lie almost entirely within the arid zone. V. C. Robinson reports that:

First, at the time of the drought years in the early 1970s, we heard much of the terrible losses of livestock and of human starvation across the West African Sahel zone virtually all the way across to the Chad-Sudan border. Then such reports reappeared in Ethiopia. One might have thought that Sudan escaped the drought, which of course it did not. The people of Sudan's western savannas were however able to escape the worst effects of the drought years by moving south, which they were able to firstly because they had no international frontier to cross in doing so and secondly because the wetter country they moved into was not already extensively occupied. This ability to move, with their stock, was often not available to peoples in western Africa.[49]

The effects of territorial restrictions are also illustrated by a recent study by Claudia Carr of the Dasanetch tribe in southwest Ethiopia.[50] Carr shows how a severe reduction in the area of their tribal lands has led to major ecological deterioration and economic disruption on the remaining tribal lands. The Dasanetch were excluded from the western and southern portions of their territory—which they traditionally depended on for seasonal grazing of their herds—after an agreement between the Kenyan and Ethiopian governments, which has since been enforced with varying degrees of vigilance by the Kenyans. Like other pastoral tribes in surrounding areas—the Turkana, Inyangatom, Kerre, Musle, Hamar, Borana, and others—the Dasanetch have maintained a strong orientation to and preference for a mobile economy based on cattle and herding. Carr sums up the consequences:

The input of territorial restriction to the system has resulted in a self-perpetuating (or runaway) deterioration within the system, especially along the lines of: (1) environmental breakdown in the plains in the form of reduction of total plant cover, invasion of bush and unpalatable plants, and disruption of natural faunal assemblages, soil erosion, and (2) economic breakdown within the major production activity, stock raising, through reduction of stock vigor, increase in disease and death, and reduced milk yields.[51]

Another potential cause of environmental degradation is the constant insecurity of land tenure that many poor people throughout the world must endure.

In both rural and urban areas, people are reluctant to take steps to protect or improve the land around them if they do not have some reasonable assurance that they will be permitted to continue occupying that land. A World Bank study of environmental sanitation in squatter settlements of San Salvador found that people express an urgent need for adequate housing, drainage systems, and water supply. However, the study noted, until the people receive assurance that they will not be evicted from the territory they occupy, "they are not willing to spend or invest any money on house improvement and environmental sanitation, including the building and maintenance of latrines."[52]

Degradation of the local environment may also be encouraged when governments exercise political power to force people to move from one place to another. As already noted, many countries—including Indonesia, Peru, and Brazil—have large-scale projects to relocate people from populated areas to less populated areas. Many of the people who participate in these "directed colonization" programs are recruited by government fiat to participate. However, numerous studies of such relocation schemes have emphasized that settlements populated by those forced by the government to move from one place to another have been far less successful than those where participation has been spontaneous and voluntary.

In the 1970s, for example, Michael Nelson surveyed twenty-four virgin land settlement projects in Latin America and found that elaborately directed government projects were most likely to face failure and least likely to result in dynamic and sustainable agricultural expansion. The self-selection process of voluntary settlements was much more likely to bring settlers who could surmount problems stemming from isolation, poor soil, and climatic hardship and create a viable long-term colony.[53]

A study of the Indonesian Transmigration efforts came to similar conclusions:

The most successful settlers have proved to be those who as voluntary migrants make their own way to a new area . . . (S)everal surveys have indicated that they are the dynamic element in the development of new areas, and despite their initial struggles show a considerable degree of success. . . . (They) make rapid advances in farming and are generally more successful in farm production than general transmigrants.[54]

Thus, when governments try to dictate where people roam or where they settle, one consequence can be a failure by those so coerced to care for their adopted environment. When territorial boundaries are manipulated or political restrictions implemented to foreclose the option of migration to peoples whose traditional environmental management strategies depend on it, or when people who settle in an area are under perpetual threat that they may lose their land, or when people are forcibly moved to new settlements, the will, the incentive, or even the ability to maintain and improve the surrounding environment may be lost.

Economic Incentives and Disincentives

In endorsing economic development as an important means of reducing the habitat destruction and overexploitation of living resources by poor people in poor countries, many individuals and organizations associated with the *World Conservation Strategy* and the *Global 2000 Report* have also rallied around the call by developing countries for the establishment of a New International Economic Order (NIEO). In general, the goals for an NIEO include: trade concessions for third world countries, stable and higher prices for third world commodities, reorganization of the international monetary system and international capital markets, increased aid from developed to developing countries, a code of conduct for transnational corporations, and greater access to western technology at more favorable terms.

Yet, the whole thrust of NIEO concerns the structure of relations between developed and developing country governments. Beyond a certain amount of rhetoric, there is little in the NIEO-related demands that would alter the relationships between individual governments and their citizens. More than the structure of North-South relations, it is the internal distributions of political and economic power in developing countries that perpetuate inequalities, control access to certain resources, and structure economic incentives and administrative interventions in manners which hold people in situations where abuse of local natural resources is an important aspect of their daily living. Changes at this level would be little affected even if the North were to agree to every demand associated with southern proposals for an NIEO.

Indeed, in many developing countries, concerted, sustainable rural development will occur only when the principles underlying the New International Economic Order are applied at a domestic level. One of the major stumbling blocks in the rural sector throughout the third world is that fiscal policies are heavily biased against producers in the agricultural economy, particularly small producers. Governments throughout the third world, much to the chagrin of development economists, continue to manipulate the terms of trade between agriculture and other sectors of the economy as a means of raising government revenues, subsidizing industrial growth, and providing cheap food to urban dwellers. The result is that farmers pay high prices for their inputs— implements, seeds, fertilizers—and receive artificially low returns on the sale of their outputs.[55]

This problem of persistent distortion of trade between city and countryside is perpetuated, in part, because of the heavy bias toward industrial growth and urban demands within the development process. The serious roadblocks this bias creates to balanced economic development as well as to efforts to raise the standard of living of the rural poor have been noted and analyzed extensively in the literature on development.[56] The implications for the rural environment are equally as profound. When rural producers cannot make adequate returns on their investments, they cannot afford to take steps that might improve their lands in the long term. Instead, they must use all of their energies and available capital to increase present consumption. The land does not get manure because people cannot afford to keep animals; crop rotation, terracing, and other sound agricultural techniques cannot be practiced.

Under such circumstances, programs to increase ecological awareness and to stimulate wider use of conservation techniques in agriculture are not likely to have widespread success. The whole structure of economic relations between the rural and urban sectors may underlie the behavior of rural producers. Until the basic incentives change, until producers believe that they have some reasonable chance of receiving some rewards for their stewardship, little progress is likely to occur in stemming environmental degradation resulting from rural food and commodity production. This is as true throughout developing countries today as it was when Adam Smith surveyed the problem of low productivity in his native Scotland two centuries ago (see Chapter 1) and wrote that:

The lands of no country, it is evident, can ever be completely cultivated and improved till once the price of every produce, which human industry is obliged to raise upon them, has got so high as to pay for the expense of complete improvement and cultivation. . . . [57]

The World Bank's 1982 *World Development Report* underscores this point, noting that:

The key to agriculture's growth among the present industrial economies was the farmer himself, who sparked a stream of cost-reducing innovations and also financed and carried out the investment in land improvement needed to exploit new technology. The evidence from a wide range of developing countries shows that farmers behave no differently today. The key factors are still the opportunity and the incentive to improve the land and with it the farmer's livelihood. [58]

Another serious hurdle to overall rural economic development also leads to environmental destruction: the tremendous underemployment of human productive potential that exists in heavily populated nations where the vast majority still till the soil or harvest other fruits of nature for their livelihood. A large portion of these laborers are surplus—that is, their marginal production is at or near zero. Overall agricultural output would be little reduced if a higher percentage of people were employed in nonagricultural rural activities or in industrial or commercial jobs in urban areas. The problem, of course, is that such jobs do not exist.

In national economic terms, this is really only slightly different than having a huge rural population of unemployed people and, in fact, many economists refer to this phenomenon as 'disguised unemployment.' At the same time, some argue that the local economic consequences are much less harmful than outright unemployment because people in essence "share" jobs and therefore distribute the rural product more evenly than if some worked and others did not.

However, the ecological consequences are unequivocally bad for at least two reasons. First, there is constant pressure to stretch nature beyond its limits—to crop marginal lands and try to get more present consumption from each piece of available land. W. Arthur Lewis, the Nobel Prize–winning economist, wrote in the 1950s that:

This sort of over-population, in addition to wasting labour frequently also reduces the fertility of the soil. . . . (There) is pressure to use every inch of ground; land is put under plough which ought to be left in forest, or which should be left for purposes of soil conservation. Then there is the temptation to over-crop the land; to take too many crops in one year, or to cut down on fallow periods.[59]

Another less remarked upon consequence of widespread rural underemployment is the fact that for the vast majority of cultivators agriculture remains a means of survival rather than a professional vocation. Careless, weak, uneducated, and hungry cultivators make poor stewards of the land. In more advanced economies, these people would be employed in menial jobs in factories and the service sector, or be on welfare, or perhaps segregated in pockets of rural poverty. In many developing countries, though, the pool of marginal cultivators vastly outnumbers the pool of farmers. This contributes to the degradation not only of marginal lands but also of good agricultural lands that would fare better under the care of people who by dint of their brawn, agronomic skills, or capital endowments are better farmers.

The implications of this latter phenomenon must be realistically considered by development planners. At present, a great deal of attention and money in the third world is being devoted to helping the masses of marginal cultivators become better marginal cultivators. This may make sense as a short-term strategy to help people meet their basic human needs in spite of the fact that the economies of their countries are stagnating and nonagricultural jobs are scarce. But in terms of a long-term strategy for development, these marginal cultivators are precisely the ones who must be moved out of agriculture in order to achieve the productivity gains that are integral to the entire economic development process. This is not a newly discovered dilemma; economist Ragnar Nurkse noted in 1953 that "it is rather hopeless to try to introduce better farming methods unless the excess population is drained off first."[60] But it is one that has not been widely addressed among the planners and executors of development policies. Here again, the stabilization and improvement of the ecological system may not come until marginal cultivators are moved from their present "jobs" into employment (either rural or urban) where they do not depend solely upon whatever daily yield they can coax from the land.

Thus, two major, systemwide economic problems that predominate in the rural sector in a large number of developing countries—pricing policy for agricultural goods and gross underemployment—are and likely will, remain fundamental contributors to long-term environmental problems such as soil erosion, loss of soil fertility, and deforestation. In areas where this is the case, the ecological well-being of the local environment may be virtually impossible to protect unless and until regressive economic policies are altered and some means are found to reduce the numbers of cultivators whose marginal productivity is low or even negative.

In some areas, though, an entire economic system may be dependent upon an activity that cannot be sustained under techniques that are not harmful to the environment. Thus, a fundamental reorientation of the local economic base may become a prerequisite for stabilizing a declining ecological zone. One possible example is the case of the Wana, a primitive tribe on the island of Sulawesi, Indonesia. The Wana economy is heavily dependent upon the collection and sale of rattan for use in making cane furniture. Rattan, a prolific vine that can grow as much as three yards per year, climbs to great heights by wrapping around the large trees in the thickly forested areas of Sulawesi.

For the Wana, there is only one economical way to harvest rattan: chop down the host trees and disentangle the vine. While the method is extremely wasteful and has led to local forest destruction near Wana villages, the Wana have yet to adopt alternate harvesting practices. To some extent, this may occur out of necessity as local forest destruction becomes excessive. But there is a real question whether, at prevailing prices for raw rattan and the technology available to the Wana, the tribe would be able to institute more expensive or significantly more time-consuming methods of harvest.[61]

Development Planning and Administration

Governments are often directly responsible for environmental deterioration in their roles as planners and executors of development projects and as the nominal protectors of public property and national heritage. Often governments simply do not have the manpower and the will to halt undesirable trends that occur as a result of greed, need, or ignorance. Allowing development projects to proceed without environmental safeguards may well be a more attractive short-term solution for governments facing immediate economic constraints; permitting unlawful abuse of natural resources may be far easier than providing alternatives for people in need or implementing the political and economic reforms that might reduce the pressures that lead to the abuse.

In Bangladesh, for example, recent studies have indicated that between 15 and 25 percent of the nation's arable land has been lost as a result of unplanned rural housing. In spite of efforts to control building construction through permit systems, the Bangladeshi government has simply not been capable of mustering the force or providing the alternatives to slow the unauthorized land invasions. The National Planning Commission predicts that these incursions could occupy over 30 percent of the fertile farmlands of Bangladesh by the year 2000.[62]

It is clear enough to the Bangladeshi government that this is a serious threat to its long-term food self-sufficiency goals, but the resources required to stop spontaneous colonization of agricultural lands would be quite large. In addition, of course, the need to satisfy the housing demands of the population probably is viewed as a more urgent demand than heading off the gradual reduction of available arable land.

Sometimes long-term environment rehabilitation programs do not succeed because governments do not afford adequate protection. In China, reforestation programs have been plagued by administrative problems and the inability of the government to police reforested areas. Chinese officials have blamed serious flooding of the Yangtze River in recent years on large-scale deforestation that continued, and even increased, following the ascendence of the Communist government. In part, the blame has been placed on unreasonable production quotas for wood and wood products during the Cultural Revolution.[63] Yet, an article in the *Sichuan Daily*, the Communist party newspaper, acknowledged that of 4.3 million trees planted in 1981 in Sichuan, only about 50,000 remained a year later. Although the article did not estimate how many had died and how many had been cut, its call for stiff punishment for unauthorized tree cutting indicated the government's concern that this was a major factor.[64]

In reality, the government is going to find it difficult to police its reforestation projects until it can provide for alternate fuel sources for China's 800 million peasants. Consequently, it recently announced a ten-year development program to find means of meeting rural energy needs through biogas, solar and wind power, geothermal sources, shale, and peat.[65]

A similar problem exists in India, where the government is trying desperately to expand social forestry programs to slow the expansion of desert in Rajasthan. The goal of planting 34 million trees was met, but officials say the mortality rate is alarming. One report noted:

Villagers oppose the declaration of any area as closed for social forestry. People often encroach on areas earmarked for development and steal fuelwood and fodder from government land. Legal action taken against offenders is a laborious process and only alienates the local community further.[66]

In addition, there are numerous examples in the developing world where local groups have strongly protested or simply ignored governmental efforts to institute conservation policies because this would amount to a forced reduction of present levels of income. In Zambia, for example, government attempts to impose new regulations in order to prevent depletion of the Lake Mweru fishery were vehemently opposed by local fishermen. In fact, opposition to the new controls on net sizes and fishing times provided a basis for incorporating the Luapula fisheries into the nationalist movement.[67]

Similarly, in many parts of Africa, coercive efforts by colonial governments to implement conservation strategies—e.g. limiting collective grazing rights on arid lands, promoting soil conservation, controlling crop disease, reducing soil erosion—led many wealthy and not so wealthy African farmers to back the efforts of nationalist politicians to overthrow the colonial regimes.[68] When over-consumption or abuse of the local environment is built into the socioeconomic structure as it was and still is in many parts of Africa, a government may find it extremely difficult to implement policies that ultimately would improve the long-term outlook for all. To date, few governments facing such dilemmas have found the will to force adjustments in the behavior of individual cultivators even when the future consequences of failing to do so are obvious.

But in some cases, governments simply lack money and commitment to provide for adequate protection of natural resources from greedy poachers. Bolivia, for example, has taken very firm legislative steps to protect threatened wildlife, especially the vicuna, and wildlife habitats. However, officials esti-mate that at least 600 forest guards are needed to enforce the legislation and only about 100 guards are currently employed. In response, one private group, Prodeno Bolivia, has actually initiated its own policing efforts until the govern-ment sees fit to provide for more forest guards.[69]

Even when adequate numbers of government agents are available, this does not necessarily result in enforcement of rules. For example, it is unlawful to export raw tree trunks from Paraguay, but it is estimated that close to one-half of Paraguay's timber exports to Brazil are unprocessed. Although the problem is to some extent one of a lack of enforcement manpower, it is also clear that large-scale bribery of Paraguayan officials is facilitating the contraband exports.[70]

In the southern zone of the Sahara, efforts to slow the incursions of the desert are hampered both by lack of government control and by some government-backed development schemes designed, ironically, to improve the welfare of local pastoralists. One observer noted recently:

Planting, reseeding, water development, and virtually every other available means to-ward improvement of the range and livestock are bound to fail unless government control can be exerted. Indeed, most development efforts that have been attempted in this region have aggravated the problem rather than cured it. Water development in areas previously protected from livestock use because of the lack of water brings destruction of these in addition to the destruction of the ones previously grazed.[71]

Chapter 6 describes these problems in more detail and outlines some sugges-tions for reducing their contributions to spreading desert encroachments south of the Sahara.

Frequently in third world countries, large development projects carried out to increase national infrastructure for the modern sector have caused local environmental hardships. In Malaysia, the construction of the Kuala Lumpur–Karak Highway in the mid-1970s (providing a link between the capital and the hinterlands of the East Coast) involved the dislocation of massive amounts of earth and the clearing of wide areas of land along the Gombak River. Yet, virtually no measures were taken to minimize land erosion and prevent excessive silt and sedimentation in the river. Within one year, siltation and flooding in the Gombak area of Selangor had ruined large areas of agricultural lands, with many village farmers forced to give up farming or move to new villages.[72] To reduce the problems of flash floods and sedimentation, the Selangor Drainage and Irrigation Department was forced to station two hydraulic excavators along the Gombak River and to spend hundreds of thousands of dollars for construction of silt traps and silt removal basins.[73] Obviously, a more cost-effective approach would have been to build antierosion measures into the original project.

Yet, development strategies for the rural, traditional sector in poor countries may also worsen existing environmental management problems. A recent report published by the Swedish International Development Agency (SIDA) took note of the many practices in Mozambique that are built into traditional patterns of living which are detrimental to the environment. In particular, the uncontrolled burning of vegetation and a number of careless agricultural practices are deeply ingrained in traditional economies of Mozambique. Most of these practices, the report said, "are compensated by homeostatic natural mechanisms when their frequency, intensity or density are as low as it has traditionally been, but can trigger disruptive chains of events if their pattern changes, usually during the initial phases of socio-economic modifications of rural communities."[74]

The SIDA report goes on to point out that the national strategy for the development of Mozambique's rural population may be inadvertently worsening the potential local ecological consequences of careless land management traditions. The Mozambique government is attempting to move a large percentage of the rural population into communal villages as part of its long-range political and economic development goals. These villages concentrate large numbers of people who were formerly dispersed over a broad area. At the same time, agricultural and other traditional economic customs cannot be altered nearly as quickly as people can be mobilized and moved. More people on less land is precisely the formula that has triggered a disruptive ecological chain of events for traditional societies dependent upon shifting cultivation and extensive land use practices rather than on preserving and restoring local vegetation and soil fertility on an annual basis. Thus, the SIDA report noted:

Problems such as higher incidence of disease, accelerated erosion and decreased soil fertility due to a shortened cycle of shifting cultivation, or extensive deforestation due to fuel and agricultural needs, are examples of the risks involved in the communal village programme.[75]

In addition to exacerbating poor environmental management practices, rural socioeconomic development schemes may bring about a disruption in traditional land use management practices which have enabled a society to perpetuate the annual productivity of the local environment. An anthropologist, Roy Rappaport, has studied the practical role of ritual in facilitating better management of the local environment among some primitive peoples. In New Guinea, Rappaport concluded in the late 1960s, an elaborate and long-standing system of rituals among the Tsembaga and other Maring "helps maintain an undegraded environment, limits fighting to frequencies which do not endanger the existence of the regional population, adjusts man-land ratios, facilitates trade, distributes local surpluses of pig . . . and assures people of high quality protein when they are most in need of it."[76]

Where this is the case, early stages of socioeconomic development, by shattering time-honored customs and traditional values, may induce people to abandon environmental management practices which were previously governed by tradition and ritual.[77] As already noted, in the Philippines the economic and social life of the Kalinga and Bantoc tribes has been based since the sixteenth century on an elaborate system of hand-built rice paddy terraces maintained on the steep mountains sloping down to the Chico River. The complex system of cultural tradition and ritual that bound them to maintain their land and their intricate infrastructure ensured not only a balanced ecosystem but an ample supply of food and cohesive social organization. However, the relocation pressures and the political turmoil that have come as a result of major river basin development projects in these tribal areas, have undermined this intricate social, cultural, economic, and ecological relationship.[78]

Ironically, while its development efforts have undermined tribal community and culture, the Philippine government is also engaged in a large campaign to increase the extent of irrigated agriculture by nearly 500,000 acres. Almost a third of this area is being improved through communal projects that seek to enmesh farmers in a broader social and economic system that facilitates communal building, operating, and maintenance. In fact, in Cavite Province, almost 40,000 acres has been irrigated by reviving a system of dikes and dams built and operated in the nineteenth century by Roman Catholic friars.[79]

As the example cited above of water hole projects in the Sahel may illustrate, development projects in certain areas may stimulate more intensive use of an area than is nature's will. Writing a number of years ago, economist Jacob Viner noted that:

There is no sense in wasting scarce resources in 'developing' areas which cannot provide a decent living for human beings, but a great deal of effort and wealth and even a greater deal of talk are being wasted on such areas.[80]

Still, decisions to "develop" regions are only partially dictated by calculations of productive potential in relation to climate, soil fertility, water availability, and other such factors. More often than not there are any number of seemingly compelling reasons for governments to push ahead with major virgin land-conquering schemes—integration of distant territories, short-term economic gain, resettlement of troublesome groups, or increasing the numbers of "loyal" groups in outlying areas for political purposes are a few noted in the chapters of this book. These justifications only rarely coincide with clear analysis of nature's potential, its deficiencies, and the knowledge at hand to maximize the former and minimize the latter for the long term.

Arthur Lewis has pointed out that virgin lands have usually been left virgin over the centuries for a good reason, such as marginal fertility, erratic rainfall, or absence of trace elements.[81] But as long as governments have other agendas than long-term maximization of productive potential, examples of project failures and of large-scale environmental devastation will probably outnumber the examples of successful virgin land development schemes.

It may even be the case that a large portion of current prosperity in a country is being generated by a strategy of abuse of renewable resources that cannot be perpetuated in the future. In some respects, much of the national economic strength of the United States during the nineteenth century was built on an unsustainable policy of exploitation. Writing on the 1880 census, for example, General Francis A. Walker noted this irony:

Down to this time our apparently wasteful culture has, as I have sought to show, been the true economy of the national strength; our apparent abuse of the capital fund of the country has, in fact, effected the highest possible improvement of the public patrimony. Thirty-eight noble states, in an indissoluble union, are the ample justification of this policy. Their schoolhouses and churches, their shops and factories, their roads and bridges, their railways and warehouses, are the fruits of the characteristic American agriculture of the past.[82]

As General Walker pointed out, this policy of exploitation may well have served the nation well in the past, but at some point a strategy of conservation and improved stewardship is necessary.

A nation that today appears to be pursuing a similar strategy of massive consumption and abuse to maximize its economic prosperity, with bold confidence that it can later settle back to a more sustainable pattern of exploitation, is Brazil. The difference is that climatic and soil conditions in much of Brazil's unconquered areas may not sustain the same abuse that North American environments did. Norman Gall has written lucidly of the challenge and the pitfalls apparent in Brazil's national strategy of extensive resource use:

Brazil's recent increases in agricultural production have not come from higher yields, as in India and Mexico, but from farming new areas. The problem with this policy of extensive cultivation is that, as the frontier pushes farther into the interior, soil quality generally becomes poorer, notwithstanding such islands of fertility as the terra roxa in central Rondonia, the wet, loamy plains of the remote Amazon state of Acre, and some areas along the Transamazon and Belem-Brasilia highways. Farming these poorer soils will demand greater energy and logistical subsidies. Thus development of large areas of the Brazilian frontier will pose an enormous economic and technological challenge, involving subsidized inputs of machinery, fuel, fertilizer, pesticides, and agricultural research. One of the great questions of the final decades of this century is whether this kind of economic development can continue at the new price of oil.[83]

SOME POSITIVE STEPS FOR DEVELOPMENT ASSISTANCE

The basic theme of this chapter is that the failure to manage natural resources and to contain the most invasive forms of environmental pollution are quite often symptoms of broader problems. The majority of people in the developing countries, after all, still live in tenuous political systems that have difficulty delivering basic services, deprive people of control over their own destinies, allocate access to resources in an inequitable manner, and have difficulty maintaining a rational framework that encourages people to save and invest with some guarantee of reward in the future. Any attempt to design strategies to reduce environmental abuse in developing countries must begin with an understanding of how intricately the various forms of resource and environmental mismanagement are interwoven into the fabric of individual political-economic systems. This concluding section looks at some of the implications that the views presented in this chapter might have for international development assistance organizations, conservation groups, and forward-looking planners in developing countries.

The United Nations, the World Bank, USAID, other development assistance organizations, and international conservationists have attempted to call attention to resource abuse problems and to help developing countries increase their capabilities to deal with them. They are furnishing more expertise and more training in resource management, assessing the environmental impacts of their development projects, providing for more infrastructure and projects designed to protect and restore the productivity of already overextended or depleted forests and soils, and working to reach out to instruct poor countryfolk and villagers how to keep themselves fed and warm without undermining their future economic well-being.

The question every one of these groups must ultimately face is whether all these actions—important though they are—will fundamentally alter the behavior of enough individuals to make a difference. Millions of individuals in developing countries continue today to take actions—whether out of economic necessity, greed, naiveté or political repression—that will reduce their material wealth in the future because they will pay more for scarce wood fuel, grow less in depleted soils, and receive fewer benefits from clogged irrigation systems and dams.

There are steps that international organizations and conservation groups can take to help people in developing countries to overcome certain resource and environmental problems. Not all remedial actions by developing country governments will threaten the power or status of vested interests. But what this analysis does point out is that there is a significant need for a broadened and more realistic assessment of how to cope with third world resource management problems on the part of developmentalists, international development assistance agencies, and world conservationists.

Ultimately the stakes in devising better approaches may be quite large. In many developing countries today, no single achievement would be more important for the welfare of the masses of poor people than the stabilization and enhancement of soil, water, and wood resources to ensure improved and sustainable production from the land. Indeed, most of the major steps necessary for sustained development—increased agricultural productivity, population stabilization, industrial expansion, diversification of exports, and reduced fiscal problems—are integrally linked to renewable resource productivity and hence management, since land and human labor are the only resources available to the masses of people in most poor countries. A few important steps are sketched below.

1. *Technical Assistance and Environmental Guidelines for Large Projects Will Not by Themselves Lead to Better Overall Environmental Management*

There is a marked tendency on the part of development assistance providers to see the dissemination of knowledge, the temporary provisions of technical experts, and the training of third world technicians as sufficient responses to serious environmental degradation in the third world. The importance of providing adequate knowledge and helping developing countries overcome what development experts refer to as the lack of "skilled human infrastructure" is immense. But as this chapter has argued, far more than ignorance and poor technical training may be at fault. Political constraints may prevent the attainment of environmental quality even where knowledge and technicians abound and "appropriate" technology and international assistance are available.

In executing large development projects, national governments are sometimes overwhelmed by pressures which cause them to ignore the principles of sound environmental management. The short-term economic and political demands faced by a regime struggling primarily to remain in power and to meet its immediate fiscal needs may compel it to embark on huge new tropical forestry projects, or to maximize revenue from upland timber production, in spite of what all of its newly trained experts say. For reasons of national prestige, a government may choose a large showcase development project, even though a smaller project with less intensive technology might make more ecological and economic sense. The interests of national governments, aid agencies, or foreign corporations may lead them, on occasion, to select inappropriate technologies for development projects. Technical assistance alone is not likely to alter any of these decisions or significantly increase the attention and resources devoted to long-term natural resource management.

Many development assistance providers, especially the multilateral banks, have been reluctant to push too hard to insist upon significant project changes on environmental grounds, preferring instead to undertake an environmental assessment and add an environmental technical assistance component to big projects. But in some cases it may become necessary, on fiscal as well as environmental grounds, to take a more activist stand in scaling down, relocating, or simply refusing to finance some projects on environmental grounds. This is not unheard of, especially within the World Bank, but the multilaterals remain extremely reticent to disrupt projects unless they are very bad indeed.

Similarly, at the microlevel of individual cultivators in many developing countries, development assistance organizations find it much easier to approach problems from a technical and technological perspective. It seems inevitable, though, that more pressure is going to have to be applied directly on developing country governments to make structural changes as well. A representative of the Ford Foundation in India, for example, said recently that in many places,

the farming systems are becoming increasingly fragile and exploitive of soil wealth. Under such conditions new crop technology, while offering a chance, can only transform agricultural stability and production if the environmental issues are also tackled—land use, community relations to resources, physical flows of nutrients, fuel and power into crop agriculture.[84]

Development assistance providers have also focused heavily on project assessment—seeking to establish and follow procedures designed to ensure that development projects do not contribute to local environmental problems. This is an important undertaking, but the concentration on environmental procedures for projects has two crucial drawbacks.

First, these procedures must be properly implemented, not only in the present, but for the duration of the development project. There is evidence that this is not occurring. For example, a recent survey of the environmental procedures and guidelines of development assistance agencies concluded that guidelines for environmental planning and assessment have "proliferated." However, the report, commissioned by the Directorate General for Development of the Commission of the European Communities, went on to state that "there was little evidence of the systematic application of guidelines in planning or assessing development activities."[85]

The second and more important problem is the fact that large development projects supported by international organizations constitute only a small proportion of the overall development effort being made in many countries and development projects in general only affect the lives of a small proportion of the entire population. More than the extent to which environmental guidelines are followed for specific development projects, the key to improved environmental management in many countries is the extent to which the underlying incentives are altered enough to induce large numbers of people to enhance the productivity of their natural environment for the future.

2. Much Greater Attention Should be Devoted to Overall Development Policy and Incentives as a Means of Reducing Local Environmental Abuse

As this chapter has sought to demonstrate, environmental problems in many developing countries are often the manifestations of bad economic and political policies that inhibit economic development in general and the improvement of the quality of life for individuals as well. Aid agencies cannot go on ignoring this fact if they wish the money they are allocating for alleviating environmental abuse to have positive results. AID's former deputy assistant administrator for Africa, Haven North, made this general point forcefully several years ago:

My first concern is that inadequate attention is being paid by developing countries to national economic and political policy issues to create an appropriate national framework for rural development. In some developing countries there has been gross mismanagement of the resources, severe economic destabilization, and inflation between 100 and 200 percent. A couple of countries in Africa face this situation now. The impact of these macro problems on rural development makes one realize that nothing that we do in the rural areas is going to succeed, in spite of how they do in their own right, unless the macro environment is supportive of that effort. While one always tries to point the finger at the developing countries' policies, it is also necessary to point the finger at the donor. I think that we should recommend that a higher priority be given to creating the national policy framework necessary for a successful rural development effort.[86]

This problem is not a new one to confront development assistance providers; anyone working in the development field is well aware that the broader framework often undermines local project success.[87] But in their environmental programs, development assistance providers still tend not to deal with the broader context and this will continue to reduce the impact of their efforts.

One USAID mission director recently emphasized the importance of a broader-than-project-assessment perspective for development assistance agencies, claiming that:

AID's overwhelming focus in environment, despite some general rhetoric to the contrary, is in preventing environmental damage from AID's small piece of the action. We therefore insist on special studies, by U.S. experts, in order to design U.S. procedures which in turn control the use of U.S. money. But (in this country) there is an environmental nightmare unfolding before our eyes. And it has nothing to do with AID projects, or all the donor projects put together. It is the result of the acts of millions (of poor people), struggling for survival: scratching the surface of eroded land and eroding it further; cutting down the trees for warmth and fuel and leaving the country denuded; diverting streams to irrigate dry land and depriving others of their water source. Over 1 billion—1 billion—tons of topsoil flows from (the) highlands each year. The answer to this problem is not feasibility studies to control each of AID's projects . . . . The answer is in *making environment part of the thinking and doing of the millions* of individual (countrymen) who must also struggle for daily survival.[88]

The important point is that environmental problems cannot be dealt with as a separate compartment. Nor are they going to be much reduced through a focus primarily on environmental management programs unless these are undertaken as part of much larger efforts to alter overall development strategies, particularly in the rural sector. However, even wholesale changes of incentives and policies may not be enough in heavily populated countries where there remains chronic and large-scale unemployment or underemployment in the rural sector.

3. *In Many Countries, the Direct Dependence of Surplus People Upon the Land Must be Broken through Rural Works Programs*

Substantial progress in improving the land management practices of people who till the soil and harvest the forests for their daily living probably cannot be made until the numbers of both are reduced. In some countries the problem is that total population is too large in relation to cultivatable land to sustain the efforts of the masses—this sort of underemployment is most prevalent in the countries of Asia and the Far East. In other countries, especially many parts of Africa and Latin America, population densities are not nearly as high but the problem is often that marginal, hilly, or fragile lands are being exploited too intensively. For the long-term productivity of natural resource systems to be stabilized, these pressures must be reduced.

In most underdeveloped, poor countries this means breaking the direct dependence of "underemployed" rural people on the land around them. The fact that the vast majority of people in poor countries still must work the land for their fuel supplies and sustenance implies enormous, if disguised, unemployment or underemployment. This is a waste of labor, but it also leads people to crop marginal lands, overtax soils, or cut trees far beyond a sustainable yield.

Obviously, the solution to this overarching problem is not coming with the growth of industrial and urban employment opportunities in sufficient numbers to allow more people to earn a prosperous living without exploiting the soil. In the context of present economic and political circumstances prevailing internationally, the only way to break the cycle of destructive unemployment in the rural sector is to initiate large programs that put rural people to work in the countryside but not in trying to secure a meal or some fuel from the land. Rather than being rewarded for overexploiting the land around them and reducing its future productive potential, people can be employed to reforest and reclaim lands, and repair or build land-based infrastructure such as dams, irrigation systems, and terraces.

Indeed, a USAID manual on rural employment generation pointed out that the projects with the greatest potential for employment generation are those that repair and restore obsolescent but directly productive assets, such as irrigation and drainage systems.[89] It went on to note:

Conservation and reforestation projects and flood embankments may not produce immediate income for people, but tend to promote increased economic activity and returns for a longer period of time, and do more to prevent future losses than to provide immediate benefits. This may be just as important a function as creating assets with new benefit flows, and the long-term benefits may conceivably exceed those of either roads or directly productive projects.[90]

The manual concluded that a "composite" picture of a country or region most in need of rural works programs is one that has a high degree of dependence on agriculture, heavy population pressures on agricultural resources, and instability in production of food crops. The major requisites for success, in addition to these problems, appear to be relatively settled population patterns and an administrative capacity sufficiently developed to provide the needed decentralized skills.[91]

The objections to such large-scale public works programs, of course, are that they are inflationary, often nonproductive, and only raise people's dependence on the public treasury. To some extent, these programs would be inflationary, since people demand more goods for consumption but do not produce any themselves. But in some areas, marginal productivity is so low that total production will not even drop when some people are removed from their daily toil.[92] Besides, as many development economists have pointed out, sometimes government-induced inflation can be an effective means of accelerating capital formation. This is particularly true if, as would be the case, otherwise unproductive labor is employed to create assets which will stimulate future production. And public works projects designed to build or improve irrigation systems, terrace sloping lands, establish village woodlots, replant forests, and reclaim degraded lands will, as much as investments in new factories, increase productivity in poor countries for the future.

Some countries, with more or less support from international organizations, have sought to establish national youth corps designed to undertake land repair and reforestation projects. The labor-intensive and arduous physical tasks of such programs do indeed make young people a logical core group. However, it is also necessary to include local people in the mobilized labor force for two reasons. First, as noted above, in many areas where such programs are needed, too many people now depend upon the land for their daily sustenance. Second, only by being in touch with these land conservation projects, will people come to better understand the forces that influence the long-term well-being of the natural systems around them. A report on youth conservation projects pointed out:

Unless there is a change in the human behavior patterns (of the local people who depend on the land) no amount of reforestation and land reclamation has a chance of halting the present destructive process. The people who are unwittingly causing the fatal deterioration of their lands must be involved in the repair efforts and they must be given the means and incentives to change their land use patterns, otherwise the process will of necessity continue.[93]

What is important to emphasize is that it is not only the provision of these projects through large capital infusions from development assistance agencies that matters. What also matters is that these projects should employ vast cadres of local people so that these people are no longer "employed" to rob the soil and the forests for a living. Development assistance organizations, as well as developing countries, have increasingly noted the former imperative but ignored the latter.

The fundamental point is that building large dams, teaching people more "ecologically sound" agricultural techniques, helping them set up village woodlots, training experts in conservation and environmental impact assessments, and numerous other existing natural resource management programs being carried out in developing countries today may all be for naught if the masses of rural people remain marginally employed on the land and squeezed by numerous incentives to damage future natural resource productivity. More than anything, then, natural resource conservation, as well as improved economic productivity in many poor developing countries, may depend on how effectively governments, with or without international assistance, can create labor-intensive, locally staffed and administered projects throughout their countrysides.

Notes

1. There is, for example, much literature on peasant reactions to changing weather patterns, particularly the onset of drought conditions. In general, traditional pastoral and agricultural systems have relied on what is described as a "minimal risk" strategy. As a result of past overextensions of the local carrying capacity, levels of environmental exploitation are kept at a "suboptimal" level as a margin of safety in the event of drought or other natural fluctuations. See N. Dyson Hudson, "Strategies of Resource Exploitation Among East African Savanna Pastoralists," in *Human Ecology in Savanna Environments*, edited by David R. Harris. (London: Academic Press, 1980.) Examples are noted also in several of the essays in Sir Joseph Hutchinson, A. H. Bunting, A. R. Jolly, and H. C. Pereira, *Resource Development in Semi-Arid Lands* (London: The Royal Society, 1977); Colin Clark and Margaret Haswell, *The Economics of Subsistence Agriculture* (London: Macmillan, 1967); and S. H. Ominde and C. N. Ejiogu, *Population Growth and Economic Development in Africa* (London: Heinemann, 1974).

2. See, for example, Hollis Chenery et al., *Redistribution with Growth* (London: Oxford University Press, 1974).

3. For an overview of the broadening of perspective by major international development assistance providers, see Coralie Bryant and Louise G. White, *Managing Development in the Third World* (Boulder, Colo.: Westview Press, 1982).

4. These points were made by the president of the World Bank, A. W. Clausen, in his speech on "Sustainable Development: The Global Imperative," the 1981 Fairfield Oxborn Memorial Lecture in Environmental Science, sponsored by the Conservation Foundation in Washington, D.C., on November 12, 1981. See Hobart Rowan, "World Bank Assisting Third World Cleanups," *The Washington Post*, November 13, 1981; and Philip Shabecoff, "Protection of Nature, Loans Tied," *The New York Times*, November 13, 1981.

5. See, for example, UNEP, *Environment and Development in Asia and the South Pacific: Experience and Prospects* (Nairobi: UNEP, 1982).

6. The numerous actions taken and programs initiated by United Nations specialized organizations before and in the aftermath of the Stockholm Conference are detailed in several chapters from David A. Kay and Eugene B. Skolnikoff, eds., *World Eco-Crisis: International Organizations in Response* (Madison, Wisc.: University of Wisconsin Press, 1972). For an update on UNEP activities, see recent UNEP annual reports.

7. See *Environment and Development* (Washington, D.C.: World Bank, November 1979); *World Bank Environmental Guidelines* (Washington, D.C.: World Bank, March 1981); *The Inter-American Development Bank and the Environment* (Washington, D.C.: Inter-American Development Bank, May 1983). For a general overview, see Robert E. Stein and Brian Johnson, *Banking on the Biosphere* (Lexington, Mass.: Lexington Books, 1979). Tripartite discussions among the World Bank, UNDP, and UNEP led in 1980 to the "Declaration of Environmental Policies and Procedures Relating to Economic Development," which has now been signed by eleven multilateral development institutions. A Committee of International Development Institutions on the Environment (CIDIE) was formed to provide specific guidance on translating this declaration into action.

8. A. W. Clausen, "Sustainable Development."

9. World Bank, *Forestry-Sector Policy Paper* (Washington, D.C.: World Bank, 1978).

10. Congress amended Section 102 of the Foreign Assistance Act of 1961, 22 U.S.C. Sec. 2151-1, and added Section 118 to the Act, 22 U.S.C. Sec. 2151 p. Section 110 of the International Development and Food Assistance Act of 1978, Pub. L. 95-424, 92 Stat. 948, further elaborated USAID's responsibilities by adding two new subsections to Section 118. Later, in 1978 and 1979, amendments to Section 103(b) of the Foreign Assistance Act, 22 U.S.C. Sec. 2151a, authorized USAID to expand its forestry and soil conservation projects.

11. USAID programs to aid developing countries with their resource management problems are described in Robert O. Blake, et al., *Aiding the Environment: A study of the Environmental Policies, Procedures, and Performance of the U.S. Agency for International Development* (Washington, D.C.: Natural Resources Defense Council, February 1979). Programs of other bilateral agencies are described in Brian Johnson and Robert O. Blake, *The Environmental Policies, Programs and Performances of the Development Assistance Agencies of Canada, the Federal Republic of Germany, the Netherlands, Sweden, the United Kingdom and the United States* (Washington, D.C.: International Institute for Environment and Development, 1979).

12. See M. Peter McPherson, "Managing Natural Resources," *AID Horizons*, February 1983, and, "Environmental and Natural Resource Aspects of Development Assistance," AID Policy Determination, signed by M. Peter McPherson, USAID administrator, on April 26, 1983.

13. M. Peter McPherson, remarks at a luncheon meeting sponsored by the International Institute for Environment and Development in Washington, D.C., March 29, 1983.

14. Office of Science and Technology, Bureau for Technical Assistance, AID, "Environmental Problems in Selected Developing Countries" (July 1971), p. 10, cited in USAID, *Environmental and Natural Resource Management in Developing Countries: A Report to Congress*, vol. 1 (Washington, D.C.: USAID February 1979, p. 16)

15. *Ibid.*, p. 1, fn 14.

16. International Union for Conservation of Nature and Natural Resources, United Nations Environment Programme, and the World Wildlife Fund, *World Conservation Strategy: Living Resource Conservation for Sustainable Development* (Morges, Switzerland: IUCN, March 1980). (Cited hereafter as *World Conservation Strategy*); U.S. Council on Environmental Quality and the Department of State, *The Global 2000 Report to the President: Entering the Twenty-First Century*, vol. 1. (Washington, D.C.: U.S. Government Printing Office, 1980), (cited hereafter as *Global 2000 Report*); and U.S. Council on Environmental Quality and Department of State, *Global Future: Time to Act:* Report to the President on Global Resources Environment and Population (Washington, D.C.: U.S. Government Printing Office, January 1981).

17. *World Conservation Strategy*.

18. *Global 2000 Report*, p. iii.

19. As quoted in *ibid.*, p. 1.

20. See for example, Julian Simon, *The Ultimate Resource* (Princeton, N.J.: Princeton University Press, 1981); and Heritage Foundation, *Global 2000 Revised* (Washington, D.C.: The Heritage Foundation, 1983).

21. *World Conservation Strategy*, "Introduction."

22. Mark August Nyirenda, "Barren Bantustans," *New African*, July 1981, pp. 16–19.

23. Andres R. Novoa and Joshua L. Posner, eds., *Agricultura de Ladera en América Tropical* (Turrialba, Costa Rica: Centro Agronómico Tropical de Investigación Y Enseñanza, Rockefeller Foundation, 1981), p. 14.

24. *Ibid.*, pp. 15–16 (The opening sections of the text were translated by the publishers.)

25. Keith Dalton, "Manila's Ecologically Awful Water and Sewerage Lines Improved," *World Environment Report*, May 5, 1980. Barbara Ward, *The Home of Man* (New York: Norton, 1976), discusses the politics of unequal distribution and access to urban services, pp. 58–59.

26. Michael Smith, "Fishing Headed for Another Big Change," *International Herald Tribune*, Special Report: Peru, June 1980, p. 105.

27. *Ibid.*

28. Colin S. Harding, "Agricultural Decline Continues," *International Herald Tribune*, p. 95; and Juan de Onis, "Belaunde Aims to Put Private Agriculture Back on Its Feet," *International Herald Tribune*, June 1980, p. 105.

29. See Clifford Geertz, *Agricultural Involution: The Process of Ecological Change in Indonesia* (Berkeley: University of California Press, 1963).

30. W. Donald McTaggert, "The Environment Consequences of Rapid Development in Indonesia," paper presented at meeting of the Association for Asian Studies, Toronto, March 1976, pp. 18–19.

31. "How the Proposed Endau-Rompin Park Came About," *New Sunday Times*, June 5, 1977. Also, Kuah Guan Oo, "Endau-Rompin: The Last Stand," *The* (Kuala Lumpur) *Star*, September 14, 1977.

32. *Ibid.*

33. Quoted in the *New Strait Times* (Malaysia), May 12, 1977, and reprinted in Consumers' Association of Penang (CAP), "Lying . . . A Forest is Dying: Do Something," undated brochure distributed by CAP.

34. Ooi Kim Kee, "The Rape of Endau-Rompin," *The* (Kuala Lumpur) *Star*, July 28, 1977. The author is grateful to Jonathan Ratner for collecting research material and reporting on the Endau-Rompin controversy from Malaysia.

35. *Ibid.* Also, Swithin Monteiro, "Question of Balance Between Nature and Humanity," *New Sunday Times*, June 5, 1977; and "Rape of Endau-Rompin Leaves Biologists Horrified," *The* (Kuala Lumpur) *Star*, August 1, 1977.

36. Alan Rake, "Ambitious 5-Year Plan Could Be Threatened," *New African*, August 1981; and Jimoh Omo-Fadaka, "Added Self-Sufficiency Is the Top Priority," *New African*, August 1981.

37. See Alaba Akinesete, "Some Pollution Problems in Nigeria," in *Pollution: Engineering and Scientific Solutions* (New York: Plenum, 1973).

38. Rake, "Ambitious 5-Year Plan."

39. Omo-Fadaka, "Self-Sufficiency Is the Top Priority," concludes his survey by noting: "The current National Development Plan fails to integrate conservation with industrial and agricultural development. There is an absence of conservation at the policy-making level."

40. Cited in Jonathan Silverston, "Weekly Report," Bureau of Program and Policy Coordination, USAID, July 11, 1980, p. 3.

41. Sheilah Ocampo, "Breaching a Dam of Despair," *Far Eastern Economic Review*, June 13, 1980, pp. 23–24.

42. Warren Hoge, "New Menace in Brazil's 'Valley of Death' Strikes at Unborn," *The New York Times*, September 23, 1980.

43. Charles Harrison, "Kenya's Destitute Turkana to Learn Desert Farming," *World Environment Report*, May 11, 1981.

44. John Worrall, "Kenya's Turkana: The Tribe That Lost Its Soul," *New African*, September 1981, p. 27.

45. John Kugblenu, "Ghana Tribes in Wave of Terror," *New African*, August 1981.

46. See Philip Carl Salzman, ed., *When Nomads Settle: Processes of Sedentarization as Adaptation and Response* (New York: Praeger, 1980).

47. G. V. Jacks and R. O. Whyte, *Vanishing Lands: A World Survey of Soil Erosion* (New York: Doubleday, Doran & Co., 1939), p. 304. See also, F. Fraser Darling and Mary A. Farvar, "Ecological Consequences of Sedentarization of Nomads," in *The Careless Technology*, edited by M. Taghi Farvar and John P. Milton (Garden City, N.Y.: Natural History Press, 1972).

134 H. Jeffrey Leonard

48. See A. T. Grove, "The Geography of Semi-Arid Lands"; Dharma Kumar, "The Edge of the Desert: The Problems of Poor and Semi-Arid Lands;" and J. Dresch, "The Evaluation and Exploitation of the West African Sahel," all in *Resource Development in Semi-Arid Lands* (London: The Royal Society, 1977), a Royal Society discussion organized by Sir Joseph Hutchinson, A. H. Bunting, A. R. Jolly, and H. C. Pereira. Also, William W. Murdoch, *The Poverty of Nations: The Political-Economy of Hunger and Population* (Baltimore: Johns Hopkins University Press, 1980), pp. 293–300.

49. Robinson's comments are appended as discussion to J. Dresch, "The Evaluation and Exploitation of the West African Sahel," in Royal Society *Resource Development in Semi-Arid Lands*.

50. Claudia J. Carr, *Pastoralism in Crisis: The Dasanetch and Their Ethiopian Lands*. University of Chicago, Department of Geography. Research Paper No. 180, 1977.

51. *Ibid.*, p. 266

52. Isabel Nieves and W. Timothy Farrell, "Appropriate Technology for Water Supply and Waste Disposal: A Behavioral Case Study: Marginal Urban Communities in San Salvador," in *Eight Case Studies of Rural and Urban Fringe Areas in Latin America*, a compendium prepared for the World Bank Research Project on Appropriate Technology for Water Supply and Waste Disposal in Developing Countries (Washington, D.C.: World Bank, Central Projects Research Staff, May 1979), p. 135.

53. Michael Nelson, *The Development of Tropical Lands* (Baltimore: Johns Hopkins University Press, 1973), pp. 261–274.

54. Soeratman and Patric Giuness, "Transmigration from Java to the Outer Islands of Indonesia," *Bulletin of Indonesian Studies* 3, no. 2 (July 1977).

55. See *Rural Development: Sector Policy Paper* (Washington, D.C.: World Bank), February 1975, pp. 29–30.

56. See Michael Lipton, *Why Poor People Stay Poor* (Cambridge, Mass.: Harvard University Press, 1977).

57. Adam Smith, *The Wealth of Nations*, Pelican Classics edition (London: Penguin Books, 1970), p. 334.

58. *World Development Report 1982*, (Washington, D.C.: World Bank, 1982), p. 39.

59. W. Arthur Lewis, *Theory of Economic Growth* (New York: Harper & Row, 1965), p. 328.

60. Ragnar Nurkse, *Problems of Capital Formation in Underdeveloped Countries*, reprinted edition (New York: Oxford University Press, 1967), p. 34.

61. Paul Spencer Wachtel, "Crocodiles, Bats, and Macaques—The Living Treasures of Sulawesi," *Asia*, January/February, 1981, pp. 24–25.

62. Ahmed Fazl, "Unplanned Housing Has Used 25% of Bangladeshi Farmland," *World Environment Report*, November 15, 1981.

63. Christopher S. Wren, "China Tries to End Loss of Its Forests," *The New York Times*, December 13, 1981.

64. *Ibid.* See also *World Environment Report*, September 28, 1981, p. 3; and *World Environment Report*, January 1, 1982, p. 2.

65. "China Reports Cooking Fuel is Scarce in the Countryside," *The Washington Post*, July 16, 1981.

64. Darryl D'Monte, "Plans to Afforest India's Biggest Desert Area Go Awry," *World Environment Report*, February 22, 1982.

67. Raymond F. Hopkins, Donald J. Puchala, and Ross B. Talbot, eds. *Food Politics and Agricultural Development: Case Studies in the Public Policy of Rural Modernization* (Boulder, Colo.: Westview Press, 1979), pp. 240–45.

68. *Ibid*.

69. Juan Leon and Harold Olmos, "Bolivia's New Government Acts to Protect Wildlife, *World Environment Report*, February 11, 1980. Personal correspondence from Reginald Hardy, overseas representative for Prodena-Bolivia, June 10, 1983.

70. "Timber, Contraband and Deforestation" *Paraguay Watch*, circulated by Jonathan Silverstone, U.S. Agency for International Development, April 27, 1981.

71. Raymond F. Dasmann, *Environmental Conservation*, 4th ed., (New York: John Wiley and Sons, 1976), p. 207.

72. "Good Earth Down Drain with Progress," *Malay Mail*, June 18, 1977; "River of Destruction," *The* (Kuala Lumpur) *Star*, June 21, 1977. A study undertaken by Persatuan Perlindungan Alam Sekitar Malaysia (Environmental Protection Society of Malaysia), "Land Management: Klung Valley's Woe" (Petaling Jaya, Selangor, Malaysia, 1977) details the serious sedimentation and flooding problems in the entire central area around Kuala Lumpur due largely to highway and housing construction.

73. "Cleaning a River to Cure Flash Floods," *New Strait Times* (Malaysia), June 13, 1977.

74. Pedro Alcantara, "A Strategy for Environmental Protection in Mozambique." Paper prepared for SIDA's Environmental Seminar, under the direction of M. Zumer-Linder, March 1980, p. 3.

75. *Ibid*.

76. Roy A. Rappaport, "Ritual Regulation of Environmental Relations Among a New Guinea People," in *Environment and Cultural Behavior*, edited by Andrew P. Vayda (Garden City, N.Y.: Natural History Press, 1969).

77. For discussions of the cultural changes brought by development in rural areas which induced changes in people's attitudes toward the land, see: Ted Lewellen, *Peasants in Transition: The Changing Economy of the Peruvian Aymara* (Boulder, Colo.: Westview Press, 1978); and William H. Durham, *Scarcity and Survival in Central America: Ecological Origins of the Soccer War* (Stanford, Calif.: Stanford University Press, 1979), esp. pp. 75–76. For discussions of changing attitude toward terracing and cropping, see I. Constantinesco, *Soil Conservation for Developing Countries* (Rome: Food and Agriculture Organization of the United Nations, 1976) pp. 41–88; and David R. Harris, "The Environmental Impact of Traditional and Modern Agricultural Systems," M. W. Holdgate, "The Balance Between Food Production and Conservation," R. W. J. Keay, "Temperate and Tropical: Some Comparisons and Contrasts," and J. G. Hawkes, "General Discussion," in *Conservation and Agriculture*, edited by J. G. Hawkes (London: Duckworth, 1978).

78. See Robert Goodland, *Tribal People and Economic Development: Human Ecologic Considerations* (Washington, D.C.: World Bank), May 1982. Also South-East Asia Resource Center, "Tribal People and the Marcos Regime: Cultural Genocide in the Philippines," *S. E. Asian Chronicle*, October 1979; J. Rocamora, "Rural Development Strategies: The Philippine Case" (Quezon City, The Philippines: Ateneo de Manila University, 1975); and Ocampo "Breaching a Dam of Despair."

79. "Philippines Stresses Irrigation to Spur Farm Yield," *The New York Times*, May 10, 1981, p. 8.

80. Jacob Viner, "The Economics of Development," in *The Economics of Underdevelopment*, edited by A. N. Agarwala and S. P. Singh (New York: Oxford University Press, 1963), p. 10.

81. W. Arthur Lewis, *Development Planning: The Essentials of Economic Policy* (New York: Harper and Row, 1966) p. 47.

82. As quoted in Charles M. Hardin, *The Politics of Agriculture: Soil Conservation and the Struggle for Power in Rural America* (Glencoe, Ill.: Free Press, 1952) p. 17.

83. Normal Gall, "Letter from Rondonia, Part II, Strategic Search," *American Universities Field Staff Reports*, 1978/No. 10, South America.

84. N. E. Reynolds, whose comments are appended as discussion to the paper by Kumar in *Resource Development in Semi-Arid Lands*, p. 53.

85. John Horberry, *Environmental Guidelines Survey* (Washington, D.C.: International Institute for Environment and Development, April 1983) pp. 2–3.

86. Haven North, "Governmental and Non-Governmental Organizations: What is Their Role in Rural Development," *Rural Development in the 1980's*, Report on the International Conference sponsored by the Office of Rural Development and Development Administration, USAID (Washington, D.C.: USAID, November 1979) p. 121.

87. An excellent, unpolemical, and still relevant article on this problem is Erven J. Long, "Institutional Factors Limiting Progress in the Less Developed Countries." In *Agricultural Sciences for the Developing Nations*, edited by Albert H. Moseman (Washington, D.C.: American Association for the Advancement of Science, 1964). Long argued that overall economic development would await profound changes in institutional structures in many countries because existing institutions often inhibit the play of incentives, inhibit the development of the capabilities of rural people, and inhibit the development and utilization of science and technology by, and suited for, local rural people.

88. Cited in M. Peter McPherson, "Managing Natural Resources," *AID Horizons*, February 1983, pp. 15–16.

89. *Creating Rural Employment: A Manual for Organizing Rural Works Programs* (Washington, D.C.: USAID, July 1977) p. 26.

90. *Ibid.*, pp. 31–32.

91. *Ibid.*, p, 19.

92. The classic exposition of the capital-creating capacity of rural underemployment is found in Ragnar Nurkse, *Problems of Capital Formation in Underdeveloped Countries* (New York: Oxford University Press, 1967) reprint of 1953 edition, pp. 32–56.

93. David Dichter, *Mobilizing Youth and Students for Reforestation and Land Reclamation* (Geneva, Switzerland: David Dichter and Associates, 1978) p. 4.

CHAPTER 4

RHETORIC AND REALITY: ENVIRONMENTAL POLITICS AND ENVIRONMENTAL ADMINISTRATION IN DEVELOPING COUNTRIES

David Morell
with Joanna Poznanski

The political dynamics of environmental action in developing countries around the world, while extraordinarily varied from one nation to the next, evince a set of common principles. As explored in earlier chapters, environmental politics are embedded within the broader fabric of these countries' basic political dynamics. That is, natural resource issues gain political salience and are resolved—or deferred—in the context of elite-mass tensions, rural-urban conflict, coexistence of centralized authoritarian concepts with decentralized political structures, and the ever-present demand for short-term economic advantage at the potential expense of serious long-term environmental damage (and long-term economic cost).

These general principles of environmental politics apply directly to the administration and implementation of the many environmental laws and programs which now exist in the various developing countries. The laws which these countries have passed in response to their environmental problems, and the administrative institutions which they have modified or created anew to carry out the provisions of these new statutes, reflect these nations' overall patterns of planning, institutional development, and public administration—their strengths and weaknesses, their successes and failures.

With rare exceptions, administration of environmental programs in developing countries is no more effective than administration of economic development efforts, social welfare programs, national security activities, and the plethora of other actions taken by their governments. Indeed, administration of environmental programs may be significantly *less* efficient than the public administrative norm. Environmental control programs, if implemented effectively, might constrain (at least in the short term) the economic advancement so desperately desired by the nation's political elite, in the name of, if not always in the interest of, the mass of the populace. If environmental controls were strictly enforced, some domestic and foreign investment might be diverted from productive expansion into purchases of pollution control devices in industry, or into adoption of more costly procedures for forestry management, energy development, or agricultural expansion. While analysts and experts may argue—possibly correctly—that the long-term benefits from environmentally-sensitive development will vastly overwhelm any short-term disadvantages associated with effective administration of environmental laws and regulations,[1] political decisions in developing countries typically are made on the basis of short-term rather than long-term considerations. Professor W. Howard Wriggins captured this thought in his work on strategies for political survival in Asia and Africa: "The ruler's imperative is to stay in power."[2]

Moreover, the potential administrative effectiveness of environmental controls often is constrained in response to the personal interests of those few individuals who dominate the country's political and economic decisions. Industrial owners and managers may find it advantageous to bribe government officials instead of buying the pollution abatement equipment needed to meet the strict requirements of an effluent discharge permit. Timber companies may receive permission from the police to clear cut a portion of a "reserved" forest, so long as they share the profits from this activity with police chieftains along some prearranged formula. In sum, the individual interests of powerful people in government agencies, state enterprises, and private corporations may impinge directly on the execution of a nation's environmental programs.

In much of the developing world, the confluence of contradictory environmental and political pressures has led to an ironic situation. As is illustrated in other chapters, visible environmental problems—particularly deterioration of air and water quality in urban/industrial locations, and to a lesser extent deforestation and soil erosion in rural/agricultural areas—have galvanized certain groups into political action. Pressures from elites concerned about pollution or wildlife preservation, and from farmers or fishermen worried about their economic survival in the face of a particular environmental threat, have been reinforced by the symbols and the incentives of the international environmental community. As a result, country after country has passed new environmental laws and has established new environmental agencies. By 1981, such institutions were nearly universal; 132 countries had identifiable environmental agencies, a vast increase from the eleven countries reporting such agencies less than a decade earlier, at the time of the United Nation's Stockholm Conference.[3] In this sense, the statutory and institutional response to the increasingly apparent environmental challenge has indeed been impressive.

Upon closer examination, however, this response—while a *necessary* prerequisite to effective environmental action in any modern nation-state—certainly seems *not* to have been *sufficient* to meet the growing environmental challenge. Many of the statutes, laws, and regulations in developing countries contain admirable rhetoric: strong environmental goals, relatively strict standards, actions designed to alleviate ecological damage or to avoid new environmental problems. In reality, however, enforcement of these laws has been weak or nonexistent, particularly in rural areas. Similarly, most of the new environmental institutions in developing countries are small or ineffectual politically in the face of their powerful civilian and military competitors for bureaucratic power and influence.

EMERGENCE OF ENVIRONMENTAL CONCERN

Only ten years ago, there was little concern or awareness in developing countries about the quality of the environment.[4] Environmental problems gained little attention. While third world governments and international aid organizations tried to stimulate economic development, they did not deal with the potential ecological consequences of such actions.[5] Concern about controlling pollution was typically seen as either irrelevant or antithetical to the problems associated with underdevelopment. "How can we speak to those who live in the villages and in the slums about keeping oceans, the rivers, and the air clean," asked Indira Gandhi, "when their own lives are contaminated? Are not poverty and need the greatest polluters?"[6]

Prior to the 1972 United Nations Conference on the Human Environment in Stockholm, many leaders from developing countries viewed the issue of environmental quality with open suspicion,[7] as a potential threat to their own industrial development.[8] The very concept of environmental control was condemned, as times with great virulence, by some developing countries—Algeria and Brazil, for example.[9]

Since the early 1970s, however, both third world governments and international development assistance agencies have devoted an increasing amount of attention to pollution problems, to broader problems of environmental degradation (such as deforestation), and to analyzing the environmental impacts of specific new development projects.[10] Indeed, some of the most aggressive opponents of environmental protection during the Stockholm era later became active in formulating their own environmental policies. While Brazil had been strongly opposed to the idea of environmental control in 1972, for example, by 1976 this country had designed several antipollution policies and had begun to express concern over deforestation in the Amazon Basin. By 1982, the World Wildlife Fund would award its highest annual prize to two Brazilians: a biologist specializing in the Amazon, and the head of the government's environmental agency. The award was presented in Brasilia personally by the nation's prime minister, whose speech favoring tighter environmental controls was broadcast nationally on Brazilian television and radio networks. Observers of Brazil's stance at Stockholm in 1972 found this event—less than a decade later—striking.[11]

One observer suggests that a revolution in third world attitudes toward the environment had occurred:

[The developing countries] are now increasingly aware of the harsh economic and human consequences that can result from failing to take into account the environmental impact of industrial development. As a result, many of these countries have not only formulated national environmental policies, but also created institutions to implement these policies. Furthermore, they are incorporating elements of environmental planning in their development process and allocating scarce funds and manpower to carry out environmental projects.[12]

The causes of such a rapid shift in environmental consciousness may be found in a combination of political pressures from the international arena and from within the developing countries themselves.

International Influences

Most of the developing countries did attend the Stockholm Conference after the agenda was widened to include substantially more than the pollution problems of industrialized societies.[13] This meeting and subsequent UN initiatives helped raise awareness of environmental problems in the third world.

Private nongovernmental organizations, national aid agencies from the developed countries, and international development organizations have conducted research and disseminated information about the environmental problems confronting developing countries. These groups emphasized that attention to such basic rural environmental problems as soil erosion, water quality, pesticide abuse, and deforestation would have a direct impact on the quality of life and the standard of living of large numbers of people in poor rural areas.[14] The World Bank and the U.S. Agency for International Development initiated procedures to incorporate environmental assessment and planning into the development projects they helped finance.[15] Development agencies stressed the economic advantages of including environmental controls in the initial calculation of project costs.[16] As World Bank President A. W. Clausen said in a 1981 speech:

It isn't that Third World countries are better able to afford environmental protection than they were 10 years ago. . . . The reason for their interest comes from an understanding that there is a long-run payoff from it. . . .

It costs a lot less, for instance, to protect the forested watershed above a new dam than to deal with a silted reservoir later. . . . Similarly, the benefits of an irrigation project can be diminished if, for lack of proper planning, it leads to an increase of schistosmiasis.[17]

The United Nations Environment Programme (UNEP), established in 1972, helped provide environmental training, and, along with other international agencies, provided assistance in environmental planning and in drafting environmental legislation. For instance, Saudi Arabia signed an agreement in 1981 with the International Union for Conservation of Nature and Natural Resources (IUCN) under which this agency provided the country expert guidance on natural resource protection and management. The program is focused on wildlife management and training, development of a national conservation strategy, and establishment of new government agencies to deal with environmental problems.[18] Similarly, IUCN and UNEP prepared a national environmental plan in 1980 for Thailand.[19]

Certain nongovernmental groups and individuals in developing countries have been influenced by international forces. Citizens of developing countries have protested air pollution and congestion in cities like São Paulo, Hong Kong, and Mexico City.[20] Middle-class conservation groups, similar in goals and orientation to some of their Western counterparts, have taken form in several developing countries. Vocal conservation organizations which work to ensure protection of wildlife and to encourage governments to preserve and enlarge national parks and wilderness areas now exist in Costa Rica, India, Kenya, Malaysia, and several South American countries.[21] As in the developed countries, growing cadres of environmental experts and scientists sometimes manage to make their voices heard in the upper echelons of governments in developing countries.[22]

During the 1970s, studies of environmental disruption in developing countries showed much more serious environmental degradation than had initially been suspected. In fact, analyses began to demonstrate that, in many cases, environmental degradation in developing countries exceeded the levels reached by developed countries—thus demanding immediate attention. The Institute of Acoustics of China's Academy of Science found that noise in Peking, for instance, was greater than in Tokyo, a city with fifteen times as many vehicles and many more industrial plants.[23] Similarly, studies on São Paulo and Cubatao, Brazil, showed that concentrations of suspended particulates were significantly higher than in typical cities in the industrial world.[24] In contrast to many developed nations in which, by the late 1970s, genuine progress could already be observed, environmental problems in developing countries were seen as becoming more serious.

Moreover, new information indicated that, for certain environmental problems, large-scale degradation existed *only* in developing countries—and had to be solved primarily by those countries themselves. Waterborne diseases are one example of environmental disruption which now exists almost entirely in developing countries. Some reports suggest that 80 percent of all illness in Africa can be blamed on poor water supply.[25] On this continent, waterborne diseases such as schistosomiasis affect many hundreds of millions of victims and are on the increase.[26] In Egypt nearly one-quarter of the population suffers from schistosomiasis.[27]

As of 1975, according to World Health Organization statistics, 62 percent of the population of developing countries (not including China)—about 1.2 billion people—did not have reasonable access to safe water supplies. Adequate domestic water supplies were not available to four-fifths of the rural and one-fourth of the urban population of the developing world.[28]

Governments of developing countries in the 1970s obtained greater information on the costs and benefits of implementing environmental policies. Initial cost estimates were grossly exaggerated. The World Bank, for example, had an early projection that installations to reduce environmental pollution from a new development project could increase its costs by 30 to 50 percent. Later calculations correct this mistake:

The additional cost actually attributable to environmental and health safeguards in "nonenvironmental" projects (i.e., exclusive of sewerage, afforestation, and other rehabilitative and control projects) has ranged from nothing to 3% of total project costs, with the high end of the range applying in instances in which precautionary measures were added when the project design was already well advanced.[29]

Environmental reviews of proposed projects also came to be seen as affordable. According to a 1980 report by the Natural Resources Defense Council, for example, the expenses of preparing an investment project review amounted to only a small part of the total costs of project design and construction.[30]

Domestic Political Pressures

As the previous chapter showed, the emergence of environmental politics in developing countries also resulted from indigenous circumstances. Governments of many developing countries had to respond to local demands for improvements in the environment. Environmental protest has increasingly become an element of regional or ethnic conflict in developing countries. It has also become a basic issue mobilizing traditionally unorganized people whose very economic survival is threatened by some form of environmental degradation. These environmental impacts can also have powerful political or economic implications, causing governments to respond with new laws or new regulations, new agencies, or stronger (if sometimes temporary), enforcement of existing rules.

To some extent, as was apparent from the analysis presented in Chapter 3, expanded environmental awareness in developing countries has been a function of a growing understanding of the nature of the environmental challenge. In the early 1970s, understanding of environmental problems in developing countries was limited. The focus was almost entirely on the pollution caused by industry; environmental degradation related to poverty and backwardness (e.g., deforestation caused by villagers), was neglected. As perceptions of environmental threats have broadened to encompass these poverty-related concerns, governments in developing countries naturally have become more inclined to accept at least the idea of conservation.

Small elite groups in some of the developing countries have had a tradition of environmental concern. These people focus mostly, however, on narrow aspects of the environmental issue, predominantly on the protection of species, areas of natural beauty, and so on. Influential individuals at times have been quite successful in meeting their elitist goals, in large part because they had the political and economic power to do so. For example, many national parks in Latin America were created in response to initiatives from large landowners. Many elites, however, have shown a distinct tendency to neglect the negative effects of their actions on other groups in the society, particularly if these negative effects arise as a result of the elite's own economic and commercial endeavors. As a result, pollution problems are often simply "transferred" from the elite to other less powerful social groups.[31]

In the last few years, concern over the quality of the environment has become more widespread, especially among urban residents. Over 80 percent of respondents from different social groups and occupations interviewed in a 1980 public opinion poll in São Paulo, Brazil, for example, considered pollution in their city to be a more serious problem than crime in the streets or the high cost of living.[32] Considering the degree to which the latter two problems have escalated in recent years, this survey response reflects not only the seriousness of environmental pollution in São Paulo, but also the growing public awareness of its deleterious consequences to the public's health and well-being. Similarly, a 1982 survey of 2000 people in Taiwan's main cities of Taipei and Kaohsiung showed widespread dissatisfaction over pollution of all kinds.[33]

To be sure, widespread ignorance about the effects of environmental disruption still persists among many people in developing countries, especially among the poor, the uneducated, and rural peasants. This ignorance often leads not only to a generalized lack of concern about environmental control, but also makes much more difficult the execution of particular government programs devoted to improved environmental quality. For example, technically successful new disinfection devices which are simple and cheap to use on rural wells often have not been accepted by villagers, who abhor the taste of chlorine in their drinking water. This has been a problem in Thailand's potable water program, supported by USAID and WHO.[34]

In a few developing countries, ordinary people have joined associations which have had an impact on their government's policies toward the environment. For example, the existing Consumer Associaton in the municipality of Penang, in northwestern Malaysia, took on a series of environmental challenges. The combination of major international shipping lanes and attractive industrial development zones makes Penang one of Asia's most industrialized areas, and one of its most polluted. Through educational seminars and mailings to 40,000 individuals and groups each month, the Consumer Association is trying to make Penang residents aware of the area's environmental problems, especially air and water pollution.[35]

Urban residents have been the most active group regarding environmental concerns. They are more likely than rural residents to express openly their interest in environmental protection, and to act in ways which ensure that their interests will be respected by local or national authorities. Urban residents' concern about their environment tends to focus on a few specific visible issues which cause negative effects on individuals immediately. This helps explain why air and water pollution from large industries attract attention, whereas conservation of soil, forests, or mineral resources less often become the focus of effective protest. Respiratory diseases and lowered private property values because of pollution immediately affect individual lives, and therefore create dissatisfaction which can lead to political action.

INSTITUTIONALIZATION OF ENVIRONMENTAL CONCERN

Developing countries in Africa, Asia, Latin America, and the Middle East have responded in various ways to this confluence of internal and external political pressures. Their responses have been both legislative and organizational. Typically a legislative framework has been created for environmental control, and new governmental organizations have been created at national and lower levels of public administration. These statutory and institutional responses have frequently been superficial, however; and their effectiveness has been quite limited.

Government Agencies for Environmental Management

Over the past decade, nearly all of the developing countries have established national organizations of some kind responsible for the conduct of environmental control functions. By the early 1980s, only a small number of developing countries still had no such organizational arrangements.

A status report prepared in mid-1982 by USAID identified the principal governmental institutions with environmental responsibilities in seventy-two developing countries.[36]

Those organizations vary in many respects, of course: in their areas of responsibility or commitment, in their methods of operation, in the effective power they can exercise, in the financial and personnel resources at their disposal, and so on. Generalizations about these environmental management institutions across the developing world as a whole, therefore, can be potentially misleading. Nevertheless, a few preliminary observations can be made about the nature of the organizational frameworks for environmental protection present in developing countries.

One can distinguish two different types of institutional arrangements. Some "specialized" organizations are devoted exclusively to regulating environmental problems; other "general" governmental organizations have instead incorporated environmental issues into their wider administrative concerns.

Many environmental organizations in developing countries are, in fact, ad hoc interministerial boards or commissions. For example, Nigeria proposed in 1982 to create a new Federal Environmental Protection Agency. The agency's board would have a chairman and fourteen "distinguished scientists" to be appointed by Nigeria's president, Shehu Shagari. The board would also include representatives from the ministries of health, housing and environment, and science and technology, and three who would represent other interest groups.[37]

India created a new Department of Environment in 1980 to take direct responsibility for monitoring and regulating pollution. The department administers the Water Pollution Control Act and legislation on air pollution. It also has direct charge of critical biosystems and marine ecosystems, to be protected against human intrusion. The new agency set up a National Eco-development Board to identify critical ecosystems and prepare blueprints for ecological preservation and restoration, especially in hilly areas. This board is headed by the secretary of the department of environment and consists of representatives of various ministries, the Planning Commission, and directors of several research institutes.[38]

Statutes and Laws for Environmental Control

While a few laws on environmental policy have been in effect in developing countries for many years, most environmental statutes in these countries were passed in the late 1960s or in the early 1970s, in response to the foreign and domestic political pressures described earlier in this chapter. Although up-to-date information on environmental legislation in developing countries is difficult to find, studies conducted in the 1970s showed that legislative frameworks for environmental control were by then quite extensive in many developing countries.[39]

Centralization of authority has been a key theme in many of these statutes. In federal systems, environmental laws have to define the respective responsibilities of the national government and the states. The extent of decentralization may even vary from one law to the next. In India, for example, the 1981 air pollution control act covers all states, whereas the water pollution law is applicable only to those states which adopt it. The air law covers a wide range of industries. State governments are empowered to identify specific areas for air pollution control and to establish standards for emissions by industries, appliances, and automobiles. The controversy over whether to build a hydroelectric dam which would flood the Silent Valley in India's southwestern hills produced major changes in that country's constitution and planning procedures regarding environment and natural resources. Major development projects with broad ecological implications thereafter had to receive concurrent approval from both the central government and the host state. The Planning Commission in New Delhi was assigned the responsibility to carry out these reviews on behalf of the central government.[40]

It is impossible to analyze environmental legislation in developing countries without direct access to the documents themselves. This has not been done for this study, and remains an interesting subject for further study by environmental economists, lawyers, and others. It is obvious, however, that the existing legislative system is the result of political processes in which the dominant interest groups with access to legislative bodies and councils of ministers can obtain favorable arrangements at the expense of underprivileged groups in society. Moreover, when powerful groups are not able to defer some adverse— from their point of view—legislative initiatives, usually they are able subsequently to place obstacles in the way of effective execution of the new regulations.

EFFECTIVENESS OF ENVIRONMENTAL CONTROLS IN DEVELOPING COUNTRIES

The growing concern about environmental protection seen in developing countries since the early 1970s has not led, unfortunately, to creation of effective systems to prevent pollution in these countries, nor of adequate procedures to control the excesses of deforestation, soil erosion, and other environmental impacts. Indeed, despite all the new laws and the new institutions, capabilities in developing countries are still well below the necessary level. This lack of administrative effectiveness remains one of the primary factors inhibiting implementation of sound environmental policies in these countries.

These institutional weaknesses do not exist in a vacuum. Indeed, the overall lack of political will and political capacity to act on environmental issues typical in so many developing countries remain the underlying force restricting effective environmental action. As a result of these political and institutional failures, levels of pollution and problems of ecological damage remain very serious throughout the developing world—and appear to be accelerating in many countries—despite the many new laws and new institutions which have been created in recent years.

Successful efforts to improve environmental quality thus remain relatively rare. From the perspective of actually implementing environmental plans and programs, the developing countries' efforts cannot yet compare to those in the developed world, nor are they adequate to meet the immensity of the evident environmental challenge. Although significant differences exist in the strictness of environmental policies being implemented in particular developing countries, examples abound of failed attempts to prevent pollution, and of excessive abuse and depletion of natural resources despite many new laws to the contrary. A few of the most important institutional and administrative shortcomings can be identified, although such generalizations must be made cautiously because of the great variation from one country to the next.

Environmental Degradation Despite Environmental Laws

Although comprehensive data do not exist, evidence suggests that serious environmental degradation is prevalent and growing in developing countries— even after the passage of new laws and the creation of new agencies. Overall commitment to coping with environmental problems remains low; instead, economic development projects and government responses to the immediate problems of poverty and disease are afforded higher priority. Administrative organization and manpower are often inadequate to cope with basic economic and political problems, let alone with environmental problems. Technical experts with knowledge of the environment are rare, and often must be brought in from developed countries. Funding is limited for all problems, especially for environmental action.

In Thailand, for example, a senior professor of environmental studies at Mahidol University pointed in 1982 to the government's inefficiency in handling pollution problems. Dr. Nart Tantawiroon said that officials were too weak and the country's laws too lax to cope with the magnitude of the problem. He criticized the penchant among Thai government agencies to draw upon foreign consultants and institutions to carry out environmental studies, which he characterized as "usually meaningless." According to Nart, Thailand's environmental impact assessment legislation had proved a "paper tiger" over the preceding seven years. The National Environment Board had hardly made its presence felt, leaving it to environmentalists to do most of the work when decisions had to be made on a proposed nuclear power plant or a soda ash factory (two major siting controversies). "The larger the magnitude of the project involved, the more powerful is the prime mover behind it; and it is too much to expect any typical civil servant to come out openly against it for fear of reprisal. He would prefer to play safe with such noncontroversial issues like garbage collection or tree planting," Nart said.[41]

In Pakistan, a recent report noted that pollution control is "disorganized and muddled, and though there have been good intentions there has been very little progress." Despite the fact that environmental control is included in the Con-current Legislative List of the 1973 Constitution, no Federal or Provincial law had been promulgated ten years later, according to the report.[42]

A similar story of inadequate government enforcement of environmental protection laws is available from Jamaica. Here a 1981 critique focused on the weaknesses of the country's Environmental Control Division. Dr. T. E. Al-dridge, writing in the Jamaican *Weekly Gleaner*, concluded that "the level of service the Division has been able to provide in controlling water quality, sewage, and industrial wastes is about twenty-five percent of requirements."[43] Interaction between development planning and environmental assessment was also apparently inadequate. Aldridge was explicit about his country's failure to deal with solid-waste problems:

The piles of stinking garbage, refuse, and other solid wastes in markets, streets, yards, gullies, open lots, and dumps of the Kingston Metropolitan Region bears loud testimony to the fact that the Division has had very little success in relieving one of Jamaica's most disgusting and serious environmental conditions.[44]

Numerous other country-by-country examples could be provided illustrating the difficulties of implementing environmental controls in developing countries. It may be more useful, however, to examine next a few specific areas of environ-mental concern.

Air pollution in developing countries is most prevalent in urban areas, as there are relatively few factories and vehicles in rural areas. Emissions legisla-tion is typically inadequate, and those laws which do exist are poorly imple-mented. Many factories do not have pollution control equipment, even if such equipment has been mandated. Because of a lack of zoning policy, pollution-intensive industry has frequently been situated immediately adjacent to resi-dential areas, reinforcing the impact of industrial air pollution. Moreover, high-sulfur coal and heavy residual oil are typically burned as fuel in power plants and factories in developing countries. This results in the release of large quan-tities of sulfur oxides and particulates into the urban atmosphere. This problem is evident in Korea, for example.[45]

A high proportion of the cars, trucks, and buses in many developing coun-tries' cities are in very poor condition, resulting in high emission rates of carbon monoxide, hydrocarbons, photochemical oxidants, lead, and particulates (from diesel engines, especially).[46] Governments seem incapable of responding effec-tively to this problem (except, interestingly, in Singapore, where the govern-ment of Lew Kwan Yew's People's Action Party has been uniquely successful in implementing automobile control measures in the downtown area).[47] Auto-mobile-related pollution is particularly severe in Bangkok, Mexico City, and

São Paulo, and is appearing in many other cities across the developing world. Furthermore, a number of these cities suffer from thermal inversions and a frequent lack of air circulation, aggravating the effects of their high air pollution levels. Mexico City's high altitude makes the situation much worse.

Extensive use of wood, dung, charcoal, or anthracite briquets for domestic cooking and heating cause further intense urban air pollution.[48] Calcutta is an especially severe example. Developing country governments have shown little capability to cope effectively with the thousands (even millions) of individual, often poor, daily polluters.

Air pollution levels in Ankara, Bangkok, Bombay, Buenos Aires, Cairo, Calcutta, Caracas, Manila, Mexico City, Rio de Janiero, São Paulo, Seoul, and Teheran are reported generally to be worse than in the large cities of the developed world, including London, Los Angeles, New York, and Tokyo.[49] The carbon monoxide level in Calcutta, for example, is reputedly twice as high as that in London or New York;[50] carbon monoxide levels in both Bangkok and Caracas are significantly higher than the internationally accepted standards.[51] Data from the Pan American Health Organization's air pollution monitoring network indicates that sulfur oxides and particulate levels in several South American cities (despite national air pollution laws to the contrary) are three to four times the limits recommended by the World Health Organization, and are increasing.[52] In Bombay, sulfur oxide levels are twice those of India's legal standards.[53] Data on sulfur dioxide pollution in 1976 showed Seoul having the worst incidence; Calcutta, Hong Kong, and Teheran also showed higher sulfur dioxide levels than did either London or Tokyo.[54] The situation in Seoul was portrayed as follows in a 1982 report:

Seoul is crammed with nearly 8 million people, making it one of the most populous cities in the world. In terms of pollution, it also ranks high among world cities.

The air over the South Korean capital is seriously polluted by high-sulfur exhaust emitted by more than 250,000 cars, briquette gas from household smoke stacks and thousands of high-rise buildings and factories using bunker-C oil as heating fuel.

A recent city-wide survey shows that sulfur content in the air over Seoul averages 0.126 parts per million, 2.5 times the maximum allowed by the Environmental Protection Law . . . the lack of money makes doubtful the successful implementation of the programs. The city has allocated only $200,000 for anti-pollution efforts in 1982.[55]

In Ankara, Turkey, in early 1982, "air pollution . . . reached disastrous proportions" despite a series of laws and plans to the contrary.

Although the pollution crisis provoked a lot of official and unofficial comment and new official promises to take more effective measures, hardly any real action followed. The situation has been deteriorating every winter for the last decade. . . .

Another factor in delaying any effective measures has been the inability of successive governments and various state agencies to decide on the best way to solve Ankara's pollution problem.[56]

Urban pollution could be lessened by siting new industry outside of existing urban areas. However, this dispersal would require effective land use planning, not evident in many developing countries. South Korea, Taiwan, and Thailand have begun to site some new industrial facilities away from urban areas, but only after pollution levels became terrible in their capital cities. Control over urban expansion is another area in which effective government response has been a rarity:

In the LDC's, efforts to decrease urban growth, short of using force, have, on the whole, not achieved success. It is becoming recognized, however, that efforts to obstruct urban growth are not only futile, but also counterproductive.[57]

Many cities in the developing world are projected to reach previously unheard of sizes, with an obviously intensified crisis over urban pollution. Mexico City and São Paulo, for example, are expected to grow to populations of 32 and 26 million respectively, over four times the present population of New York.[58] Although the environmental stresses placed on these cities will be minor in comparison to the public service stresses, they will still be considerable. Moreover, the use of high-polluting wood, dung, and coal as the main sources of cooking and heating fuel further increases the probability of dangerously high urban air pollution levels.

This pattern of urban pollution is also apparent with respect to noise. The Tenth International Acoustics Conference held in 1982 labeled Rio de Janeiro the world's noisiest city, followed by São Paulo and then by New York City. Rio's Copacabana area was one of the worst in the city; here noise was deemed so bad that it could cause "irreversible medical damage including deafness and tachycardia [rapid heart action]."[59]

Problems of contaminated water show a similar story—lack of effective enforcement of those regulations which do exist, and consequently serious degradation of water resources.[60] A few specific cases can help illustrate this situation. By the late 1970s, forty-two of Malaysia's sixty-five major rivers were heavily polluted and another sixteen were moderately polluted[61]—in spite of water pollution control laws which are some of the most impressive environmental statutes in the developing world. In the Sugut River area, phenomenally high heavy-metal concentrations were caused by drainage from a strip mine. Despite its laws, the Malaysian government neither closed the mine nor curtailed its activities.[62]

Only 34 percent of Pakistan's 83 million people have clean, piped drinking water, and only 13 percent have sewage and drainage facilities, according to Ghulan Iskaq Khan, minister for finance and planning, speaking to a United

Nations water conference in Islamabad. Khan noted a wide disparity between urban and rural facilities. In urban areas safe water was available to 72 percent of the population and sanitation to 42 percent; in rural areas access to clean water was available to 20 percent while only 2 percent had any sort of sanitation facilities.[63]

Analysis presented in the *Global 2000* report illustrated the lack of response to problems of water pollution:

Few LDC's have invested heavily in urban and industrial waste treatment facilities. As a result the waters below many LDC cities are often thick with sewage sludge and wastes from pulp and paper factories, tanneries, slaughterhouses, oil refineries, chemical plants and other industries. One consequence of this action is declining fishing yields downstream of LDC cities. For example, the inland catch in the eastern provinces of Thailand, 686 tons in 1963, fell to 68 tons by 1968, and it is thought that water pollution, particularly from Bangkok, was the main cause of the decline.[64]

In India's eastern province of Orissa, effluent containing chlorine has driven hundreds of farmers off their land. According to one report, polluted water from a chemical factory

enters irrigation channels from the river in Ganjam district and bleaches paddy plants. Fish have also been severely affected. Fishermen, farmers and students have complained that provisions of the Industries Act and the Orissa River Pollution Act are not being invoked against the factory.

A Parliamentary committee had asked the factory to remove the pipe leading to the river and had ordered the Orissa River Board to take preventive measures, but nothing has been done so far.[65]

Deforestation is another type of severe environmental concern in many developing countries (see Chapter 5). Here, too, one frequently sees weak enforcement of those laws which have been passed to try to lessen impacts on remaining forest resources. If the rate of deforestation in Thailand continues without effective government intervention, for example, the country's forests could vanish completely by early in the twenty-first century. Yet the rate of depletion is expected to increase rather than to decrease in the near future, despite clear preservationist laws. Thailand passed laws in the 1970s which set strict controls on cutting timber without a permit and on exporting teak, and which protected government forestry preserves. To date, unfortunately, enforcement of these laws—often due to corruption of the police and other law enforcement officials—has been minimal at best.

Evaluation of the extent to which a particular country is actually implementing its environmental control laws is quite difficult, as we have seen. This is a complex topic for which neither acceptable criteria nor reliable data are readily available. Some possible indicators include the extent of resources (budget, personnel, etc.) actually devoted to environmental control (e.g., investment in pollution-abatement equipment, number of people working in environmental agencies); the degree of rigorousness of the environmental regulations imposed by the central government, or by local organizations dealing with environmental control; or the degree of sophistication of institutional frameworks for environmental action.

When efforts to improve environmental quality are judged by the monetary expenditures made by developing countries, they appear insignificant. The World Bank has estimated that in contrast to the 2.5 percent of its gross national product that the United States devoted annually to environmental actions from 1978 to 1980, not one out of a group of forty less developed countries studied devoted more than 0.3 percent of its GNP to the same purpose.[66] Brazil has been estimated to devote only 0.065 percent of its national income to environmental protection.[67] Although developing countries are showing more concern about environmental pollution than they did before, they still give low priority to this issue in their national economic development programs.

Money is in short supply for nearly every type of public expenditure program in developing countries. Funds for new projects must be rationed and expensive technological imports kept to a minimum. Environmental programs rank as a relatively low priority, and are subject to substantial cutbacks in the budgetary competition. In South Korea, many government projects designed to improve the environment have been revised or canceled by drastic budgetary cuts. In 1980, for example, only 13 percent of the funds necessary to set up the Office of Environment responsible for carrying out antipollution activities were allocated to the Ministry of Health and Social Affairs. Among the projects eliminated were one to provide funds to assist factories in purchasing antipollution equipment, and another to build new sewage disposal facilities.[68]

Weak enforcement of environmental standards is frequently rationalized on economic grounds: "it's too expensive"; "it's a luxury"; "we can't afford it in a poor country." However, here the issue of long-term vs. short-term perspective becomes critical. The cumulative effects of pollution on natural resources can be substantial. Effluent from factories, for example, has been known to destroy downstream and estuarine fishing industries. Another example of such a cumulative impact is the deforestation and irreparable erosion for an area due to poor forestry management. If these cumulative impacts are weighed, environmental control can be seen to be cheaper in the long run than is lack of control. Yet political and administrative decisions are typically made on the basis of short-run considerations or relative costs and benefits. This helps explain the absence of aggressive enforcement of environmental regulations.

Contextual analysis of environmental requirements similarly shows that environmental policy in developing countries remains comparatively to excessively permissive, although there are substantial variations among them in the rigorousness of the standards being imposed. In 1976, the United Nations

Conference on Trade and Development (UNCTAD) meeting in Geneva examined the degree of rigorousness of national environmental policies in forty different countries, including twenty-five developing nations. Each nation's policies were evaluated on a scale from one (strict) to seven (tolerant). The mean score for developed countries was 3.1, while for developing countries it was 6.1. Despite the predominance of the "tolerant" category, four developing countries did place in the "stricter" categories: Chile, Colombia, Israel, and Singapore (among the developed countries, Japan, Sweden, and the United States were classified in this group).[69]

To evaluate the developing countries' concern for effective environmental control, it is not enough to compare their efforts to those of the developed countries. Instead, one needs to contrast the intentions particular countries declare with the efforts they actually put into completing the programs necessary to meet these goals. For instance, the Egyptian government officially stated in 1971 that its new water pollution control programs would avoid an annual economic loss of 214 million Egyptian pounds (some 8 percent of GDP) due to waterborne diseases. Ten years after that statement was made, however, serious public health problems persisted.

Generally, it appears that the developing countries as a group spend significantly less than is necessary to control the increasing pollution of their environments. Environmental policy is just beginning to emerge in rapidly growing countries such as Brazil, Mexico, and South Korea, and it will be some time before it gains prominence in poorer countries like Bangladesh or Ethiopia. The reason for this situation is not just the fact that developing countries lack the economic resources to deal more seriously with environmental problems, however. While awareness of environmental problems and passage of new environmental statutes are certainly vital first steps, major obstacles continue to hinder the implementation of programs that would bring this environmental degradation under control. Until these obstacles are removed or surmounted, progress toward environmental quality in the third world will continue to be, at best, grudging; awareness and concern are not enough by themselves. Some of the obstacles are also familiar in the industrialized countries: inadequate information, shortages of trained specialists and technicians, and a perennial lack of equipment and funds. In developing countries, however, such deprivations tend to be relatively more serious.[70]

The Politics of Inadequate Implementation

To a large extent, the failure to implement those environmental laws which have been passed—weak though many of them may be—reflects the basic political characteristics of developing countries. Their political dynamics and the nature of their systems of public administration help explain these countries' difficulties in putting sufficient effort into effective environmental control.

In most developing countries, the public bureaucracy plays a dominant role in organizing and directing the development process; environmental management is certainly no exception. Moreover, the fundamental nature of many environmental problems—the "tragedy of the commons" and the "free rider" problem, for example—makes effective actions in this area heavily dependent on an active role for public administration. The private marketplace, alone, is clearly inadequate to the task.

In spite of many differences, most developing countries' administrations are controlled by a modern, industrially oriented, externally dependent urban elite. This elite has an inherent tendency to neglect environmental issues unless they imperil industrial development (e.g., lack of water for industrial purposes). The elite's primary goals are retention of political power and rapid industrialization. This pro-industrial ideology typically encompasses both market (capitalist) and centrally planned (socialist) economies.

The rural areas, in particular, are visualized by the ruling elites as synonymous with backwardness, and often are treated as areas to be ignored or exploited. As a result, elites do not pay enough attention to achieving balanced interregional development, to increasing agricultural production, or to resolving environmental problems in rural areas. In this conflict between urban and rural areas, the latter usually lose since their residents are weakly organized and politically underrepresented within the mechanisms of public administration. And when substantial rural representation does exist, it usually comes from narrow groups of landowners.[71] Other rural residents in most cases have had no opportunity to establish their own strong political institutions.

Urban residents in developing countries are relatively eager to accept the industrial ideology of their elites, since growth of production would mean more modern-sector jobs for them. Also, groups representing particular income and social strata tend to act separately against that pollution which affects them directly. For example, inhabitants of high-income residential areas act separately from the urban poor, with little cooperation between their related efforts. In this sense, the low value attached to environmental issues by the public administration apparatus in developing countries may derive from the unequal participation of different groups in the political process. A greater degree of participation in politics may therefore be a necessary condition to making any government capable of responding effectively to environmental problems.

To date, experience shows that governments seldom, if ever, undertake serious environmental policies in the absence of significant political pressure from groups within society (or from foreign governments). Environmental control is thus identical to all the other kinds of economic and social policies. Any government's natural strategy is simply to wait and see what pressures actually develop and then respond accordingly. All administrative bureaucracies try to avoid changes to their routine activities. This has certainly been true in the United States, Europe, and Japan. In the developing world, rhetoric has been the principal response to the first phase of political pressures—international and domestic—for environmental action; further pressures will be needed to move into aggressive implementation of the many new laws and regulations.

Participant political institutions are, generally speaking, less evident in developing countries than in the developed ones, a fact which helps explain why the former have been more passive in their attempts to protect the environment through implementation of environmental laws. Because the elite controls power so totally in most developing countries, the overwhelming majority of the population has had no meaningful way to articulate its interests, let alone to compel the administrative machinery to respond to its needs.

Analysis of the basic characteristics of political and public administration systems in developing countries suggests that effective environmental protection here is even more problematical than it is in developed countries. Public administrators have a strong urge to avoid the political conflicts inherent in controversial issues. Environmental policy is typically very controversial, especially if the controls have the potential actually to be effective. While adroit political maneuvering among the many competing interests is necessary to minimize the political tensions that inevitably grow between these diverse interests, public administrators in developing countries seldom have been able or willing to use such talents to pursue long-run environmental objectives.

The political conflicts which emerge during implementation of environmental policy can be illustrated by the debates which have taken place in São Paulo, Brazil.[72] Here the state assembly, controlled by the opposition *Movimento Democratico Brasileiro*, rejected a petition from the state governor to create a special fund to finance installation of pollution-abatement equipment in factories. The opposition claimed that the fund was designed to channel large amounts of public resources to private industries that could easily cover the costs of the necessary pollution control equipment by themselves. Similarly, a state project to finance (at interest rates well below the existing rate of inflation) the manufacture, purchase, and installation of equipment to treat industrial wastes was turned down by the state assembly in 1979. The grounds for criticism were that the plan would direct most of the funds to a small number of the largest private corporations, which could most easily cover the additional costs of pollution control equipment on their own. Brazil's National Confederation of Industry (NIC) registered its discontent with President Figueiredo in 1981 over the country's new environmental law, labeling it as "unjust intervention." The new law gives state governors the power to fine and close down polluters after they have been warned. CNI further charged that industry was being subjected to a multiplicity of federal, state, and municipal laws.[73]

In most developing countries, policy formulation and implementation are highly centralized, in line with prevailing administrative tradition. Even when governments have realized that particular policy areas—such as environmental protection and control of resource degradation—are excessively centralized, and try to delegate some decisions to lower levels of the administrative apparatus, such efforts often have not been very successful. While one faction of the government has tried to decentralize decision making, others in the central power structure have fought to retain the traditional balance of authority. The traditionalists' views typically prevail, especially when potential participants at the local level are not able strongly to demand a larger share in the decision-making process.

Peru's regional planning efforts between 1968 and 1977, for example, illustrate how a declared program to decentralize regional development decisions can fail, largely because of strong built-in tendencies toward centralization. Despite the military government's decision to delegate more authority to local administrative divisions, regional planning remained definitely "top down" and may in fact have become even more centralized.[74]

Effective environmental control requires proper integration of environmental policy with other fields of public intervention. This requirement is frequently difficult to meet in developing countries, which may not be able to formulate coherent economic development strategies. In the least developed countries, one sees almost a total absence of relevant development strategies. Overall development policy elsewhere is often ill-prepared, or is vulnerable to disruption due to political instability.

Even if a country has designated a particular administrative body to be responsible for administration of environmental controls, this agency typically suffers from a lack of cooperation by other authorities. For example, a spokesman for South Korea's Office of Environment disclosed that:

. . . the country's Environmental Preservation Law makes it compulsory for any chief of an administrative office which has control over large construction projects to consult with the Office of Environment before the final plans are worked out. However, most government offices start such projects without consulting the Office of Environment. . . . For example, the state-run Industrial Site and Water Resource Development Corporation's scheme to construct a dam in the estuary of the Naktong River . . . is expected to cause serious damage to rare migratory birds in the area, but the Office of Environment only learned of the project through newspapers.[75]

Institutions dealing with environmental control in developing countries are unable to meet their goals because they are short of specialists who could organize an environmental monitoring system, for example; or gather environmental data; or control execution of environmental programs. For instance, while China's water management and sewage systems have impressed many Western visitors, this country has fewer than 600 university-trained ecologists (in per capita terms, nearly 100 times fewer than in the United States).[76] Administrative personnel in environmental agencies are often unable to react quickly to new situations, to make clear decisions, and to execute environmental policies as strictly as necessary. In some countries, the absence of skilled personnel means that even the best political intentions cannot be translated into practical actions. Many examples of this can be found among developing countries.[77]

Moreover, low-skilled administrators are often placed in demanding organizational frameworks. In the environmental field, many organizational arrangements have been introduced by foreign advisers, often as copies of organizations designed for environmental protection in developed countries. This reflects a more general trend in developing countries, where, according to Green:

> Many apparently well-designated institutions are, on closer observation, all too clearly transplants from the industrial economies hopelessly ill-adapted to the least developed countries . . . The end result is very often an intolerably high administrative overhead combined with a poor ability to understand problems well enough to make pertinent decisions and with still less genuine efficacy in the satisfaction of basic needs.[78]

Politics and Environmental Administration

Since nearly all less-developed countries by now have established some form of regulatory framework, the important question is whether their environmental regulations can be enforced. Enforcement typically is much more difficult than merely passing laws. Enforcement of environmental regulations in developing countries is a relatively haphazard process, one which responds strongly to the political power of those who violate the regulations and which depends on the extent to which the government comes under effective pressure to take action to stop pollution and environmental degradation.[79] Enforcement at times is arbitrary in ways which appear to have more to do with political considerations than with concern for the environment. Multinational corporations whose facilities may be cleaner and more modern than those of local companies may be singled out as pollution scapegoats when a government is under pressure to take action.

In Mexico, for instance, many pollution laws are ineffective because the fines are negligible and enforcement is sporadic.[80] Although many multinational corporations involved in heavy manufacturing claim that their pollution control measures exceed Mexican standards,[81] Bayer's Mexican subsidiary, for one, realized the vulnerability of foreign firms when the Mexican Health and Welfare Secretariat (SSA) summarily closed its plant, ostensibly because the facility lacked an operating permit. SSA issued a statement accusing the company of polluting the country's air and of endangering the health of its workers. The company denied the pollution accusations, saying that its plant was a modern facility equipped with the latest abatement equipment.[82] According to a report in *Business Latin America,* SSA's harsh reaction to the Bayer facility was related to the government's need to find a "pollution scapegoat" to hold up to the public following pollution problems actually created by a domestic firm that did business with Bayer.[83] While all of this action may have been important for the

Mexican government, it contributed little if anything to improving the environment. The government officials did not have the political will to crack down directly on the real culprits, very possibly because of close political ties between government officials on the one hand and Mexican industrialists on the other. Bayer was a far easier political target than the local firm.

Numerous political impediments hinder enforcement of environmental standards in developing countries. Indeed, while the fundamental causes of many serious environmental problems in the third world may be poverty and lack of knowledge, the failure to overcome them in many cases constitutes a political, even more than an economic or technical, dilemma. Political constraints may prevent the attainment of environmental quality even where "appropriate" technology and international assistance are available. National governments are sometimes overwhelmed by pressures which cause them to ignore the principles of sound environmental management. The short-term economic and political demands faced by a regime struggling primarily to remain in power and to meet its immediate fiscal needs may compel it to embark on huge new tropical forestry projects, for example, or to maximize revenue from upland timber production, in spite of the obvious implications of these actions for the future. In one case, a vice-president of a multinational timber company has spoken privately of his company's experience in one developing country in Southeast Asia where the government, under enormous pressure to increase its foreign exchange revenues, ordered the company to ignore its normal approach to long-term forestry management and instead to clear cut millions of acres of tropical forest. Here, short-term national interests came directly into conflict with long-term local and national needs.[84]

The interests of national governments, aid agencies, or foreign corporations may lead them, on occasion, to select inappropriate technologies for development projects.[85] For reasons of national prestige, a government may choose a large showcase development project even though a smaller project with less intensive technology might make more ecological and economic sense.[86] Some spokesmen for developing countries contend that projects funded by bilateral or international aid agencies have in some instances imported inappropriate technologies as part of aid packages put together to meet organizational needs.[87] In this sense, multinational corporations intent on selling their pesticides, fertilizers, machinery, or other products have contributed to the environmental problems of poor countries.[88]

Environmental laws and regulations in much of the third world must be implemented through administrative and governmental mechanisms which are vastly different from those in the industrialized countries. These mechanisms have evolved to fulfill certain functions in their societies, functions frequently far removed from any objective measure of effective performance. Instead, their principal goals revolve around access to status and prestige, dominance by one ethnic group over another, or the availability of extensive financial rewards. Factionalism, patron-client relationships, personalism, and corruption, while present everywhere of course, play a relatively larger part in third world politics.[89] Conversely, litigation and judicial interpretation are generally less significant influences on the formulation of environmental policy in third world states.

Environmental decisions in developing countries are obviously embedded in their broader political dynamics. In countries under military rule, for example, environmental policy can only be implemented if the military leaders perceive these problems and choose to address them.[90] Implementation of environmental policy in systems dominated by a single political party requires a commitment to environmental quality from the party's highest leaders, and from cadre at various levels. Where ethnicity is a dominant factor in a country's political life, this will certainly affect environmental decisions. Nigeria is one example of this phenomenon. Here clean-up of an oil spill in the eastern provinces and decisions on extension of the electricity[91] grid were both affected by considerations of ethnic balance. A similar pattern is evident in Malaysia.[92]

Passing new environmental laws, by definition, is of limited value in a bureaucratic polity controlled by officials of the executive branch. Here the top officials' personal decisions will determine environmental and political outcomes.[93] In these political systems, either a parliament does not exist at all, or its authority is sharply constrained. In either event, it becomes difficult for problems of environmental quality to gain political salience.

Groups with environmental grievances may have no choice but to take to the streets in protest. Yet even in these cases the personalism endemic to the political leadership of many developing countries takes on great importance. Activists must deal with the existing power structure. Like other single-interest political groups, environmental activists often have to focus their protests on a few key leaders, such as a prime minister, a provincial governor, or a leading general; they cannot afford to divert their limited political power and economic resources.[94] They have to reach those leaders who have the power to bring about change. Until these leaders become convinced of the need to respond, effective government action is unlikely.

At times, activists have advanced their environmental objectives by exploiting factional conflicts within a bureaucratic polity. In Thailand, for example, proposed construction of a major new soda ash factory at Laem Chabang on the Gulf of Siam was blocked by citizen protests. The effectiveness of pressures on government sponsors of the project was enhanced by reliance on differences between leaders of political party groupings within the cabinet headed by Prime Minister General Prem Tinsulanonda.[95] Factional politics dominated the debate over this controversial project. As the *Far Eastern Economic Review* summarized:

The soda ash plant, one of the Asian industrial projects adopted in 1977, was originally to be sited at Laem Chabang, near the resort beaches of Pattaya. Environmentalists and resort operators, however, claimed that effluent from the factory would destroy valuable marine ecology and despoil Pattaya's income-generating beauty. The Chart Thai party and, in particular, Industry Minister Chatichai Choonhavan, strongly supported the Laem Chabang site. The Social Action Party (SAP) of Deputy Prime Minister Boonchu Rojanasathien, however, favoured the deepwater port of Sattahip to the south, a move favoured also by environmentalists and the prime minister's advisory council.

There were political overtones too: Laem Chabang is an SAP stronghold and the siting of the soda ash project there would alienate people from the party while gaining votes from business groups in the area for the Chart Thai.[96]

Protection of an estuary or control of deforestation may enhance the interests of a particular factional leader. This kind of alliance between environmentalists and the factional leader may help advance specific environmental interests. Similarly, environmental groups may design their actions to support the roles of individual technocrats or experts in key government positions who are already sympathetic to ecological goals.

Bringing a lawsuit against a government agency may be impossible or meaningless in a country with a dominant military junta or single political party. In India, by contrast, a 1981 Supreme Court judgment upheld the rights of citizens to sue municipal authorities; according to one observer on the scene, this "could have wide impact on the control of slums and chemical pollution in Indian cities."[97] In most developing countries, however, judicial systems lack autonomy; critical decisions are made by leading party cadre or by military leaders. And even where courts function with a sizable degree of institutional coherence,[98] the absence of specific statutes obviously makes it more difficult for legal challenges to be effective against government agencies that have made environmental mistakes. In a few instances, litigation may appear to be the best response to an environmental problem within a developing country. This would be most likely to occur where a country has already created basic environmental legislation, providing the statutory basis for a court challenge. Then, international groups with extensive litigation experience might be able to provide important assistance to local environmental groups. In one case, for example, the Natural Resources Defense Council worked with groups in the Philippines to prepare a legal challenge to a proposed nuclear reactor.[99] With these few exceptions, however, courts have not become a primary arena of action for environmentalists in developing countries.

While some 133 countries now have national environmental agencies of one kind or another, many of these agencies are very small, weak institutions—one-person offices or interagency coordinating committees with no independent authority. Since personalism is an important characteristic of politics in many developing nations, the leadership which individuals impart to environmental agencies is critical to a country's success in coping with environmental challenges. The leaders of national environmental boards are seldom effective, powerful individuals able to exercise great influence over their nation's economic and regulatory policies. Frequently, the trained scientists and engineers who understand their country's environmental needs are unable to exercise significant political power.[100]

As in the industrialized world, media coverage of open protests is often critical to the success of an environmental action. In developing countries, however, radio and televison typically fall under direct government control and, therefore, little independent news reporting exists. Obviously, explicit censorship of the news, or indirect influence over broadcasters, enables governments to keep news of environmental protests off the air waves.[101] Newspapers and magazines are a different matter, however, as they are frequently able to cover demonstrations and protest movements, and contain accounts of damage to the environment.[102] When particular papers are linked to individual political leaders or parties, as is often the case, their patron's own factional advantage may be enhanced by publishing news about a specific environmental controversy. In many less developed countries, environmental groups seek out opportunities in publications of various kinds. The press often has great impact, especially in capital cities.[103]

TOWARD EFFECTIVE IMPLEMENTATION OF ENVIRONMENTAL POLICIES

While there is no question that the level of awareness about their environmental problems has increased markedly in developing countries over the past decade, it is quite another matter, as we have seen, to conclude that these countries are actually moving closer to alleviating these problems. Indeed, the evidence suggests that the contrary may be true. Industrial pollution is worsening in most developing countries in spite of all their new laws, policies, regulations, and government agencies. And of even greater significance for human welfare and long-term economic development, sporadic but growing evidence exists of the potentially catastrophic rural environmental problems of soil erosion, desertification, and deforestation. Many third world governments continue to clear cut forests and to perpetuate policies and incentives that lead to massive losses of fertile agricultural soils, even when governing elites are aware that such policies are turning once-productive lands into deserts. These forms of environmental degradation are often exacerbated by the poverty of millions of people who must eke out a living by overtaking already fragile natural resources.

This chapter has traced the growth in awareness of particular environmental problems in the third world, and has explored the limited extent to which this awareness has been translated into remedial action through new laws and new institutions. Numerous barriers continue to hinder progress in coping with environmental problems in developing countries.

The Political Salience of Environmental Problems

Frequently, the effectiveness of governmental response to a particular public policy problem varies with the visibility of the problem—its political salience. This "issue-attention cycle"[104] has been evident with respect to environmental politics in developing countries. As noted earlier in this chapter, the pollution so visible in urban areas and in some non-urban industrialized areas has combined with growing pressures from the international arena to cause one country after the next to pass new environmental laws and to create new environmental institutions. The issue gained sufficient political salience so that it could no longer be ignored. Institutional and statutory response was forthcoming.

Enforcement of these environmental laws has been sadly lacking; as we have seen, administration of environmental programs has been ineffectual. The response to the visible environmental challenge was superficial. While it was adequate to forestall political demands for immediate action, it was inadequate to quell the growing environmental degradation. Institutional barriers to effective environmental action still dominate. Yet as urban and industrial pollution accelerate in Bangkok, Mexico City, Lagos, and elsewhere, one can certainly anticipate that the issue-attention cycle will once again return environmental issues to a central focus. Eventually, growing political pressures will produce demands for more effective administration of environmental programs, just as they earlier compelled the initial responses.

Environmental politics in rural areas, associated with deforestation, soil erosion, and waterborne disease, illustrate many of the same themes of the issue-attention cycle—but at a much earlier stage. Here the more subtle forces of ecological deterioration stand in contrast to the highly visible problems of urban-industrial pollution. The political weaknesses of most rural people and the massive difficulties in implementing diffuse programs across vast rural areas combine to constrain the political salience of rural environmental issues.

Indeed, the most intractable barriers to environmental quality in developing countries arise in the rural sector. Here many of the problems of environmental degradation demand much more complicated and far-reaching solutions than merely enacting and enforcing regulations. The misuse of drylands and steeply sloping land in the continuous pursuit of food production in much of the third world is causing large-scale erosion and desertification. This further reduces the land's capacity to produce food in the future, and increases the need to utilize and abuse even more marginal lands. This vicious cycle, in which short-term survival requirements lead to environmental degradation which increases long-run poverty, is repeated in the search for wood.

The basic energy source for the rural population's domestic needs is wood. Increasing population results in deforestation to meet energy demands and increased land requirements for food production. This leads to a vicious circle of soil erosion, floods, lower agricultural productivity and further deforestation . . . . (W)ater resources have to be developed for irrigation purposes. Unscientific development has led to complete diversion of low flows on the one hand and water logging on the other, leading to serious resource depletion and environmental problems. Similarly, people live in filthy conditions without adequate management of human and solid wastes, causing serious health hazards.[105]

In such instances, governments can try to pass laws that forbid agricultural activities and the cutting of wood in certain places; but such regulations rarely are effective. As numerous observers have pointed out, few governments in developing countries are very effective in administering programs in rural sectors far removed from administrative centers.[106] In Africa, government programs intended to reduce deforestation and desertification by trying to prevent people from cutting trees for fuel use are circumvented by an elaborate system of bribery and patron-client arrangements.[107]

More importantly, many of the problems of environmental degradation in rural areas are deeply rooted in these areas' political and economic processes. As noted, the people who both create the immediate problems and suffer their consequences have shown little propensity to organize in protest to environmental degradation. While fishermen have organized to protest pollution of their fishing areas, farmers have organized to protest damage to their land from mining wastes, and students have organized to demand curbs on a particular industry's air pollution, most peasant farmers have been unable to extricate themselves politically from the complicated web of relationships in which they are both the perpetrators and the victims of deforestation and soil erosion. The ambiguous visibility of the environmental problem and their relationship to it renders effective political action difficult. The fundamental cause of their abuse of the environment, however, is not so much their lack of awareness as it is their marginal political and economic status. The ultimate barrier to solving the problems of rural environmental degradation in many developing countries may be that the solutions to these problems would involve far-reaching social reforms that few governments are in a position to undertake, certainly not in the absence of effective political pressures from the mass of the rural citizenry. Thus ecological devastation accelerates despite the superficial laws passed to curtail it.

Flexible Enforcement and Public Administration

A government's policy choices to alleviate environmental degradation will rarely if ever be guided solely by consideration of the optimal steps that could be taken from an ecological perspective. Instead, a wide range of political, institutional, and bureaucratic constraints—many of which have been identified in this chapter—drastically narrow the scope of policy options available for environmental management.

Governments in developing countries have many standards on their books that simply *cannot* be enforced. Given this situation, those concerned with environmental management in these countries must ask themselves quite seriously whether it is better to have many strong regulations that simply go unenforced, or to have instead a small number of strategically selected enforceable regulations that begin to change behavior in conscious increments.

In a few countries, this dilemma has led already to calls to simplify and loosen some regulations in order to encourage compliance with others. The philosophy of simplicity has been embraced by Egypt, as one example. In trying to cope with the country's serious problems of industrial pollution, Egyptian authorities have reportedly decided to reduce the stringency of many environmental standards while trying to secure compliance with at least the most critical of their regulations.[108] This practice may become more widespread. It is hoped that countries will set priorities in accordance with the magnitude and severity of the pollution emanating from particular sources. In the United States, for example, while the National Pollutant Discharge Elimination Systems (NPDES) waste water permit program applies legally to all sources, permit issuance procedures and enforcement priorities have focused on the largest dischargers, and on others located on particularly important bodies of water. Given the developing countries' problems with effective environmental management, setting such priorities would seem essential.

No public administration apparatus can do everything at once; priorities have to be established and choices made. The danger, of course, is that personal favoritism and political opportunism will overwhelm criteria designed around ecological priorities. Foreign firms may be easier enforcement targets than their larger domestic counterparts, especially if the indigenous corporation has close affiliations with the dominant political party or the nation's ruling military junta. Regional and ethnic issues or the intricate balances of bureaucratic politics may take precedence over environmental threats in defining the parameters of environmental administration. Nevertheless, as pressures build for effective, rather than just superficial, environmental action, clear implementation priorities will have to be set as the basis for the next phase of the issue-attention cycle.

In many developing countries—and in the industrial world as well, of course, though perhaps to a lesser degree—corruption provides the prevalent mechanism for nonenforcement of applicable laws, standards, and regulations. Bribery of law-enforcement officials is commonplace; obviously, enforcement of environmental rules will be no different from other laws. Thailand, for example, has for several decades had strict statutes controlling tree cutting, and has identified extensive "reserved forest" areas in which all cutting is prohibited. Typically, however, peasants bribe police or civil administrative (district officers) officials in exchange for their tolerance in local tree cutting (to repair their wooden houses, for example); and large lumber firms bribe police and

Forestry Department officials in order to conduct commercial timbering operations in supposedly reserved forests.[109] James Thomson's chapter in this volume illustates a similar problem in the Sahel.

The prevalence of corruption in so many developing countries constrains the choice of effective approaches to environmental implementation. In its own way, however, corruption is a kind of flexible enforcement mechanism. And this factor needs to enter into environmental planning. Administrative and regulatory devices like discharge permits, for example, seemed doomed to failure—the cost of a bribe will typically be less than the cost of strict conformance with the permit's conditions. Similarly, police enforcement of forest-protection laws seems likely to produce dubious results in the face of pervasive bribery (except in enriching members of the police force).

Social anthropologist Emilio Moran conducted a detailed study of the ecological and economic impacts of development in Brazil's Amazon region, especially the colonization of the tropical rain forest by small-scale farmers. He concluded that flexible implementation is essential if the Amazon is to be developed within its environmental constraints:

> The question which is central to the future of the Amazon region is whether or not the structure of the Brazilian bureaucracy is capable of adjusting its policies. . . .
>
> The Amazon will continue to be exploited, sometimes poorly, sometimes disastrously, and in time, perhaps, wisely. The monolithic developmental strategies used until now may give way to the needed flexible strategies capable of incorporating diversity of local conditions into the execution of projects designed to exploit the land, provide jobs and income, and achieve the multiple goals pursued by citizens and nation alike. These multiple goals will not be achieved easily. They can be made a part of policy only when there is change in the bureaucratic structures around which Brazil is organized as a nation.[110]

An Integrated Framework for Planning

With varying levels of sophistication, all developing countries throughout the world now devise economic development plans, characteristically of a five-year basis. These plans pinpoint growth priorities, identify critical constraints and barriers, and allocate government (and sometimes private) resources along the pattern deemed most likely to achieve the desired development targets during the plan period. Typically these plans are prepared by a central planning office within the prime minister's office. In Thailand, for example, this function is performed by the National Economic and Social Development Board within the office of the prime minister. India's Central Planning Commission is an autonomous body independently established by the parliament.

Actual implementation of the plan depends, among other factors, on the administrative and political relationships between the planning agency (and the five-year plan) on the one hand, and the budget bureau (and the annual government budget) on the other. The budget process normally links development planning objectives with expenditures of public monies for specific purposes.

Many developing countries have tried to introduce new planning methods into the decision-making process. Often, however, these efforts have created only an illusion of coordination among different projects and decisions. According to research by Caiden and Wildavsky, based upon one month's interviewing in each of twelve countries, planning in many developing countries is totally irrelevant and powerless. Plans are accompanied by restrictive and inappropriate budgetary systems in which departmental competition and the tactics of self-preservation prevail over rational allocation of resources.[111] By insulating themselves from daily administration and from procedures for actual project execution, these planning systems and agencies have simply produced a series of documents which are not subsequently implemented. While generally true for economic development planning, this lack of implementation seems particularly apparent for environmental control plans.

In the 1980s, many developing countries will be preparing national environmental plans for the first time, and those countries with an initial environmental plan will be revising these documents in light of recent implementation experience. If these plans are to be a successful guide to the national effort at pollution abatement and at prevention of ecological destruction, it seems essential that they be coordinated closely with the economic development plan, and with emerging strategies for energy use in those countries (the transition away from petroleum toward biomass, for example, will have enormous environmental implications).

Coordination has not been apparent in most countries to date. Economic and environmental plans typically are devised by different government agencies, each pursuing different goals. Potential contradictions between a nation's strategies for development and for environmental protection need to be identified, debated, and—it is hoped—resolved in the interest of sustainable development; this is rare at present, however. Since the environmental planning process is so new, many of the plans—Thailand's, for example—are being prepared by outside experts rather than by officials of the country itself.[112] This renders coordination of plan targets and of implementation approaches even more difficult, and reduces the likelihood that the environmental plan's provisions actually will be carried out. The siting, land use, and industrial promotion aspects of the development plan require close scrutiny from an environmental perspective, to ensure their basic compatibility with the nation's underlying environmental constraints.

In many countries, it might be preferable to meld the incipient environmental planning effort directly into the nation's ongoing economic planning process. Environmental issues might become a separate chapter or component (like transportation or manpower) of the overall economic development plan. While the specific details of environmental planning might gain somewhat less visibility in such a combined effort, the ability to achieve greater coherence of economic and environmental objectives would seem well worth it.

The Political Basis of Effective Environmental Management

As developing countries have begun to cope with environmental problems, several common features have become apparent. Most significant is the enormous gap between the passage of laws and the creation of new institutions, on the one hand, and the strict enforcement of those laws through effective environmental management, on the other. As the late Barbara Ward (Lady Jackson) noted in the foreword to Erik Eckholm's *Down to Earth: Environment and Human Needs:*

In retrospect the 1972 Stockholm Conference should have been more of a turning point than it became. . . . the series of UN Conferences that followed . . . had a common pattern—governments agreed on the nature of a problem and agreed on the solutions. But their actions rarely matched their promises. [113]

She saw the problem primarily as a lack of political will. [114]

The developing countries have generally concentrated on abatement of pollution from new industrial sources, rather than on planning for environmentally sound development and on preservation of scarce natural resources. Where regulations have been promulgated and enforced, the principal targets have been industrial smokestacks or discharge pipes. In spite of the efforts of numerous international organizations, problems of soil erosion, deforestation, and contamination from agricultural pesticides continue to be neglected by these governments—and by most estimates continue to worsen throughout the developing world. To date, administration of environmental programs has been a failure in this vital sphere of the world's ecological challenge.

As in much of the industrialized world, environmental action in developing countries has been characterized by ad hoc responses to crises rather than by continuing execution of coherent public policies; problems are ignored as long as possible. The issue-attention cycle of environmental politics has led to initial, superficial responses to profound threats. This political phenomenon reinforces the tendency to respond to visible problems of pollution rather than to insidious long-term environmental degradation, especially in rural areas.

National institutions created to deal primarily with problems of industrial pollution have been intergovernmental—councils, committees, task forces—rather than ministerial or departmental. Most have had few staff resources, small budgets, and relatively limited power to devise and enforce regulations. Coordination, compromise, and cooperation with existing agencies have been favored over independence, autonomy, and confrontation.

The ability of both ad hoc and previously organized citizen groups to bring significant public pressure on the political system frequently determines whether a government will respond to a problem. In particular, enforcement of existing laws or regulations seems to depend in large measure on the extent of effective citizen pressure. This is particularly important—and particularly difficult—in dealing with environmental issues in rural areas. Citizen environmental action in developing countries seldom stresses coherent, continuous enforcement of environmental laws or planning for long-term balance between man and ecosystem. Cumulative environmental degradation thus perpetuates the cycle of poverty in rural areas, rapid migration to urban growth centers, and growing pollution pressures there as well.

National institutions created to deal primarily with problems of industrial pollution have been intergovernmental—councils, committees, task forces—rather than ministerial or departmental. Most have had few staff resources, small budgets, and relatively limited power to devise and enforce regulations. Coordination, compromise, and cooperation with existing agencies have been favored over independence, autonomy, and confrontation.

The ability of both ad hoc and previously organized citizen groups to bring significant public pressure on the political system frequently determines whether a government will respond to a problem. In particular, enforcement of existing laws or regulations seems to depend in large measure on the extent of effective citizen pressure. This is particularly important—and particularly difficult—in dealing with environmental issues in rural areas. Citizen environmental action in developing countries seldom stresses coherent, continuous enforcement of environmental laws or planning for long-term balance between man and ecosystem. Cumulative environmental degradation thus perpetuates the cycle of poverty in rural areas, rapid migration to urban growth centers, and growing pollution pressures there as well.

Emergence of strong public advocacy for environmental action on rural problems may be more important than any other factor in achieving sustainable development in the third world. Despite growth in general environmental awareness, more profound changes in the political dynamics of these countries may be essential to bring renewed attention to the connection between poverty and environmental degradation, and to provide the political basis for effective implementation of environmental programs.

Notes

1. See International Union for Conservation of Nature and Natural Resources, United Nations Environment Programme, and World Wildlife Fund, *World Conservation Strategy* (March 1980); and Lester Brown, *Building a Sustainable Society* (New York: Norton, 1981).

2. W. Howard Wriggins, *The Ruler's Imperative: Strategies of Political Rule in Asia and Africa* (New York: Columbia University Press, 1971).

3. "The Year In Review: America Abdicates As Others Assert Ecological Leadership," *World Environment Report* 7, no. 26 (December 15, 1981): Also see Center for International Environment Information, *Government Agencies with Environmental Responsibilities in Developing Countries* (New York: CIEI, April 15, 1980).

4. See H. Jeffrey Leonard and David Morell, "Emergence of Environmental Concern in Developing Countries: A Political Perspective," *Stanford Journal of International Law* 17, no. 2 (Summer 1981): 281–313.

5. An early attempt to point out the interrelationships between environment and development was made at the Conference on the Ecological Aspects of International Development, convened by the Conservation Foundation and the Center for the Biology of Natural Systems (Washington University) at Airlie House, Warrenton, Virginia, on December 8–11, 1968. The papers presented at this conference are published in M. Taghi Farvar and John P. Milton, *The Careless Technology: Ecology and International Development* (Garden City, N.Y.: Natural History Press, 1972).

6. Quoted in Alan S. Miller, *A Planet to Choose* (New York: Pilgrim Press, 1978), p. 49. See also, *Development and Environment*, a report submitted by a panel of experts convened by the Secretary General of the United Nations Conference on the Human Environment, at Founex, Switzerland, June 4–12, 1971 (Stockholm: Kungl, Boktryckeriet, P. A. Norstedt, and Soner, 1971), p. 6 (hereafter cited as *Founex Report*). Sri Lanka's ambassador to the United Nations, at that time president of the United Nations General Assembly, spoke for the majority of developing countries during the early 1970s when he said:

> Developing countries have of late been warned of the price that has to be paid in the form of environmental pollution for industrial development. All developing countries are aware of the risks, but they would be quite prepared to accept from the developed countries even 100 percent of their gross national pollution if thereby they could diversify their economies through industrialization.

Hamilton Amerassignhe, quoted in Farrar, Thomas, Boksenbaum, and Soule, "The Pollution of Asia," *Environment* 13, no. 10 (October 1971): 11.

7. During much of the planning period for the 1972 Stockholm Conference, it appeared that most developing countries would not participate. The issue of whether and how developing countries could become involved in the international debate about the environmental crisis was discussed, among other topics, at a series of meetings convened in 1971 to plan for the conference. These meetings included: "International Organization and the Human Environment," cosponsored by the Institute on Man and Science and the Aspen Institute for Humanistic studies, held at Rensselaerville, New York, May 21–23, 1971; "The Crisis of the Human Environment and International Action," sponsored by the International Studies Program, University of Toronto, held at Toronto, Canada, May 25–27, 1971; "Sixth Conference on the United Nations of the Next Decade", sponsored by the Stanley Foundation, held at Sinaia, Romania, June 20–26, 1971; "First International Environmental Workshop," cosponsored by the International Institute for Environmental Affairs and Aspen Institute for Humanistic Studies, held at Aspen, Colorado, June 20–August 6, 1971; "Panel of Experts on International Organizational Implications," convened by the Secretary General of the United Nations Conference on the Human Environment, held at Geneva, Switzerland, July 8–9, 1971; "International Legal

and Institutional Responses to the Problems of the Global Environment," cosponsored by the Carnegie Endowment for International Peace and the American Society of International Law, held at Harriman, New York, September 25–October 1, 1971; and "The UN System and the Human Environment," sponsored by the Institute for the Study of International Organization, University of Sussex, held at Brighton, England, November 1–4, 1971.

Concern in developing countries over the political implications of paying attention to environmental problems is evident in *Summaries of National Reports on Environmental Problems* (Washington, D.C.: Woodrow Wilson Center for Scholars, 1972), and in T. L. Hargrove, ed., *Law, Institutions and the Global Environment* (Leiden: A. W. Sigthoff, 1972), pp. 81–83.

In the end, most developing nations participated in the discussions and resolutions of the Stockholm Conference. See United Nations, *Report of the Secretary General on the United Nations Conference on the Human Environment*, Stockholm, Sweden, 5–16 June 1972 (UN Doc A/CONF 48 and Add.1, Add.1/Corr.1 and Add.2.) (1972), hereafter termed *UN Report*).

8. See especially Joao Augusto de Araujo Castro, "Environment and Development: The Case of the Less Developed Countries," *International Organization* 26 no. 2 (Spring 1972): 401–416. Spokesmen for the third world expressed at least four major concerns. First, they feared that their trade would be adversely affected as developed countries adopted lead and sulfur standards for fuel, and purity standards for a whole host of other products. In addition, third world countries believed that the high cost of environmental clean-up and protection programs in the developed countries might significantly reduce the amount of aid available for development assistance. They feared that the capital costs of development would increase as developed countries established new standards for factories and technology being transferred to the developing world. Finally, developing countries saw that the infusion of sophisticated pollution control technologies would not only add to development costs but would worsen the problem of inappropriate technology already facing them. These four fears are summarized in the *Founex Report*, pp. 11–12.

9. Hargrove, *Law, Institutions and the Global Environment*, p. 82.

10. Whitman Bassow, "The Third World: Changing Attitudes Toward Environmental Protection," *The Annals of the American Academy of Political and Social Science*, 444 (July 1979): 112–113.

11. Russell Train, Speech to the Stony Brook–Millstone Watersheds Association, Princeton, New Jersey, April 15, 1982.

12. Bassow, "The Third World," p. 113.

13. *UN Report*. For a description of how the Stockholm agenda was broadened, see Lawrence Juda, "International Environmental Concern: Perspectives of and Implications for Developing States," in *The Global Predicament: Ecological Perspectives on World Order*, edited by David W. Orr and Marvin S. Soroos (Chapel Hill, N.C.: University of North Carolina Press, 1979), pp. 90–107.

14. See Robert E. Stein and Brian Johnson, *Banking on the Biosphere?* (Lexington, Mass.: Lexington Books, 1979); Brian Johnson and Robert O. Blake, *The Environmental Policies, Programs and Performances of the Development Assistance Agencies of Canada, the Federal Republic of Germany, the Netherlands, Sweden, the United Kingdom, and the United States*, draft report (Washington, D.C., and London: International Institute for Environment and Development, 1979); and H. Jeffrey Leonard, *Environmental Training*

in Developing Countries: A Study of the Practices of Major National and International Development Financing Agencies (New York: The Center for International Environment Information, September 1980). These works provide a description of the numerous environmental management programs and consciousness-raising activities undertaken by international, national, and nongovernmental organizations. Also see United Nations Environment Programme, *Ecodevelopment* (GC/80), January 15, 1976; and World Bank, *Environment and Development*, June 1975. For a more recent perspective on the relationship between environment and development, see IUCN et al., *World Conservation Strategy*.

15. See Stein and Johnson, *Banking on the Biosphere;* Johnson and Blake, *Environmental Policies;* and U.S. Agency for International Development, *Environmental and Natural Resources Management in Developing Countries—a Report to Congress* (February 1979). (This report is the final product of a project organized by the Science and Technology Division of the Library of Congress, PAS No. ZA/DSB-000-1-79.) Albert Printz, environmental coordinator for the USAID, says: "Now we are focusing more on the environmental impediments to development in entire sectors because unless progress is made on these broader problems, many development projects will not be successful." Quoted in Leonard, *Environmental Training in Developing Countries*, p. 7.

16. See Stein and Johnson, *Banking on the Biosphere* and World Bank, *Environment and Development*.

17. Hobart Rowan, "World Bank Assisting Third World Cleanups," *The Washington Post*, November 13, 1981.

18. *World Environment Report*, March 2, 1981 (New York: Center for International Environment Information).

19. International Union for Conservation of Nature and Natural Resources, *Conservation for Thailand: Policy Guidelines* (Morges, Switzerland: IUCN, 1979). Report prepared for the National Environment Board of Thailand.

20. Examples of such protests are found in "The War on Pollution Spreads Worldwide," *Business Week*, September 27, 1976, p. 86.

21. See Thaddeus Trzyna and Eugene Coan, *World Director of Environmental Organizations*, Sierra Club Special Publications, International Series, no. 1, 2nd edition (Claremont, Cal.: Sequoia Institute, 1976).

22. See, for example, "90 Irate Mexican Specialists Quit Clean Air Section," *World Environment Report* 5, no. 25 (October 22, 1979); and "Mexico's Air Quality Program Gets A Presidential Boost," *World Environment Report* 5, no. 26 (December 3, 1979). Scientists can sometimes be more effective than bureaucrats in securing results. For example, Dr. Jose Goldemberg, director of the Institute of Physics at the University of São Paulo, made the following comment in responding to an earlier version of this material: "The head of the Federal Environmental Protection Agency is a former professor at the University of São Paulo and he is a fairly disillusioned and powerless figure in the administration. Our society (Brazilian Association for the Advancement of Science) has probably done more for the environment by political pressure than by him working from the 'inside.'" Letter to David Morell (December 5, 1980).

23. V. Smil, "Environmental Degradation in China," *Asian Survey* (August 1980) p. 780. Similiar measurement in other Chinese cities, such as Shanghai, Tianjin, Wuhan, Hangzhou, Guanzhou, Chongging, Najing, and Harbin showed that the average decibel levels were much higher than in New York, London, Rome, and Tokyo.

24. See V. Thomas, A. E. Comune, and J. Rizzieri, "Control of Industrial Air Pollution in São Paulo: Evaluating Costs, Benefits and Spatial Effects." Paper presented at the second Urban and Regional Economics Seminar, FIPE, University of São Paulo, August 4–6, 1980, p. 63.

25. T. Land, "Water: Scourge or Salvation?", *Africa Report* (November–December 1980), p. 7. According to Land, these decreases paradoxically were encouraged by the construction of man-made lakes and irrigation systems typically considered to be instruments of economic progress.

26. Y. Rovani, "The Problem of Water Supply and Waste Disposal," *World Development Report* (January 1981), p. 17.

27. T. View, "Health and Environment," in "Cost-Benefit Analysis-Land Reclamation in Egypt," edited by B. Cassidy et al., mimeograph (nondated), p. 9.

28. USAID, *Environmental and Natural Resources Management, p. 14.*

29. *World Bank, Environment and Development*, p. 12.

30. Natural Resources Defense Council, Inc., *Aiding the Environment* (Washington, D.C.: NRDC, 1979), p. 77.

31. For a U.S. equivalent, see William Tucker, "Environmentalism and the Leisure Class," *Harper's*, December 1977, pp. 49–56, 73–80.

32. Thomas, Comune, and Rizzieri, "Control of Industrial Air Pollution in Sao Paulo," p. 2.

33. Michael Boydell, "Taiwan Has Set Up An Ambitious EPA," *World Environment Report* 8 no. 5 (March 15, 1982), 3.

34. See Richard Frankel and David Morell, "Project Evaluation in Developing Countries", *Modern Government and National Development*, January–February 1973, pp. 22–29.

35. P. G. Hollie, "Malaysia Confronts Environment Issues," *The New York Times*, January 25, 1981, p. 15. Also see David Lee, *The Sinking Ark: Environmental Problems in Malaysia and Southeast Asia* (Kuala Lumpur: Heinemann, 1980).

36. USAID, "Environment and Natural Resources Policies and Programs—status Report" (Washington, D.C.: USAID, 1982).

37. J. N. Obinegbo, "Nigeria Plans Federal Eco-Protection Agency," *World Environment Report* 8, no. 5 (March 15, 1982): 3.

38. Darryl D'Monte, "India's Environment Agency To Administer Pollution Laws," *World Environment Report* 7, no. 20 (September 28, 1981): 6.

39. See especially H. and J. M. Johnson and R. Gour-Tanguy, *Environmental Policies in Developing Countries* (Berlin: Erich Schmidt Verlag, 1977).

40. Richard Tucker, "Special Report: Indian Environment Planning—1981," Sierra Club, International Earthcare Center, *International Report* 10, no. 7 (March 15, 1982): 1–2.

41. "Government Inefficient in Fighting Pollution," *Bangkok Post*, March 9, 1982. Report in *TIC News*, March 19, 1982, pp. 2–3.

42. Mohammed Aftab, "Analysis—Pakistani Pollution Control: Big Plans and Little Progress," *World Environment Report* 7, no. 22 (October 30, 1981): 8. Emphasis added.

43. Dr. T. E. Aldridge, "Environmental Control: Successes, Failures, Future Direction," *The Jamaican Weekly Gleaner*, February 2, 1981, p. 30.

44. *Ibid.*

45. K. C. Kim and C. Rho, *Korean Environment and Natural Development* (Seoul: Korean Atomic Research Institute, 1975), p. 45.

46. J. Parikh, "Environmental Problems in India and Their Possible Trends in the Future," *Environmental Conservation* 4, no. 3 (1977): 192.

47. Lee, *The Sinking Ark*.

48. Kim and Roh, *Korean Environment*, p. 45.

49. USAID, *Environmental and Natural Resources Management*, pp. 81, 106.

50. *Ibid.*, p. 81.

51. Gregory Provan, "The Role of Environmental Planning in LDC Development." Paper prepared for "Environmental Politics and Policies," Politics 341/ Engineer 341, Princeton University, December 1981, p. 24.

52. R. Haddad, "Contaminación del Aire: Situación Actual en la America Latina y el Caribe," in *Proceedings of the Symposium on Environmental Health and Development in the America*, PAHO Serie Technica 19 (1976): 129–137.

53. Parikh, "Environmental Problems in India," p. 192.

54. Provan, "Environmental Planning in LDC Development," p. 22.

55. "Seoul, Korea, Issues Anti-pollution Orders," *World Environment Report* 8, no. 5 (March 15, 1982), 4.

56. Sam Cohen, "Ankara Smog Scare May Happen Again," *World Environment Report* 8, no. 6 (March 30, 1982): 3 Emphasis added.

57. P. M. Hauser, *World Population and Development* (Syracuse: Syracuse University Press, 1979), pp. 48–49.

58. United Nations, *Trends and Prospects in Urban and Rural Population: 1950 to 2000* (New York: United Nations, 1975).

59. "Rio de Janeiro Is World's Noisiest City," *World Environment Report* 8, no. 5 (March 15, 1982): 5.

60. Sierra Club, International Earthcare Center, *International Report* 10, no. 7 (March 15, 1982): 3.

61. V. Sardar, "The Fight to Save Malaysia," *New Scientist* 87 (September 1980): 702.

62. *Ibid.*

63. Mohammad Aftab, "Pakistan Proposes Clean Water and Sanitation Measures," *World Environment Report* 8, no. 4 (February 28, 1982): 2–3.

64. *Global 2000 Report*, p. 269.

65. *World Environment Report*, 8, no. 22 (November 7, 1980): 3.

66. Rowan, "World Bank Assisting Third World Cleanups."

67. Thomas, Comune, and Rizzieri, "Air Pollution in São Paulo," p. 70.

68. "On Asia," *World Environment Report* 5, no. 19 (October 22, 1979): 8.

69. Ingo Walter, "Environmental Attitudes in Less Developed Countries," *Resources Policy* 4 (September 1978): 200–204.

70. Leonard, *Environmental Training in Developing Countries*, pp. 4–12.

71. R. Steppacher, B. Zogg-Waltz, and H. Hatzfeldt, eds., *Economics in Institutional Perspective* (Lexington, Mass.: Lexington Books, 1977), pp. 189–192. See also G. W. Wynia, *The Politics of Latin American Development* (Cambridge: Cambridge University Press, 1978), pp. 45–52.

72. "Brazilian Battle Over Control of Pollution," *Latin American Economic Report* 7, no. 31 (August 10, 1979): 273.

73. *World Environment Report* 7, no. 18 (September 28, 1981): 2.

74. T. M. Hilhorst, "Regional Planning in Peru, 1966–1977: Top-down or Bottom-up?", (The Hague, Institute of Social Studies), *ISS Occasional Papers*, no. 83, September 1980, pp. 26–29.

75. *World Environment Report* 7, no. 13 (July 13, 1981): 7.

76. Smil, "Environmental Degradation in China," p. 787.

77. C. H. Gundel, "Experiments with Communism in Southern Africa," *Swiss Review of World Affairs* 30, no. 6 (September 1980).

78. Smil, "Environmental Degradation in China," p. 780.

79. See Thomas Gladwin, "Environmental Policy Trends Facing Multinationals," *California Management Review* 20, no. 2 (1977): 81; R. M. Lesaca, "Pollution Control Legislation and Experience in a Developing Country: The Philippines," *Journal of Developing Areas* 8, no. 4 (1974): 541; Walter, "Environmental Attitudes in Less Developed Countries," and Norman Wood, "The Environmental Movement in the Developing Economies," *Rivista Internazionale di Science Economiche e Commerciali* 24, May/June (1977): 467–477.

80. "The War on Pollution Spreads Worldwide," *Business Week*, p. 86; and Wood, *Ibid.*, p. 473. J. Juergensmeyer and E. Blizzard, "Legal Aspects of Environmental Control in Mexico: An Analysis of Mexico's New Environmental Law," *Natural Resources Journal* 12, no. 4 (1972): 580–595, provide an ex ante view of pollution enforcement which casts doubt on Mexico's ability to enforce its environmental regulations strictly.

81. *Business Week, Ibid.*

82. "Mexico Forces Plant Closure," *Business Latin America*, August 30, 1978, p. 274.

83. *Ibid.*

84. Confidential interview, Washington, D.C., April 14, 1979.

85. See "Less Expensive and More Appropriate Technologies for the Developing Countries," *Development and Socio-Economic Progress* (July–September 1980), 43–58.

86. For a description of twenty-four development projects, many of which illustrate this phenomenon, see Michael Nelson, *The Development of Tropical Lands: Policy Issues in Latin America* (Baltimore, Md.: Johns Hopkins, 1973) pp. 71–141.

87. "Less Expensive and More Appropriate Technologies," pp. 43–58.

88. See Mark Dowie, "The Corporate Crime of the Century," *Mother Jones* 11, no. 11 (November, 1979), p. 22; Mark Dowie and Steve Minkin, "The Charge: Genocide," *Mother Jones* 11, no. 11 (November, 1979), p. 26; David Weir, "The Boomerang Crime," *Mother Jones*, 11, no. 11 (November, 1979), p. 40. For articles on the policy problems raised by the export of hazardous wastes to developing countries, see Kathleen Agena, "Hazards International: No Easy Solution Is Possible," *The New York Times*, April 27, 1980, Section E, p. 9; Bill Richards, "U.S. Fights Export of Hazardous Waste," *The Washington Post*, January 26, 1980, Section A, p. 4.

89. Arnold Heidenheimer, ed., *Political Corruption: Readings in Comparative Analysis* (New York: Holt, Rinehart, Winston, 1970).

90. For background information on the role of the military in the politics of developing nations, see Henry Bienen, *Armies and Parties in Africa* (New York: Africana Publishing Co., 1978); Morris Janowitz, *The Military in the Political Development of New Nations* (Chicago: University of Chicago Press, 1964); Abraham Lowenthal, *Armies and Politics in Latin America* (New York: Holmes & Meier, 1976); *The Role of the Military in*

Underdeveloped Countries, John Johnson, ed., (Princeton, N.J.: Princeton University Press, 1964). Unfortunately, no specific information is available in the literature on environmental politics under military regimes.

91. Presentation by Henry Bienen, Seminar on Environment and Development, Woodrow Wilson School of Public and International Affairs, Princeton University, Princeton, N.J. (January 20, 1980).

92. Lee, *The Sinking Ark*.

93. For a description of a bureaucratic polity controlled by officials of the executive branch, see Fred Riggs, *Thailand; The Modernization of a Bureaucratic Polity* (Honolulu: East-West Center Press, 1966).

In this kind of political system, passage of new statutory provisions will be far less significant than the decisions of bureaucratic leaders, both military and civilian.

94. Cynthia Enloe, *The Politics of Pollution in Comparative Perspective* (New York: David McKay, 1975), pp. 322–23.

95. Frank Oliver, "Eco-politics in Thailand May Stop a Major Soda Ash Project," *World Environment Report* 6, no. 23 (November 17, 1980): 2–3.

96. *Far Eastern Economic Review*, December 12, 1980, Vol. 110, no. 51, pp. 44–45.

97. *World Environment Report* 7, no. 3 (January 19, 1981): 5.

98. Thailand provides one example of a judicial process which retains sharp autonomy from military rule and the pervasive corruption of the country's overall political dynamics. See David Morell, "Power and Parliament in Thailand: The Futile Challenge, 1968–1971." Ph.D. diss., Princeton University, 1974.

99. The legal assistance provided by NRDC attorneys was facilitated by the fact that the Philippine legal system and its Atomic Energy Act are both modeled on U.S. statutes and procedures. Telephone conversation with Jacob Scherr, NRDC staff attorney February 13, 1981.

100. This point is made by spokesmen for several international organizations that have sponsored training programs to build environmental management skills in developing countries. See Leonard, *Environmental Training in Developing Countries*, p. 22.

101. Such censorship was apparent during much of the period that the author spent doing field research on politics in Thailand, especially after the November 1971 military coup d'etat. See David Morell, "Thailand: Military Checkmate," *Asian Survey* (1972), 156–167.

102. Johnson, "Aid for Third World Environment," p. 239.

103. For an example of how the press has been used to generate support for a group seeking to prevent pollution of its water by a new sewer system outlet, see Talton Ray, *The Politics of the Barrios of Venezuela* (Berkeley: University of California Press, 1969), pp. 96–97.

104. Anthony Downs, "The Issue-Attention Cycle and the Political Economy of Improving Our Environment," in *The Political Economy of Environmental Control*, edited by Joe Bain and Warren Ilchman (Berkeley: Institute of Business and Economic Research, University of California, 1972), pp. 9–23.

105. Chaturvedi, "Second-Best Technology as First Choice," *Ambio* 8 (1979): 75.

106. On the problems of administration in rural areas, see Robert Chambers, *Managing Rural Development: Ideas and Experiences from East Africa* (Uppsala: Scan-

dinavian Institute of African Studies, 1974); and Uma Lele, *The Design of Rural Development: Lessons from Africa* (Baltimore: Johns Hopkins Press, 1975).

107. James Thomson, "Ecological Deterioration: Local-Level Rule-Making and Enforcement Problems in Niger," In *Desertification: Environmental Degradation In and Around Arid Lands,* edited by M. Glantz (Boulder, Colo.: Westview Press, 1977).

108. "Egypt Is Easing Its Eco-laws So That Industry Will Comply," *World Environment Report* 6, no. 8 (May 5, 1980).

109. David Morell, "The Functions of Corruption in Thai Politics." Paper presented at the Bi-Annual Meetings of the International Political Science Association, Edinburgh, Scotland, 1976.

110. Emilio Moran, *Developing the Amazon* (Bloomington: Indiana University Press, 1981), pp. 227, 229–230.

111. Naomi Caiden and Aaron Wildavsky, *Planning and Budgeting in Poor Countries* (New York: Wiley, 1971).

112. IUCN, *Conservation for Thailand.*

113. Barbara Ward, "Foreword," in Erik Eckholm, *Down to Earth: Environment and Human Needs* (New York: Norton, 1982). Emphasis added.

114. See R. M. Green, "The Role of the State as an Agent of Economic and Social Development in the Least Developed Countries," *Journal of Development Planning* 6 (1974): 7–8.

Three Key Environmental Problems: Deforestation, Desertification, Pollution

CHAPTER 5

THE POLITICAL ECONOMY OF TROPICAL DEFORESTATION

George Ledec*

Tropical moist forests, presently covering some 8 percent of the earth's land surface, are disappearing at a rate apparently unequaled in the earth's history. This unprecedented assault on one of the world's major biomes is of human origin. The specific causes of recent tropical deforestation are varied, complex, and deeply rooted in the economic, social, and political problems of the developing countries of the tropics. Moreover, the developed world is stimulating deforestation through a variety of international economic linkages. This chapter examines the importance of tropical deforestation; the specific causes and their underlying political and economic incentives; and the barriers and political dynamics involving efforts to control the problem.

As used here, the term "tropical moist forests" (TMFs) means evergreen or partly evergreen terrestrial forests, in areas of the geographic tropics receiving not less than 100 mm. of precipitation in any month for two out of three years.[1] This definition therefore includes lowland rainforests and hill, montane, subalpine, and freshwater swamp forests. However, this definition deliberately excludes mangroves (saltwater swamp forests), which face a unique set of management problems, owing to their special ecology, economic potential, and pressures for destruction. Also excluded are the "open forests," woodlands, and savannas of more arid regions (such as the Sahel), as well as the forests of nontropical developing countries (such as Nepal).

TMFs occur in three principal global regions: Latin America (primarily South America, but also Central America, southern Mexico, and the Caribbean), 54

*The author gratefully acknowledges the following people who kindly provided comments and criticisms: Gloria Davis, Susanna Hecht, Anne La Bastille, Norman Myers, James Nations, Bruce Ross, John Spears, Thomas Stoel, Scott Perkin, and Robert Vincent.

TABLE 1
Mid-1970s Distribution of TMF Area by Region and Country

Region	Estimated TMF Area (km²)	Percent of Total*
Latin America and the Caribbean	**5,900,000**	**54**
Bolivia	300,000	3
Brazil	3,000,000	27
Colombia	360,000	3
Ecuador	180,000	2
Guyana	200,000	2
Peru	650,000	6
Venezuela	350,000	3
Other countries	860,000	8
Africa and the Indian Ocean	**2,100,000**	**19**
Cameroon	130,000	1
Congo (People's Republic of)	100,000	1
Gabon	200,000	2
Zaire	1,000,000	9
Other countries	670,000	6
Asia, Australasia, and the Pacific	**3,000,000**	**27**
Burma	365,000	3
Indonesia	800,000	7
Malaysia	231,000	2
Papua New Guinea	400,000	4
Philippines	115,000	1
Thailand	132,000	1
Other countries	957,000	9
Total:	11,000,000	100

*Sources: *The World's Tropical Forests: A Policy, Strategy, and Program for the United States* (1980), (Washington, D.C.: U.S. Department of State, Publication No. 91117, 1980); and Norman Myers, *Conversion of Tropical Moist Forests* (Washington, D.C.: National Academy of Sciences, 1980).

percent of world total; Africa (primarily Central and West Africa and Madagascar), 19 percent; and the balance (Southeast and South Asia, northern Australia, and Oceania), 27 percent. As is indicated in Table 1, some two-thirds of the earth's area of these forests occurs in only nine countries: Bolivia, Brazil, Colombia, Peru, and Venezuela in Latin America; Zaire in Africa; and Burma, Indonesia, and Papua New Guinea in Southeast Asia. In addition to these, the following countries are believed to have 100,000 square kilometers or more of TMF cover: Ecuador and Guyana in Latin America; Cameroon, the People's Republic of the Congo, and Gabon in Africa; and Malaysia, the Philippines, and Thailand in Asia and the Pacific. The other countries that have TMF cover are listed in Table 2. While their TMF areas comprise only a small proportion of the world's total, these latter countries should not be neglected, as their TMFs are locally important and often biologically unique.

TABLE 2
Countries With TMF Area of Less Than 100,000 km²

Latin America and the Caribbean

Belize
Costa Rica
Cuba
Dominican Republic
El Salvador
French Guiana
Guatemala
Haiti
Honduras
Jamaica
Lesser Antilles: mainly Dominica, Grenada, Guadeloupe, Martinique, St. Lucia, and St. Vincent
Mexico
Nicaragua
Panama
Puerto Rico (U.S.A.)
Suriname
Trinidad and Tobago

Africa and the Indian Ocean

Benin (Dahomey)
Central African Republic
Equatorial Guinea
East Africa: relict (mostly montane) TMF patches in Kenya, Tanzania, Rwanda, and Uganda
Ghana
Guinea
Indian Ocean: Mauritius, Reunion, and Seychelles
Ivory Coast
Liberia
Malagasy Democratic Republic (Madagascar)
Nigeria
Sierra Leone
Togo

Asia, Australasia, and the Pacific

Australia
Brunei
China (Yunnan province)
Democratic Kampuchea (Cambodia)
India
Lao People's Republic (Laos)
Pacific Islands (most extensive TMF stands in New Caledonia (France), Fiji, Hawaii (U.S.A.),
      Solomon Islands, Western Samoa, and New Hebrides)
Sri Lanka
Vietnam

Source: Adapted from International Union for Conservation of Nature and Natural Resources, *World Conservation Strategy*, map no. 1 (Gland, Switzerland: IUCN 1980)

Significantly, almost all of the world's TMFs are in developing countries. While developing countries (tropical or otherwise) have many forestry problems in common, TMFs are especially prone to certain management problems, owing to their unique ecology. They are usually situated on agriculturally marginal soils, they have more limited potential for recovery following disturbance than most other forest types, and their (usually) high diversity of tree species greatly complicates commercial forestry efforts.

EXTENT AND RATES OF TROPICAL DEFORESTATION

"Deforestation" can entail total elimination, or mere modification (e.g., thinning) of the original forest cover. As used here, "deforestation" or TMF removal generally refers to outright elimination of a TMF area resulting from both conversion to non-forest uses and forest cutting that exceeds regrowth rates.

Official figures as to rates of tropical deforestation vary considerably. The most pessimistic estimates are in the recent *Global 2000* study by the U.S. Council on Environmental Quality, which projects that if current trends continue, roughly one-half of today's remaining TMFs will be eliminated by the year 2000.[2] A country-by-country study published in 1980 by the U.S. National Academy of Sciences suggests that about 20 million hectares of primary TMF are being eliminated or severely damaged each year.[3] This would represent an annual loss of nearly 2 percent.

In contrast, a more recent study prepared by the United Nations Environment Programme (UNEP) and Food and Agriculture Organization (FAO) estimates the annual global loss of TMFs to be only 0.6 percent.[4] This study had access to much data that have only very recently become available, through the use of such technologies as LANDSAT (satellite) remote sensing, side-looking radar (mounted on high-flying aircraft), and aerial photography, in a number of important TMF countries.

Although a wide spectrum of the relevant scientific community believes that TMF removal is taking place at a rapid—and unsustainable—rate, much debate continues about which of these studies is most accurate. Some criticize the *Global 2000* and National Academy of Sciences studies as being too pessimistic.[5] Others say the FAO study, despite much high-quality information, may be unduly optimistic because it does not adequately distinguish between untouched primary forest, logged-over primary forest, and second-growth forest. Also, it appears that FAO was obligated to accept unverifiable official figures from national governments to supplement its use of remote sensing and similar technologies.[6] From our perspective, what is most important is that at the local level in many developing countries, TMF destruction is indeed occurring and, as is noted below, his significant ecological, economic, and political consequences. This fact is not disputed.

TMF destruction is not spread evenly across the globe. A number of countries have already lost a majority of their TMF cover, and the remainder is disappearing rapidly. These countries include Bangladesh, El Salvador, Ghana, Haiti, India, Nigeria, the Philippines, Sierra Leone, and Thailand. In other countries, a major TMF endowment still remains, but is rapidly disappearing. These countries include Brazil (varies by region), Colombia, Ecuador, Indonesia, and Malaysia. In still others, deforestation is proceeding, but at more moderate rates. These countries include Bolivia, Burma, Cameroon, and Papua New Guinea. There are only a few countries where deforestation pressures are still light or virtually nonexistent, namely Guyana, Suriname, French Guyana, Brunei, Zaire, People's Republic of the Congo, Central African Republic, and Gabon. This great variation in remaining TMF area and deforestation rates implies vastly different forest management problems and goals for the various countries.

Consequences of TMF Loss

The cutting of trees in TMFs serves many desirable economic purposes. However, when deforestation is excessive, the harms can be significant, in both the short and long run. Tropical deforestation may damage human welfare and the prospects for long-term economic development in the third world. The global loss of TMFs could also have significant repercussions for citizens of the developed world. The key policy issues thus concern not whether TMFs should be utilized at all, but what types of uses are most desirable under differing circumstances.

The most obvious benefit of TMFs is their provision of wood and other forest products. One of the most important products is fuel wood (firewood and charcoal). No less than one and a half billion people in developing countries derive at least 90 percent of their energy requirements from fuel wood, while another billion meet at least 56 percent of their energy needs in this manner.[7] In addition, there is rapidly growing demand within TMF countries for paper, building materials, poles, and a wide variety of industrial products (from wood and other forest products, such as rattan).[8] TMFs also supply food (fruits, nuts, honey, fish, and wild animals) to more than 200 million people who live within them or on their margins.[9] Moreover, the international trade in tropical hardwoods can be a major source of foreign exchange and employment in developing countries. Of course, all of these "consumptive" uses of TMF products are sustainable over the long term only if harvesting is not excessive.

Of perhaps even greater importance are the "public goods" provided by TMFs in their natural or near-natural state. Many of these benefits result from the relationship between TMFs and a vital resource: fresh water. By retaining water and releasing it gradually throughout the year, TMFs help maintain reliable, permanent supplies of high-quality water. Thus, they reduce flooding and mitigate the effects of droughts. At the same time, they stabilize soils and help prevent erosion.

The developing world is replete with examples of major economic and human dislocations resulting from the impact of deforestation on watersheds. For example, deforestation upstream is jeopardizing the continued operation of the Panama Canal, which suffers from heavy sedimentation and a lack of sufficient water during the dry season.[10] The canal is Panama's most important economic asset. This deforestation is also affecting the quality of drinking water in Panama City.[11] In some rural areas, deforestation can damage human health by forcing people to drink from polluted streams when wells become dry.[12] Upstream deforestation has contributed to the clogging of urban sewers in Port-au-Prince, Haiti.[13] Numerous hydroelectric projects have been affected by deforestation. For example, the useful life of the Philippines' Ambuklao Dam has been cut from sixty to thirty-two years.[14] Deforestation has also led to daily electricity rationing in Bogota, Colombia, by causing the Guatavita hydroelectric complex to operate at only one-sixth of normal capacity.[15] Typhoon damage in the Philippines amounts to roughly $20 million per year, through floods and landslides that are greatly intensified by deforestation.[16] Deforestation also reduces the productivity of irrigated agriculture, due to sedimentation of irrigation works and a lack of water during the dry season. This especially affects "high yield" farming, such as of "Green Revolution" rice in Indonesia, Malaysia, and the Philippines.[17]

In addition to these watershed functions, TMFs are important to the continued high productivity of many fisheries. For example, in the Amazon Basin, fallen fruit from floodplain (varzea) forest trees is necessary for the survival of many species of fish, a principal source of animal protein in the region.[18] In many countries, soil erosion resulting from tropical deforestation threatens the fishery potential of coral reefs, by covering these highly productive underwater ecosystems with a layer of silt.[19]

TMFs are biologically the richest ecosystems on earth, containing some 40 to 50 percent of all species on earth.[20] Many of these species have very localized distributions, and are therefore extremely vulnerable to habitat destruction (more so than most temperate-zone species). The Global 2000 study by the U.S. Council on Environmental Quality indicates that if relatively pessimistic projections for loss of primary forest cover are realized, some 15–20 percent of all plant and animal species on earth are likely to become extinct by the year 2000; this represents the loss of 500,000 to 600,000 species. (Tropical deforestation would be responsible for one-half to two-thirds of these extinctions.)[21] Many more species are likely to be lost in the next century if TMF destruction continues unabated; it is possible that over half of all species of plants and animals that exist today will have disappeared by the year 2100.[22] Dr. Norman Myers, an internationally known conservation authority, estimates that an average of one species per day is presently becoming extinct, and this rate is accelerating, primarily as a result of TMF destruction.[23] This raises the possibility that tropical deforestation will irreversibly alter the course of evolution on this planet.

In addition to the aesthetic and ethical implications, such large-scale destruction of species may have major, though unquantified, economic consequences (in the form of lost opportunity costs) for mankind. Tropical forest species are very important to man as sources of medications, industrial products, genetic inputs to agriculture, and as subjects of research in all the fields of applied biology. For example, over 40 percent of all prescriptions written in the United States contain one or more drugs of natural origin; TMFs are the earth's principal depository of drug-yielding plants.[24] The recently discovered *Copaifera langsdorfii*, a tree species that grows in the Amazon Basin, yields a sap that can be used directly in diesel engines. A new species of perennial corn *(Zea diploperennis)* with significant potential for boosting worldwide food production was recently discovered growing in a montane forest area of Jalisco, Mexico.[25] In fact, it is estimated that perhaps only about one-sixth of all TMF species have ever been catalogued and given a Latin name by scientists, much less screened for economically useful properties.[26] Therefore, though impossible to quantify accurately, a huge potential exits for TMFs to provide economic benefits for future generations. These benefits, all potentially renewable, may not be realized if tropical deforestation continues unabated.

In some of the more remote TMFs (such as the Amazon Basin, Central Africa, and New Guinea), there are still tribes of indigenous people practicing traditional means of livelihood that have changed little for centuries. Although it is by no means the only disruptive consequence of modernization, tropical deforestation can destroy these people's livelihood by eliminating or altering their habitat. In the Amazon Basin, the population of Indians with traditional lifestyles has declined since 1900 from about 1 million to 100,000. Since these people have accumulated a wealth of knowledge concerning various practical uses of otherwise unknown TMF species, their physical or cultural demise also results in the loss of a great deal of valuable knowledge.[27]

The possible climatic effects of tropical deforestation are both regional and global. On the regional level, it is likely that some TMFs generate much of the local rainfall due to their role in evapotranspiration (vaporization of water by means of evaporation and transpiration from plants). For example, recent studies of the Amazon Basin suggest that the rainforest generates approximately 50 percent of the region's rainfall.[28] Beyond a certain point, deforestation in the Amazon Basin would not only "dry out" the remaining forest; some fear it could set off an irreversible drying trend that could affect all of South America (east of the Andes).[29]

It is also possible that the global climate will be severely affected by TMF loss, due to an increase of atmospheric carbon dioxide (CO_2) levels. It is known that atmospheric CO_2 concentrations are increasing, and that a significant portion of the world's carbon is stored in the wood of TMFs. It is believed that the CO_2 released by the clearing and burning of wood from TMFs may be roughly equivalent to the CO_2 contribution from burning fossil fuels (although neither activity is likely to affect atmospheric oxygen concentrations significantly). The possible consequences of increasing atmospheric CO_2 are varied and extremely speculative. A commonly cited scenario is the "greenhouse effect," where the increased CO_2 produces a global warming trend which could greatly reduce agricultural productivity in, for example, the North American grain belt. Furthermore, such an increase in the earth's mean temperature could melt the Antarctic and Greenland icecaps, thus raising the ocean levels substantially and imperiling such heavily populated coastal areas as New York City and Bangladesh. On the other hand, if the earth is entering a natural long-term cooling trend (for which there is some evidence), the greenhouse effect could be a beneficial compensation. The issue is further complicated by the unknown consequences of the "albedo effect," which is an increase in the amount of solar radiation reflected by the earth. (Forests absorb more sunlight than do deforested areas.)[30] Thus, the climatic effects of tropical deforestation are extremely uncertain, though potentially catastrophic; however, by the time they are conclusively proven, it may be too late to do much about them.

Principal "Losers" from Tropical Deforestation

The harms of tropical deforestation outlined above affect a variety of people in different ways. The affected groups can be rural or urban, rich or poor, living at deforestation sites or downstream from them, residents of tropical or nontropical countries, and members of present or future generations. Moreover, they can be harmed in either an acute or in a diffuse, general manner.

In TMF countries, the persons harmed most acutely by deforestation are usually poor and rural. These include primitive tribal people who are totally dependent upon the forest for their livelihood; peasants living in or near forested areas who need fuel wood, forest foods, and various forest products for homes and cottage industries; farmers (poor or otherwise) who suffer from soil erosion and degraded land at the deforestation site, and from floods and impaired irrigation works downstream; and both inland and coastal fishermen.

The persons affected less acutely by deforestation within TMF countries are often urban and not necessarily poor. They include city dwellers who suffer from impaired electricity and water supplies. Some deforestation affects national economic development prospects in general, but relatively few individuals acutely. Outside of TMF countries, the most acutely affected present-day groups are scientists and tourists interested in TMF flora and fauna (there are also such persons within TMF countries, to varying degrees). Otherwise, the "losers" from tropical deforestation tend to be in the future: residents of both developing and developed countries who could enjoy the medications, industrial products (including timber), and other benefits of TMF species; and all the people who could be adversely affected by deforestation-induced climatic changes.

This breakdown of persons adversely affected by deforestation helps to explain why the process is continuing and (in some countries) accelerating. The most acutely affected contemporary "losers" from tropical deforestation (i.e., the rural poor) tend not to be of primary political significance to national policy makers. In the extreme case, indigenous tribal people are not even part of a cash economy, and often encounter antipathy from government officials and the general public (as in Brazil).[31] Also, a major portion of the costs of severe tropical deforestation will be borne by future generations, who, of course, have no voice in today's policy decisions.

It should also be noted that not all of the harms of tropical deforestation are completely irreversible. Certainly, the losses of TMF species and physical or cultural extinction of tribal people (along with the knowledge of TMF uses which they possess) are completely irreversible. The possible climatic effects are probably irreversible (although they might be mitigated by rapid reforestation). However, if the initial loss of soil is not too great, the watershed services and wood products from TMFs can be restored (totally or partially) through reforestation. The time scale for such a recovery varies by location and type of forest product or environmental service sought. However, reforestation is generally an expensive and risky undertaking with few immediate payoffs, as is discussed below. As such, reforestation of land that was unwisely deforested is a distant "second-best" alternative to preventing deforestation in the first place.

CAUSES OF TROPICAL DEFORESTATION

Slash-and-Burn Agriculture

"Slash-and-burn agriculture" refers to the process, practiced by peasants and some indigenous tribes, of clearing forest lands to grow food (or cash crops on a very small scale). The clearing process involves cutting and then burning the forest (although some logs may be sold locally). Slash-and-burn farming is believed by some to be the most important direct cause of TMF removal.[32] It is an important cause of deforestation in all major TMF regions; it is less significant in those countries where rural populations are small relative to cultivated land area. Some of the countries in which slash-and-burn agriculture is most pronounced are Brazil, Colombia, Indonesia, Kenya, Malagasy Republic, Papua New Guinea, Peru, the Philippines, Thailand, Uganda, Vietnam, and most of the countries of West Africa and Middle America[33] (Mexico and Central America).

Slash-and-burn agriculture has several different forms and types of practitioners. One of these forms, shifting cultivation (known also as "swidden" and by various other names), has been practiced for millennia, often on a sustainable basis, by various TMF-dwelling peoples. The process involves felling and burning a small patch of forest, growing two or three successions of food crops, and then abandoning the depleted soil to repeat the process at a nearby site. It is necessary to move on every few years because most TMF soils are unable to sustain permanent agriculture, particularly of annual crops. This is because, unlike most temperate areas, most of the nutrients in a TMF are in the biomass itself (mostly in the trees), *not* in the soil.[34] After abandonment of a site, secondary vegetation takes hold, ultimately producing a healthy forest again. Thus, if population densities are sufficiently low, the process can be sustained indefinitely. However, in many TMF areas, population densities of these traditional farmers are no longer sufficiently low, in part because modern health practices have lowered mortality, but not natality, among these people. As a result, fallow cycles have become too short, soils are rapidly being exhausted over large areas, and the shifting cultivators are forced to migrate out of the area (often to new areas of TMF, if they are available).

However, traditional shifting cultivation is no longer the main form of slash-and-burn agriculture in most TMF areas. Instead, the forest is now being invaded by large numbers of land-seeking peasants, who practice slash-and-burn agriculture because they lack a satisfactory alternative form of livelihood. These peasants are usually migrants from rural (rather than urban) areas. They often colonize new TMF lands because their present lands can no longer support them due to drought, ecological degradation, or population growth. For example, many of the illegal slash-and-burn cultivators in the Ivory Coast's Tai National Park are immigrants from drought-stricken Mali and Upper Volta to the north.[35]

Because they are not culturally adapted to forest environments, these recent arrivals tend to be much less careful in their treatment of the land than traditional shifting cultivators. Unlike shifting cultivators who clear small patches in the midst of a forest, these immigrant peasants often advance in "pioneer fronts" against the forest edge, leaving behind them a mosaic of degraded croplands and brush growth, where there is no near-term prospect of natural forest regeneration. In Peru, the process has been graphically described as follows:

The populations overflowing from the (Andes) mountains down to the Amazon plains do not settle there, but advance like a slow-burning fire, concentrating along a narrow margin between the land they are destroying and about to leave behind, and the forests lying ahead of them.[36]

Why are so many slash-and-burn peasants now colonizing TMF areas? One important underlying cause is the rapid population growth characteristic of most

TABLE 3
Estimated Annual Population Growth Rates for Major TMF Countries*

Country	Percent Annual Growth
Bolivia	2.5
Brazil	2.4
Burma	2.4
Cameroon	2.3
Colombia	2.1
Congo (People's Republic of)	2.6
Ecuador	3.1
Gabon	1.1
Guyana	2.1
Indonesia	2.0
Malaysia	2.3
Papua New Guinea	2.8
Peru	2.7
Philippines	2.4
Thailand	2.0
Venezuela	3.0
Zaire	2.8

Source: *1981 World Population Data Sheet* (Washington, DC: Population Reference Bureau).
*Countries with 100,000 km² or more of TMF.

TMF countries (See Table 3). Thus stabilizing (rural) population size is important for a long-range solution to the deforestation problem. However, rapid population growth in TMF countries is usually taken as a given for at least several more decades, because these countries' populations have a very high proportion of young people about to enter their child-bearing years. Therefore, efforts to control slash-and-burn agriculture often stress more intensive management of existing cultivated lands, to relieve pressures on fragile TMF areas from populations that are certain to continue growing.

However, population growth alone cannot be blamed for peasant encroachment on TMF lands. The land tenure situation is another critical factor. In many TMF countries, inequitable distribution of existing prime agricultural lands induces peasants to invade agriculturally marginal TMF lands and practice slash-and-burn agriculture. For example, in Guatemala (a country with rapid deforestation), 2.2 percent of the population owns 70 percent of the land suited for permanent agriculture. Meanwhile, 85 percent of Guatemala's rural families either own no land or own too little to support themselves.[37] According to a report by the United Nations Food and Agriculture Organization (FAO), in Latin America, as a whole, 7 percent of the population controlled 93 percent of the arable land in 1975.[38] With good agricultural land unavailable to them, these marginal peasants open up new TMF lands for subsistence cultivation, even though these lands are usually unsuited for this purpose. Some argue that if the agricultural lands already in production in TMF countries were redistributed more equitably, the need for peasants to colonize new forest lands would be greatly reduced.

In addition to uneven access to land, a lack of employment opportunities in nonagricultural sectors compels many persons to colonize TMF lands. A number of conservationists argue that one good way to reduce colonization pressure on TMF lands is to encourage the development of labor-intensive manufacturing and other industries, to generate alternative employment for would-be forest farmers. Therefore, successful strategies of expanding nonagricultural employment in developing countries could help significantly reduce pressures for subsistence farming on TMF lands. In view of this, many conservationists endorse efforts to increase economic growth in developing countries (with the exception of those development activities that encourage deforestation, discussed below). The list of priority actions to promote such non-forest development in the 1980 World Conservation Strategy of the International Union for Conservation of Nature and Natural Resources (IUCN) closely resembles many of the recommendations of the New International Economic Order. The IUCN recommendations include trade liberalization, including the removal of all trade barriers to goods from developing countries; increase of development aid to a minimum of 0.7 percent of each developed country's gross national product; an increase in the proportion of development aid going to the poorest developing countries (with annual per capita incomes under $300); reform of the international monetary system to favor developing countries; and more rapid progress towards disarmament (to siphon fewer funds away from development activities).[39]

Although they represent the lowest income strata of society, slash-and-burn peasants are not able to colonize extensive TMF areas without indirect assistance from wealthy and powerful interests: national governments, development aid agencies, and multinational corporations. The required assistance takes the form of roads, which make entry into TMF areas possible. (River transportation has provided access to some TMF areas for years, but is not now the principal means of access to most sites of TMF colonization.) The mere building of a road into virgin TMF land is usually sufficient to encourage "spontaneous migration" by land-hungry peasants. Even widening or otherwise improving an existing road can have this effect, by providing would-be slash-and-burn farmers with improved access to a market for their surplus produce. Spontaneous colonization along new roads is common in all TMF countries with significant populations of landless rural people.

Aside from merely building penetration roads, national governments and international aid agencies often sponsor integrated settlement projects for TMF areas, providing a wide range of infrastructure and financial incentives for colonists. These resettlement projects are notable for their lack of long-term viability, because the TMF sites settled tend to be agriculturally marginal. A significant number of TMF countries have such large-scale integrated resettlement projects; two of the most notable are Indonesia and Brazil.

The largest integrated resettlement program affecting TMFs is in Indonesia, where the government is presently assisting transmigration from crowded Java (also from Bali, Madura, and Lombok) to the less populated and heavily forested "outer islands," especially Sumatra and Kalimantan (Borneo). The present target is to move 100,000 per year, until 2 million families, or 12-15 million people, have been translocated. [40] The program is intended to entail settlement of between 2 and 10 million hectares, of which a significant proportion is presently forested. However, good-quality agricultural soils of all types on TMF lands are believed to account for less than 5 percent of the presently unoccupied land area of the outer islands. [41] Moreover, government-sponsored transmigration sites are often explicitly not in areas of good soils, because these are usually occupied by local people or by earlier spontaneous migrants. [42] The World Bank is the major international donor assisting this massive scheme; it plans to lend up to $350 million for this purpose during Indonesia's Third Five-Year Plan. [43]

The official reasons given by the Indonesian government and the World Bank for undertaking this enormous project are mostly demographic and economic. The project will help relieve overcrowding on Java to some extent; however, Myers points out that even the most ambitious annual transmigration goals are substantially less than Java's annual population increase of 2.6 million. [44] The economic objectives are to increase domestic food production, relieve poverty (on Java), and develop underutilized land resources. Unfortunately, it is uncertain that these productivity objectives can be achieved in the long run on soils which are unsuited to the types of agriculture planned. Food crop yields on most transmigration sites have already been disappointingly low. [45] Another likely motivation for government support of the program is political in nature: the transmigration program may help to reduce potential political unrest on Java, by offering free land to the poor. Indonesia's junior minister for transmigration affairs has stated:

Transmigration can reduce the possibility of social unrest and political upheaval that might occur in densely populated areas as a consequence of low standards of living and unemployment. [46]

Norman Myers states the point even more succinctly: "People don't riot when you put them in the forest." [47]

Brazil's most ambitious resettlement project was the Transamazonica Highway, a network of primary roads extending for 6,000 kilometers in the Amazon Basin (Amazonia) (with another 6,000 kilometers of feeder roads). A catalyzing event in the decision to build the road may have been the visit of President Emilio Garrastazu Medici to Brazil's impoverished northeast during a major drought in 1970. Shortly afterwards, he ordered construction of the highway (which was absent from previous transportation plans) to open the virgin jungle to land-hungry northeastern peasants. [48] In his words, Amazonia was "a land without men for men without land." [49] The settlement program was soon scaled down to a planned 100,000 colonists per year (roughly one-tenth of the northeast's annual population increase). By 1975, however, only 50,000 colonists had settled (fewer than half of them from the northeast), and many of these left the area within a few years. In 1979, Brazilian officials conceded that the planned settlements were less than 7 percent successful, primarily because of unsuitable soils (although disease also played a role).[50]

Since the disappointments of this resettlement project, Brazilian government officials have become more realistic about Amazonia's limited agricultural potential. However, they are still intent on occupying the area. A major motivation of the military government appears to be a desire to settle Brazil's borders with its Amazon neighbors (eight countries), to help ensure that any future riches found in Amazonia will not provoke territorial disputes. There is considerable mystery concerning Amazonia's potential mineral and other wealth, but many Brazilians view it as a possible way to pay off the country's enormous foreign debt, second largest in the third world.[51] In any event, the failure of the Transamazonica project has not meant an end to large resettlement schemes in Amazonia; the government is presently planning Project Polonoroeste, an integrated colonization project projected to clear nearly 2 million hectares of natural vegetation (largely TMF) in Rondonia and Mato Grosso, along the Bolivian border. However, the area has a higher proportion of agriculturally suitable soils than most of Amazonia.[52]

As is almost always the case with large colonization projects, the Brazilian government received international support, with funds from development aid agencies and construction equipment from multinational corporations. The Transamazonica Highway was backed by a World Bank loan of $400 million. The Belem-Brasilia highway (which opened up another portion of the Amazon TMF) received $4 million via the U.S. Export-Import Bank, while the Caterpillar Corporation sold Brazil $47 million in construction equipment. Similarly, the Santarem-Cuiaba highway was supported by a U.S. Agency for International Development donation of $8.4 million.[53]

Whether they only build a road or also promote colonization more actively, governments of TMF countries enable deforestation to occur by providing immigrant peasants with access to the forest. Resettlement of the poor in TMF areas is politically preferable to land reform or income redistribution, since it does not directly threaten national elites. In addition, it gives citizens the impression of a "positive sum game" of economic growth, rather than a "zero sum game" of redistribution. (To the extent that the deforested land cannot sustain the intended agriculture, the "positive sum" image is an illusory one, of course. But this only becomes evident some years later.) Road and resettlement projects may also increase the central government's control over outlying areas, by connecting them with major cities, by populating them with loyal ethnic groups and by reducing the risk of a territorial dispute with bordering countries.

Government officials can also receive considerable economic benefits from large roads and other public works projects; the bigger the project, the bigger the potential kickbacks from contractors. Another example of the ways in which corruption encourages deforestation via road-building is the Aceh Road project in Sumatra, Indonesia, funded jointly by USAID and the Indonesian government. The road penetrated the Gunung Leuser National Park, thus promoting access to slash-and-burn peasants in one of the most biologically important TMF areas in Indonesia. (Two hundred families have settled illegally in the park since the road was built.)[54] The road will, however, provide improved access to the town of Blangkejeren, located in a major marijuana-growing area. A representative of an international organization has said that such access will enable corrupt government officials to "control" (i.e., have a greater share of the proceeds from) this illegal activity.[55]

Large road and other public works projects also have considerable publicity value for the national government. They arouse nationalistic pride in the citizenry and help impress foreign visitors from multinational corporations and international lending organizations. In addition, government leaders seem to derive satisfaction from "taming the wilderness." These appear to be major motivations behind the environmentally destructive and economically lavish *Conquista del Sur* (Conquest of the South, i.e., the rainforest) program of roads and water projects being promoted in Venezuela.[56] In Brazil, the Amazon rainforest is often called "Green Hell," and the development of Amazonia is referred to as "our moon shot."[57] Especially in the less densely populated TMF countries, the "frontier philosophy" prevails when virgin forest areas are considered.

It is evident that while subsistence slash-and-burn agriculture is practiced by the poor, it is assisted (directly or indirectly) by national governments and other powerful institutions. Unfortunately for TMF conservation and sustainable management efforts, governments are much better at abetting slash-and-burn agriculture than at controlling it. Although in many government-owned TMF areas, clearing a "homestead" is not only lawful but actively promoted, much slash-and-burn activity in TMFs is illegal.

On officially protected public TMF lands, effective removal of illegal slash-and-burn agriculturalists is the exception, not the rule. Dr. William Webb's analysis of the situation in the Philippines helps explain why.[58] First, the *police power* of the forestry department is reluctantly applied by local officers, who know that the slash-and-burn peasant is not evil, but merely trying to make a living. If an arrest is made, the courts are reluctant to impose stiff fines; judicial officials realize that, following any fine or jail sentence, the peasant is likely to resume his former practice, for lack of suitable alternatives. At the political level, little effort is made to compel the police or judicial levels to operate more effectively, because people are less of a short-term political liability when they are living in the forest than when they are unemployed in cities and towns.

A number of other factors are also important. It is politically risky and administratively difficult to enforce the law when there are large numbers of violators, as is often the case with slash-and-burn agriculture. In Thailand, the government is reluctant to enforce laws against cultivation in protected areas in part because the slash-and-burn farmers might thereby be persuaded to join insurgent forces.[59] (On the other hand, the presence of political insurgents can keep multinational timber corporations out of some TMF areas.) There are often inadequate enforcement personnel, equipment, or other administrative infrastructure, because most governments are unwilling to devote scarce financial resources to a problem that is usually perceived as less than acute. In rural areas, low population densities make the marginal efficiency of enforcement resources low in relation to urban areas. There are often problems of access because of factors such as washed-out roads; it is hard to catch people living in the jungle! There are often bureaucratic problems. In Thailand, for example, more than half of the forestry department personnel are stationed in Bangkok, because office jobs offer higher pay and prestige than field work.[60] Finally, there is corruption in most forestry departments.

Myers estimates that at least 140 million people were engaged in slash-and-burn agriculture in TMF areas in the mid-1970s. Although the overall populations in TMF countries will increase 60–65 percent by the year 2000, he estimates that the number of slash-and-burn peasants could more than double, due to lack of alternative employment opportunities and land degradation in non-forested areas.[61] Several of the actions necessary to minimize slash-and-burn deforestation have already been suggested. Efforts should be made to increase nonagricultural employment opportunities, promote land reform and income redistribution, and stabilize population size in TMF countries. Environmentally unsound forest penetration roads and colonization projects should be explicitly discouraged. A special effort should be made to persuade development aid agencies that the high initial costs (typically $5,000 to $20,000 per family settled), deforestation, and frequent lack of long-term viability of many larger-scale colonization projects make them unsound; aid agencies are less dependent upon these projects for their political survival than are TMF government elites.

Technical solutions to slash-and-burn deforestation should also be pursued. The productivity (and employment potential) of existing agricultural lands, outside of forest areas, can be increased. Another approach is to obtain greater productivity from nutrient-poor TMF soils, thus reducing the need for subsistence peasants to move on again every few years. The techniques generally used to stabilize shifting agriculture fall under the rubric of "agroforestry," which can be an ecologically sustainable management system for TMF land that combines agricultural crops, tree crops, and forest plants and/or animals simultaneously or sequentially. Various forms of agroforestry are practiced sustainably by indigenous forest-dwelling cultures, even on impoverished tropical soils. For example, the Lua of northern Thailand grow at least 120 different crops, including seventy-five food crops, twenty-one medicinal crops, twenty plants for ceremonial or decorative purposes, and seven for weaving and dyes—thus achieving a partial mimicry of the diversity of natural forests.[62] This contrasts markedly with efforts by immigrant peasants to grow monocultures of corn, manioc, or upland rice along the Transamazonica highway! It is possible to introduce agroforestry successfully to slash-and-burn peasants; one apparent success story is in eastern Mindanao, Philippines, where a national timber corporation, PICOP, with World Bank assistance, is encouraging peasants to grow fast-growing commercial pulpwood species (sequentially with food crops) on deforested company lands.[63] PICOP agrees to buy all the wood that these farmers grow.[64] The effectiveness of agroforestry projects in reducing slash-and-burn deforestation will depend on the extent of additional site-specific research and the scale and effectiveness of implementation.

Commercial Timber Exploitation

Commercial timber exploitation, primarily for internationally traded species of tropical hardwoods, is a cause of deforestation in most TMF countries, although it is far more important in some countries than others. The main tropical hardwood producers (each with output exceeding 1 million cubic meters per year) are Indonesia, Malaysia, the Philippines, Papua New Guinea, Brazil, Ivory Coast, Colombia, Ecuador, Gabon, Ghana, Nigeria, Costa Rica, Burma, and Thailand.[65] Commercial timber harvesting is most significant as a cause of deforestation in Southeast Asia, which accounts for about three-fourths of international trade in tropical hardwoods. Commercial timber exploitation is believed to be the single greatest cause of deforestation in several countries, including Indonesia.[66] On the other hand, Amazonia and Central Africa have had little of their forest area exploited for tropical hardwoods, largely because they lack well-developed infrastructure and are more distant from seaports. However, the rapid depletion of more accessible TMF regions, along with cheaper harvesting technologies, are likely to make these more remote areas increasingly vulnerable to future exploitation.

The export of tropical hardwoods is a major source of revenue for some TMF countries, though by no means for all of them. For Indonesia (the world's largest exporter), tropical hardwoods provide 30 percent of all foreign exchange earned from non-oil exports. For Burma, tropical hardwoods provide 25 percent of all foreign exchange. Other countries which currently depend on tropical hardwood exports as a major portion of their foreign exchange include Malaysia, People's Republic of the Congo, Liberia, and Ivory Coast.[67] Between 1954 and 1979, global tropical hardwood exports increased in value from $272 million to $4.7 billion. (This represents a growth rate far faster than for the overall international trade in forest products.) Tropical hardwoods have become one of the five most important revenue earners among commodities produced by the developing world, earning about as much foreign exchange as sugar, cotton, or copper.[68]

The final markets for exported tropical hardwoods are Japan (53 percent of the total); Western Europe (32 percent); and the United States (15 percent). Tropical hardwoods consumed in the United States are a luxury good, accounting for less than 2 percent of the volume of wood consumed. They are used chiefly by the mobile home, residential home, boat building, and furniture industries, for such products as decorative interior paneling, mouldings, and other millwork products, boat decking and fixtures, and fine furniture.[69]

There are ready substitutes for tropical hardwood products; for example, decorative paneling can be made from domestically produced softwoods (such as pine or Douglas fir) with a plastic overlay. Alternatively, U.S. species of native hardwoods can be used. However, the attractiveness of tropical hardwood species to consumers and (most importantly) high domestic labor costs in the United States discourage the use of these substitutes.[70] It has been suggested that efforts by U.S. environmentalists to preserve the nation's hardwood forests for recreational and aesthetic purposes have increased the demand for imported tropical hardwoods.[71] However, this argument appears to be without much foundation, since under 3 percent of the country's hardwood stands are on public land that has been withdrawn from logging.[72] Over four-fifths of U.S. imports of tropical hardwoods originate in Southeast Asia, principally Indonesia, Malaysia, and the Philippines. In western Europe, the situation is rather similar: imported tropical hardwoods are primarily used for luxury products similar to those in the United States, although most of western Europe's tropical hardwood consumption is supplied by west Africa, rather than Southeast Asia.[73]

Of developed countries, Japan is by far the most dependent on imported tropical hardwoods. Among Japan's imports, wood now ranks a strong second to oil; the country depends on overseas sources for more than two-thirds of its wood.[74] In Japan, in contrast to Europe and the United States, tropical hardwoods serve more than "luxury" purposes; they are used in a wide variety of wood products, including pulp and paper. For example, one of Japan's sources of pulp is the Gogol Valley of Papua New Guinea, where TMF is clear-felled on a 681 square kilometer logging concession and made into woodchips. The woodchips are then shipped directly to Japan, where they are made into pulp and paper by the Honshu Paper Company.[75]

A former FAO forestry official has said that Japan has the most clearly defined and "rational" long-term forestry strategy of any nation. Japan wants to avoid being heavily dependent on other countries for wood (as it is with OPEC countries for oil), and is therefore building up its domestic timber production capacity. Currently, some 67 percent of Japan's total land area is forested, and roughly half of this amount is in fast-growing softwood plantations. By the year 2000, Japan will be largely self-sufficient in wood products; meanwhile, it is importing wood from Southeast Asia, Papua New Guinea, Australia (northern Queensland), and North America (including southeastern Alaska).[76]

Most TMFs are characterized by a very high diversity of tree species, of which relatively few have high commercial value. These valuable species (with trade names like teak, mahogany, rosewood, and meranti) constitute the bulk of the international trade. For example, in west Africa about ten tree species (out of more than 300) account for over 70 percent of total exports.[77] Thus, commercial logging usually employs selective cutting techniques rather than clear cutting (except for such products as woodchips, as noted above). If only the commercially desired species were affected, the result would be only a modification of the original TMF ecosystem, rather than its destruction or gross degradation. Unfortunately, modern selective logging techniques often damage much of the remaining forest beyond (near-term) recovery, far more often than is the case in temperate forests. One reason for this difference is that lianas ("Tarzan vines") and other climbing plants connect each TMF tree with others. Thus, when one TMF tree is felled, it tends to break or pull down several others with it. Moreover, the heavy machinery usually used in TMF logging inadvertantly breaks limbs and scrapes bark off many "unwanted" TMF species; such injuries are often fatal to these trees, which are highly susceptible to attack by pathogens. In addition, this machinery often compacts or scrapes off the thin TMF soil, thereby preventing forest regeneration.

If careful logging techniques were employed, some estimates indicate that the damage to the residual forest could be cut in half.[78] Examples of such techniques are to replace some of the heavy machinery with manual labor or elephants (still widely used in Burma), and to sever the attached lianas prior to felling a tree. According to studies in Sabah, Malaysia, severing of lianas prior to selective cutting could reduce logging damage by 20 percent, at a very reasonable cost of $2 per tree (or $0.25 added to the price of each cubic meter of exported logs).[79] Indonesia has recently imposed a system of charging timber concessionaires $4 for each non-marketed tree destroyed or damaged by careless logging practices.[80] (The effectiveness of this system remains to be seen.) In most other TMF countries, the incentives are presently lacking for logging companies to use any forest-conserving techniques, regardless of their cost.

TMF logging also promotes deforestation through the construction of logging roads, which provide access to new lands for slash-and-burn agriculturalists, who complete the deforestation process. This synergism complicates efforts to estimate the amount of TMF area that is deforested as a specific consequence of commercial logging. While logging companies often seek to remove slash-and-burn peasants from unlogged areas with valuable timber species, they have little incentive to do so in cut-over areas.

The ecological difficulties associated with sustained yield harvesting of tropical hardwoods also encourage deforestation. Even when care is taken during selective cutting not to damage the residual forest, a successive harvest of desired hardwood species is by no means assured within what many TMF countries perceive as a reasonable time frame. The viability of natural regeneration forestry as a TMF management scheme is the subject of great controversy among tropical ecologists and foresters. Some scientists argue that TMFs, at least in many areas, are fragile ecosystems that cannot withstand the type and scale of disturbance associated with commercial utilization.[81] Others believe that natural regeneration forestry has great potential for the sustained-yield production of tropical hardwoods, but that more research is needed.[82] It is known that tropical hardwoods in natural forests grow quite slowly. The time scale for complete regeneration varies greatly by location and species, but can be on the order of 100 years or more.[83] Notwithstanding these uncertainties, natural regeneration forestry offers great hope as a sustainable economic use of TMFs that preserves much of their natural diversity. In Sarawak, Malaysia, a form of natural regeneration forestry, featuring "liberation thinning" and other silvicultural techniques, apparently can renew tropical hardwoods on a forty-five-year rotation basis, while still providing good wildlife habitat.[84] However (as is noted below), most commercially valuable TMF areas around the world are logged far more rapidly than even a forty-five-year rotation period would permit.

Natural regeneration forestry can also involve the harvesting of "secondary species" (those species that lack high value on international markets). Their highly heterogenous composition reduces their commercial attractiveness. However, new processing technologies are making profitable the clear cutting of secondary species for wood chips or fuel wood pellets.[85] The effect of such "full-forest harvesting" on future TMF conservation prospects is unclear. Such harvesting does reduce the massive waste of wood that now occurs (largely through burning), thereby presumably reducing the pressure to exploit virgin forests for pulp and similar commodities. Also, since many secondary species grow faster than highly valuable tropical hardwoods, there exists a potential for sustainable natural regeneration forestry with more frequent harvests than are possible with most highly valued (but slow-growing) tropical hardwoods. On the other hand, these new technologies make profitable the clear cutting of TMF areas hitherto considered unprofitable for harvesting, because of low stocking densities of highly valued hardwoods. For these reasons, the development and use of full forest harvesting technologies will be viewed with great interest by forestry officials, timber industry representatives, conservationists, and other interested parties.

In lieu of natural regeneration forestry, tropical hardwood plantations can be implemented in cut-over TMF areas. When grown in monoculture or intensively managed polyculture plantations, tropical hardwoods reach harvestable size sooner and grow in much greater densities than under natural regeneration. However, such plantations are presently pursued on a very small scale: *Triplochoton* is grown in the Ivory Coast, *Terminalia* in the People's Republic of the Congo, *Okoume* in Gabon, *Maesopsis* in Uganda, and true teak *(Tectona grandis)* in Burma, India, and Java.[86] The very limited (often experimental) scale of these plantations, relative to the TMF area being logged, is due to a number of factors. Because tropical hardwoods are primarily a luxury product, there is some uncertainty about future demand. Possible changes in consumer tastes or declining relative prices of substitutes could greatly alter today's demand patterns. Even more important are the ecological and economic problems associated with plantation forestry; these are much greater in the tropics than in most temperate regions. Most TMF soils have poor structure and low fertility. Even fertilizer applications, when economically feasible, often have unsatisfactory results. Problems with insect pests and plant diseases that threaten all monoculture plantations are especially pronounced in the tropics: the variety of potential pests and diseases is much greater, and there is no winter season to disrupt their proliferation. Moreover, plantations are very expensive, they are initially very labor-intensive, require continual care, and have a relatively long-term payback period.[87] It is therefore not surprising that most timber companies and TMF governments prefer the immediate and lucrative benefits of logging natural TMF to the uncertain rewards of investing in a second crop of tropical hardwoods.

Replacement of cut-over TMF with plantations of fast-growing tree species for "general purpose" industrial wood (such as poles, construction lumber and plywood, and pulp and paper), and for fuel wood, is adopted more frequently than hardwood plantations. The trees most often planted are various species of pine, Eucalyptus, and "melina" *(Gmelina arborea)*. These plantations are susceptible to more or less the same ecological problems as tropical hardwood plantations. They also require heavy initial expenditures. However, the payback period is shorter (typically five to fifteen years). Moreover, there is little doubt about future demand for the product. The spread of literacy is causing a rapid increase in demand for paper in developing countries; for example, by the year 2000, Southeast Asia is expected to require five times as much paper as in 1974.[88] Rapid increases in population and urbanization are resulting in accelerating demand for construction lumber and other wood products. Moreover, demand for general-purpose industrial wood in developed countries continues to grow, albeit at a slower rate. According to FAO projections, worldwide consumption of wood for all purposes will grow from 2.5 billion cubic meters in 1967 to 4 billion cubic meters in 1994.[89]

Although plantations of fast-growing species in TMF countries greatly outnumber tropical hardwood plantations, they are still a minor form of land use for cut-over TMF areas. In fact, Spears says that most TMF countries meet their domestic demands for industrial wood through imports, and are likely to continue doing so for at least two decades. He estimates that the only TMF countries likely to have a significant surplus of plantation-grown wood (over 1 million cubic meters per year) for export by 1990 are Brazil (which has most of its plantations outside of TMF areas), Kenya, Madagascar, and Fiji.[90] The principal reasons why reforestation of cut-over TMF areas with fast-growing plantations species has been so limited are the ecological limitations noted above (many plantations have failed for this reason), high initial costs, a long payback period relative to most other investments, and a lack of domestic processing facilities.

Although the replacement of TMF areas with plantations (tropical or otherwise) is commonly called "reforestation," the resulting man-made forest does not provide many of the environmental services of natural TMFs. The watershed and climate stabilization functions of TMFs are also served by plantations (albeit usually to a lesser extent, since the trees are smaller). However, the fuel wood, forest foods, and other forest products used by local people (indigenous tribes or otherwise) are usually not provided by industrial plantations. (Frequently, plantation managers hire guards to keep local people out.) Moreover, man-made plantations have little biological diversity compared to natural TMFs. This is understandable, since reforesting cut-off TMFs means replacing the most biologically diverse ecosystems on earth with very simple ones, where usually only one species is encouraged. However, plantations are seen by many conservationists as a means of meeting national demand for fiber, providing foreign exchange (if the wood is exported), and providing local employment (often to would-be slash-and-burn agriculturalists). Therefore, these plantations can reduce some of the pressures on existing TMFs (although they cannot replace, at least in the near term, the revenues obtained from logging tropical hardwoods in natural TMFs).

Unfortunately, most plantation projects in TMF areas begin by clearing the primary forest, rather than reforesting degraded land. (These plantations are often financed by development aid agencies.) There are several reasons for this pattern. First, degraded land is more difficult to work with in silvicultural terms because of soil fertility losses and erosion. Second, the commercially valuable tropical hardwoods present in a primary TMF help to meet the initial costs of the plantation. Third, deforested or degraded land is more likely to be occupied by peasants, who are expensive to relocate (in both economic and political terms).[91] The result is that, instead of reducing deforestation pressures on natural TMFs, industrial wood plantations often increase it.

An interesting example of a huge and unsuccessful industrial wood plantation is the billion-dollar pulpwood investment along the Jari River in Amazonian Brazil. Conceived and originally owned by U.S. billionaire Daniel Ludwig, the Jari project covers an area roughly the size of Holland and may be the largest project ever undertaken by a private citizen without recourse to capital markets. Although the project features some kaolin mining, wet rice cultivation, and cattle grazing, the principal component is growing monocultures of melina and Caribbean pine for pulpwood. The project has its own pulp mill, built in Japan and floated by barge to its present site. Without any prior selective harvesting, virgin TMF is cut and then burned in the dry season to make room for the plantations. The project's annual forest-clearing fires are large enough to create their own thunderstorms.[92]

The Jari project is proof that industrial wood plantations in the humid tropics need more than economies of scale to be successful. Ludwig finally decided to sell his project, which has been unable to recover even its annual operating costs, much less the huge initial investment. A major reason for the economic failure is the disappointingly low melina yield, owing to the region's characteristically poor tropical soils. There have also been huge cost overruns, because the Brazilian government has refused to finance any of the infrastructure (such as roads, schools, and police) needed to support Jari's 9,500 employees.[93] Nonetheless, in ecological terms, this pulpwood project has fared better than many in the humid tropics; most of the Jari plantations have not been devastated by insects or disease, and the soils have permitted at least some successful harvests.

Owing to lucrative foreign exchange revenues from tropical hardwood exports on the one hand and the uncertainties and long-term payoff associated with natural regeneration forestry (or even plantations) on the other, TMF country governments are inclined to liquidate their "forest capital" on a one-shot basis. Thus, TMFs are "mined" unsustainably, rather than treated as a renewable resource. This attitude towards TMFs was aptly expressed by Fiji's "Conservator of Forests," A. K. Oram, in 1971:

The balance of advantage would appear to be strongly in favor of felling and selling as much timber as possible. If it were possible to do so efficiently, it is arguable that it would be desirable to fell all of the natural timber over, say, the next five years.[94]

The desire of TMF country governments for short-term revenues (which imply increased foreign exchange, economic growth, and, hence, political survival) is not the only reason for the rapid felling of tropical hardwoods. Corruption among government officials is also important. Corruption results in the logging of officially protected TMF areas (such as watershed forests and nature preserves). Corruption means that regulations intended to minimize damage to the remaining trees under selective logging are often ignored. It also means that slash-and-burn peasants can, through bribes, obtain access to areas from which they are supposedly excluded.

The incentives for corruption are great. Corruption is a form of "bureaucratic capitalism," in which government officials can translate their political power into wealth. It can also help keep government officials in power; a lucrative timber concession is a convenient way to co-opt would-be political troublemakers. It also often represents a continuation of traditional, particularistic patterns of behavior in developing countries where official legal institutions are still relatively unimportant. The importance of corruption in accelerating deforestation rates can be seen in Indonesia, the world's largest exporter of tropical hardwoods. According to FAO forestry officials, the amount of unrecorded (illegal) sales of Indonesian hardwoods each year approximately equals the recorded sales.[95]

In addition to meeting the private financial goals of government officials, tropical hardwoods exploitation, legal and otherwise, benefits logging companies handsomely. For example, Myers reports that one foreign logging company in Indonesia earned more than a 25 percent return on its entire initial investment in one year.[96] Both multinational corporations (MNCs) and wholly owned national enterprises are active in logging tropical hardwoods. However, the former (often in joint ventures with national companies) are relatively more important, because they are the primary source of the capital needed for TMF logging. The MNCs active in Southeast Asia are largely from Japan, Singapore, South Korea, Taiwan, the Philippines, and the United States. Western European companies are particularly important in West Africa.

Around the world, MNCs and other corporations tend to approach TMF logging with a "cut and run" attitude. The incentives promoting this approach include uncertain political stability in most TMF countries (hence, the risk of future expropriation), uncertainty about future markets for luxury tropical hardwoods, and "the time value of money" (which implies that revenues from unrenewed tropical hardwoods are worth more now than in the future). At times, government officials, eager for foreign exchange or illegal personal gain, can pressure logging companies to cut TMF faster than they would otherwise. This was the case with one MNC in a Southeast Asian country.[97] Also, competition among logging companies for the limited TMF resource encourages rapid and ecologically unsound cutting practices. One source familiar with the Weyerhaeuser Corporation has said that company officials might not oppose "reasonable" environmental standards, if all of their competitors were also forced to comply.[98] Interestingly, out of roughly 450 national and multinational companies operating in Indonesia, Weyerhaeuser is apparently the only one that has undertaken any reforestation efforts (this has been with fast-growing species, on a relatively modest scale.)[99]

It is clear that prevailing political and economic incentives strongly favor rapid logging of tropical hardwoods for short-term gain. A decision to forgo a significant portion of the potential short-term revenues from logging tropical hardwoods in order to preserve future options requires a greater degree of political will than most TMF country government leaders have been able to muster. Still, several measures might help maximize the revenue obtained from the forest that is cut. If a desired amount of foreign exchange can be provided from a smaller area of forest cut, it can be argued that, at least at the margin, the pressure on the remaining TMFs will be somewhat reduced. (This is notwithstanding corruption and the legitimate desire among government leaders to seek ever greater revenues.) The more revenues available from the forest industry, the easier it will be for any *relatively* farsighted government leader to withdraw some forest land from short-term logging.

Two means that are commonly suggested for maximizing tropical hardwood revenues for TMF countries are an OPEC-style cartel and increased domestic processing. The idea of a cartel to raise tropical hardwood prices has been discussed informally at meetings held under the auspices of the United Nations Conference on Trade and Development (UNCTAD).[100] A cartel arrangement can appear feasible if one considers that the export of tropical hardwoods is dominated by a handful of countries. (Almost 80 percent of all exports come from Indonesia, Malaysia, and the Philippines). However, there are major barriers to initiating an effective cartel. As noted above, substitutes for tropical hardwood products are readily available. Also, tropical hardwoods are not a homogeneous product; the commercial qualities of different species vary greatly. Moreover, even if an effective cartel were implemented, the effects on TMF conservation are uncertain. The higher prices resulting from a cartel would increase revenues per area of forest cut, but they could also stimulate logging in more remote areas previously considered unprofitable (especially in Amazonia and Central Africa).

Increasing domestic processing appears to be a more promising approach. Presently, much of the timber exported from TMF countries still takes the form of unprocessed logs. An estimated 92 percent of the volume of Indonesian timber exported in 1980 was in raw logs.[101] Most of the processing was done in Japan, Taiwan, South Korea, and Singapore.[102] Since the value of a log exported raw often more than triples when it is processed into sawed lumber, plywood, or veneer, by not processing most of its timber, Indonesia forfeited a sizable potential increase in foreign exchange.

Realizing the potential revenue gains, a number of TMF countries have enacted policies designed to increase local processing. The most significant case is in Indonesia, where the May 1981 Triministerial Decree severely restricted the export of raw logs, thereby mandating local processing. (Since domestic processing facilities are still limited, the result has been a significant decrease in logging.)[103] This decision was made despite such obstacles as protective tariffs applied by countries like Japan to processed wood (but not raw logs) and the fact that local processing facilities sometimes need a minimum fifteen to thirty years guaranteed supply of timber to justify the investment, whereas rapid deforestation is making such assured supplies unlikely in many areas.

In addition to increasing the revenues per TMF area cut, this encouraging increase in domestic processing can reduce deforestation pressures in other ways. By providing local employment near forested areas, it offers an alternative to subsistence slash-and-burn cultivation. It also increases the public perception of TMFs as a valuable long-term resource. The presence of processing facilities also encourages long-term forestry management to ensure a permanent wood supply, either through plantations or natural regeneration forestry Finally, the presence of local processing facilities could reduce the waste of wood from logged-over areas. By investing further in processing facilities in TMF countries, MNCs and development aid agencies might help to replace the wasteful "creaming" of TMFs for log exports with a more efficient and even more lucrative form of forest utilization.

However, the hope of countries like Indonesia to increase revenues and use their timber supplies more slowly by doing more of their own processing is not easily accomplished. Despite lower labor costs, timber processing is currently often more expensive in TMF countries because of higher costs for infrastructure; purchase, installation, and maintenance of imported equipment; wages of overseas management experts; and other inputs. In addition, multinational countries may simply decide to do more business with countries without local processing requirements. Thus, one of the side effects of Indonesia's decision has been to increase the interest of MNCs in logging neighboring Papua New Guinea, which does not yet require local processing.[104]

Cattle Raising

The raising of beef cattle on pastures created from cleared rainforest lands is an important cause of TMF loss, mainly in Latin America and the Caribbean. In Amazonian Brazil and much of Central America, it is the single greatest cause of deforestation.[105]

Cattle ranching in TMF areas involves a thorough removal of the original vegetation, after which various species of grass (usually of African origin) are planted. A number of methods are used to clear the forest. One system, especially common in Middle America, is for the cattle rancher to take over lands held by slash-and-burn agriculturalists. This takeover comes about either through purchase or coercion. The typical pattern is described succinctly by geographer James Parsons:

After one or two crops of maize, rice, or yuca are harvested from the forest clearing, declining soil fertility, invasive weeds, and noxious insects combine to force the colonist to sell out to a second wave of settlers or speculators who follow behind, consolidating small holdings into larger ones for the exclusive purpose of raising beef cattle.[106]

As James Nations points out, the three primary causes of TMF destruction often operate in tandem in Latin America: logging companies bulldoze roads through TMFs to extract a few species of valuable hardwoods, landless peasants use these roads to colonize the area and grow subsistence or cash crops, and cattle ranchers often follow.[107]

Consequently, cattle ranchers use slash-and-burn peasants as inexpensive (or free) labor for clearing their TMF lands. An example of this phenomenon recently took place in the lowlands of Chiapas, Mexico, where cattlemen acquired legal title to large tracts of virgin TMF. In a temporarily surprising move, the ranchers encouraged peasants to settle on this land and apply to the government for *ejido* (communal land) status. After the peasants had cleared the land, but before they had received legal title, the ranchers expelled them and turned the land over to beef cattle production. The evicted families were thereby forced to move further into the forest and clear more land for subsistence.[108]

It is important to note that, when using this land-clearing strategy, cattle ranchers are not merely the opportunistic beneficiaries of deforestation by slash-and-burn peasants; rather, the ranchers are often the most important driving force of deforestation. By converting slash-and-burn agricultural plots to pasture, they preclude future reuse of these lands through shifting cultivation. Therefore (as in the Chiapas example), they speed up the clearing of new lands. Furthermore, cattle ranchers often take over smallholder farms on lands that are capable of supporting permanent agriculture. In Costa Rica, many such small farmers who have been driven off their lands have taken up subsistence slash-and-burn agriculture in the forested Talamanca Mountains, Osa Peninsula, San Carlos, and Limon areas, while others have migrated to urban slums.[109]

While taking over previously cleared TMF lands is effective for ranchers in areas with large peasant populations, other methods are used in such sparsely settled areas as Amazonia. In Brazil, large-scale cattle ranchers often clear their newly purchased TMF tracts first by "chaining." This process uses two large tractors to topple trees by pulling a heavy 100-meter chain between them. Once the forest has been bulldozed or chained, it is burned to prepare the land for the planting of pasture grasses.

Unfortunately, cattle pastures created by clearing TMF are difficult to sustain, due to soil erosion, compaction by cattle hooves, nutrient depletion, and the inevitable invasion by persistent weeds (some poisonous to cattle) that soon outcompete the pasture grasses.[110] As a result, the pastures tend to be productive for only about six to ten years.[111] Thereafter, the ranchers clear more TMF land, thus practicing a very large-scale form of "shifting cultivation."

Prevailing economic incentives perpetuate these wasteful practices. TMF lands are very cheap to purchase (Daniel Ludwig paid $.75 per acre for his Jari property).[112] SUDAM, Brazil's federal agency which promotes Amazonian development, even granted generous tax incentives for forest clearing. Labor costs are also very low, because little labor is used. In Amazonian Brazil, estimates indicate that only one job is created for each $63,000 invested in cattle ranches; this is the lowest employment/expenditure ratio of virtually any type of development project.[113]

In addition to low investment costs, the immense profitability of cattle ranching on TMF lands is due to the heavy international demand for beef. In Central America, deforestation for cattle pastures can be linked to beef consumption in the United States. For example, James D. Nations says Costa Rica annually exports between one-half and two-thirds of its annual beef production, principally to the United States.[114] Ironically, the high beef prices offered by U.S. importers are causing per capita beef consumption in Central America to drop.

For example, between 1959 and 1972, beef production in Costa Rica doubled, but annual per capita beef consumption fell from twelve kilograms to less than nine. Similar decreases in domestic per capita beef consumption have occurred in Guatemala, Nicaragua, Mexico, and El Salvador.[115]

In the United States, beef imports have risen by 137 percent in the last twenty years. Probably the most important factors in this increase have been the growth in demand for convenience foods and the rapid proliferation of fast-food restaurants (which grew at an annual rate of 25 percent in the mid-1970s). In 1979, 10 percent of all beef consumed in the United States was imported. Most of this imported beef came from Australia and New Zealand (where it is usually not produced at the expense of forests). However, 17 percent of U.S. beef imports came from tropical Latin America (mostly from Central America). Thus, while U.S. beef consumption is the greatest impetus for tropical deforestation in Central America, less than 2 percent of the beef consumed in the United States comes from this region.[116]

A growing proportion of cattle ranching in TMF areas (particularly in Amazonia) is carried out by MNCs. In Brazil, Volkswagen outdistances other foreign cattle investments at $35 million. Another huge operation belongs to a Brescan-Swift-Armour-King Ranch consortium, which owns 720 square kilometers of Amazonian Brazil. Other MNCs directly involved in Amazonian cattle ranching include many from the United States and Japan, Liquigas from Italy, and George Markhov from Austria.[117] In addition, many MNCs promote cattle ranching on TMF lands, even if they are not directly involved. For example, the Latin American Agribusiness Development Corporation (LAAD), incorporated in Panama, was created in 1970 with investments from over a dozen U.S.-based MNCs, including Bank of America, Cargill, Caterpillar Tractor, Ralston Purina, and Goodyear. LAAD provides loans to a variety of private agribusiness enterprises in Latin America, including beef production operations in Belize and Panama.[118]

Nonetheless, the great majority of cattle raising on TMF lands is carried out by domestic entrepreneurs. In Amazonian Brazil, most of the ranches have wealthy absentee owners. In most of Central America, this is also the case. For example, in Costa Rica, the beef ranching industry is dominated by upper-class citizens, many of whom retire to their ranches on weekends to ride horses. In Latin America, owning land and cattle fosters both social standing and political power.[119] In the words of one Costa Rican resident:

Cattle raising is part of the country's Spanish heritage. You're a man if you raise cows. You have prestige. You can put on a cowboy hat and ride around your ranch in a Range Rover. A man who raises corn cannot be proud in the same way. Prestige is more important than money.[120]

The political power of Costa Rica's cattle ranching elites is suggested by the text of former President Rodrigo Carazo's Plan of Action for Renewable Natural

Resources.[121] Although the statement primarily addresses deforestation and the resulting soil erosion, it scarcely mentions cattle raising, which is the dominant cause of TMF elimination in the country.[122] Although Costa Rica is renowned for its conservationist policies with regard to TMFs and other ecosystems, its ambassador to the United States habitually lobbies in Washington for higher beef import quotas.[123]

No discussion of cattle ranching projects in TMF areas would be complete without an account of development aid agencies. Foremost is the World Bank, which has provided loans (amounting to hundreds of millions of dollars) for livestock (principally beef cattle) production in Bolivia, Brazil, Colombia, Ecuador, Guyana, Peru, and every country in Middle America except El Salvador. Another important lender is the Inter-American Development Bank (IDB) which has also provided loans for livestock (largely cattle) development in a majority of TMF countries in Latin America. In addition, USAID indirectly assists cattle ranching in TMF areas by funding programs for eradicating such native cattle pests as screwworms, ticks, and vampire bats.

Some claim the United States should limit the import market for beef raised in TMF areas to reduce the degree of deforestation resulting from cattle raising for export. Since the United States provides such an important market, they say, this could reduce deforestation pressures significantly in tropical Latin America.[124] If such a ban were enacted, beef consumption in Central America would increase, though probably not enough to offset the loss of production for the U.S. market, because U.S. importers offer higher prices than most Central American residents can afford (as noted above). Similarly, other current importing nations would probably not make up the full difference. Japan obtains most of its beef from Australia and New Zealand, while western Europe imports only 7.8 percent of the beef it consumes, mostly from Canada and Oceania. Were a U.S. ban enacted for beef imports from tropical Latin America, Shane argues that higher transportation costs and the high beef import tariffs currently imposed by European nations would probably make beef production in tropical Latin America less profitable than at present.[125] The U.S. government has yet to consider seriously imposing such import restrictions. Interestingly, the principal interest group behind reducing beef imports thus far has not been an environmental organization, but rather the National Cattlemen's Association, which seeks economic protection from beef imports. Its efforts have not been enough to ban imports; only to have quotas set for each country from which the United States imports beef.[126]

An alternative approach to reducing deforestation is to increase the productivity of existing pastures, through improved range management and animal husbandry techniques. Beef cattle could be raised more intensively, like dairy cattle, which are raised in, for example, Costa Rica without promoting deforestation (because they are kept on small, carefully managed plots and have food brought to them).[127] However, such techniques will not be adopted until TMF land ceases to be so cheap. The most important policy levers in TMF countries for encouraging less wasteful pasture utilization (and deforestation) therefore appear to be land use taxation and regulation. However, TMF country governments will not impose disincentives for pasture expansion unless they perceive the costs of deforestation to exceed the economic benefits (including foreign exchange) of beef production, and unless they can overcome the influence of powerful cattle ranching interests. If TMF country governments were to enact disincentives for pasture expansion, their efforts would certainly be more successful if livestock development loans from aid agencies and private institutions were to become less readily available, and if the overseas market for beef could be dampened.

Fuel Wood Gathering

Some 80 percent of all wood consumed in tropical countries is used as fuel (firewood and charcoal), largely to meet household cooking needs.[128] Fuel wood is also used for heating (in the high-altitude tropics), drying fish and agricultural produce, and a variety of small industries. The demand for fuel wood in developing countries is growing faster than population, because rising petroleum prices are making kerosene, a common substitute, unaffordable for many persons. Nonetheless, fuel wood gathering is a relatively minor factor in the global disappearance of TMFs[129] because these forests have a high density of wood per unit area, and because many residents of TMF areas meet their needs with firewood from home gardens. Fuel wood gathering is much more important in the ecological degradation or outright elimination of dry forest areas, such as in the Sahel, where wood grows more slowly. (Mangroves also suffer heavy depredations, because mangrove charcoal burns exceptionally well.)

While fuel wood cutting accounts for a small proportion of global TMF loss, it is nonetheless an important cause of deforestation in select TMF areas. These areas include high-elevation TMFs (such as in the high Andes, where wood grows slowly) or TMF areas with high population densities.

Although the use of firewood in rural areas is of major importance, growing urbanization in TMF countries has increased the relative importance of charcoal (which is much less bulky to transport than firewood). Thus, TMF cutting for charcoal production is a booming industry near many urban centers. For example, near timberline in Costa Rica's Talamanca Mountains along the Pan American Highway, small-scale operators clear cut primary forest (often on very steep, erodable slopes), produce charcoal at the same site, and transport it by truck to San Jose. This entire operation is carried out illegally on forest reserve land, but the government makes little or no effort to stop it,[130] due apparently to a lack of political will.

The elimination of TMF for fuel wood is especially unfortunate in view of the much larger volumes of TMF wood that are wasted in logging operations or burned for land clearance. With the development of advanced wood processing technologies (such as "fuel wood pellets") and increasing commercialization of fuel wood cutting, there is some hope that future fuel wood demands will be met from the utilization of "waste wood," rather than the cutting of primary forest. However, the proper economic incentives will have to emerge (or be created through governmental intervention), before such increased efficiency of wood utilization can occur.

Commercial Agriculture

Commercial agriculture, of rubber, bananas, palm oil, coffee, cocoa, or other cash crops, is widespread in TMF countries. However, such crops require relatively good soils, which represent only a fraction of the soils that support existing TMF stands. (The size of this fraction is disputed.) For this reason, as well as a variety of marketing constraints,[131] comparatively little TMF has been eliminated in recent years for this purpose. However, growing such cash crops on good soils can imply indirectly forcing slash-and-burn peasants to clear TMFs on marginal soils.

Although clearing of TMFs for commercial agriculture (excluding livestock) accounts for relatively little deforestation on a global scale, it is a very important cause of TMF loss in some areas with good soils. The coastal wet forests of Ecuador have been largely replaced with banana and palm oil cultivation in less than a decade.[132] In peninsular Malaysia, agriculture, primarily rubber and palm oil plantations, is intended to replace 35 percent of the original forest cover. The federal government justifies this measure on the grounds that commercial agriculture provides far more employment than forestry (currently, 1 million jobs versus 30,000).[133] Plantations of palm oil and other commercial crops have also converted sizable tracts of TMF in West Africa.

Additional Deforestation Causes

A number of other factors are locally important in TMF destruction, but are not major deforestation causes on a global scale. *Large dams* inundate many TMF areas, including such biologically unique ones as has been proposed in India's Silent Valley.[134] At the same time, the presence of a reservoir is a major reason for protecting the surrounding watershed forests to prevent siltation. *Mining* projects can deforest unique TMF areas. For example, Mount Nimba, at the junction of Liberia, Ivory Coast, and Guinea, contains over 200 animal species found nowhere else, as well as high-grade iron ore deposits.[135] Modern *warfare* can also eliminate or degrade TMFs; in Vietnam, aerial defoliation by the U.S. military destroyed or damaged between 20,000 and 50,000 square kilometers of TMF.[136]

Principal beneficiaries of tropical deforestation

As the above discussion demonstrates, tropical deforestation does not occur in the absence of major economic and political incentives. The elimination of TMFs has a diverse set of beneficiaries, who can be rural or urban, individuals or institutions, and domestic or foreign.

Perhaps foremost among the beneficiaries of deforestation are TMF country government leaders for whom deforestation serves as a short-term "safety valve" that alleviates political pressures resulting from an unwillingness or inability to confront major economic and political problems effectively. Rather than promote effective land reform, population control, and a sufficient expansion of modern-sector employment, governments can allow growing numbers of otherwise unemployed peasants to practice slash-and-burn agriculture in TMF areas. Rather than meet the political demands of the poor, governments can disperse them to TMF areas by using resettlement projects. If they are unable to achieve sufficient economic growth by other means, governments can generate needed foreign exchange by promoting unsustainable logging or cattle ranching. If they have trouble controlling the economies or politics of remote areas, governments can build forest-penetrating roads and populate these areas with loyalists. Thus, deforestation helps to keep government officials in power (and increases their personal wealth if they are corrupt). By acting as a "safety valve," deforestation also delays the implementation of needed economic adaptations and political reforms. Such changes will be necessary in the future, because the deforestation safety valve will surely not last any longer than the forests.

Although low-income fuel wood cutters and slash-and-burn peasants are short-term beneficiaries of deforestation to the extent that they have a temporary livelihood, their destruction of the resource base that sustains them will force them to seek alternative employment in the future. The more unambiguous beneficiaries of deforestation are from higher-income groups. They include all persons that stand to lose from any of the policies that are alternatives to continued deforestation (most notably, land reform). They include the shareholders of MNCs and national firms, which earn high profits from short-term liquidation of the forest resource, as well as such wealthy private individuals as cattle ranchers. They also include affluent consumers, particularly in developed countries, who consume such products as hamburgers and elegant wood paneling. Of course, the varied costs of deforestation are "externalities," not included in the prices of these products. Under prevailing political and economic incentives, these costs are shifted to the present-day "losers" from tropical deforestation and to future generations.

EFFORTS FOR CONSERVATION AND IMPROVED MANAGEMENT OF TMFS

Despite the powerful economic and political forces that promote deforestation, an encouraging number of actions have been taken in recent years to promote more ecologically sound and sustainable TMF uses. The most important actors in TMF conservation and improved management efforts have been TMF country governments and development aid agencies. Their actions have been influenced markedly by other actors: a variety of UN and other international organizations, nongovernmental organizations, scientists, the media, and even elements of the general public.

Before examining efforts at controlling TMF destruction, it is important to note that a handful of TMF countries are experiencing very light or negligible deforestation pressures, even in the absence of concerted conservation efforts. These countries are listed in Table 4. The size (and hence total TMF area) and *per capita* gross national product (roughly reflecting the level of overall development) of these countries vary widely. However, as shown in Table 4, all of these countries (except oil-rich Brunei) have very low population densities; therefore, there is relatively little destructive slash-and-burn pressure on TMF lands. Furthermore, in all of these countries commercial harvesting of timber or agricultural products on TMF lands is relatively light. This can be due to the relative inaccessibility of major TMF tracts (as in Central African Republic, Congo, French Guiana, Guyana, Suriname, and Zaire), or to the abundance of alternative sources of foreign exchange. (Gabon has extensive uranium and manganese deposits; Brunei has substantial oil reserves that provide tax revenues well in excess of government expenditures.[137])

In all of the world's other TMF countries, however, deforestation pressures are significant, although (as noted above) they range from moderate to extreme. Hence, the option of mere "benign neglect" of a country's TMFs usually does not exist, and conservation policies become necessary to prevent unwise deforestation. The degree of governmental "conservation consciousness" with respect to TMFs varies greatly among countries. It is very difficult to rank governments according to their concern for TMF conservation. However, in virtually every TMF country, deforestation (if serious) has aroused some concern among government officials. (The oft-repeated contention that conservation is not a concern in developing countries is simply not true.) On the other hand, in no TMF country has the government's commitment to conservation been sufficient to solve the deforestation problem (if one initially existed).

Governmental Initiatives

Most notably in the past five years, TMF country governments have taken a variety of actions to combat deforestation. These measures include the estab-

TABLE 4
TMF Countries Experiencing Little or No Deforestation Pressure

Country	GNP Per Capita (US $)	Population Density (Persons per kilometer)	Existing TMF Area
Brunei	10,680	35	5,000
Central African Republic	290	3	—
Congo (People's Republic of)	630	4	100,000
French Guiana	—	—	86,000
Gabon	2,600	2	200,000
Guyana	560	4	200,000
Suriname	1,500	3	140,000
Zaire	260	12	1,000,000

Sources: *World Development Report, 1980* (Washington, DC: World Bank), pp. 110–111; *World Table (1980)* (Washington, DC: World Bank); *1980 World Bank Atlas* (Washington, DC: World Bank); and Norman Myers, *Conversion of Tropical Moist Forests* (Washington, DC: National Academy of Sciences, 1980).

lishment of protected TMF areas, regulations affecting logging techniques and the size of allowable harvests, assessment of possible deforestation impacts of development projects, increased land use planning and land capability surveys, establishment or enlargement of forestry and environmental protection agencies, among others. The effectiveness of these efforts has usually been limited; for example, many TMF areas are protected only on paper, due to the on-the-ground difficulties in controlling slash-and-burn agriculture, logging, and fuel wood cutting. Nonetheless, the very existence of such efforts reflects significant and growing pressures felt by government officials to control deforestation.

Government officials in TMF countries have a variety of motivations for promoting forest conservation. One of the most important is a response to economic development problems encountered because of watershed destruction, depletion of valuable timber, or development failures on poor TMF soils. Severe flooding, landslides, and siltation of reservoirs in the Philippines were apparently largely responsible for President Marcos's declaration that the state of the country's forests constitutes a national emergency.[138] In Malaysia (presently a major wood exporter), fears that the peninsula will need to import wood by 1990 apparently helped bring about a partial ban on raw log exports. In Brazil, the tremendous failure of the Transamazonica Highway, numerous cattle ranches, and other forest-clearing projects have made government officials more concerned about the effects of deforestation. In the words of one Brazilian scientist:

They (the government officials) are still motivated more by what works and what doesn't than by ecological enlightenment, but they've been burned in the Amazon and they aren't stupid.[139]

The Brazilian government has responded to its increased concern by establishing some 12 million acres of new TMF national parks, tightening a law that no landowner may cut more than 50 percent of the forest land that he owns, and terminating SUDAM's official financial incentives for Amazonian cattle ranching.[140]

Nationalistic pride can sometimes be an important factor in promoting forest conservation measures, particularly the establishment of protected TMF areas. In Costa Rica, the land expropriation necessary for establishing Corcovado National Park (an important TMF area) was made politically much easier by the fact that the owner was an unpopular American.[141] National parks in developing countries can also be important for national prestige; a national park system can have an aura of "modernness," in much the same manner as a new highway or dam project. As a consequence of nationalism, it is also easier to protect a TMF area if it is also an important historical site (such as Guatemala's Tikal National Park), or features spectacular scenery (such as Venezuela's Angel Falls, located in the Gran Sabana National Park). Nationalism can also encourage TMF conservation in other ways. For example, in Indonesia, greater governmental concern for improved forest management seemed to arise after many visiting foresters were unimpressed by what they learned of the country's forestry practices during the Eighth World Forestry Congress, held in Jakarta in 1978.[142]

A number of other motivations exist specifically for establishing protected TMF areas. One of these is to promote tourism (and the accompanying revenues). The potential for tourism was an important consideration in the development of Costa Rica's system of protected TMF areas. Other TMF areas where tourism is important include the Tijuca Forest on the outskirts of Rio de Janeiro, Brazil; several TMF nature reserves in Java (including Cibodas and Pangandaran); and the Caribbean National Forest near San Juan, Puerto Rico. However, the potential for tourism is usually not a sufficient motivation for protecting TMF areas, because the revenues that can be generated are often small, relative to alternative forest uses. For example, the prohibition of commercial logging in peninsular Malaysia's Endau Rompin Park entails a short-term opportunity cost of $450 million in timber revenues;[143] tourism cannot hope to provide comparable revenues. A related problem with tourism in TMF areas is that although abundant, wildlife is usually difficult to see (in contrast to such areas as the plains of East Africa). Of course, excessive numbers of visitors can also be environmentally destructive.

At times, establishment of a TMF national park can be used to assert a territorial claim, in a manner similar to TMF frontier settlements. This appears to be one reason behind Panama's proposed Darien National Park along the Colombia border. Panama also has outlined plans to establish a joint TMF "friendship park" with Costa Rica.[144]

In addition to such motivations as these, governments can promote TMF conservation in response to pressures from a wide range of interest groups. A variety of domestic nongovernmental organizations (NGOs) promote TMF conservation within their respective countries. In Ecuador, a well-organized NGO named NATURA is active in environmental education and other activities related to TMF protection. NATURA's membership consists largely of middle-class persons with an interest in nature.[145] The same characteristics apply to a number of NGOs in India, including the Indian Society of Naturalists. These groups have actively and successfully opposed the Silent Valley Dam, which would have flooded much of a unique TMF area in the state of Kerala.[146] In Malaysia, the vocal Environmental Protection Society of Malaysia (EPSM) and other NGOs helped publicize (and thereby stop) illegal logging in Endau-Rompin National Park. EPSM is interested in a broad range of environmental and consumer protection issues.[147] In Brazil, NGOs concerned about the rights of Indian tribes have helped prevent deforestation in parts of the Amazon. Partly due to their efforts, a 16 million acre TMF reserve has been established to safeguard the homeland of the 10,000 remaining Yanamamo Indians.[148]

In some countries, the scientific establishment is particularly important in promoting TMF conservation. For example, scientists of Brazil's National Institute of Amazonian Research (INPA) have been pivotal in stressing the importance of conservation and recommending sites for protected areas to government officials.[149] A variety of student and youth groups assist TMF conservation efforts. For example, the government-supported National Youth Movement in Costa Rica enlists student volunteers in the protection of TMF parks during school vacations. These young people often become champions of TMF conservation as a result.[150]

Occasionally, tribal peoples organize politically to oppose deforestation by outsiders. For example, in south Bihar, India, aboriginal hill people have illegally destroyed government-sponsored teak plantations to protest the replacement of the natural forest. These tribal people obtain firewood, fruit, seeds, leaves, and herbal medicines from the natural forest, but are unable to use the teak.[151] In Papua New Guinea, the Binandere tribe of shifting cultivators has successfully resisted repeated efforts by multinational corporations to cut timber on their land. The Binandere use threats of violence to keep the MNCs off their land. In 1979, a Binandere village magistrate had the following response to a proposed logging scheme by a combined Hong Kong and Saudi Arabian company:

I warn you that this is the last meeting of its kind. The Binandere conquered tribes to occupy its territory. From now on if any clan collaborate with foreigners to exploit us and our resources, those collaborators including politicians, will be our enemy and there will be killings. In doing so the Binandere will kill off itself and the land will be empty of its owners. Until then the foreigners will not use our land.[152]

Notwithstanding such instances as these, accounts of successful resistance by forest-dwelling people to deforestation by outsiders are comparatively rare.

International Attention

In addition to such domestic pressures as these, international pressure from foreign NGOs has at times successfully promoted TMF conservation. The World

Wildlife Fund, IUCN, and a number of smaller international conservation NGOs have played an important catalytic role in many TMF conservation efforts. For example, a number of U.S.-based organizations donated more than $100,000 in 1975 and 1976 to the Costa Rican government for preservation of the Corcovado TMF. Although park establishment cost the Costa Rican government $1.7 million (primarily to relocate slash-and-burn squatters), the relatively small U.S. funding was critical because it kept the Corcovado conservation effort alive until government funds became available. Moreover, this international show of support helped provide this conservation project with the political legitimacy it needed in Costa Rica.[153] Of course, international conservation efforts need to be carried out with great sensitivity for politics in the TMF countries concerned, to avoid arousing resentment or concerns about "imperialism."

A number of factors seem to emerge as necessary (if not sufficient) conditions for significant governmental efforts at TMF conservation. One of these is the availability of good information about the extent of deforestation, its damaging consequences, and appropriate corrective measures. For example, in both Thailand and the Philippines, governmental concern about deforestation increased markedly when good data became available, as a result of LANDSAT remote sensing, aerial photography, and other sophisticated techniques.[154] In many TMF countries, such as Malaysia and Brazil, the press is important in disseminating such information, even when it is under government censorship. In fact, environmental issues in such countries often receive considerable attention from the press, because these issues are seldom perceived as important to national security, and, consequently, their discussion is less frequently censored.[155]

Another important factor in encouraging governmental concern appears to be political stability. TMF conservation and improved management involve long-term benefits, and a certain degree of political stability is necessary before long-term considerations become important. For example, Costa Rica has had an unusually high degree of political stability, as well as a conservation program that compares favorably with most countries of the world, developing or otherwise. On the other hand, a high degree of political instability appears to be one important factor in the relative lack of concern about deforestation in Bolivia; the government there is usually too preoccupied with just trying to stay in power.

Perhaps most important is the presence of dedicated and competent individuals promoting conservation within the TMF country concerned. A recent AID report on forestry problems and related donor agency activities in developing countries concluded:

Successes are nearly always based on the efforts of one key individual, whether donors are involved or not. That key individual is usually a local person. Donor successes do not usually occur without such an individual.[156]

In addition to TMF country governments, bilateral and multilateral development aid agencies have become more concerned about tropical deforestation. At the same time that they continue to support a wide range of projects that promote deforestation (including penetration roads, resettlement schemes, cattle raising, logging, and commercial agriculture), these agencies are becoming increasingly active in efforts to promote ecologically sound TMF uses. One of the reasons for their increased concern is a growing awareness of the damaging consequences of deforestation for development prospects. Some of this increased awareness has arisen within the agencies themselves; some has been the result of effective advocacy campaigns by outside groups. For example, the Natural Resources Defense Council and several other U.S. environmental NGOs have been instrumental in making AID more responsive to TMF conservation needs. This was accomplished partly by working through the U.S. Congress to give AID a statutory mandate to address deforestation problems.

Aid agencies have responded to the deforestation problem through a variety of projects. Some of these are directed at reducing encroachment pressures by peasants on the remaining TMF areas. These projects include agroforestry, plantations of fast-growing species for fuel wood and other local uses, soil erosion control and intensification of agriculture on existing croplands, and development of "cottage industries" to provide employment alternatives to would-be forest farmers. Others involve training and institution-building activities, to develop within TMF countries the trained personnel and effective institutions needed for improved forest management and conservation. Others support TMF related research, especially monitoring of existing forest cover and land capability studies of TMF areas. In a few cases, aid agencies give direct assistance to the protection of national parks, as the World Bank is doing for the Dumoga National Park, Sulawesi, Indonesia.[157]

At present, the TMF management policies of major development aid agencies can be described as schizophrenic. For example, the World Bank provided $200,000 over three years to the World Wildlife Fund–Indonesia program for TMF conservation; at the same time, it was assisting large-scale deforestation in the country via the massive transmigration program.[158] At the same time that it provided financial support to the TMF conservation efforts of NATURA in Ecuador, AID was planning a resettlement project that would cause significant deforestation in the Pichis-Palcazu region of Peru.[159] While FAO is developing a nature conservation master plan for the TMF areas of Indonesia,[160] it is also promoting deforestation via cattle raising in a number of Latin American countries.[161] Other such agencies engaged in a variety of TMF-related activities include the Inter-American Development Bank, Asian Development Bank, and the aid agencies of Australia, Canada, France, Holland, Japan, New Zealand, Norway, Sweden, Switzerland, United Kingdom, and West Germany. Taken as a whole, their projects run the gamut from directly promoting conservation to wasteful deforestation.[162] In general, however, development aid agencies are much more concerned about controlling deforestation than ever before.

One of the major impediments to a more conservation-oriented approach by aid agencies is a lack of broad enough cost-benefit analysis techniques for TMF utilization. Not surprisingly, these agencies are strongly motivated by considerations of economic efficiency in their selection of projects. Unfortunately, the short-term economic benefits of deforestation, such as timber or agricultural commodities, receive the most attention in economic analyses, because they are so easy to measure. The economic harms of deforestation, while very real, are much more difficult to calculate in dollar terms. It is difficult to estimate the economic damages resulting from the loss of watershed services, especially since the extent of flooding, landslides, siltation, loss of fisheries, or other consequences is often not known until after the deforestation has occurred. It is even more difficult to assign realistic values to the loss of biological diversity, destruction of tribal cultures, or possible changes in climate due to deforestation. Moreover, present economic analysis techniques discount future costs and benefits, but not present ones. Since most of the economic costs of deforestation are long term, while the benefits are immediate, the costs are thereby given very short shrift. Given the heavy bias of these techniques against the future, it is possible to give high marks for economic viability to a project that clears a forest for ten years or less of cattle raising or other agriculture and then leaves degraded, totally unproductive land for many generations thereafter. An end to deforestation abuses by aid agencies is not likely until economic analysts conclude that ecologically unsound land development activities are ultimately counterproductive, even when they are economically beneficial in the short term.

Aside from development aid agencies and conservation NGOs, a number of United Nations organizations have become increasingly concerned about tropical deforestation. Through such activities as its sponsorship of international meetings to address deforestation problems (1979 and 1982), UNEP has been important in raising the level of international concern. UNCTAD is studying various approaches to increasing the efficiency of utilization of TMF wood that is harvested, and to develop an "international reforestation fund." The "Man and the Biosphere" (MAB) program of the United Nations Education, Scientific, and Cultural Organization (UNESCO) is sponsoring a number of interdisciplinary TMF applied ecological research projects. Moreover, it has begun to establish an international network of protected ecosystems (including TMFs) called Biosphere Reserves.

International organization and some governments have also begun to show some interest in a large-scale international financing mechanism for TMF conservation. The rationale for such an "international fund" is that while TMF conservation is important to the longer-term economic well-being of developing countries, it can be somewhat expensive in the short term. Moreover, many of the international benefits of TMF conservation, including future medications, industrial products, and inputs to agriculture from TMF species, would accrue largely to the devloped countries. Therefore, based both on their "ability to pay" and expected future benefits, developed countries should be encouraged to contribute to such an international fund. Such a fund still appears some distance from becoming a reality, but it has been discussed at UNEP-sponsored and other international meetings, where officials from the United States[163] and a number of European countries have indicated interest in such a scheme. Furthermore, on-the-ground mechanisms already exist for using the money efficiently; the MAB Biosphere Reserves program is a case in point. An international conservation fund could do much to increase the scale and effectiveness of the conservation actions already being taken by many financially pressed TMF country governments.

As indicated above, private enterprise (consisting of MNCs and others) plays an important role in tropical deforestation. Since deforestation is presently so profitable, these firms can be expected to continue their destructive activities until the economic incentives disappear. Short of elimination of the TMF resource or unforeseen changes in demand patterns for commodities such as tropical hardwoods and beef, market forces will not be sufficient to remove deforestation incentives. Governmental actions, in terms of enforceable regulations and taxation incentive schemes, are needed. At the same time, it would be useful to assist businesses with an economic stake in TMF conservation. For example, since TMF plants are the raw materials for so many medications, drug companies should be encouraged to obtain "exploration and exploitation rights" for plant collecting on TMF lands. Such a system would, of course, require considerable negotiation among the companies and TMF country governments. Furthermore, it is possible that drug patent laws in the "parent" countries of these companies would have to be changed. To the extent that TMF conservation provides short-term, marketable economic benefits, businesses should be encouraged to exploit them in an ecologically sound manner.

CONCLUSIONS

Tropical deforestation is proceeding at an alarming pace because the political and economic incentives that promote it are so great. Many of the projects that encourage deforestation, especially roads and resettlement activities, are politically very attractive to the leaders of TMF governments, especially by providing the "safety valve" noted above. Deforestation is also extremely profitable economically, under prevailing economic incentives and international trade patterns. This is in spite of the fact that economic consequences of deforestation, especially in developing countries, are often disastrous even in the present, and promise to be far worse in the future.

Meanwhile, efforts to control tropical deforestation have had relatively minor success because they have been belated, of limited scale and scope, and largely ineffectual. The barriers to conservation and environmentally sound TMF utilization are still enormous. The available data concerning the rates, extent, and consequences of deforestation are often poor, and scientific authorities are often in disagreement about them. For this and other reasons, most leaders of TMF countries perceive the deforestation problem as less than urgent. Available knowledge about ecologically sound, sustainable alternatives to destructive TMF uses is still limited. The benefits of TMF conservation are usually diffuse (watershed services, for example, are a "public good"), difficult to measure, and largely in the future. Meanwhile, the costs of conservation directly affect important constituencies, are very easy to measure, and occur in the present. This is true of both direct costs (such as patrolling protected TMF areas) and opportunity costs (such as forgoing the revenues from timber exports).

The most seriously affected "losers" from tropical deforestation usually lack political influence; this is most true of the "losers" who belong to future generations! Moreover many of the most acutely affected present-day victims of deforestation (rural peasants) are also perpetrators. Finally, to the extent that sincere efforts to control deforestation are made, their effectiveness is impeded by weak institutions, lack of trained personnel, insufficient budgets, and widespread corruption.

Despite these immense barriers, the disappearance of most TMFs is not a foregone conclusion, even in countries where present deforestation pressures are heavy. While a significant loss of TMFs is inevitable in all three major TMF regions, it is still possible that many major TMF areas will be conserved for the benefit of present and future generations. A recent U.S. government report on tropical deforestation demonstrates the huge difference in projected remaining TMF area by the year 2000 under the "best case" and "worst case" scenarios; respectively, between 82 and 49 percent of today's TMFs will survive.[164]

Just *how much* TMF area will survive mankind's present onslaught will depend upon the actions of a variety of actors. It will depend on how much TMF country government officials can avoid perceiving these forests as a short-term resource to be "mined" or as worthless areas that should be converted to cattle raising or similar uses; how much they can avoid condoning or encouraging migration by peasants to TMF areas; how well they alter the economic incentives that promote deforestation by MNCs and domestic entrepreneurs; how willing they are to invest scarce resources in TMF conservation activities with long-term payoffs; how successful they are in promoting population control, land reform, and labor-intensive development; and how well they can control corruption within their ranks. It will depend on how much development aid agencies pursue projects that relieve the pressure on TMFs, instead of increasing it. It will depend on how much international lending institutions (whether aid agencies or private banks) will provide credit for such constructive activities as rehabilitation of degraded lands, rather than such destructive ones as cattle pasture expansion on TMF lands. It will depend on how much the governments of developed countries are willing to subsidize TMF conservation via an international fund or other means; how much they agree to international economic reforms and increased development aid; how much they are willing to regulate the TMF-related abuses of their MNCs; and whether they implement certain policies concerning imported TMF products (for example, elimination of tariff barriers on processed wood and restriction of beef imports). It will depend on how effective domestic and international NGOs (and relevant United Nations agencies) are at spreading vital information and persuading TMF government officials (and other decision makers). It will depend on how much the scientific community can, through research, provide timely solutions to TMF management problems, and how effectively it can disseminate research results to policy makers and development planners. It will depend on how many successful tribal uprisings occur to oppose deforestation. Last but not least, it will depend upon the economic environment in which MNCs and national companies will operate: whether the prevailing incentives that promote deforestation will change, and how much industry interest will develop in environmentally benign forms of TMF exploitation (such as drug plant collection). Thus far, the records of most of these actors have been disappointing from the standpoint of TMF conservation. Nonetheless, significant progress has been made in some areas. Although severe deforestation pressures are likely to continue for the foreseeable future, there are encouraging signals that a significant TMF area might nonetheless withstand the present onslaught and survive for the benefit of present and future generations. The long-term sustainability of economic development in some tropical countries may depend to no small extent upon the care with which their TMF resources are managed.

Notes

1. This definition was adapted from Cynthia Mackie, *NRDC Tropical Moist Forests Conservation Bulletin No. 1* (Washington, D.C.: Natural Resources Defense Council, May 1978), p. 2; and from Norman Myers, *Conversion of Tropical Moist Forests* (Washington, D.C.: National Academy of Sciences, 1980).

2. *Global 2000 Report*, Vol. 1, p. 36.

3. Myers, *Conversion of Tropical Moist Forests*.

4. United Nations Environment Programme, *Global Assessment of Tropical Forest Resources* (Nairobi: UNEP, GEMS Pac Information Series No. 3, April 1982).

5. See, for example, Ariel E. Lugo and Sandra Brown, "Are Tropical Forests Endangered Ecosystems?" Unpublished paper, ca. 1980, available from the Institute of Tropical Forestry, Rio Piedros, Puerto Rico.

6. These criticisms were voiced by Dr. Norman Myers during a conversation in Washington, D.C., February 1983.

7. National Academy of Sciences, *Firewood Crops* (Washington, D.C.: National Academy of Sciences, 1980), p. vii.

8. World Bank, "Forestry Sector Policy Paper" (Washington, D.C.,: World Bank, 1978), p. 16.

9. *Statement of the International Union for Conservation of Nature and Natural Resources*, Experts Meeting on Tropical Forests (Nairobi: United Nations Environment Program, 25 February–1 March 1980).

10. Frank Wadsworth, "Deforestation—Death to the Panama Canal," *Proceedings of the U.S. Strategy Conference on Tropical Deforestation* (Washington, D.C.: U.S. Department of State and Agency for International Development, 1978), pp. 22–24.

11. Robert Allen, *How to Save the World* (London: Kogan Page, 1980), pp. 55–56.

12. For example, this is believed to be a significant problem in the Lesser Sundas Islands of Indonesia. (Conversation with Robert Pratt, chief, Office of Health and Nutrition, U.S. Agency for International Development, Jakarta, Indonesia, August 13, 1981).

13. Conversation with Mike Berge, U.S. Agency for International Development Washington, D.C., July 1980.

14. USAID, *Environmental and Natural Resources Management*.

15. *World Environment Report*, March 16, 1981, p. 7.

16. *Overview Document*, Experts Meeting on Tropical Forests (Nairobi: United Nations Environment Programme), 25 February–1 March 1980, p. 26.

17. Allen, *How to Save the World*, p. 56.

18. *Supra*, fn. 9.

19. International Union for Conservation of Nature and Natural Resources, *World Conservation Strategy* (Gland, Switzerland: 1980), chapter 2.

20. *Statement of the International Union*.

21. *Global 2000 Report*, p. 37.

22. National Academy of Sciences, *Report of Committee on Research Priorities in Tropical Biology* (Washington, D.C.: National Academy of Sciences, 1980).

23. Norman Myers, *The Sinking Ark* (New York: Pergamon Press, 1979), pp. 3–5.

24. See Allen, *How to Save the World*, p. 102; and *Overview Document*, p. 28.

25. *Statement of the International Union*.

26. National Academy of Sciences, *Priorities in Tropical Biology*. For further examples of economically useful TMF species, see Myers, *Sinking Ark*, pp. 57–79.

27. Tom Horton, "Effort to Protect Indians May Be Too Little, Too Late," *The Baltimore Sun*, September 21, 1980.

28. E. Salati, et al., *Recycling of Water in the Amazon Basin: An Isotopic Study* (Piracicaba, Brazil: Division of Environmental Science, Center of Nuclear Energy and Agriculture, 1978).

29. Unpublished proceedings of a small tropical forests "meeting of experts," IUCN, Gland, Switzerland, December 1979.

30. For more in-depth discussions, see George M. Woodwell, "CO_2–Deforestation Relationships." In *Proceedings of the U.S. Strategy Conference on Tropical Deforestation* (Washington, D.C.: U.S. Department of State and Agency for International Development, 1978), pp. 34–37; Alan Grainger, "The State of the World's Tropical Forests," *The Ecologist* 10, no. 1 (January 1980), p. 49; *The World's Tropical Forests: A Policy, Strategy, and Program for the United States* (Washington, D.C.: U.S. Department of State Publication No. 9117, 1980); and *Statement for the International Union*.

31. Cultural Survival *Newsletter* (Cambridge, Mass.) Vol. 4.

32. Norman Myers estimates that up to 10 million hectares of primary TMF are removed annually by slash-and-burn agriculture, *Conversion of Tropical Moist Forests*, p. 25.

33. *Ibid.*, p. 26.

34. The paradox of TMF soils which can sustain a luxuriant growth of rainforest, but no more than two or three crops of, e.g., corn, is widely documented. See, for example, *World Conservation Strategy*, pp. 23–24; *Overview Document*, p. 9; Peter Raven, *Tropical Rain Forest: A Global Responsibility* (St. Louis: Missouri Botanical Gardens, 1979).

35. "S.O.S.: Save the Tai," *IUNC Bulletin* (Gland, Switzerland: International Union for Conservation of Nature and Natural Resources) 12, no. 3–4 (March–April 1981), p. 10.

36. Marc Dourojeanni, "Conservation Strategies for Tropical Rain Forests, With Special Reference to National Parks and Equivalent Reserves," in *Proceedings of IUCN Thirteenth Technical Meeting* (Gland, Switzerland: International Union for Conservation of Nature and Natural Resources, 1975).

37. James D. Nations, Correspondence to Thomas Stoel, Natural Resources Defense Council, Washington, D.C., July 8, 1980.

38. Erik Eckholm, *The Dispossessed of the Earth: Land Reform and Sustainable Development*, Worldwatch Paper No. 30 (Washington, D.C.: Worldwatch Institute, 1979), p. 11.

39. See Myers, *Sinking Ark*, pp. 278–283 and *World Conservation Strategy*, Chapter 20.

40. Conversation with Gloria Davis, Transmigration Officer, World Bank, Washington, D.C., September 1982.

41. Myers, *Conversion of Tropical Moist Forests*, p. 73.

42. Andrew Vayda, "Human Ecology and Human Settlements in Kalimantan and Sumatra: Patterns and Problems." Paper presented at the East Kalimantan Man and Biosphere Program Workshop, Samarinda, Indonesia, March 24, 1978.

43. Conversation with Gloria Davis, September 1982.

44. Myers, *Conversion of Tropical Moist Forests*, p. 73.

45. Personal interviews with Paul Weatherly, former environmental advisor for Indonesia, U.S. Agency for International Development, and Jeffrey McNeeley, former World Wildlife Fund—Indonesia representative, Washington, D.C., April 1981.

46. Joan Hardjono, "Assisted and Unassisted Transmigration in the Context of Repelita III Targets," *Prisma* (Jakarta, Indonesia), No. 18 (September 1980), p. 4.

47. Personal interview with Norman Myers, international environmental consultant, Washington, D.C., April 1981.

48. Norman Gall, "Letter from Rondonia," *American Universities Field Staff Reports*, 1978/No. 12, p. 9.

49. Myers, *Conversion of Tropical Moist Forests*, p. 121.

50. *Ibid.*

51. Edward Meadows, "Brazil Stretches its Wings," *Fortune*, April 20, 1981, p. 113.

52. *Programa Integrado de Desenvolvimento do Noroeste do Brasil—Area de Influencia da Ligacao Rodovaria, Cuiaba—Porto Velho—1979* (Brasilia: Ministerios dos Interior, Agricultura, e Transportes).

53. Grainger, "State of Tropical Forests," p. 15.

54. Personal interview with Jan Wind, World Wildlife Fund representative in charge of conservation at Gunung Leuser, Bogor, Indonesia, September 1981.

55. Personal interview with an anonymous source in Washington, D.C., April 1981.

56. Julian Steyermark, "Future Outlook for Threatened and Endangered Species in Venezuela." In *Extinction Is Forever*, edited by Ghillean Prance (New York: New York Botanical Garden, 1977), p. 134.

57. Myers, *Sinking Ark*, p. 138.

58. William L. Webb, "Development of Incentive Control of Shifting Cultivation." Transactions of the National Conference on the Kaingin Problem, Manila, Philippines, March 12–13, 1964.

59. Myers, *Conversion of Tropical Moist Forests*, p. 111.

60. Allen, *How to Save the World*, p. 132.

61. Myers, *Conversion of Tropical Moist Forests*, p. 23–26.

62. P. Kunstadter et al., eds., *Farmers in the Forest: Economic Development and Marginal Agriculture in Northern Thailand* (Honolulu, Hawaii: University Press of Hawaii, 1978).

63. Myers, *Conversion of Tropical Moist Forests*, p. 96.

64. "Agro-forestry at PICOP." Brochure from Paper Industries Corporation of the Philippines, Makati, Rizal, Philippines (1976).

65. John Spears, "Can the Wet Tropical Forest Survive?" Address given at the Annual General Meeting of the Commonwealth Forestry Association (United Kingdom), April 1975.

66. Jeffrey McNeeley. Correspondence to Thomas Stoel, Natural Resources Defense Council, Washington, D.C., July 1980.

67. Spears, "Can Wet Forest Survive?"

68. See Myers, *Conversion of Tropical Moist Forests*, p. 39; *World's Tropical Forests*, p. 12; and *Overview Document*, p. 12.

69. *World's Tropical Forests*, pp. 1, 36.

70. These points were made in a conversation with Thomas Martin, Economics Bureau, U.S. State Department, Washington, D.C., December 1979.

71. *Overview Document*, p. 11.

72. Conversation with Gary Wetterberg, Office of International Park Affairs, National Park Service, Washington, D.C., August 1980.

73. Myers, *Conversion of Tropical Moist Forests*, p. 35.

74. *Ibid.*

75. John Zerbe et al., *Forestry Activities and Deforestation Problems in Developing Countries* (Washington, D.C.: U.S. Agency for International Development, 1980), pp. 72–73.

76. See footnote 29.

77. Spears, "Can Wet Forest Survive?"

78. *Overview Document*, p. 43.

79. S. Hadi and R. S. Suparto, eds., *Proceedings of Symposium on the Long-Term Effects of Logging in South-East Asia* (Bogor, Indonesia: Regional Center for Tropical Biology, 1977).

80. Personal interview with Dr. Soeriaatmadja, Deputy Assistant Environment Minister, near Bandung, Indonesia, August 16, 1981.

81. Alf Leslie, "Where Contradictory Theory and Practice Co-Exist." *Unasylva* 29, no. 115 (1977), p. 4.

82. See footnote 29.

83. "Vanishing Forests," *Newsweek*, November 24, 1980, p. 122.

84. Personal interview with Ken Proud, World Wildlife Fund, Indonesia, Bogor, Indonesia, July 3, 1981.

85. *Overview Document*, p. 7.

86. See Spears, "Can Wet Forest Survive?"

87. *Ibid*.

88. Myers, *Conversion of Tropical Moist Forests*, p. 39.

89. Erik Eckholm, *Planting for the Future: Forestry for Human Needs*, Worldwatch Paper No. 26 (Washington, D.C.: Worldwatch Institute, February 1979), p. 7.

90. Spears, "Can Wet Forest Survive?"

91. See footnote 29.

92. Gwen Kinkead, "Trouble in D. K. Ludwig's Jungle," *Fortune*, April 20, 1981.

93. *Ibid*.

94. As quoted in Myers, *Conversion of Tropical Moist Forests*, p. 89.

95. See footnote 55.

96. Myers, *Sinking Ark*, p. 196.

97. H. Jeffrey Leonard and David Morell, "Emergence of Environmental Concern in Developing Countries: A Political Perspective," *Stanford Journal of International Law* (June 1981).

98. Personal interview with an anonymous source in Washington, D.C., May 1979.

99. William E. Knowland. Correspondence to Peter D. Martin, Institute of Current World Affairs, Hanover, New Hampshire, October 29, 1978; and *World's Tropical Forests*, p. 36.

100. See footnote 70.

101. *Report on the Timbering and Wood-Processing Industries of Indonesia: Part One*, (Jakarta: United States Agency for International Development, American Embassy, April 1980), p. 4.

102. *World's Tropical Forests*, p. 12; and footnote 70.

103. Robert Vincent, forester, United States Agency for International Development. Correspondence to George Ledec, Jakarta, Indonesia, August 1981.

104. Personal interview with John C. Low, Papua New Guinea environmental official in Christchurch, New Zealand, October 1981.

105. Douglas R. Shane, *Hoofprints on the Forest: An Inquiry into the Beef Cattle Industry in the Tropical Forest Areas of Latin America* (Washington, D.C.: Office of Environmental Affairs, U.S. Department of State, March 1980), p. 15; Myers, *Conversion of Tropical Moist Forests*. pp. 44; and, Nations, footnote 37.

106. James J. Parsons "Forest to Pasture: Development or Destruction?" *Revista de Biologia Tropical* 24, no. 1, p. 122.

107. James D. Nations, *The Future of Middle America's Tropical Rainforest* (first draft), (San Cristobal de las Casas, Chiapas, Mexico: Center for Applied Human Ecology, May 1980), p. 5.

108. *Ibid*., p. 21.

109. Stephen Schmidt, " 'Sacred Cow' Causing Ecological Disaster in Costa Rica, Local Experts Say," *The Tico Times* (San Jose, Costa Rica), Nov. 3, 1978, p. 12.

110. Robert Goodland, "Environmental Ranking of Amazonian Development Projects in Brazil," *Environmental Conservation* 7, no. 1, p. 19.

111. Myers, *Sinking Ark*, p. 170.

112. Kinkead, "Ludwig's Jungle," p. 105.

113. Goodland, "Environmental Ranking."

114. Nations, *Future of Middle America*, pp. 33–34.

115. *Ibid*. Also, Shane, *Hoofprints on the Forest*, p. 89.

116. *Ibid*., p. 100. Virtually all of the imported beef used in the United States is "lean" (grass-fed) beef. Because this beef was not feedlot-fattened, it lacks the "marbling" prefered by American consumers for table cuts and is rarely used for steaks or roasts. Instead, it is used for "manufacturing purposes," including frankfurters, sausages, canned stews and soups, frozen dinners, and pet and baby foods. However, the majority is used in hamburger and ground beef (which account for 25 percent of all U.S. beef consumed). Although the giant McDonald's Corporation reportedly uses no imported beef, other U.S. hamburger chains (including Burger King, Jack-in-the-Box, Roy Rogers, and Bob's Big Boy) do. As a result, this peculiar relationship to tropical deforestation has been called the "hamburger connection." *Ibid*., pp. 109–113.

117. *Ibid*., p. 70; and Myers, *Conversion of Tropical Moist Forests*, p. 124.

118. Shane, *Hoofprints on the Forest*, pp. 48–51.

119. Myers, *Conversion of Tropical Moist Forests*, p. 124; Myers, *Sinking Ark*, pp. 145–146; and Goodland, "Environmental Ranking," p. 10.

120. Schmidt, "Sacred Cow," p. 12.

121. President Rodrigo Carazo, *Plan of Action for Renewable Natural Resources* (unofficial translation) (San Jose, Costa Rica: National Press, Publication No. 3, 1978).

122. Myers, *Sinking Ark*, p. 142.

123. Joseph A. Tosi. Correspondence to S. Jacob Scherr, Natural Resources Defense Council, Washington, D.C., February 22, 1971.

124. Shane, *Hoofprints on the Forest*.

125. *Ibid*., p. 127.

126. *Ibid*., pp. 100–103.

127. Schmidt, "Sacred Cow," p. 13.

128. *World's Tropical Forests*, p. 12.

129. Myers, *Conversion of Tropical Moist Forests*, p. 48.

130. Personal interview with a local landowner at Cerro de la Muerte, Costa Rica, January 25, 1979.

131. Spears, "Can Wet Forest Survive?"

132. Myers, *Conversion of Tropical Moist Forests*, p. 142.

133. *Ibid*., p. 82–83.

134. G. M. Oza, Indian Society of Naturalists. Correspondence to George Ledec, Natural Resources Defense Council, Washington, D.C., June 1, 1980.

135. Myers, *Sinking Ark*, p. 42.

136. Myers, *Conversion of Tropical Moist Forest*, p. 116.

137. *Ibid*., and Spears, "Can Wet Forest Survive?"

138. Zerbe et al., *Forestry Activities*, p. 79; and Myers, *Conversion of Tropical Moist Forest*, p. 101.

139. Tom Horton, "Ambitious Assault on the Amazon Runs into an Ecological Minefield," *The Baltimore Sun*, September 14, 1980.

140. Myers, *Conversion of Tropical Moist Forest*, p. 125; and "Brazil Sets Aside Ecological Preserves: Parks Limits Burning to Save Rain Forest," *The Baltimore Sun* September 19, 1980.

141. Gary Hartshorn. Correspondence to Peter Martin, Institute of Current World Affairs, Hanover, New Hampshire, September 4, 1978.

142. Personal interview with R. Michael Wright, World Wildlife Fund–U.S. Washington, D.C., June 11, 1981.

143. Myers, *Sinking Ark*, p. 262.

144. George Ledec and Lynda K. Williamson, *NRDC Tropical Moist Forests Conservation Bulletin No. 2* (Washington, D.C.: Natural Resources Defense Council, December 1979), p. 6.

145. See footnote 144.

146. See footnote 136.

147. Personal interview with Gurmit Singh, Environmental Protection Society of Malaysia, Washington, D.C., August 1980.

148. Horton, "Effort to Protect Indians."

149. Thomas E. Lovejoy, "Brasil Trip Report." World Wildlife Fund–U.S., Washington, D.C., March 21, 1976.

150. Mario A. Boza, "Costa Rica: A Case Study of Strategy in the Setting Up of National Parks in a Developing Country," *Proceedings of the Second World Conference on National Parks* (Gland, Switzerland: International Union for Conservation of Nature and Natural Resources, 1974), p. 187.

151. "Indian Aborigines Fight Teak Planters in Bihar," *World Environment Report* 5, no. 11 (May 7, 1979), p. 1.

152. John D. Waiko, "'Yu No Baggarapim Em Tasol,' The Woods in Papua New Guinea, for 'Leave the Trees Alone,'" *Uniterra*, February 1980, p. 5.

153. See footnote 143.

154. See footnote 29, and Myers, *Conversion of Tropical Moist Forests*, pp. 98, 108, 112.

155. William Knowland. Correspondence to Peter Martin, Institute of Current World Affairs, Hanover, New Hampshire, August 31, 1980.

156. Zerbe et al., *Forestry Activities*, p. 78.

157. See footnote 66.

158. *Ibid.*

159. Personal interview with S. Jacob Scherr, Natural Resources Defense Council, Washington, D.C., June 11, 1981.

160. See footnote 84.

161. Shane, *Hoofprints on the Forest*, p. 46.

162. Zerbe et al., *Forestry Activities*.

163. *Bill L. Long, U.S. State Dept., and F. Bryan Clark, U.S. Agriculture Dept. Correspondence to Mostafa Tolba, U.N. Environment Programme, Nairobi (1980).*

164. *World's Tropical Forests*, p. 16.

CHAPTER 6

THE POLITICS OF DESERTIFICATION IN MARGINAL ENVIRONMENTS: THE SAHELIAN CASE

James T. Thomson

This chapter analyzes desertification in the African Sahel, its consequences, and the probabilities for remedial action. The Sahel is the territory fringing the desert edge of the southern Sahara from the Atlantic coast to the Indian Ocean. This arid belt includes much of Mauritania, Senegal, Mali, Niger, Chad, and Sudan. Sahelian conditions exist also in northern Upper Volta, northern Kenya, and parts of Ethiopia and Somalia.

Desertification can be defined as "desert encroachment."[1] More complex definitions exist, but all share the essential focus on the spread of arid areas.[2] When desertification strikes, renewable resources—soil, water, pastures, and woodstock—can be eroded to the point of sharply lowered productivity or even destruction. Desertification is a virulent form of environmental degradation.

This chapter concentrates primarily on desertification in Niger,[3] although comparative references are made to other Sahelian countries. Within the limited Niger framework, causal factors, natural and human, are noted first. A second section reveals the dynamics of desertification-promoting micropolitical and microeconomic strategies adopted by various actors to maintain or better their living standards and power positions. The consequences of desertification for rich and poor, urban and rural, herders and farmers are also explored. The third section assesses the systemic barriers and incentives to antidesertification efforts. It explains the positive and negative roles that political actors will probably play in this regard, as well as the deadening effort of administrative overcentralization on environmental entrepreneurship. A final section draws on the preceding materials to evaluate the probabilities for constructive antidesertification policies and actions.

DESERTIFICATION AND ITS CAUSES

The cumulative impact on fragile environments of desertification caused by numerous human causes can be powerful. But non-human, natural factors exert profound influence as well. Of these, meteorological ones dominate in the Sahel, since gross amounts of rainfall and annual fluctuations therein structure the basic environmental characteristics of an area as well as setting the parameters for environmental upgrading.

The Sahel strip, roughly 500 kilometers wide north to south, receives from four to twenty-four inches of rainfall annually.[4] It can be subdivided into two parallel east-west bands, with the northern part receiving up to eighteen inches of annual rainfall and the southern part getting from eighteen to twenty-four inches.

The northern, or "high" Sahel, consists mostly of steppe-like terrain. Grasses cover most of the land; scrub trees grow only in occasional seasonally watered valleys. This zone until very recently was exploited only by pastoralists raising camel, cattle, and small ruminants. The most important groups are the Twareg,[5] Fulbe,[6] Tubu, and Maures in the western half of the Sahel, and Arabic-speaking peoples in the eastern half. At present, particularly in central Niger, some herders are turning to agriculture, along with southern immigrants to the steppes.[7]

The more southern "Sudano-Sahel" strip presents a different setting. The woodstock (all sorts of ligneous vegetation) here contains real trees, as well as stunted specimens and bushes. Remnants of precolonial forests include trees which attain heights of more than one hundred feet. Many parts remain reasonably well wooded. In others, deforestation has advanced to the point where, besides scrub brush, only the largest specimens still stand. These are either protected by law or too difficult to work comfortably with hand tools. Deforestation is particularly pronounced around urban centers, where the demand for fuel wood and construction materials has ballooned with the dramatic expansion of city populations.

Most Sudano-Sahelians live by farming, although agropastoralists do exist.[8] Some pastoralists still spend part of the year in the zone, but mounting pressure from the extension of peasant agriculture is forcing them out.[9] The stock held by the agropastoralists and peasant farmers consists mainly of thousands of tiny herds of goats, belonging to single individuals, often women; sheep, owned and herded by transhumant shepherds; and cattle, owned again in small herds by large numbers of individuals and often herded in large groups by single hired cow-herds. Camels are rare.

For a long time, people have been concerned about the southward movement of the Sahara Desert. This concern reflects a gradual, fluctuating process of desiccation which dates back to the height of the last Saharan rainy epoch around 9,000 B.C. These pluvial years (10,000–5,000 B.C. followed a much drier period, comparable to the present, which desiccated the region from about

20,000–15,000 B.C.[10] During the pluvial period, rainfall in the Tibesti Mountains of Chad varied between twenty-four inches and forty-eight inches annually (current precipitation there is less than four inches).[11] Big game—elephant, giraffe, and bison—was abundant, and herders exploited the whole central Saharan area under a temperate climate regime.

The subsequent desiccation has been largely caused by natural factors. Two distinct processes are involved: long-term, fluctuating aridity; and periodic droughts, cycles of which have proven very hard to determine.[12] The underlying factors are complex, but they are clearly related to global meteorological events.[13]

While man may not bear the primary blame for the long-term desiccation of the Sahara and the adjacent Sahel, desertification is now being fostered by human activities. Desert-like conditions have leap-frogged ahead, far south of the actual Saharan *tenere* (sand dune) border.[14] In the vulnerable steppe areas and farther south, herders, farmers, agropastoralists, and woodcutters try to make a living in a rough environment and often abuse the woodstock, pasture, and soil resource bases. This impairs the environment's water retention capability, enhances the impact of desiccation, and magnifies the threat of wind erosion and the generalized resource impoverishment. Periodic droughts intensify these processes.[15]

No Sahelian country is rich.[16] Few even have marketable mineral resources.[17] Only Niger and Mauritania now enjoy anything like a mineral boom and none can boast more than a bare margin of survival security, particularly in light of unchecked population growth rates. Spreading desertification and overexploitation of renewable resources will intensify human suffering in both the short and long term. As resources erode, even with outside assistance, drought relief and postdrought reconstitution of herds, grain stores, woodstock, soil resources, and groundwater reserves all become more difficult and costly.[18]

The escalating desertification sharpens the struggle for existence, imposing higher costs on the weaker members of the community, notably the children. Malnutrition debilitates physical and mental capacities and leaves individuals vulnerable to many virulent diseases which still persist in the Sahel.[19] In addition, urban communities, already ill-equipped to handle escalating city populations,[20] confront an influx of rural refugees no longer able to sustain themselves on the land.

To stem desertification, soil, water, wood, and grass resources must be stabilized and then expanded or upgraded to meet increasing demand. Soils must be protected and reconstituted so that during good years, rainfed agriculture can meet or exceed the population's nutrition requirements and produce security stocks for the bad years that are sure to come.

Water resources, properly managed, *can* render agricultural production partially independent of short-term rainfall fluctuations. Large-scale dam projects, of the sort planned or underway for the Senegal and Niger Rivers in particular, will not necessarily achieve this result.[21] With certain modifications, however, they may help. Small-scale water management projects (earth and rock dams, microcatchments, and seasonal watercourse improvements[22]) can permit more productive exploitation of even small amounts of rainfall. Reducing runoff and improving surface-water infiltration could stabilize or even raise the ground water tables, and so enhance the possibilities of dry-season gardening and crop production.

The woodstock needs to be protected and restored throughout the Sahel, not only to satisfy increasing consumption, but to defend the steppes and fields against wind erosion.[23] Trees also function as fertilizer pumps, returning to the surface natural and artificial nutrients leached down through the topsoil beyond the reach of field crop roots.[24] This cuts the need for costly fertilizer inputs and relieves the stress on local soils as well.

Pastures may be beyond restoration in some areas as a result of soil compaction and generalized desiccation.[25] Perennial grasses suffer particularly in this regard, although they form a small percentage of Sahelian pastures.[26] The more prevalent annual grasses are hardier and can survive during dormant years of inadequate moisture before springing to life following a brief summer shower. But most observers conclude that pasture management will be extremely difficult without more structured organizations among Sahelian pastoralists.[27]

If herders' organizations can be established and pasture management efforts undertaken with the pastoralists' willing cooperation, pastures can probably be reestablished in at least some areas where they are now degraded.[28] But this will be difficult unless more control is exercised over farming—the location of fields and the total amount of land cultivated—within the managed area, in addition to controlling grazing.

POLITICAL DYNAMICS OF DESERTIFICATION

The dynamics of the prevailing geopolitical circumstances push Sahelians to adopt a variety of resource exploitation strategies that are designed to secure their short-term welfare. However, these strategies inevitably hurt their chances of perpetuating their economic well-being, to say nothing of improving their living standards over the long run.

The more arid "high" Sahel and more humid "Sudano-Sahel" sub-regions have different local economies: largely agricultural in the Sudano-Sahel, largely pastoral in the arid Sahel. Each has its own dynamic, but they tend to interact and mutually affect each other, especially where the demand for renewable natural resources exceed the supply.

Sudano-Sahelian Agricultural Zone

Villagers are mainly peasant farmers. At present, most are struggling to raise enough millet and sorghum to maintain from harvest time a two and one-half-year reserve of staple grains in their silos.[29] Few are not meeting this goal. For instance, in three Inuwa[30] canton villages (south-central Niger), many people had emptied their silos by the beginning of the 1981 summer agricultural season (when increased work output demands increased food input). From 20 to 50 percent of the household heads were liquidating their possessions to purchase grain.[31]

Often cited as an example of successful efforts at food self-sufficiency among Sahelian states,[32] Niger experienced another deficit year in 1980.[33] While a national shortfall does not directly suggest localized famines, it indicates mounting pressure on the peasants. Numerous observers corroborate the peasant dilemma.[34]

Those who do attain reserves of agricultural products and get ahead of the game—often those who own the best-manured fields closest to the villages[35]—tend to speculate in staple grain price fluctuations, a time-honored strategy in Hausaland on both sides of the franco-anglophone divide.[36] Some invest in animal traction equipment, ostensibly to increase agricultural productivity. But more often the equipment goes unused for agricultural purposes; the real motivation for purchasing equipment is access to a farm cart which is (correctly) seen as the money-maker, and thus the key to timely payment of debt installments.

Others, less fortunate, less industrious, or less skillful, try to survive or develop food reserves by bringing more (marginal) land into cultivation, thus increasing the surface exposed to wind and water erosion. More peasants now use fungicides, hybrid seeds, and chemical fertilizers. But price barriers and distribution difficulties prevent many peasants from adapting these innovations, and in any case it is unlikely that these measures alone will reestablish the fundamental equilibrium, even in average years, to say nothing of drought years. Yields are falling as the agricultural system reaches the limits of its productive potential.[37] The falling yields correlate with the impairment of the environment's capacity to absorb punishment and rebound from abuse. Efforts to improve agricultural productivity have a chance to succeed only if coupled—closely—with effective programs for the restoration of renewable resources. Chemical dressing of degraded soils does *not* exhaust the list of such programs, though many development projects still seem to proceed on this assumption.

Where land has become rare (certainly not everywhere[38]), individuals put more land under cultivation more often. Earlier, fields were farmed and then left fallow in a one-to-three ratio. Cultivation ceased before soils were totally exhausted, usually within ten years after field clearing, while fallows lasted as long as thirty.[39] The second-growth bush which recolonized the fallows enriched the soil, preparing it for further cultivation.

Such is not now the case in the land-short areas, where severe shortening of fallows, or continuous cultivation of land to which no appreciable fertilizer inputs, either natural or chemical, are added leads to soil degradation.[40]

When large areas were still fallowed, wood for building and fuel posed no problem. Plentiful supplies existed close at hand to meet rural needs. Only in urban centers did construction and fuel woods pose problems, and there demand typically elicited adequate supplies through networks of vendors and woodcutters extending out along main feeder roads.

In the face of this plenty, farmers clearing bush for cultivation normally uprooted, fired, or cut all but the largest trees. This made farming easier, added nutrients to the soil when rains leached resulting ashes, and reduced crop losses in areas otherwise shaded out by trees during the growing season. Fields occurred in isolation within large fallows surrounding the close-cultivated area of each village; the adjacent bush sheltered them from erosion. The fields were later fallowed and rapidly reclaimed by natural regeneration.

As farmed surfaces expanded, clean clearing of fields deforested large areas through a multitude of small-scale, individual actions. In many parts of the Sahel, adult specimens constitute most of what remains of the ligneous cover on cultivated fields. Lands stripped of second growth undergo erosion and soil-mining. Simultaneously, the price of wood is skyrocketing in response to increasing—and now perceived—shortages.

Sudano-Sahelian herders face a dilemma; land-hungry farmers have largely taken over their traditional grazing areas.[41] Herders, forced out by lack of pastures, gradually withdraw to more marginal areas.[42] Crop residues might conceivably replace the nutrient value of the bush and fallow pastures eliminated by spreading field agriculture,[43] but local farmers now gather and stock crop residues for their own animals in many parts of the Sahel. Thus stubble is no longer available in large amounts as a free food for transhumant herds. Pastoralists also seek less cultivated areas to avoid the fines imposed in many Sahelian states for animal-caused crop or garden damage.[44] Falling stock populations in the agricultural zone remove an important nutrient input—manure—from the local regenerative cycle.

Local institutions—land tenure, tree tenure, legal systems, and administrative structures—profoundly affect the existence strategies of peasant farmers, agropastoralists, and transhumant herders in the southern zone population. Land tenure in Niger, for example, reflects complex interactions between customary rules, modified by imported Islamic principles, national legislation, and presidential declarations. It reflects as well the application of these rules and edicts through two separate court systems, civil and administrative. The latter include everything from village moots up to tribunals presided over by county-level administrators (subprefects.)[45]

In general, land in Niger is individually held, heritable, and subject to contractual relations such as loan, mortgage, and sale[46] (in some parts of the Sahel, e.g., Yatenga, Upper Volta, commercial land transactions remain fairly rare).[47] Land has come on the market increasingly during recent years,[48] but land transactions occurred in some parts of Niger, e.g., Inuwa district, as early as the 1920s.[49] Up until the 1974 Niger coup d'état, land litigation flourished as various ..ctors tried legal ploys, in addition to outright purchase, to increase their land holdings.[50] This destabilized land tenure relations, especially in jurisdictions where powerful local chiefs could impose biased "conciliation" settlements favoring the highest bidder or the best-connected litigant.

Seyni Kountché, the leader of the 1974 coup, reacted to end these practices by a fiat ruling. The ruling vested effective use rights in anyone who currently cultivates a field.[51] In general, Kountché's ruling may be said to have dampened "entrepreneurial" litigation. The real basis of land use now in Niger is usufructuary rights. Possession is at least nine points of the law. In many instances, land-rich peasants are now rapidly rotating tenants or refusing land loans to tenants who are less well supplied, for fear of losing their fields in eventual suits to dislodge recalcitrant tenants. In some situations, appropriate reallocation of land has been impeded.[52] This may also discourage present occupiers who are unsure of tenure prospects from investing in soil protection, manuring, or chemical fertilizer and other conservation measures,[53] thus aggravating soil impoverishment.

Trees located on nonstate lands in Niger are divided into two classes; protected and nonprotected. The forestry code provides for "customary rights" of wood collecting, when the product is for individual use, but in practice, these rights can be severely limited by other provisions.[54] Furthermore, when wood is to be cut from a protected live tree of some size, peasants are advised to get authorization from a forestry official "to avoid unpleasant surprises" (e.g., a nasty fine).[55]

Contemporary "tree trouble cases" in heavily populated south-central Niger suggest that changes have begun to occur in tree tenure rights. Until very recently, an abundance of trees and the national forestry code (as applied locally by many forestry guards) dissuaded individuals from planting trees.[56] Wood was in fact common property, free to whoever harvested it. Foraging peasants took from the bush and others' fields as well as from their own.

These negative incentives may be overcome by individual responses to the growing wood penury, either through the gradual development of an effective "common law" of individualized tree tenure, or through the modification of the state forestry code.

In the Sudano-Sahelian region of Niger, administrative and civil courts process almost all land tenure litigation. The administrative system includes, at the top, *arrondissement* (county) courts, with traditional district courts and village moots in the local jurisdictions. In addition, independent Muslim legal entrepreneurs (*malam*, pl. *malamai* [Hausa]) frequently offer their services as conciliators.

The administrative courts handle the lion's share of the land tenure cases. Cases sometimes go on appeal as high as the civil system justices of the peace or primary court judges. But most are resolved by administrative tribunals.

Until very recently, the forest service retained practically exclusive control over tree tenure cases. Foresters usually handled code infractions through warnings (for minor offences) or by administrative fines imposed and accepted through "amicable" proceedings.[57] Enforcer and violator often bargain out a bribe price less costly than the fine (but more profitable to both in terms of money in pocket), under terms of which the offence is "forgotten."[58] Widespread nonenforcement of the code results.[59]

More recently, local village moots have (surreptitiously) heard some tree-related disputes. This developing common law of tree tenure does not impose fines or damages—at least for the moment. Instead it quietly buttresses the field owner's (or user's) right to control the trees on his property.

The Niger policy and administrative network, a unified system, centers on the national administrative hierarchy. The chain of command originates with Col. Seyni Kountché, the military head of state brought to power by his 1974 coup d'etat. It runs down through the minister of interior, seven departmental prefects, and thirty-two arrondissement subprefects. Within each arrondissement jurisdiction, a number of traditional sedentary and nomad chiefs, styled *collaborateurs*, and below them several appointed village and tribal headmen, are expected to carry out their superiors' orders.

At each administrative level, technical specialists (livestock, agriculture, hydraulic infrastructure, cooperatives, rural extension, adult literacy, etc.) implement policy under the administrators' tutelage. At the national level, the council of ministers articulates policy. At the departmental and arrondissement levels, specialists participate in administrative technical committees which pass on issues of implementation and occasionally make propositions of their own. At the district and local levels, subordinate technical cadres supervise action programs elaborated by their superiors.

Despite efforts to decentralize the policy-making and administrative system, it remains (a) highly centralized in terms of main policy initiatives and (b) quite closed to popular input. Kountché knows the dangers of overcentralization.[60] Indeed, a major thrust of the "Development Society" concept he currently advocates proposes increasing popular participation in decision-making processes.[61] A close collaborator puts a rather sharper point on the problem:

> We won't be able to change anything if we continue to neglect the overwhelming majority of Nigerians on the pretext that they won't understand anything about development or because, quite simply, they are unenlightened.[62]

It is problematic whether Development Society initiatives will effect changes in policy making and implementation. At the moment, viewed by peasants looking up from the bottom, the administration appears very distant and very powerful indeed.

To date, the Niger policy preference for a top-down, interventionist approach to development problems has led to highly structured, heavily controlled development projects. Very little leeway has existed for local entrepreneurs to resolve local problems autonomously. The Niger policy has fostered peasant dependence on the state apparatus rather than independent self-help activities and the kinds of local decision-making capabilities which must underlie these. This is a common control strategy throughout the third world.[63]

Sahelian Pastoral Zone

The Niger pastoral zone lies within the sub-Saharan steppe region; its economy is now centered on extensive pastoralism. Stock-raising in the pastoral zone follows one of two basic strategies. Some people constantly herd their animals, moving them when necessary to new pastures or healthier environments. Others permit their herds to roam, using isolated water sources as magnets to hold the stock in an area, thus avoiding having to invest in either herding or fencing. Herd composition is structured to maximize the adaptation to various environmental niches while meeting the herders' consumptive needs. Complex institutions spread the risks and increase the long-term survival chances of the humans who depend on the herds.[64]

Pasture management in the area has been complicated by the expanding livestock populations coupled with the breakdown of traditional mechanisms (frequently, the control of the water rights) that previously prevented overgrazing.[65] Informants in the central Nigerian pastoral zone agree that more wells now exist than ever before, confirming the increases in the human and animal populations.[66]

In some southern pastoral zone areas, the pastures are threatened by an influx of southern farmers and agropastoralists.[67] Pastoral zone ex-herders, forced by stock losses to take up farming, are also diminishing the pasture base.[68] These new farming populations have tended to create scattered fields in pasture areas. Unless the animals are closely herded, the pastures adjacent to the fields are then effectively off limits to stock owners if the farmers can claim compensation for animal-caused crop losses.[69] Farmers and agropastoralists have also colonized the better-watered valleys, where the pastoralists have commonly dug shallow wells to meet their own and their stock's water needs. Conflicts between the two groups for control over these spaces now arise with more frequency in some areas.[70]

Effective pastoral zone land tenure reflects the contemporary *formal* base rule of unlimited access to a common property pasture area. This contrasts sharply with the precolonial division of the pastoral zone into a set of smaller common properties, managed by particular groups (tribes, lineages, families, even confederations of tribes).[71] Other factors have aggravated the *induced disorganization* of pasture management practices. Niger government policies favor the digging of boreholes to tap fossil waters in areas otherwise unusable during the dry season for lack of water. Some administrators and group chiefs require herdsmen to compensate pastoral zone farmers for crop damages, thus removing a strong institutional disincentive to agricultural extension into the pastoral zone. Government-imposed land tenure rules in the pastoral zone, coupled with the influx of immigrants to the steppes, thus help to cause high Sahelian environmental degradation. Finally, government policies promoting range management may encounter serious difficulty because pastoralists currently have few opportunities for collective action.

By contrast with the Sudano-Sahelian agricultural zone, the pastoral zone is not legally open year-round to all comers. Almost all herding groups have a dry season home range—although some shift gradually over a period of years, as herders remain full time in areas which earlier served only as rainy season pastures.[72] But home ranges cannot now be defended as exclusive properties, at least by the formal terms of pastoral zone land tenure. Areas where a shallow water table permits well construction by traditional techniques tend to be subdivided according to family or camp control of watering points. Administrative authorities can prevent interlopers from digging new wells in the immediate neighborhood,[73] but do not always do so.[74] Overcrowding, or at least a reduction in the pasture available to initial occupants, that results from the arrival of additional herds often provokes tensions.

In many areas, the water table cannot be tapped by traditional methods. Pastures there can be exploited regularly only if boreholes are drilled into deep fossil aquifers. While no theoretical reason exists why such wells could not be allocated to specific user groups, in practice the government has insisted they be open to all users. Thus, any herder can water his stock at a borehole and graze his animals on the surrounding pastures. As a result, forage is often quickly exhausted, and pastures may be permanently degraded, though evidence on this point remains inadequate.[75]

This danger is now clearly recognized. Increasingly, a modified well borehole method is adopted that reduces the danger of overexploitation by reinstating the human labor constraint on water availability. Water is pumped mechanically from fossil aquifers to a deep, modern, wide-bore well. Herders can always get water from the well, but must raise it manually. This slows the extraction and reduces the number of animals which can be watered, decreasing the pressure on the adjacent pastures.

Such artificial but automatic restraints on grazing pressure cannot be employed everywhere throughout the zone. Shallow water tables in some areas permit traditional wells. Institutional constraints on grazing pressure could substitute for technical ones. But institutions must operate in a reliable fashion to achieve the goals assigned to them. Weak institutional control structures, both within the administration and among pastoral groups, make this unlikely in the Niger pastoral zone.

The pastoral zone legal system governing the resource management centers on administrative law procedures. Administrators sitting as judges resolve cases, as do gendarmes who police the zone. Cases can be taken on appeal to

the civil courts, but those revolving around allocation of water rights and imposition of civil restitution for crop damages tend to begin and end within the
administrative courts. Because nomadic groups are underrepresented, particularly at the all-important subprefectoral level, farmers often find it easy to
collect compensation for crop losses. This is true although such actions violate
the express provisions of Law 61-05, which delimits the pastoral zone and
specifically forbids farmers to be compensated for losses sustained within the
zone. Knowledge that they can extract damage payments leads at least some
farmers to deliberately court confrontation by placing their fields in pastoral
zone areas heavily used by herdsmen. [76]

The general politico-administrative framework found in the southern agricultural zone is replicated in the pastoral zone. The same effective emphasis on
centralized decision making and top-down efforts at development are apparent.
But significant differences exist, reflecting communications difficulties in the
pastoral zone caused by great distances, poorly developed road systems, widely
dispersed population, etc. The character of Sahelian pastoral life, with its
inevitable aspect of at least some seasonal migration to favorable pastures,
further complicates things, as do ethnic antagonisms.

Many Niger officials consider contact with pastoralists pointless because they
are so "unreliable." Other administrators believe meaningful contact is possible
only if herders are sedentarized. Such propositions reflect thorough ignorance of
mobility as the most efficient manner of exploiting harsh, arid steppe environments. [77] Some officials, however, are better informed. [78] At any rate, relationships between civil servants and Niger pastoral zone herders remain distant and
often strained, as is common elsewhere in the Sahel. [79]

OUTCOMES OF POLITICO-ECONOMIC STRATEGIES IN MARGINAL ENVIRONMENTS

The relationships between people and natural resources that prevail in the Sahel
help some and expose others to risk and hardship. And the evolution of Sahelian
environments during recent decades partially reflects the strategies people have
pursued for survival or gain, given the exposures and opportunities they face as
individuals. This is no new phenomenon in the Sahel. As Baier argues, Tuareg
social structure clearly enabled nobles, especially those heading powerful
lineages, to organize exploitation of resources and capital to minimize the
impact of environmental calamities on their immediate families. [80]

Losers: The Marginal and Most Exposed

Thus, the losers in these games tend to be the poorest individuals. They cannot
fall back on a reliable government-operated social security net. Whether they

herd, farm, or do mixed farming, they remain constantly vulnerable to personal reverses. In the dry season, they *have* to go on labor migration, to earn money and to preserve inadequate food stores for the farming season. Then during the rains, they must typically hire themselves out to cultivate others' crops at critical points while their own languish for lack of proper attention.[81] The chance of an accident or sickness menaces them perpetually. When it occurs, family members may suffer crippling hunger if they cannot liquidate their possessions for food. At harvest time, what they reap in their fields falls far short of production on well-tended land. This poverty cycle can easily devastate a family over a short period of years.

Fragmentation of extended families also increases the Sahelian peasant's vulnerability to natural disasters.[82] Kinship support as an institutional safety net was weakened by the start of the 1970s drought. In part, this widespread pattern was fostered by cash cropping. Many young men found they could make it on their own by using the proceeds of peanut or cotton sales to finance tax payments and purchase basic necessities no longer produced within the family unit.[83] They demanded their share of the family patrimony before the father died or relinquished the economic leadership of the larger unit. When the drought struck, many could no longer pool their efforts to accomplish joint tasks or share the hardships on an equal basis. The institutional structure was no longer there. It was every man for himself, and the devil did take some of the hindmost.[84]

The poorest members of herding societies face a similar dilemma. Those with few animals or—more important for short-run family welfare—few milking animals, may have to sell so many beasts under drought conditions (or watch them progressively weaken and die) that reproduction can no longer meet the family's consumption needs and preserve the herd capital.[85]

If the herds of some pastoralists are stricken by scattered epizootics or an unusually high proportion of male calves, they can hope to reestablish themselves through recourse to indigenous stock gift and loan institutions.[86] But these mechanisms help far less when a major disaster sharply reduces the overall herd size in a large area. Marginal herders then face much greater difficulty regaining a working capital of livestock to support family needs and provide for increase.[87]

Now, during drought disasters, stricken peasants and herders can no longer rely on free goods—fruits, seeds, etc.—formerly available from common bush land. Especially in the most heavily populated regions of the Sudano-Sahelian zone, very little unclaimed bush remains. On the arid steppes, game herds, which earlier offered stock-poor nomads an alternative food source, have been largely decimated, both through over-hunting (soldiers, tourists, and others as well as nomads) and through the destruction of their habitat.

Only the cities and some rural regions of the humid savanna and rain forest to the south offer employment and a chance to earn one's keep. Demand for such positions in drought periods is likely to outstrip supply.

Winners: Doing Well by Others' Misfortunes

Joel Migdal argues that economic differentiation appears in peasant societies with the introduction of new opportunities which only some can exploit. New technology often initiates this differentiation process. General reverses in the fortunes of a community, which nonetheless strike families differentially, may likewise leave some comparatively stronger than others. In many cases, those able to benefit from others' misfortunes—by acquiring their land or their labor in the context of a patron-client relationship—can do so simply because they fortuitously enjoy a certain security cushion *at the time* disaster does others in.[88]

Government officials, who often control natural resources and access to them through the offices they hold, clearly have such a cushion. They can exploit legal determining powers exercised in the normal course of their duties to define what law will be effective in a particular situation.[89] Agricultural extension agents, quasi-cooperative managers salaried by the state, livestock agency personnel, public health workers, state marketing company clerks, and general administrators all enjoy chances to manipulate rules to enhance their own incomes, social prestige, political power, or all three.[90]

Forestry guards, the field agents for Sahelian conservation services, exemplify those who can benefit, as Thomas Hobbes put it in *Leviathan*, by manipulating "Unnecessary lawes, which are not good lawes, but trappes for money."[91] They exploit forestry code provisions to shake down wood users.

Other officials, employed as livestock agency personnel, sell water illegally to herders who congregate around high steppe boreholes. Instead of shutting pumps during much of the dry season to reduce the pressure on surrounding pastures, as officially required, well operators run pumps daily (or nightly, as the case may be) in return for herders' bribes.[92] Against government policy, they thus facilitate exploitation and eventually, overexploitation of pastures: herds congregate on the steppes where water is found.

In the Niger agricultural zone, wealthier individuals often secure animal traction equipment loans. It is difficult for most peasants to take advantage of such subsidies—currently amounting in Niger to $900 for a pair of oxen, a cart, plow, harrow, and other cultivation accessories. Many poorer peasants, whose annual cash income may not exceed $200, are understandably hesitant to go so far into debt.[93]

Wealthier individuals, who can take the risks along with the credit, thereby gain a strategic advantage: subsequently they can finance the purchase of chemical fertilizer with the proceeds of improved crop outputs and particularly, the returns from dry-season cartage. This permits them to rebuild impoverished soils and develop important grain reserves. They can either speculate with these reserves on the lucrative internal staple grain black market,[94] or use them as an inducement to attract or consolidate clients' support.

In the Niger pastoral zone, some Tuareg chiefs systematically encourage farmer and mixed-farmer immigration to the pastoral zone. They also urge herders devastated by the 1970s drought to take up cultivation in the immediate vicinity of their residences.[95] A simple logic explains this apparently paradoxical strategy of herding chiefs and nobles converting scarce pasture lands to agricultural uses.

Tuareg leaders derive personal benefits from this development, whatever eventual difficulties it may cause by eliminating pastures for marginal herders in their own and other ethnic groups. Three prominent benefits include: increases in the chiefs' tax revenues through the inscription of agricultural immigrants on their tax roles; increase in their entourages, and therefore in their reputations as powerful individuals; and access to local sources of millet, the staple grain which now bulks large in pastoral zone diets and which herders often cannot obtain from the state-run grain marketing agency. Farmers seeking a Tuareg patron, whatever their ethnic group, will probably sell him millet at attractive prices in return for his protection.

Increasing his dependent following—in addition to those who merely pay taxes through him to the administration—may help a chief consolidate control over an entire pasture area for his own ethnic group or personal clientele. Other herders not administratively subordinate to him may be driven from the area by a combination of illegal fines (which his clients never face) imposed for crop damages, and manipulation of public policy concerning the location of wells.

The latter tactic involves chiefs lobbying to have public wells placed next to privately owned ones controlled by other ethnic groups. The public well destroys whatever may remain of the traditional, quasi-private pasture management system in its immediate vicinity. By encouraging his clients to flood the area, the patron chief can temporarily run down the pasture base. If he has the political connections with administrators and others necessary to sustain the strategy at his rivals' expense, the combination of illegal fines and a dwindling critical resource may lead non-client herders to seek more abundant pastures elsewhere.[96]

Agricultural and intermediate zone residents now being forced from their lands by falling crop yields, or seeking to move into areas where agropastoralism is possible, represent an important resistance to eventual government attempts to stem immigration to the pastoral zone.[97] Some powerful Twareg chiefs might well fight immigration controls and attempts to end cultivation as threats to their own diversification strategies. Common herders might also resist controls on cultivation: many now want some family members to farm while others herd, to reduce their overall exposures at least in "normal" times, if not in bad drought years.[98]

Environmental Consequences

In the agricultural zone, several major trends can be discerned. Poor peasants' efforts to survive by cultivating lands more and more marginal in character—

either those already farmed too long without adequate fertilizer inputs, or low grade areas (hillsides, eroded surfaces, extremely arid sites)—pose a severe threat to the Sudano-Sahelian soil base. Cultivation techniques—clean-clearing fields—are adapted to the traditional bush fallow system. They cease to be viable once high percentages of land are kept under continuous cultivation. Field extension under current circumstances means woodstock destruction, sharply reduced natural regeneration, and intensified degradation of the soil base as it is more fully exposed to wind and water erosion.

Field extension has also destroyed pasture areas, forcing herdsmen to remove their animals to less populated regions. This may or may not reduce manure inputs to local fields. If local animals now consume all crop residues, there is probably not much to choose between the intestinal tracts of local beasts and those of transhumant animals.

Agricultural development programs such as irrigated and dryland productivity projects, seed hybridization, and producer credit operations have often benefited individuals at the expense of small groups or communities, with the practical result that the poor majority is increasingly marginalized.[99] Agricultural pursuits in the Sudano-Sahelian region are becoming less and less viable for large numbers of peasants.

Two consequences follow: emigration to urban areas or to other (coastal) countries, where opportunities are perceived to be more promising; or emigration to the Niger pastoral zone (herders, farmers, and agropastoralists alike). In the latter case, intensified exploitation of the pastoral zone provokes further environmental degradation there.

In political terms these developments create and strengthen patron-client alliances. Poor peasants and herders seek patrons for protection. They are thereby largely removed from the pool of potentially mobilizable individuals who might engage in pro-environmental political action at some future point: patrons do not want to reduce their leverage by stemming the environmental degradation which has driven clients to them in the first place. This same process, not surprisingly, can be identified in the history of some Sahelian agricultural development projects: environmental degradation increases clientele for an otherwise unsatisfactory role.[100]

The dry-season carrying capacity of the Niger pastoral zone is again strained less than ten years after the last major drought. Pastures improved when grazing pressure plummeted in the mid-1970s. But reconstituted herds, exploiting grazing leeways opened by the government's public water policy, may again be hindering the natural regeneration of pasture areas. Farming in the pastoral zone merely aggravates the situation.[101]

Winners' short-term strategies to promote their personal welfare may therefore be self-limiting over the medium term. The pastoral zone environment may be so fragile that dust bowl conditions will set in again, wiping out current profits. In that case, the pastoral zone chiefs will suffer somewhat from a decline of the herding economy. But, agricultural zone merchants, cattle owners, and government officials may well escape severe personal reverses from a decline or even collapse of pastoral zone herding. They may simply reorient their commercial activities into more profitable channels, or continue to draw government salaries. The herders who do not enjoy such flexibility and margins of security will not so easily ride out a renewed decline in the pastoral zone economy provoked by drought and/or environmental degradation.

Government efforts, through a drilling program to create more public boreholes, may succeed in opening up dry-season pastures hitherto inaccessible for lack of water. If the program succeeds, seed reserves for perennial grasses may be eliminated over wide areas. Spreading deforestation also threatens the pastoral zone, as woodcutters press further out into common lands of the pastoral steppes to supply fuel to southern cities.[102] This further magnifies the adverse impact of even small droughts.[103]

Given this situation, three outcomes can be envisaged:

1. Sahelian environmental management via imposition of woodcutting, farming, and grazing controls through political action by government and/or herders,
2. Environmental management as a consequence of herd ownership concentration and effective subdivision of Sahelian rangelands into (large) private, rationally managed parcels, or
3. A dustbowl, with grave resource impairment or even final destruction of the pastoral zone as a viable habitat.

The first outcome seems at present unlikely because government policies concerning self-help and local-level development do not now foster the effective local organizations indispensable to the sustained maintenance of grazing controls.[104]

Another possible outcome of this process would be the elimination of smaller herders (or their generalized reduction to the status of hired cowboys) and the concentration of control over Sahelian herds in the hands of a few major stock raisers. The latter might be traditional Tuareg nobles, southern merchants, or government officials. Members of a smaller ownership group might then successfully partition the Niger Sahel into exclusive ranges, each managed by a single owner for maximum sustained yield. Such a goal would presumably require close attention to the maintenance of ecological balances, especially the relationship between herd size and carrying capacity.

Finally, if this result, with its explicit marginalization of most herding peoples now operating in the Niger pastoral zone, is not forthcoming, and the institution of better environmental management proves infeasible, a Sahelian dustbowl may be nature's answer to continued abuse. Destruction of the pasture resource will impose, as suggested, serious and far-reaching social costs.

ENVIRONMENTALLY ORIENTED POLITICAL ACTION

Given the political dynamics already described, qualified skepticism is justified about long-term Sahelian environmental prospects. Those at the bottom of the ladder who are most exposed to the problems created by the excessive abuse of marginal lands have limited possibilities for political action to insulate themselves, share the risks more broadly, or reduce the strains on the environment. There are, however, a few potential incentives which might motivate individuals to undertake environmentally relevant political action in the Sahel and a few groups which may become more effective advocates for the Sahelian environment. The political impediments and potential for action are explored in this section.

In Niger, possibilities for political action are currently limited to highly individualistic forms of self-help and patron-client interactions designed to extract services from the government. Political parties have been formally banned since the 1974 coup. Thus even the half-blocked channel[105] of political input which the single Niger party (PPN-RDA) offered from 1960 to 1974 has been eliminated. Voluntary associations are extremely limited in number, working membership, and scope of activity.

The government's much-advertised Development Society program[106] provides in principle for a system of "apolitical" democratic centralism. Collective organizations at various levels in the hierarchy are designed to promote participation and popular input to political decision-making processes. They also aim to increase the degree of "self-help" implementation of policy decisions.

This appears highly problematic. If the whole effort is not stillborn through a combination of mediocre institutional design and bureaucratic inertia, it will doubtless suffer the same communication and participation weaknesses which plagued the Niger PPN-RDA party before 1974, as well as similar parties in many other African states.

The Development Society *may* have been cynically conceived by the regime as a means to consolidate government control over both stable (peasant) and elusive (pastoral) groups in the Niger population. Yet nothing indicates that the population will be more deceived about current regime goals than they were about those of the PPN-RDA. Passive resistance will again be the standard popular counter-strategy when rural people disagree with particular goals.

Extended family breakdown in Niger agricultural societies has seriously undercut local potential for effective, collectively organized and executed self-help projects.[107] In consequence, voluntary self-help activities are not often able to mobilize large numbers of people to create public goods of general benefit (e.g., wells, village woodlots, other forms of environmental management).[108] Instead, such actions take the form of *individual* migration to a shrinking bush frontier, often on the high steppes, or the pursuit of personal success in commerce, sometimes in agriculture. Most *collective* self-help activities are really quasi-voluntary and clearly shaped by administrators.[109] Such projects reflect not local perceptions, but decisions that top-level administrators take. They hardly offer rural dwellers a way to shape environmental policy.

When such projects directly address ecological and conservation issues, they are often so badly designed and executed from a sociopolitical perspective that they simply abort any possible popular identification with government policy goals.[110] They rather lead individuals to avoid involvement if possible with, say, village woodlots and convince them to cut their losses after an initial "voluntary" participation by letting seedlings die.[111]

Barriers to Political Action

The most general, impenetrable, and pernicious barrier to political action for ecological or any other ends in the Sahel is simple government unwillingness to see it happen unless co-opted and controlled by *les autorités*.[112] This generalized administrative suspicion of autonomous organized activity creates major structural difficulties for political entrepreneurs concerned with organizing people around specific interests, for example, poverty. As well, serious social and political skill deficiencies, particularly literacy, further discourage political action.

In Niger as elsewhere in francophone Sahel, officials have inherited and made their own the French colonial administration's antipathy to group activity not government sponsored. By definition, the most worthy "voluntary" associations are those expressly established to realize regime goals. Other voluntary associations are tolerated only so long as they organize their activities in government-defined channels and do not contest government policies, especially by disrupting the peace. This view of voluntary associations reflects French administrative tradition dating back to at least the seventeenth century.[113]

Antagonisms inherent in the colonial situation between black and white, imperialist and conquered, governors and subjects, reinforced the concern to break up and eliminate autonomous, unco-optable private groups as potentially seditious organizations. Independent governments in most francophone Sahelian states, even more insecure about their ability to control the situation they inherited from the colonial power at independence, have followed suit with a vengeance. Aristide Zolberg's account of early postindependence (1960–1963) institutional engineering in the Ivory Coast remains highly instructive concerning these tactics.[114] So also does Niger legislation concerning conditions of legal association.[115] All Niger groups (public and private) must conform with relatively onerous administrative registration requirements to achieve the status of a legal organization.

The generally fragile regimes of postindependence francophone West Africa sought by all means within their power to clamp a hold on any form of continuing organization. As a result of elites' nation-building aspirations (regularly perceived by groups not represented or underrepresented in the national power bloc as exercises in ethnic imperialism), almost all faced opposition. Out-groups often sought merely to replace ruling elites, rather than to make good on separatist claims. Both aspirations struck incumbents as equally dangerous and illegal, whence the rash of one-party-state declarations (often before legal inde-pendence was achieved).[116] Nondominant ethnic groups and other potential opposition sources such as unions and student associations continue to face the jaundiced eye of administrators and regime leaders alike.[117]

These circumstances have encouraged Sahelian regimes, military and civil-ian alike, to take extreme measures to control and hamstring political power at the local level. Widespread absence of autonomous local government is thus a casualty of central government fears of letting go. State by state, from bottom to top, the subprefectoral/refectoral bureaucratic structure which controls 90 per-cent of the Sahelian population reports directly to a minister of the interior or to his military head of state.

The orientation of low-ranking civil servants is not out but up, to those who may decisively influence their career possibilities. They do not often look to the individuals they administer for clues about salient issues. Initiative for ac-tivities almost always derives from a superior echelon, if not from the center itself, rather than originating from local people's perceptions of problematic situations which, to be set right, require political or governmental action.

Only the rarest of local officials wants to attract attention to himself by making policies or autonomously initiating collective efforts to handle local problems. Given the centralized framework and bias of the system, it smacks of presumption, if not insubordination, when a local official identifies a local problem and then tries to mobilize people to do something about it.[118]

Neither local officials nor local residents fail to identify pressing issues relating to renewable resources, such as failing wood reserves, soil erosion, pasture degradation, and the like. People whose livelihood and welfare depends on these resources can hardly ignore reduced availability.

But generalized perception of scarcity does not lead automatically to reme-dial *collective* action in contemporary Sahelian systems. Feasible *individual* responses can be expected, e.g., leaving seedlings which sprout naturally in cultivated fields to mature, or terracing land to slow runoff and halt erosion. By contrast, because collective responses currently face enormous organizational costs, they are much less likely. Initiative for action has to come from higher up, or at least appear to originate there. In practice, this means a Niger subprefect—of which there are thirty-two in the entire country of five million inhabitants—has to accord the project his backing.

Effective support requires time and allocation of scarce administrative re-sources. These demands compete with all other interests, concerns, and duties on the subprefect's schedule. Given his key—and time-consuming—role in the administrative system, chances of his giving effective backing to more than a very limited number of local resource management operations shrink to insignificance.

This same barrier to action recurs across the entire range of technical service agencies active in Niger—the quasi-co-operative union, credit associations, agricultural and livestock extension, adult literacy, and forestry departments among others—whose activities the subprefect in principle coordinates. Arrondissement technicians cannot handle all the tasks the centralized organization system lays at their doorstep. So the majority of renewable resources, effective management of which requires collective action, simply degenerate for lack of effective attention.

Rural people are prevented so regularly from taking action that few ever get to the point of envisaging solutions. Rather, they immediately—and accurately—conclude that constructive collective action is not feasible, unless and until an administrator or technician takes the matter in hand. And then, given the press of problems, one has to worry whether he (or his successor in the post) will follow up in adequate fashion to see the task through to completion.

Regime officials often urge peasants and herders to demonstrate their interest in their country's future by conserving its resources.[119] Administrators admonish people to "reforest" or "do soil conservation" on a voluntary basis.

But peasants living with undesirable consequences of local underorganization know all too well the limits of voluntary action in preserving unregulated common property resources. In their own villages and in neighboring communities they personally know individuals ready to act as free-riders when investment in resource preservation is proposed. Peasants often despair of controlling these people because they so frequently lack effective enforcement mechanisms, aside from social pressure. The latter is much weakened, furthermore, by the disintegration of the extended family structure.

This holds for development of communal water control systems,[120] pasture management where the commons cannot be subdivided into individual or small-group parcels, village woodlots,[121] and soil conservation measures which must be applied to natural ecological units extending across more than one piece of property.[122]

This gross and generalized failure of Sahelian governments (and donor organizations) to confront adequately the basic problems of common property resource management leads then with painful inevitability to otherwise avoidable outcomes. The system as structured cannot handle the myriad management problems involved in restoring degraded local environments, *even though many of these are not technically difficult*. Proper management would require a vast multiplication of decision points, empowering local governments to organize, control, and sustain the long-term collective action demanded by renewable resource management in the Sahel or elsewhere, whether particular efforts are themselves individual or collective in nature.

Local governments capable of managing renewable resources with sufficient flexibility to be effective have to be autonomous, not dominated by a ponderous, immobilized administrative hierarchy. And they have to be authorized in a general, blanket fashion to move to manage such resources by setting up and upholding resource use regulations. Sahelian regimes' suspicions of uncontrolled and unco-opted local organizations probably make development of local government power politically infeasible.

The generalized poverty of Sahelian peasants and herders distracts them from environmental issues whenever they become seriously worried about feeding themselves, paying taxes, and meeting their other immediate needs. Lack of cash precludes certain efforts to intensify agricultural systems. Unfortunately this poverty limitation cannot be overcome merely by transfering national or foreign donor funds to local communities or individuals. It matters intensely how such funds are supplied and controlled once received; all too often they generate local dependence on outside initiatives in resource management problems, rather than strengthening local capacity to deal with the problem.[123]

Illiteracy, ignorance of French (the official language of most West African Sahelian states), and lack of accounting skills reduce peasant and herder ability to promote their viewpoints in negotiations with administrators, as do the status disparities between those who hold power and those who do not. Their ignorance of civil law and formal norms governing civil servant conduct reinforces this weakness in relationships with administrators. Generally, peasants know they are without effective recourse against abuse of power, and so decide to avoid such situations in the first place.

Incentives to Defend the Environment

Given such barriers, the potential for incentives which do or could motivate people to ecological concerns and action is constrained. Institutional motivations can be designed to promote "ecological awareness" by cutting costs to individuals of sustained yield management of renewable resources. But the effectiveness of such incentives, or more basically, their politico-legal feasibility, depends on two preconditions. First, as noted, autonomous local government must become a reality, to facilitate organization of management operations on a meaningful and viable local scale, and to handle user regulations enforcement.

Second, peasants and herders must perceive resource scarcities and view them as gravely threatening. So long as the people—the Sahelian peasants, herders, and bureaucrats—believe that the renewable resource reserves are adequate, or that they can escape the adverse effects of perceived shortages by geographical or career shifts, talk of conservation or resource development is irrelevant. Only when a resource crunch squeezes them personally can such people justify changing their resource consumption and management patterns (if the organizational costs of effecting the change are not excessive). The many pressing needs they face *right now* obscure the necessity to plan renewable resource futures if it means that the wood and soil crucial to producing today's dinner will come up short. The same holds for the grasses eaten by the herds which hold pastoral families together. Once people begin to wonder what they will do when the small remaining amounts of grass, wood, soil, or water disappear, motivations to invest in future supplies begin to make sense.

Assuming these two preconditions can be met, the best incentives to ensure sustained-yield renewable resource management would take the form of efforts to guarantee personal returns to individual investments in increasing or maintaining future supplies of a perceived scarce resource. Reforestation in some areas of Niger, for example, could be more easily and more effectively encouraged by changing the current forestry code to individualize tree tenure. Foresters now legally control the use of fifteen important tree species on private lands as well as in state forests. Understaffed, under-funded, and undermotivated, foresters by and large fail miserably in accomplishing this task. The roughly five million peasants and herders who live in rural Niger represent a potentially much more effective wood use regulation force than do the less than 400 forestry department employees (247 in 1978).[124] This holds both in terms of numbers—physical presence in rural areas—and in terms of potential interest in protecting individualized parts of the common property woodstock. At present, however, rural dwellers have no official role either in regulating demand or in promoting investment in woodstock supplies. Despite some exceptions, little individual investment in new woodstock increments now occurs.

Privatizing tree tenure would not alone generate reforestation efforts.[125] In many parts of the Sahel, residence and work patterns preclude full-time casual (and costless) surveillance of a village's entire land area. Consumers can take wood from many fields without being seen. Nonetheless the direct incentive to defend one's trees would, in wood-short areas, almost certainly increase the risks of taking without asking if the local government were competent to enforce property rules and impose realistic penalties for proven violations.

Given heavy grazing pressure, effective pasture management requires institutional incentives to engage in *collective* use regulation, rather than the largely individualistic approach appropriate for many reforestation activities. Collective control is dictated by the uncertainty of rainfall in the high Sahelian steppes. Unless enormous areas were to come under individual, or company, or state ranch control, no one herder could support his herd annually entirely on his "own" pasture (some limited and defined area allocated to him for his exclusive use). Thus areas sufficiently large to ensure members adequate grass in most years somewhere within the unit's boundaries must be established, and allocated to named and known associations of herders. But allocation of access rights is only the beginning of a solution.[126]

Grazing rights must be exclusive, i.e., available only to association members, who would then have power to keep others off. Grazing rights to surplus grass could be auctioned off to non-group members or traded to other associations as part of a long-term strategy to assure adequate grass even in bad years. But in all cases, grazing rights must be enforceable.

Once such associations are in place, rights accorded, and enforcement procedures operational (no easy task),[127] effective incentives to maintain or upgrade pasture quality will influence considerably herder calculations about herd size and overgrazing. *If* conservation this year reduces probabilities that herds will have to be cut in future years, *if* investments in pasture improvement mean herd sizes can later be increased, *if* government—and donor-controlled—livestock and range management projects do not impose actions so onerous they alienate herders, pastoralists may be induced, within the limits of technical constraints, to modify their survival strategies. But this all remains problematic.[128]

Other possibilities exist to heighten effective environmental concern among herders. Conversion of the infamous boreholes of the high Sahel, which induce localized but intense overgrazing, to borehole wells would activate economic and technical disincentives to exceeding the carrying capacity of the surrounding pastures. It would also be possible in some Sahelian areas to reinforce traditional pasture management systems based on water point control.

In some situations, mere provision of better information (often conditioned on improvements in extension networks, which may currently be inadequate or nonexistent) about effective or improved conservation techniques such as terracing and contour plowing may suffice to motivate action.[129] Other situations require, for improved soil management, a combination of: better information, e.g., concerning the value of windbreaks in cutting aeolian erosion; appropriate species and inexpensive planting techniques, plus policy changes vesting the ownership of trees in planters or land owners; and the creation of local soil conservation authorities capable of taking nonvoluntary decisions to organize collective antierosion efforts which individual attempts cannot realize on the basis of willing consent.

Associated attempts to intensify agricultural production, temporarily relieving the stress on parts of the arable soil base, can be undertaken. But they may require—if rural dwellers are to benefit—more labor-intensive activity than has to date been the case in most development projects. Furthermore, the participants must be associated with planning the operations from the beginning, and they must know the terms and conditions of participation. This is indispensable if the participants' long-term commitment to sustained soil management within the project framework is to be achieved.[130] It will require greater concern with the participants' welfare as opposed to the interests of international donors, national governments, urban populations, and large-scale companies.[131]

The same holds for watershed management operations: in some situations, better information will suffice; in others, policy changes that vest control over conserved water in those who create the management devices will be needed in addition to better information about low-cost, improved construction techniques. Legislation will probably also be necessary to force other potential beneficiaries to shoulder their fair share of the investment costs for particular local projects.[132]

The desire to achieve national food self-sufficiency may motivate some Sahelian elites to better environmental management. All Sahelian leaders face the economic constraint of buying extremely high-priced staple grain on the international market. Foreign aid food grants may be inadequate in the future to cover Sahelian national grain production shortfalls.

Elites can then decide to import expensive grains at the risk of mortgaging the country's future (even in mineral-rich states such as Niger, imported food costs can wreak havoc with budget provisions and development projects financed by domestic funds). They can accept famine, perhaps outright mass starvation and the opprobrium and destabilizing effects associated therewith. Or they can move to manage the environment for greater productivity, and seek ways to motivate greater peasant food production and improved distribution. For committed nationalists, or those elites who have made mass food security a fundamental justification for their seizure of government power (Niger's Seyni Kountché fits both categories),[133] arguments for achieving national food self-sufficiency appear overwhelming.

National elites may not place environmental protection high on their list of action priorities. But they may be induced to stress ecological issues by foreign donor willingness to finance projects focused directly on environmental issues. Reorientation may also come through donor insistence that other projects, e.g., agricultural development or livestock and range management efforts, incorporate substantial environmental components. Elites may or may not be interested in the environmental aspects. However, if the elites desire other values that come with the projects (i.e., jobs for themselves and subordinates, material, budget support, perks, etc.), donors have bargaining power to buy action on environmental issues.

Such interactions and the elites' own observations of national soils departing on wind- or water-borne transnational voyages, fuel wood price increases outstripping inflation, etc., may transform their sense of the urgency of environmental protection for their own political welfare. This is probably the most salient consideration for those at top levels of national power. In the long run, their individual social and/or economic welfare may hardly be directly affected by degradation of renewable natural resources, but the potential indirect effects on political stability at the state or national level may prompt greater elite concern.

Administrators at the level of prefect and subprefect, and technical counterparts, may find they can enhance their bureaucratic careers by seizing environment issues once concern about the environment has received blessing at the national level. A newsworthy, environmentally relevant project demonstrating an official's initiative may merit him a promotion over the heads of his peers and beyond the regular rank advancement he is practically guaranteed with additional years of civil service employment.[134] Those intent on advancement will thus see in environmental issues incentives as strong as in any other issues which will potentially lead to promotion.

Potential Environmental Advocates

Structural constraints in contemporary Sahelian systems limit the set of potential environmental advocates to pinnacle power figures. All other elites will remain mere sycophants mouthing the leaders' formulas and planting the same old doomed exotic tree species until and unless a fundamental political reorientation occurs on high. That change must be, specifically, not regionalization but localization. Localization must be valid, in turn, not just for environmental problems but for other issues which legitimately fall within the purview of viable local governments. Otherwise, such jurisdictions will probably not command the respect necessary to enforce environmental regulations.

Inevitably, such a change risks exposing central government officials to messages and pressures they would prefer to avoid. Popular pressure in some cases would conceivably exceed the annoyance level and develop into significant local vetoes on central policy makers' options. Thus the likelihood of such a change occurring in the near future remains small.

Given the costs, individual peasants and herders are not likely to become active environmental advocates. Some may act to preserve their part of the environment, but they will not often seek to attract attention, or actively set an example. The most one can hope for in this regard is that individuals will take action on their land to stem erosion, promote reforestation, encourage infiltration of surface waters, and protect or restore pastures. If enough individuals engage in these activities, they may eventually lay the groundwork for a change in public policy. But they will not articulate it, except and unless localization reduces costs to them of environmental political entrepreneurship.

CONCLUSIONS: ARE EFFECTIVE ANTIDESERTIFICATION POLICIES PROBABLE?

It has been argued here that effective environmental activities in the Sahelian states depend on localization of decision making about antidesertification efforts. Other factors (rural dwellers' perceptions of dwindling supplies of certain natural resources; technical difficulties in planting and maintaining tree seedlings; upgrading pasture areas or constructing and effectively exploiting contour dike systems; severe poverty, etc.—will clearly influence the evolution of the environment if localization becomes a reality and individuals have the opportunity to confront resource management problems on a collective as well as an individual basis. But without localization, little if any joint effort will be expended on stabilizing local milieus in the Sahelian zone: in individual user's terms, return will not justify the investment in voluntary collective action.

The critical question thus is whether localization is likely. As suggested, several systemic factors work against it: administrators' ingrained perception of their "duty" to exert control over all problems in any way related to the public good as they define it, and a correlative distrust of autonomous local organization; a distaste for the inconveniences associated with popular input into policy making, and a positive dislike of having to answer popular demands; a lack of strong incentive to initiate new, i.e., environmentally relevant, projects at the sub-national levels. These impediments hinder local-level entrepreneurship centered on environmental problems.

Balanced against these are a few incentives for elites to change their policies. In particular, a concern for achieving food self-sufficiency and foreign donor insistence that environmental problems be faced may provoke new elite initiatives when coupled with an observation of the environmental degradation. But prospects are not bright.

In Niger as elsewhere in the Sahel, other political problems and dramas influence environmental issues. President Seyni Kountché, the key decision maker in the contemporary Niger political system, officially wants to decentralize policy formulation and implementation. The desire to decentralize is not, however, tantamount to a policy of creating autonomous local power centers capable of dealing with many of their own public policy problems.

Kountché formally supports increased popular participation in policy formulation and implementation. But he envisages this as an innovation within constraints established by existing structures. Peasants and herders, organized in Development Society cooperatives and youth groups, will funnel their opinions on various problems (identified either at the local level or at supra-local decision centers) up through a series of consultative assemblies to the center. Decisions taken and ratified at the center will then be sent down the hierarchy for implementation.

Kountché presumably does not want to localize power beyond his regime's ability to control effective decisions at canton and village levels for several reasons. First, sub-regional cadres are thought to be unable to handle development tasks correctly. Conventional wisdom suggests that most of them lack adequate training, discipline, and initiative. But their unproductive behavior can perhaps be better explained by civil servants' accurate perception that peasant clients of the bureaucracy (to say nothing of herders) have no recourse against them if they do nothing. Francophone African civil service regulations preclude superiors from placing much of a premium on productivity in most cases, and peasants cannot insist on performance, so things move slowly indeed.

Second, Kountché mistrusts certain ethnic groups. Ethnic antagonisms between the Hausa and Djerma tribes concerning the Djerma's minority control of key government posts since independence, despite the former group's numerical dominance, are historical facts in Niger. But they now pale by comparison with north/south, black/white, sedentary/pastoral antagonism, especially given Libya's present irredentist policies concerning all Saharan Twareg groups.

The conflict which underlies these antagonisms predates the colonial era by centuries. While certain important Niger Tuareg groups (e.g., the Kel Ewey) collaborated productively with black Sahelian sultanates, others, particularly the Ouillimmedan confederation tribes, did not. This same sort of conflict persists in Mauritania, Mali, and Chad, three other important Sahelian states.

Niger's main mineral resource, uranium—upon which hangs a good part of the country's economic future—derives entirely from northern, traditionally Twareg, ethnic areas. These same regions lie within easy striking distance of Col. Muammar Qaddafi's Libyan regime. Qadaffi has made crystal clear his willingness to help the Niger Tuareg to rid themselves of a black government. In radio broadcasts in late 1980, in contacts through agents with Tuareg on labor migration north into Libya, and very recently in granting political asylum to several important Niger Tuareg civil servants, he has left no doubt about his position.

Kountché's reaction has been to move beyond the traditional administrative policy of posting civil servants outside their home areas by sending a number of Ouillimmeden Tuareg into their native region in northwest Niger with a mandate to "show what they can do." This is a partially bold move; but at the same time, Kountché is forcing the pace of co-operativization in the Niger pastoral (Tuareg) zone. This latter policy will almost certainly encounter effective passive resistance and find an ineffectual end. But it indicates the president's continuing concern to establish some form of reliable control over the people of the pastoral zone, in order to direct what happens there and to keep himself fully informed about events in the region.

This same concern applies—if with less urgency—to the black ethnic groups of the country. For this reason, contemporary regionalization and Development Society policies are unlikely soon to be converted into power localization policies. But until the peasants have active rather than passive vetoes on government programs and bureaucrats' activities, they are just as unlikely to undertake the sorts of environmental management efforts upon which their own salvation ultimately depends. They can do some things on an individual basis, as the need and the possibility of action is perceived. But such responses will not suffice to stem the negative developments of creeping and leap-frogging desertification which are converting Sahelian lands to Saharan desert.

Notes

1. A. T. Grove, "Desertification in the African Environment," in *Drought in Africa/ Sécheresse en Afrique*, 2, edited by David Dalby, R. J. Harrison Church, and Fatima Bezzaz (London: International African Institute, 1977), p. 54.

2. H. N. Le Houérou, "The Nature and Causes of Desertization," in *Desertification: Environmental Degradation in and around Arid Lands*, edited by Michael H. Glantz (Boulder, Colo.: Westview Press, 1977), pp. 17–21.

3. Niger, located between Nigeria to the south and Algeria to the north, encompasses a small strip of arable land along its southern frontier and a vast block of Saharan territory which makes up the bulk of the country.

4. Jean Copans, ed., *Sécheresses et famines du sahel* (Paris: François Maspero, 1975), I, pp. 5–6.

5. Edmond Bernus, *Touaregs nigériens*, Mémoire No. 94 (Paris: O.R.S.T.O.M., 1981); and Stephen Baier, *An Economic History of Central Niger* (Oxford: Clarendon Press, 1980).

6. Marguérite Dupire, *Peuls nomades: étude descriptive des Wodaabe du sahel nigérien* (Paris: Institut d'ethnologie, 1962).

7. Le Houérou, "Nature and Causes," p. 26.

8. Guy Nicolas, "Un village bouzou du Niger: étude d'un terroir," *Cahiers d'outremer* 15 no. 58 (April–June 1962), 138–65; James T. Thomson, "Law, Legal Process and Development at the Local Level in Hausa-speaking Niger: A Trouble Case Analysis of Rural Institutional Inertia." Ph.D. diss., Department of Political Science, Indiana University, Bloomington, Ind., 1976; Richard W. Franke and Barbara H. Chasin, *Seeds of Famine: Ecological Destruction and the Development Dilemma in the West African Sahel* (Montclair, N.J.: Allenheld Osmun, 1980), p. 48; and S. Diarra, "Les strategies spatiales des eleveurs-cultivateurs peul du Niger central agricole," in *Maîtrise de l'espace agraire et développement en Afrique tropicale: logique paysanne et rationalité technique*, Actes du colloque de Ouagadougou, December 4–8, 1978 (Paris: O.R.S.T.O.M., 1979), pp. 87–91.

9. Richard W. Franke and Barbara H. Chasin, "Peanuts, Peasants, Profits, and Pastoralists: The Social and Economic Background to Ecological Deterioration in Niger," *Peasant Studies* 8, no. 3 (Summer 1979): 1–30; interviews with Brah Gourgoudou, traditional chief of Mirriah Arrondissement Fulbe nomad canton, and with Tambari Liman, traditional chief of Mirriah Arrondissement Kel Ewey Tuareg nomad canton, both at Zinder, Niger, February 2, 1981.

10. Grove, "African Environment," p. 54.

11. Baldur Gabriel, "Early and Mid-Holocene Climate in the Eastern Central Sahara," in *Drought in Africa/Sécheresse en Afrique*, 2, ed. by David Dalby, R. J. Harrison Church, and Fatima Bezzaz (London: International African Institute, 1977), p. 65.

12. Grove, "African Environment."

13. D. J. Shove, "African Droughts and the Spectrum of Time," in *Drought in Africa/ Sécheresse en Afrique*, 2, ed. by David Dalby, R. J. Harrison Church and Fatima Bezzaz, (London: International African Institute, 1977), pp. 38–53.

14. Youssouf Kalillou, "Cette sécheresse que l'on cherche a juguler," *Sahel Hebdo* (Niamey, Niger) 234 (August 4, 1980): 20.

15. Le Houérou, "Nature and Causes," pp. 17–38; and Michael H. Glantz, ed., *Politics of a Natural Disaster: The Case of the Sahel Drought* (New York: Praeger, 1976).

16. CILSS [Comité inter-états de lutte contre la sécheresse au sahel]/Club du Sahel, *Recueil de statistiques socio-économiques pour les pays du sahel* (Paris: OECD, 1978), p. 56.

17. Roger Murray, "Uranium: The Search Continues," *African Business* 20 (April 1980): 12–13; Franke and Chasin, *Seeds of Famine*, pp. 177–79.

18. G. M. Higgins, A. H. Kassam, L. Naiken and M. M. Shah, "Le potentiel agricole de l'Afrique," *CERES* 83 (September–October 1981): 16–19; Assane Saadou, "Le directeur général des eaux et forêts au Sahel Hebdo: atteindre et sensibiliser le plus grand nombre de populations," *Sahel Hebdo* (Niamey, Niger) 234 (August 4, 1980): 24.

19. Thierry Brun, "Manifestations nutritionnelles et medicales de la famine," in *Sécheresses et famines du sahel*, ed. by Jean Copans (Paris: Francois Maspéro, 1975), I, 75–108.

20. CILSS/Club du Sahel, *Recueil de statistiques*, pp. 10–11.

21. Franke and Chasin, *Seeds of Famine*, pp. 192–94, 214–218; see also Roger Meunier, "L'aide d'urgence et les nouveaux projects de développement." In *Sécheresses et famines du sahel*, ed. by Jean Copans (Paris: Francois Maspéro, 1975), I, 125–27.

22. Arlene Blade, "Agro-Forestry Project (Vol. 93) Project Description." OXFAM, Ouahigouya, Upper Volta. Unpublished ms., 1980; Etienne Verneir, Philippe Amirault, and Emmanuel Bricks, "Petite hydraulique rurale: rapport d'activités, session 1980/81." Association française des volontaires du progrès, Séguénéga, O.R.D. du Yatenga, Upper Volta. Mimeographed report.

23. A. Aubréville, "Les forêts de la colonie du Niger," *Bulletin de la comité d études historiques et scientifiques de 1 AOF* 19, no. 1 (March, 1936), 46–47, 58–69.

24. Gunnar Poulsen, "Man and Tree in Tropical Africa: Three Essays on the Role of Trees in the African Environment," Pamphlet No. IDRC–101e. (Ottawa, Canada: International Development Research Centre, 1978), 24; Anon., "Le Discours du ministre du développement rural—'planter un arbre c'est nourrir un homme,'" *Sahel Hebdo* (Niamey, Niger) 234 (August 4, 1980): 26–28.

25. Le Houérou, "Nature and Causes," pp. 21–22, 25–26.

26. Henk Bremen, "Rangeland Productivity and Exploitation in the Sahel: To Improve Development Aid for Sahelian Livestock Farming, Soil Poverty Has to Be Recognized as a Major Bottleneck," in *Productivité des pâturages sahelians: une étude du sol, des végétations et de l'exploitation de cette ressource naturelle*, edited by F. W. T. Penning de Vries and M. A. Djiteye (Wageningen, The Netherlands: Pudoc, forthcoming), p. 7.

27. James T. Thomson, "Nigerien Herder Associations: Institutional Analysis and Design" (report submitted to Niger Range and Livestock Project, USAID/Niger, Niamey, Niger, June 9, 1981); Henk Bremen, A. Diallo, G. Traoré, and M. M. Djiteye, "The Ecology of the Annual Migrations of Cattle in the Sahel," in *Proceedings of the First International Rangeland Congress*, August 14–18, 1978, Denver, Colorado (Denver, Colo.: Society for Range Management, 1978), p. 595; Bremen, "Exploitation in the Sahel," discusses technical constraints limiting pasture management possibilities.

28. This and the preceding paragraph are based, in addition to references cited, on an interview with Bernard Peyre de Fabregues, agrostologist specializing in Sahelian

forage plants, associated with the French Institut d'Elevage et de Medicine Veterinaire Tropical (I.E.M.V.T.), at Zinder, Niger, June 26, 1981.

29. Ralph H. Faulkingham, "Ecological Constraints and Subsistence Strategies: The Impact of Drought in a Hausa Village, A Case Study from Niger," in *Drought in Africa/ Sécheresse en Afrique, 2,* ed. by David Dalby, R. J. Harrison Church, and Fatima Bezzaz, (London: International African Institute, 1977): p. 150.

30. A pseudonym.

31. Information supplied to me by research assistants permanently residing in those towns; June 1981.

32. CILSS/Club du Sahel, *Recueil de statistique,* p. 78.

33. Abdoulaye Boureima, "Produits vivriers : le seuil de la Tolérance," *Le Sahel* (Niamey, Niger) May 28, 1981, 3.

34. Claude Raynaut, "Lessons of a Crisis," in *Drought in Africa/Sécheresse en Afrique, 2,* ed. by David Dalby, R. J. Harrison Church and Fatima Bezzaz (London: International African Institute, 1977), pp. 17–29) Guy Nicolas, "Remarques sur divers facteurs socio-economiques de la famine au sein d'une société subsaharienne," in *Drought in Africa/Sécheresse en Afrique, 2,* ed. by David Dalby, R. J. Harrison Church and Fatima Bezzaz (London: International African Institute): pp. 195–96; Franke and Chasin, *Seeds of Famine;* Warren J. Enger "Niger Agricultural Sector Assessment," (Niamey, Niger: USAID, 1979) Vol. I "Synthesis," xi.

35. Claude Raynaut, "Programme de recherche multidisciplinaire dans la région de Maradi (Niger): méthodes et premiers résultats," in *Maîtrise de l'espace agraire et développement en Afrique tropicale; logique paysanne et rationalité technique,* Actes du colloque de Ouagadougou, December 4–8, 1978 (Paris: O.R.S.T.O.M., 1979), pp. 432–434.

36. Poly Hill, *Studies in Rural Capitalism in West Africa* (Cambridge: Cambridge University Press, 1970), p. 155.

37. CILSS/Club du Sahel, *Recueil de statistiques,* p. 78, Table II.4; Jean-Yves Marchal, "Système agraire et évolution de l'occupation de l'espace au Yatenga (Haute-Volta)," *Cahiers de l'O.R.S.T.O.M. Série Sciences Humaines* 14, no. 2, 141–149; Raynaut, "Lessons of a Crisis," pp. 17–29; Enger, "Niger Sector Assessment," I, 14–33.

38. Faulkingham, "Drought in a Hausa Village," p. 149.

39. Marchal, "L'espace au Yatenga," p. 145; Peter Hammond, *Yatenga: Technology in the Culture of a West African Kingdom* (New York: Free Press, 1966), pp. 33–34.

40. John W. Sutter, "Social Analysis of the Nigerien Rural Producer," in "Niger Sector Assessment," ed. by Warren J. Enger (Niamey, Niger: USAID, 1979), II.D, pp. 24–25; Jean-Yves Marchal, *Société, éspace et désertification dans le Yatenga (Haute-Volta), ou la dynamique de l'escape rural soudano-sahélian* (Paris: O.R.S.T.O.M., 1982), II, 418.

41. B. Toutain, "Situation de l'élevage dans le sahel voltaique face a l'extension de l'escape agraire," in *Maîtrise de l'espace agraire et développement en Afrique tropicale: logique paysanne et rationalité technique,* Actes du colloque de Ouagadougou, 4–8 décembre 1978 (Paris: O.R.S.T.O.M., 1979), p. 195.

42. See interviews mentioned in footnote 9. Interview with M. Levif, Section Vétérinaire, Ministère de la Coopération, Paris, May 18, 1981, commenting on the extensive destruction of traditional flood recession pastures in the Niger River's inland delta around Mopti in Mali; interview with John Heermans, USAID technician, Niger

Forestry and Land Use Planning Project, concerning grazing pressure on state forest lands east of Niamey, Niger, after development of irrigation schemes in Niger River bottoms destroyed formerly prime dry season pastures for area herders, Niamey, May 19, 1981; Angelo B. Maliki, "Etude socio-démographique sur la population wodáabé et fulbe de la région du projet NRL" (Niamey, Niger: USAID/Niger, Niger Range and Livestock Project, n.d. [1981]), pp. 1–15. In addition, land cases brought to defend traditional public grazing grounds in the Zinder area of Niger reflect this same dynamic of competition between herders and farmers (or between stock-owning farmers and land-hungry agriculturalists).

43. Toutain, "Situation de l'élevage."

44. Interview with Patrick Paris, pastoral sociologist, Niger Centre-Est Livestock Project (World Bank), Tanout, Tanout Arrondissement, Zinder Department, Niger, January 30, 1981.

45. Thomson, "Law, Legal Process and Development," pp. 99–115.

46. Sutter, "Nigerien Rural Producer", II.D., pp. 67–69.

47. Marchal, "Société, espace et désertification" II, 363.

48. PNUD (Programme des nations unies pour le développement), Projet NER 77/001; Ecole nationale d'administration de Niamey, "Les régimes fonciers du Niger: leur évolution et leur impact sur le développement de la production agricole" (Niamey, Niger: E.N.A., 1978), pp. 29–54.

49. Interview with M. T., Dajin Kowa (pseudonym), Mirriah Arrondissement, Zinder Départment, Niger, June 12, 1981.

50. Thomson, "Law, Legal Process and Development", pp. 235–80.

51. Club du Sahel, "Analyse du secteur forestier et propositions: Le Niger," Sahel D(81) 132; (Paris: Club du Sahel [OCDE/CILSS]), II, 61.

52. Interview with Counsellor D. F., Inuwa, Inuwa Canton, Mirriah Arrondissement, Zinder Department, Niger, June 14, 1981.

53. PNUD, "Les régimes fonciers du Niger," pp. 39–40.

54. Niger, Law No. 74–77 of March 4, 1974, Arts. 16, 22.

55. Asko, "La coupe du bois: une des causes de la desertification," Sahel Hebdo (Niamey, Niger) 234 (August 4, 1980), 18; cf. Niger, Decree No. 74-226/PCMS/MER/CAP of August 23, 1974, Art. 8.

56. James T. Thomson, "Ecological Deterioration: Local-Level Rule-Making and Enforcement Problems in Niger," in Desertification: Environmental Degradation in and around Arid Lands, edited by Michael H. Glantz (Boulder, Colo.: Westview Press, 1977), pp. 57–79.

57. Asko, "La coupe du bois," 18.

58. Club du Sahel, "Analyse du secteur forestier," II, 134.

59. Thomson, "Ecological Deterioration," pp. 64–71.

60. Niger Conseil militaire suprême, No. 01/PCMS/CAP (circular from President Seyni Kountché to ministers criticizing lack of consultation with subordinate levels in planning ministry activities), 1979.

61. Seyni Kountché, "Allocution prononcée par son excellence le colonel Seyni Kountché, président du conseil militaire suprême chef de l'état à l'occasion de la première réunion de la commission nationale de mise en place de la société de développement," (text of speech, Niamey, March 17, 1980) p. 6.

62. Anon., "Réflexions sur la société de développement," Sahel Hebdo (Niamey,

Niger) 214 (February 25, 1980), 29 [article quoting then-Minister of Youth, Sport, and Culture Djermakoye Moumouni Adamou] (my translation).

63. Samuel P. Huntington and Joan M. Nelson, *No Easy Choice: Political Participation in Developing Countries* (Cambridge, Mass.: Harvard University Press, 1976), pp. 38–39.

64. Jeremy Swift, "Disaster and a Sahelian Nomad Economy," in *Drought in Africa*, edited by David Dalby and R. J. Harrison Church (London: International African Institute, 1973), pp. 73–76. Anonymous [Angelo B. Maliki], "La tradition du habbanaae chez les Wodáabé région d'Abala, Niger." Unpublished ms., "Fraternité-Wodáabé," Abala, Niger, 1974.

65. Michael M. Horowitz, "The Sociology of Pastoralism and African Livestock Projects," A.I.D. Program Evaluation Discussion Paper No. 6. (Washington, D.C.: USAID, Office of Evaluation/Bureau for Program and Policy Coordination, 1979), pp. 50–52.

66. Interview with Dakoro Arrondissement Subprefect, Dakoro, Dakoro Arrondissement, Maradi Department, Niger, February 20, 1981.

67. Kevin Milligan, "Aerial Survey of Human, Livestock and Environmental Conditions in a Central Region of the Pastoral Zone of Niger," Preliminary Report No. 1, July 1981 (Prepared for the USAID/Niger Range and Livestock Project, Addis-Ababa, Ethiopia: International Livestock Centre for Africa, 1981), p. 17.

68. Concerning the validity of figures and data about pastoral practices and societies, see the trenchant caveat in USAID, Bureau for Africa and Office of Evaluation/Bureau for Program and Policy Coordination, "The Workshop on Pastoralism and African Livestock Development" (Prepared by the Institute for Development Anthropology; Washington, D.C.: USAID, 1980), pp. 5–6.

69. Interview with Rea, Wodáabé *lamido* (group chief) Gourbobo, Tanout Arrondissement, Zinder Department, Niger, January 30, 1981; interview with Mouhamadoune Abdourahabi, Nigerian Livestock Service Agent, road between Edouk and Abalak, Tchin Tabaraden Arrondissement, Tahousa Department, Niger, February 9, 1981.

70. Interview with Rea, Wodáabé *lamido* (group chief), Gourbobo, Tanout Arrondissement, Zinder Department, Niger January 31, 1981.

71. Heinrich Barth, *Travels and Discoveries in North and Central Africa, Being a Journal of an Expedition Undertaken under the Auspices of H . B . M .'s Government in the Years 1849–1855* (London: Frank Cass, 1965; first published 1857: Longmans Green), I, 276–92; Horowitz, "Sociology of Pastoralism," pp. 47–54; Maliki, "Etude socio-démographique"; Jean Gallais, *Le Delta intérieur du Niger: étude de géographie régionale* (Dakar: IFAN, 1967), 362–371; Gilles Laine, "Evolution du régime foncier dans une société d'éleveurs nomades. Le cas des Twareg Kel Dinnik dans la région de Tahoua (Niger)," in *Enjeux fonciers en Afrique noire* (Paris: ORSTOM/Karthala, 1982), pp. 196–97.

72. Maliki, "Etude socio-démographique."

73. Interview with Dakoro Arrondissement Subprefect, Dakoro, Dakoro Arrondissement, Maradi Department, Niger, February 20, 1981.

74. Interview with Tanout Arrondissement Subprefect, Mai Moussa Dikouma, Belbedji, Tanout Arrondissement, Zinder Department, Niger, January 31, 1981.

75. Horowitz, "Sociology of Pastoralism," pp. 29–31; USAID, "Workshop on Pastoralism," pp. 8–10.

76. Interview with Mouhamadoune Abdourahabi, Nigerian Livestock Service Agent, road to Edouk, Tchin Tabaraden Arrondissement, Tahoua Separtment, Niger, February 6, 1981.

77. Z. A. Konczacki, *The Economics of Pastoralism: A Case Study of Subsaharan Africa* (London: Frank Cass, 1978), pp. 7–10; USAID, "Workshop on Pastoralism," pp. 7–8; UN Conference on Desertification, "Transnational Project on Management of Livestock and Rangelands to Combat Desertification in the Sudano Sahelian Regions (SOLAR)" (New York: United Nations, 1977).

78. Ari T. Ibrahim, "Exposé au séminaire sur la gestion des coopératives organisés par l'ACCT: efforts d'organisation des éleveurs au Niger" (Niamey, Niger: Ministère du développement rural, Direction du service de l'élevage et des industries animales, 1978).

79. Horowitz, "Sociology of Pastoralism," pp. 32–35.

80. Baier, *An Economic History*, pp. 33–34.

81. Guy Nicolas, *Circulation des richesses et participation sociale dans une société hausa du Niger* (Canton de Kantché), 2nd ed. (Bordeaux, France: Editions de Centre Universitaire de Polycopiage de l'A.G.E.B., 1967), pp. 20–41, esp. 36–37; and Robert B. Charlick, "Power and Participation in the Modernization of Rural Hausa Communities." Ph.D. diss., Department of Political Science, University of California, Los Angeles, 1974, p. 231.

82. Jean-Yves Marchal, "The Evolution of Agrarian Systems in Yatenga," *African Environment*, II, 4 and III, 1, November, 1977): 82; but see Charlick, "Power and Participation," pp. 163–67, for a contrary argument.

83. Sutter, "Nigerien Rural Producer," pp. 30–33 and literature cited there.

84. See, for example, Brun, "Manifestations nutritionnelles."

85. Gudrun Dahl and Anders Hjort, *Having Herds: Pastoral Herd Growth and Household Economy* (Stockholm: Department of Social Anthropology, University of Stockholm, 1976), pp. 132–59.

86. See, e.g., Anon [Maliki], "La tradition du habbanaae"; Dahl and Hjort, *Having Herds*, pp. 70–71.

87. Interview with Mouhamadoune Abdourahabi, Nigerian Livestock Service Agent, road to Edouk, Tchin Tabaraden Arrondissement, Tahoua Department, Niger, February 6, 1981.

88. Joel S. Migdal, *Peasants, Politics and Revolution: Pressures towards Political and Social Change in the Third World* (Princeton, N.J.: Princeton University Press, 1974), pp. 133–55.

89. James T. Thomson, "Capitation in Colonial and Post-Colonial Niger: Analysis of the Effects of an Imposed Head-Tax System on Rural Political Organization," in *The Imposition of Law*, edited by Sandra B. Burman and B. E. Harrell-Bond (New York: Academic Press, 1979); James T. Thomson, "Food Politics at the Local Level: Niger and Upper Volta Approach Food Security," in *Food and Climate Review, 1979*, edited by S. K. Levin (A Publication of the Food and Climate Forum; Boulder, Colo.: Aspen Institute, 1980), pp. 39–50.

90. Interview with Mouhamadoune Abdourahabi, Nigerien Livestock Service Agent, Edouk, Tchin Tabaraden Arrondissement, Tahousa Department, Niger, February 7, 1981, concerning manipulation of state grain sales by government employees; interview with informant I. Z., Inuwa (pseudonym), Mirriah Arrondissement, Zinder Department,

March 2, 1979, concerning Mirriah Arrondissement head nurse's embezzlement of funds earmarked for purchase of village first aid kit medicines.

91. Thomas Hobbes, *Leviathan, or the Matter, Forme and Power of a Common-Wealth Ecclesiasticall and Civill*, reprinted from the Edition of 1651 with an Essay by the Late W. G. Pogson Smith (Oxford: Clarendon Press, 1909), p. 268.

92. Interview with Wodáabé herder in Tamaya bush area, Tahoua Department, February 13, 1981, concerning herdsmen's strategies to obtain borehole water from Tamaya well operator.

93. CILSS/Club du Sahel, *Recueil de statistiques*, p. 58; World Bank, *1979 World Bank Atlas: Population, Per Capita Product and Growth Rates* (Washington, D.C.: World Bank, 1979), p. 12.

94. Niger, *Plan Quinquennal, 1979–1983* (Niamey, Niger: Imprimerie Nationale, 1980), pp. 307, 312; Thomson, "Food Politics at the Local Level," pp. 47–48; Thomson, "Nigerien Herder Associations," pp. 239–242.

95. Interview with Mauhamadoune Abdourahbi, Nigerien Livestock Service Agent, Edouk, Tchin Tabaraden Arrondissement, Tahoua Department, Niger, February 7, 1981; and interview with informant I.Z., Inuwa (pseudonym), Mirriah Arrondissement, Zinder Department, March 2, 1979.

96. Interviews with Patrick Paris, pastoral sociologist, Niger Centre-Est Livestock Project (World Bank), Tanout, Tanout Arrondissement, Zinder Department, January 30, 1981, and Zinder, Zinder Department, Niger, February 2, 1981, concerning evolution of pastoral conditions in Tanout Arrondissement; interview with Tanout subprefect Mai Moussa Dikouma, Belbedji, Tanout Arrondissement, Zinder Department, January 31, 1981, rejecting assertions made in the text.

97. Interview with Harouna Mayaou, Department Planning Bureau head, Tahoua, February 16, 1981, concerning political impediments to implementation of agricultural activity in the pastoral zone; see also Thomson, "Nigerien Herder Associations," pp. 177–90.

98. Abraham S. Waldstein, "Government Sponsored Agricultural Intensification Schemes in the Sahel: Development for Whom?" (Prepared for the USAID "Papers on Sahelian Social Development" series under contract REDSO/WA 78-139; Abidjan, Ivory Coast; USAID/REDSO, 1978), pp. 31–32 for a Senegalese case.

99. Raynaut, "Lessons of a Crisis;" Franke and Chasin, *Seeds of Famine*, pp. 165–227.

100. Waldstein, "Development for Whom?" pp. 14–17.

101. Milligan, "Pastoral Zone of Niger," pp. 16–17, indicates that the encroachment of farming into the pastoral zone in central Niger is most severe along the southern fringe of the zone. In an area of roughly nine million hectares, square in form and bounded by Agadez, Tassara, Tahoua, and Tanout, 15 percent of 930 grid squares showed some cultivation. Most extensive areas of cultivation are now located around Belbedji and Dakoro in the southeast of this area, and around Tahoua, Tchin-Tabaraden, and Abalak. Around Tahoua, 7,000 square kilometers are currently farmed. The total area surveyed (by low-flying airplane, with observers using standardized observation techniques) was 81,923 square kilometers. Though no total of land under cultivation was calculated, it appears likely that it exceeds 10 percent of the area. Declining precipitation averages as one moves north may discourage further expansion of agriculture into the very high

steppe lands, but this is not certain. See Thomson, "Nigerien Herder Associations," p. 1979; Niger, *Plan Quinquennal*, pp. 548–549.

102. UN Conference on Desertification, "Transnational Project," pp. 10–12.

103. Interview with Bernard Peyre de Fabregues, agrostologist specializing in Sahelian forage plants, associate with the French Institut d'Elevage et de Médicine Vétérinaire Tropical (I.E.M.V.T.), at Zinder Department, Niger, June 26, 1981.

104. Since this article was originally written, the Niger Range and Livestock Project, now based in Tahoua, Tahoua Department, Niger, has launched some dozen herders cooperatives in the project zone (see footnote 103, above); initial results are quite encouraging, but the longer-term difficulties facing these organizations are not negligible.

105. "Half-blocked" because the party never really did respond to the needs of much of the population. See, in this regard, Charlick, "Power and Participation," pp. 72–80; Thomson, "Law, Legal Process and Development," pp. 121–22; Richard Higgot and Finn Fuglestad, "The 1974 Coup d'Etat in Niger: Towards an Explanation," *Journal of Modern African Studies* 13, no. 3 (September 1975): 383–398.

106. Kountché, speech, March 17, 1980. Seyni Kountché, "Message addressé à la nation par son excellence, le colonel Seyni Kountché président du conseil militaire supreme, chef de l'état, à l'occasion du 20ème anniversaire de l'indépendence du Niger" (text of speech, Niamey, August 2, 1980).

107. Sutter, "Nigerien Rural Producer," pp. 30–33.

108. Charlick, "Power and Participation," pp. 134–138.

109. Robert B. Charlick, "Participatory Development and Rural Modernization in Hausa Niger," *African Review* 2, no. 4 (1972): 522; Thomson, "Law, Legal Process and Development," pp. 209–216.

110. Waldstein, "Development for Whom?" pp. 88–89; James T. Thomson, "Bois de Villages (Niger): Report of an Investigation Concerning Socio-Cultural and Political Economic Aspects of the First Phase of the Project and Design Recommendations for a Possible Second Phase" (Report submitted to the International Development Research Centre, Ottawa, Canada, February 5, 1980).

111. Thomson, "Bois de Villages," pp. 22–23, 37–38.

112. Charlick, "Power and Participation," pp. 84–85; Thomson, "Law, Legal Process and Development," pp. 281–290.

113. Alexis de Tocqueville, *The Old Régime and the French Revolution*, trans. by Stuart Gibbs (Garden City, N.Y.: Doubleday Anchor, 1955; first published 1856), pp. 41–51.

114. Artistide R. Zolberg, *One-Party Government in the Ivory Coast*, rev. ed. (Princeton, N.J.: Princeton University Press, 1969; first published 1964), pp. 250–268.

115. Niger, Ordinance 75–11 of March 13, 1975.

116. Gilles Dugué, *Vers les états-unis d'Afrique* (Paris: Editions "Lettres Africaines," 1960), pp. 151–162; Ali A. Mazrui, "Whatever Happened to the African One-Party State?" Paper presented at the 77th annual meeting of the American Political Science Association, New York, N.Y., September 3–6, 1981).

117. Zolberg, *One-Party Government*, pp. 296–320.

118. Thomson, "Law, Legal Process and Development," pp. 295–296; Thomson, "Capitation in Colonial," pp. 215–218.

119. Cissé Ibrahim, "Raisons et conséquences de la désertification," *Sahel Hebdo*

(Niamey, Niger) 83 (June 20, 1977): 6–10; Anon, "Opération 'Sahel Vert,'" *Le Sahel* (Niamey, Niger), 4, no. 986 (July 22, 1977): 1, 8.

120. James T. Thomson, "Sahelian Tragedies of the Commons Revisited: The View from Ground Zero." Unpublished manuscript.

121. Thomson, "Bois de Villages," p. 10.

122. Although the number of forestry department employees has grown since 1978, it remains under 400 as of 1983. Marchal, "Evolution of Agrarian Systems," pp. 82–85.

123. Waldstein, "Development for Whom?"

124. Niger, *Plan Quinquennal*, pp. 206–217.

125. James T. Thomson, "Public Choice Analysis of Institutional Constraints on Firewood Production Strategies in the West African Sahel," in *Public Choice and Rural Development*, edited by Clifford S. Russell and Norman K. Nicholson (Washington, D.C.: Resources for the Future, 1981), pp. 127–149.

126. Jim Knight, a former Niger Range and Livestock Project Research Associate, argues persuasively that all these actions could merely succeed in making herders more dependent upon government civil servants. Interview, Niamey, Niger, January 8, 1981. Unless associations are carefully designed, and the designs faithfully implemented, they might simply serve as vehicles for more politically powerful herders to drive those less well connected from previously common pasture areas.

127. Thomson, "Nigerien Herder Associations."

128. USAID, "Workshop on Pastoralism," pp. 6–11.

129. James T. Thomson, "Traditional Soil Conservation Techniques and Government Soil Erosion Control Programs in the Yatenga Region (Upper Volta) of the West African Sahel." Paper prepared for presentation at the annual meeting of the American Society for Public Administration, New York, N.Y., April 16–19, 1983.

130. Waldstein, "Development for Whom?" esp. pp. 6–23; Jean-Yves Marchal, "L'Espace des techniciens et celui des paysans; histoire d'un périmetre antiérosif en Haute-Volta," in *Maîtrise de l'espace agraire et développement en Afrique tropicale: logique paysanne et rationalité technique*, Actes du colloque de Ouagadougou, December 4–8, 1978 (Paris: O.R.S.T.O.M., 1979), pp. 245–252.

131. Raynaut, "Lessons of a Crisis," pp. 26–28.

132. Thomson, "Traditional Soil Conservation."

133. Thomson, "Food Politics," pp. 39–42.

134. Interview with Rhony Issoufou, then Mirriah Arrondissement subprefect, Mirriah, Zinder Department, Niger, January 29, 1981, concerning his own career history. He was promoted within a month to prefect, apparently on the strength of his performance concerning environmental projects in Niger, among other things.

CHAPTER 7

POLITICS AND POLLUTION FROM URBAN AND INDUSTRIAL DEVELOPMENT

H. Jeffrey Leonard

For the advanced nations of the Western world, rapid economic development during the late nineteenth and early twentieth centuries went hand-in-hand with increasing industrialization and urbanization. In part owing to this historical experience, there has been a nearly universal trend within the third world to associate affluence and an improved quality of life with rapid rates of industrial development and an accompanying expansion of cities to provide a concentrated pool of industrial labor, market outlets, transportation, infrastructure, services, leisure opportunities, and culture. Yet, in their rush to achieve rapid economic growth by recreating the factories and cosmopolises of the industrialized countries, it is quite easy for developing country governments to lose sight of the side effects that accompanied industrialization and urbanization, and subsequently demanded extraordinary remedial efforts in all the advanced nations.

As readers of Charles Dickens or Upton Sinclair know, no Western nation achieved its present level of industrial development and urbanism without great human suffering and enormous environmental devastation. In a recent historical account of pollution in the United States, Martin Melosi summarized the situation in the typical nineteenth-century industrial city:

As the undisputed centers of economic dynamism in the United States, industrial cities flourished. Yet their overcrowded tenements, congested traffic, critical health problems, smoky skies, mounds of putrefying wastes, polluted waterways, and unbearable noise levels attested to the price they had to pay for such success.[1]

Melosi and his colleagues demonstrate in vivid terms that pollution of the air, water, and land may actually reach its most serious proportions in societies at a relatively early stage of rapid economic expansion. This is when the captains of industry and government, and indeed the population at large, may be most desperate to secure present growth at any future costs and most reluctant to make current investments to reduce long-range expenditures or provide social benefits if they mean any sacrifice in short-term output.

Anyone who has had occasion to travel to different parts of the globe in recent years will verify this fact: the worst cases of rampant and unmitigated pollution of the environment are found not in the urban areas of advanced industrial countries nor in the poorest countries, but in and around the cities of those countries which have recently commenced rapid industrial expansion and economic growth. Melosi's description of an American city of a century ago could be applied to a growing number of large urban areas in the industrializing world today. Indeed, pollution, generally assumed to be a problem of advanced industrial societies, has reached far worse proportions than it ever did in the West in such rapidly expanding cities as Ankara, Jakarta, Lagos, Bangkok, Mexico City, São Paulo, Seoul, and Bombay.

This chapter explores the nature and magnitude of key industrial and urban-related pollution problems in rapidly developing nations. In addition to examining the complex causes and the far-reaching economic and public health consequences, it outlines some of the forces pushing developing country governments to respond to these problems. Finally, while questioning the efficacy of many efforts to reduce rampant pollution, some broad public policy choices are discussed for developing country governments seeking to affect the level and distribution of pollution and to reduce some of the costs associated with pollution.

SHOULD RAPIDLY DEVELOPING COUNTRIES CARE ABOUT POLLUTION?

Despite the obvious prevalence of serious urban and industrial pollution problems in the rapidly growing countries of the third world, many observers have argued that such externality problems are only of secondary importance to countries still struggling to achieve rapid economic growth:

It is often said that improvement of the environment is really the special problem of developing nations. The developing world, it is argued, lacking resources and facing the urgent need to industrialize and to provide minimal public services, cannot afford the luxury of additional investment to enhance the environment. Developing countries, the argument goes, would like nothing better than to find themselves in the situation of the developed nations. They want heavy industry, large urban centers, higher national and per capita incomes and so on. If these aims entail air and water pollution, traffic congestion, noise, mental stress and all the other problems and maladies that are endemic to the urbanized areas of the world, well, such are the costs of being rich and one has to be rich before one can start to channel part of the national income towards the solution of environmental problems.[2]

The problems of industrial pollution and urban squalor and congestion are thus frequently seen not as objective problems but as ones of perception. They are dealt with as if they only come into cognitive existence after economic growth and relative affluence have provided people with the luxury of thinking about improving the quality of their lives instead of only thinking about providing for day-to-day subsistence. Not only can developing countries supposedly not afford to deal with pollution problems, it is pointed out that the masses are unlikely even to perceive such problems until they share in the economic growth which presumably results from urban and industrial expansion.

The Case against Concern about Pollution

Once economic growth has reached the level where people desire quality of life improvements and where "nonproductive" investments are affordable, then some of the proceeds can be diverted into the physical environmental improvements that people demand. This certainly is the pattern followed by most Western nations during the past two centuries. First the environmental sacrifices were made; then the resulting industrial pollution, urban squalor, poor housing conditions, public health hazards, and inefficient land use patterns were addressed after affluence was attained.

There is, of course, a great deal of logic to this sequence. Pollution and squalor are difficult problems to prevent in countries where people are very poor and industrial enterprises are in their fledgling stage. In the early phases of industrial development, countries (and private companies) depend heavily on maintaining high rates of savings for capital accumulation and on keeping the costs of labor, raw material, and other aspects of production as low as possible. Pollution—the disposing of wastes or by-products from industrial processes into air, water, or adjacent land—is another important means of minimizing costs for industries and governments. A backyard tannery or a low-technology food processing plant might never even get off the ground if, from the outset, it had to make provisions for treating and neutralizing its effluent before sending it into a nearby stream. Furthermore, waste treatment implies a degree of technical efficiency and control over the production process that may not be present for many small, makeshift industrial projects that may be heavy polluters—iron foundries, cement plants, tanneries, food processing operations, for example.

The argument is often made that from nature's point of view, too, it is not as necessary for a country at an early stage of industrial and urban development to be seriously concerned about controlling pollution. All natural systems have a certain "assimilative capacity" to absorb, dilute, and degrade most industrial pollutants and urban wastes. In underindustrialized countries the limits of this capacity generally have not been reached. A rushing river, a tidal estuary, a windy knoll, or even an uninhabited hillside may be able to dissipate pollutants naturally with few noticeable effects where the assimilative capacity of the natural environment has not been exceeded.

Thus, pollution control technology for factories or elaborate municipal waste treatment facilities would only duplicate at great waste of scarce capital resources what nature can accomplish. As a country reaches a stage of industrial development where nature's assimilitive capacity is being taxed (implying that substantial economic growth is taking place), pollution control steps can be implemented incrementally. Although this is an argument for careful location of urban developments and industrial facilities based upon ecological data and experience (a difficult enough task), it is quite frequently cited as a reason why developing countries not only cannot afford, but also do not need, advanced pollution control measures.

Why Some Problems Need Attention Now

All of these points—that developing countries can no more afford to pay pollution control costs than they can afford to pay high labor costs, that poor people are unlikely to be concerned about pollution, and that developing countries generally have large, unused "assimilative capacities"—doubtless have some validity in theory when applied to an entire country. There are, however, a number of mitigating factors that make pollution problems in certain areas of developing countries more serious and people more aware of them than was the case for the now-industrialized nations during their early stages of development.

First is the fact that with transfers of capital, technology, and knowledge, and international demand for a wide range of industrial goods, developing countries today have undertaken a far wider range of industrial activities in a much shorter period of time than occurred for the first industrializers. The concentration of pollution problems from this telescoping of the time sequence for industrial development is significantly complicated by several other industrial development trends.

Large, heavy industries of the sort that may generate problematical air emissions or water effluent tend overwhelmingly to be located in a very small number of heavily industrialized, urbanized enclaves in most developing countries. Although total industrial pollution for a developing country may still be quite low by modern standards, the level of pollution in these areas of concentrated industry is often far higher than the worst levels recorded in the most industrialized areas of the West.

In addition, as many observers of international industrial location patterns have pointed out, firms in particular industries—especially those producing for world markets—have a remarkable propensity to locate in close proximity to each other. They tend to cluster not only in the same countries, but often at nearby factory sites. There are many reasons for this "piggyback" effect: availability of raw materials, marketing opportunities, oligopolistic behavior, enticements from governments, labor force specifications, etc. The result is that in a particular area total industrial pollution may again be relatively low, but it may be primarily a few high-volume pollutants.

Moreover, because industrializing nations today can establish what Albert Hirschman refers to as "last" industries first—by importing technology and intermediate materials from abroad and performing the final touches for re-export—they are faced with the more subtle and pervasive forms of industrial pollution commonplace in many highly sophisticated industries that have burgeoned in the advanced developed countries since World War II. Thus, simultaneously with the more obvious forms of industrial pollution—such as thick black smoke, noxious water effluent, and hazardous industrial work conditions—many industrializing countries today must cope with "invisible" pollution problems such as industrial carcinogens carried by air and water, and toxic substances which contaminate landfills and water. This is particularly true for countries which are building industries relying on organic chemistry— petrochemicals, plastics, pesticides, fuels, solvents, pharmaceuticals, man-made fibers, paints, etc.

All these factors tend to mean that industrial pollution in developing countries is highly concentrated in location and type, but widely diversified in scope and complexity. These problems are further exacerbated by the fact that the sheer numbers of people and the volumes of pollutants associated with the urban environment—sewage, solid waste, air pollutants—are exponentially greater in third world cities today than they were in the cities of Europe and America during their periods of helter-skelter development.

One key reason is that the rapid growth period for third world cities has occurred in conjunction with an international explosion in the numbers of vehicles utilizing what is far and away the biggest worldwide polluter of the air: the internal combustion engine. But the automobile is not the only problem. In most large third world cities, urban services such as water supplies, sewer systems, and solid waste disposal facilities are nonexistent or inadequate. Many large third world urban areas are plagued by congestion problems because of their size, the rapidity of their growth, and the inability to adapt street configurations and traffic flows to the exploding numbers of automobiles. Even in the best planned developing country urban areas, huge haphazardous squatter settlements, often on the most hilly or polluted fringes of the city, only complicate the general problems of pollution, squalor, and congestion.

At an early stage in their economic development, many rapidly expanding countries are being confronted with a range of environmental pollution and health problems equally as broad and of similar or greater magnitude as those which provoked intense concern in the advanced industrial countries in the past decade or two. Yet prevailing levels of affluence, technical capability, scientific know-how, and institutional specialization in most third world countries are obviously far below those in the advanced countries. Thus, the intensity of many pollution problems that are apparent in rapidly industrializing and urbanizing nations increases the risk that environmental pollution will at some point become a serious drag on future development—by impinging on the economic productivity of people, capital, and raw material inputs. There are, doubtless, many instances where some form of pollution control or environmental protection is a luxury which a newly industrializing country can ill afford. The primary concern of this chapter, however, is to identify significant economic and public health side-effects that can, even with very poor data available from these countries, be clearly linked with rampant environmental pollution in many of the world's most quickly industrializing and urbanizing nations.

THE MAGNITUDE AND CAUSES OF POLLUTION

Although accurate, nationwide surveys are almost nonexistent, it would be difficult to exaggerate the magnitude of the pollution problems in many large urban areas of rapidly developing countries. Circumstances do vary from country to country and city to city, but water pollution tends to be the most intractable problem, because the adverse effects of water pollution often are more tangible and more cumulative than other problems, and because they carry over beyond the urban sector.

Water Pollution

Untreated organic waste is the major source of water pollution in most large urban and industrial areas in the third world. Natural organic matter poses difficulties for two key reasons. First, excreta or decaying animal matter are frequently the vectors or food supplies for a wide variety of enteric diseases and intestinal parasites. Second, waste animal, vegetable, and synthetic organic matter use up the oxygen available in water—their decay creates a high biochemical oxygen demand (BOD)—which can kill or drive away fish and other marine life and undermine the use of water for humans.

The largest source of organic waste is municipal sewage. Very few rapidly growing cities have adequate sewerage systems; fewer have plants to treat the wastes once collected. In greater São Paulo, for example, over 10 million kilograms of sewage, 99 percent of which is untreated, pours daily into the Tiete, the Pinheiros, and Tamanduater Rivers. Largely as a result, the Tiete leaves São Paulo with zero percent oxygen in the water.[3] In all of Latin America, it is estimated that less than 10 percent of municipal sewage is treated.[4]

Even in areas where sewage treatment facilities are more widely available, large amounts of raw organic waste go untreated. In India, for example, it is estimated that close to 40 percent of the urban population is linked into sewerage facilities and many large cities (Calcutta, Bombay, Delhi, Jaipur, Amritsar, and Indore) have either primary or secondary treatment plants. Yet, in the mid-1970s only 10 percent of Bombay's sewage was being treated, with the rest being dumped directly into the sea. In Calcutta, too, only a small portion of municipal sewage was being treated prior to flowing into the Hugly River.[5]

In major cities without adequate sewerage systems and sewer treatment facilities, human wastes are frequently disposed of through individual septic tanks, soakage pits, or holding tanks which are periodically collected. Yet, this is frequently only an indirect means of discharge into streams, rivers, underground aquifers, or coastal waters. In the absence of a central sewage system for Lagos, Nigeria, most modern residential dwellings and many older ones are equiped with septic tanks or soakage pits, and many large buildings and factories now have their own small sewage treatment plants. Yet, all these systems require periodic desludging and the sludge is generally stored in large lagoons and then transmitted into the open sea.[6] Similarly, Seoul, South Korea, relies heavily on a system of periodic collection of human wastes from residential holding tanks. Yet, it is estimated that as a result of spillage at collection and large-scale spillage and seepage at disposal sites, large amounts of untreated domestic wastes reach the Hon River, which is virtually lifeless when it exits the metropolitan area.[7]

Second only to municipal waste as a contributor of organic waste to bodies of water are agriculture-related processing industries. Although frequently the advanced industrial manufacturing industries receive attention as the worst polluters, it is almost invariably the agroindustrial facilities that cause the most serious industrial-related water pollution problems in rapidly expanding countries. The particular agricultural products vary among countries: coffee in Kenya, palm oil in Malaysia, tapioca in Thailand, sugar cane in Brazil, olives and sunflowers in Spain. Although agriculturally dependent, the processing plants for such primary industries tend to be located on rivers and streams in close proximity to urban areas.

In some cases, such agricultural industries outstrip even domestic sewage as a cause of water pollution. In Malaysia, for example, the palm oil and natural rubber industries have been dubbed the country's number-one polluters. In 1980, it was estimated that the BOD created by effluents from palm oil mills alone equaled the total BOD level from the wastes of the entire population of peninsular Malaysia.[8] Although there appears to have been some improvement in recent years, forty-two main rivers in peninsular Malaysia are said by the government to have been seriously threatened by palm oil pollution. Moreover, the quantity of effluent discharged is expected to rise dramatically in a very short period of time—from 284 tons BOD per day in 1981 to 500 tons BOD per day by 1985![9]

In Thailand, discharges of 80,000 kilograms per day of waste from liquor distilleries leaves the Chao Phyraya River with a zero percent oxygen content near Klong Toey Port.[10] Rapid expansion of sugar processing mills along the Mae Klong River in western Thailand had the same effect in the 1970s until some steps were taken to reduce effluent discharges.[11] The water problems caused by food processing industries were graphically demonstrated in 1977 in Porto Feliz, Brazil, when a sugar cane plant dumped enough raw waste into the river to send thousands of fish desperately jumping out of the water for air, as hundreds of residents and tourists gathered along the shore to watch the spectacle.[12]

While contributing to BOD levels, the water pollution problems of industrial facilities outside the primary agricultural industries are also caused by chemical effluents (which poison water for human and animal use), suspended solids (which reduce the light penetration and increase the turbidity of the water), and heavy metals (which build up slowly in the receiving waters and may have long-term pathogenic or mutagenic effects throughout the aquatic food chain and on its final consumer, man).

Because they generally operate locally owned, low-technology, low-margin plants, firms involved in producing basic goods for domestic use—leather goods, pulp and paper, textiles, cement and other construction materials, basic metal products—frequently contribute heavily to water pollution by all these means. Few small- and medium-scale industries have any procedures for treating chemical wastes or for removing heavy metals and suspended solids prior to discharge into receiving waters. This is not only because they cannot afford to take such steps, but because they tend to be highly dispersed in their location and find it difficult to take advantage of joint industry or industrial estate waste disposal facilities. As a result, in many countries, the cumulative industrial waste from localized, small-time, generally domestically owned and operated producers constitutes the most serious non-biological industrial water pollution problem.[13]

It is very difficult to assess accurately the total waste from these sources, since they are so spread out, or the contributions of particular firms, since discharge is often done piecemeal or at odd times of day. Yet, the results of chemical discharges are often clear enough from a visual standpoint. In Kanpur, India, for example, the local tannery opens its floodgates at about one-week intervals and for several days afterward the Ganges River is black for miles downstream.[14] The 40,000 industries in the greater São Paulo area dump an estimated thirty-six tons of chemical pollutants into the city's rivers each day. Although many large-scale chemical, steel, and other manufacturing firms operate in São Paulo, the majority of the chemical pollution is contributed by small- and medium-scale producers.[15]

Tailings from the mining sector and from cement factories and various basic mineral processing facilities contribute most clearly to the problems of suspended solids in waterways. The Klang River in Malaysia receives an estimated 1,000 tons per day of solids, mostly from mines' and quarries' discharge and runoff, enough to make it virtually unusable downstream.[16] Garbage and junk from urban areas add considerably to BOD, chemical, heavy metal, and suspended solid problems in rapidly growing urban areas. In Jakarta, Indonesia, for example, it has been estimated that 30 percent of all urban refuse goes uncollected and instead ends up in the canals, klongs, and other water bodies.[17]

As a result of increased industrial production, the rivers and bays of many third world cities are also accumulating higher concentrations of toxic metals. Reports in recent years, for example, have noted significant buildups of mercury, lead, cadmium, copper, chromium, and other heavy metals in almost every industrializing nation of Southeast Asia. In Malaysia, the Juru and Klang River basins were found to have high enough concentrations of mercury, chromium, lead, and cadmium to exceed international standards set by the World Health Organization.[18] Similar problems have been noted in United Nations, USAID, or national government reports for Thailand, Taiwan, and South Korea; in all these countries, high measures of toxic metals, especially mercury, have been found not only in waterways, but in the tissue of fish, animals, and humans.[19] Electroplating firms have frequently been major contributors of toxic materials to waterways. Until recently, the electroplating industry in Delhi dumped a ton of cyanide, and numerous other toxic metals, into the Jamuna River each day.[20] In Brazil, satellite reconnaissance photos indicate that about fourteen tons of toxic waste are dumped into Rio de Janeiro's Guanabara Bay daily. The photos show gigantic pollution plumes extending about ninety miles long, twelve miles wide, and fifteen feet deep being swept out to sea from the bay. In addition to the toxic waste, experts estimate that this pollution consists of a daily input of about 1,500 tons of suspended solids, 3,000 tons of solid garbage, 60,000 liters of oil, and untold amounts of liquid effluent.[21]

Large-scale, heavy industries—such as steel plants, oil refineries, petrochemical production—do not as yet account for the bulk of the water pollution in most rapidly developing countries. There are two reasons. First, these industries do not claim the highest proportions of total industrial production and hence effluent. But second, most of these industries are the first to get access to or install for themselves some form of water treatment devices, frequently with direct support and tax incentives from national governments.[22]

Nevertheless, water pollution from these sources is rising and, owing to the tendency of industries to cluster, is quite significant in strategic enclaves. The three large oil refineries along the shores of Guanabara Bay in Rio de Janeiro, for example, cause major additional water pollution problems above those created by small-scale industry and urban wastes, although Petrobras, the Brazilian oil company, is currently working to install new antipollution treatment systems.[23] Most advanced industrializing nations have at least one area where large industries are clustered as in the marshlands of northern New Jersey. Bilbao in Spain, Cubatao in Brazil, and Penang in Malaysia are a few places where the pollution created by big industries—some national companies, others multinational ones—dwarfs all other sources of water pollution.

Air Pollution

Although more isolated than water pollution, air pollution has increased dramatically in all large cities of rapidly growing countries. A recent USAID report noted that air pollution is a serious and growing problem in the major cities of Latin America, singling out especially Mexico City, Caracas, Lima, Santiago, São Paulo, Rio de Janeiro, and Buenos Aires. What is significant, the report stated, is that air pollution problems in all of these cities "far exceed similar problems in the U.S."[24] Moreover, air quality is deteriorating at very high rates in some cities. Mexico City, already known for having one of the worst air pollution problems in the world, suffered nearly a 50 percent increase in the level of air contamination in 1979 alone.[25]

Despite its generally high level, however, air pollution is variable even within individual urban areas. A recent study of Rio de Janeiro emphasized this point clearly, showing that the mountain splitting the city forms a wall and an air flow pattern that sweeps the highest concentrations of air pollution into the Zona Sul (the ocean side of the city.)[26]

Natural surroundings, altitude, climate, and daily weather patterns can significantly affect the rate of dissipation of air pollution as well. Thus, whatever absolute problems Mexico City may face owing to the vast amounts of pollutants released each day, its air pollution dilemma is significantly aggravated by circumstances prevailing in the bowl-shaped Valley of Mexico. The valley's high altitude, lack of air circulation, long dry season, and frequent thermal inversions make it an even poorer natural environment than Los Angeles or Denver for dissipating air pollutants. By contrast, a city such as Dublin, Ireland, where rainfall is frequent and prevailing Atlantic breezes constant, may suffer far fewer ills from air pollution than its pollutant emission levels might suggest.

In most large cities, lead has rapidly become a very significant air pollutant; other compounds found in dangerously high levels in the atmosphere above urban areas include sulfur dioxide, carbon monoxide, nitrogen oxide, various hydrocarbons, and fly ash and other suspended particulates. The principal dangers of these air pollutants are that they may damage human body tissue and the nervous system, cause eye irritation, bring increased respiratory diseases and cancer rates, burn or kill vegetation, corrode buildings and vehicles, and eventually contribute to water and land pollution.

Motor vehicle traffic is now one of the most significant contributors to air pollution in many large urban areas, owing both to proliferating numbers of automobiles and to the use of old, antiquated buses and trucks to transport people and goods around urban areas. In Malaysia, the Division of the Environment estimates that about 635,000 tons of pollutants are released into the country's atmosphere annually and that more than 45 percent of that amount is contributed by transportation vehicles.[27]

Lead pollution levels—virtually all attributable to the internal combustion engine—are many times higher in most downtown areas of major industrializing nation cities than they are in urban areas of western Europe and the United States. In Rio, for example, 30 percent of the measurements taken show lead levels several times larger than those recognized as safe.[28] One reason is that large urban areas in developing countries have a lot of cars—nearly a million in Rio, over two million in Mexico City—and with congestion as bad as it is, the cars do a lot of sitting in traffic.[29] But this is only part of the problem. Most automobiles, trucks, and buses are old and virtually none have pollution control equipment. A recent report estimated that in India and other developing countries, moving vehicles generated at least two or three times more pollution per unit than in the advanced nations.[30]

Another problem is that lead content in gasoline is extremely high in many countries. Brazil and Malaysia, for example, both permit their petroleum companies to add almost .85 grams of lead per liter of petrol in order to boost octane ratings.[31] Limits in advanced countries are much lower: the U.S. limit is .34 grams per liter; Britain's is .45; Japan's is .26; and Sweden's is .15. One reason for permitting high lead content is that the other method for raising octane levels is to recycle some of the gas produced when petroleum is fractionated and to further refine the gasoline. However, in many developing countries shortages of gas for cooking and heating preclude this option.

Sulfur dioxide levels in Rio also measure anywhere from ten to several hundred percent higher than safe levels set by international authorities, and levels in São Paulo are estimated to be at least 25 percent higher than in Rio.[32] In Seoul, the average index of sulfur dioxide in the city registers 0.275 parts per million, which is more than five times the permissible level set by the government for discharge.[33] Measures of sulfur dioxide in the air of two other South Korean cities, Pusan and Ulsan, exceed legal levels by even greater margins.[34]

The fact that high sulfur content motor fuel is used in many countries partially explains the high levels of sulfur dioxide pollution. In Brazil, for example, the heavy motor fuel used after the 1973 oil crisis contains up to 5 percent sulfur, far higher than the 2 percent allowable in the United States and the 2.8 percent in West Germany. Yet, automobiles are only a small part of the problem—only about 9 percent of the more than 200,000 tons of sulfur dioxide measured in Rio's air in 1977 were thought to have originated from auto exhaust.[35] Most of the rest came from stationary sources—factories and industrial plants. Rio's leading sulfur spewers were oil refineries (44,000 tons); followed by asphalt plants (12,700); rubber factories (10,700); cement factories (9,400); steel plants (8,000) and a variety of small industries.[36] In Seoul and many other cities, heavy oil burned in home heating units and, even more significantly, in large thermal power generating plants, are among the leading causes of sulfur dioxide pollution.[37]

Automobiles and other transportation vehicles are also major contributors of carbon monoxide, hydrocarbons, and nitrogen oxide. Surprisingly, one major cause of hydrocarbon pollution is leakage of fumes from moving vehicles and gasoline stations. Authorities in Rio de Janeiro, for instance, estimate that .5 percent of the 1.8 billion liters of motor fuel sold from gas stations in 1977 evaporated into the atmosphere.[38] Large industries, especially steel producers, fertilizer plants, petroleum refineries, and petrochemical plants also add large quantities of hydrocarbons, carbon monoxide, and nitrogen oxide to the air.

One of the most visible forms of air pollution in developing country cities comes from the burning of raw coal, wood, charcoal, or even animal dung by households for cooking and heating purposes. Thick hazes of dark smoke are common in many cities and towns, especially in the evenings and mornings of winter months.[39] The hidden pollutants from domestic fires may be more dangerous, however. Delhi and other cities of India register highly toxic levels of carbon monoxide as a result.[40] In Seoul, domestic use of "ondol" (anthracite briquet) heating and cooking systems ranks only slightly behind automobiles as a contributor of carbon monoxide.[41]

In India, power generating stations are also large air polluters. A detailed study in Bombay found high proportions of suspended particles from coal burning stations, including Benzo (A) pyrene (a carcinogenic benezene-containing hydrocarbon), mercury, cadmium, and arsenic.[42]

Another major source of particulates in the air, in addition to fly ash from homes and power generating stations, are from stone quarrying operations which pulverize and break up rock material for construction purposes. Of the 65,000 tons of particulates released daily into Rio's air, more than 60 percent consists of powdered rock from quarrying operations.[43] Other significant contributors of particulate matter are the cement and the asphalt industries that also proliferate in rapidly expanding areas. In Malaysia, dust at one cement plant, the Rawang Cement Factory, was estimated to fall on the immediate area at a rate of 100 kilograms per hour.[44]

Solid Waste

The solid waste problem is increasing in Latin America and other developing regions at a rate far greater than population, in large measure because of greater household consumption of consumer goods and increased use of unit and convenience packaging of consumer items.[45] It is also shifting in content. Increasing amounts of plastics, aluminum cans, and other nonbiodegradable items are being used, and some of these items emit toxic fumes when burned. In addition, municipal disposal facilities have had to accommodate in recent years to handling growing amounts of sludge or dust material containing toxic substances left over from newly acquired industrial processes.

Although few figures are available regarding the amounts of solid wastes actually generated in developing countries, it is clear that disposal techniques have changed little in spite of the changing makeup of garbage. According to Malaysia's Ministry of Science, Technology and Environment, approximately 3.7 million tons of municipal waste are collected and disposed annually in the country, 44 percent by landfill, 24 percent by open burning, less than 1 percent by incineration, a small amount dumped into rivers and seas, and some 30 percent disposed of haphazardly. Solid waste disposal requires over M$60 million each year, and accounts for a loss of about M$44 million worth of recoverable materials and even more in unnecessary social costs.[46]

However, in Malaysia and virtually every other rapidly industrializing country, it is difficult to really quantify the solid waste volume or disposal method. Generally, solid wastes—including junk, such as old automobiles, household refuse, and solid wastes from industrial processes—are dumped into rivers, streams, or lakes, or heaped together in open "tips." In most cases, waste disposal sites are not selected or supervised by a governmental unit. Wastes are merely dumped at convenient locations. The dumps provide habitats for rats and insects. In addition, they can lead to the leaching and seepage of toxic and noxious materials into water supplies. Haphazard waste disposal also causes serious problems for local residents because of smoke pollution from open burnings. This has become a problem of major dimension near Mexico City's Santa Cruz Meyehualco dump.[47]

ECONOMIC, PUBLIC HEALTH, AND POLITICAL CONSEQUENCES

One of the reasons why externalities are often ignored in the development process by public as well as private actors is that the precise costs in terms of present and future GNP are virtually impossible to calculate. Nobody has any idea how much of a drag present pollution problems are on the economies of developing nations nor how much future capital expenditure will be necessary to offset the damages. Yet, there are a number of striking examples of severe local economic disruptions and public health problems in many rapidly developing nations that can be more or less quantified and can hardly go unnoticed. These "costs" are highly skewed, of course, in that they are rarely paid by those who create the problems and are generally borne disproportionately by certain geographic or economic groups of people. While this remains the rule, there also appear to be an increasing number of cases where groups which see themselves as the "losers" from pollution, or leaders who believe they can gain by taking up the cause of these groups, have successfully sought redress from pollution via the political process.

Economic Impacts

Pollution caused by the urban and industrial sectors frequently spills over and directly impinges on other sectors of the economy. Three sectors in particular are affected; all depend heavily upon the health of the natural environment— especially the water—for their continued prosperity. These are the fishing, the agricultural, and the tourist industries.

Small-time fishermen who earn their livelihood fishing in inland waterways and along the bays, inlets, and coastlines have been perhaps the hardest hit of all by the massive increases in the volume of water pollution being discharged in rapidly industrializing and urbanizing nations. Fish catches have almost without exception fallen off steadily in the bays and rivers below major third world cities in recent years. In Rio's Guanabara Bay, for example, the three major colonies of local fishermen who earn their livelihood catching the bay's fish, shrimp, lobster, and other shellfish have reported declining catches as pollution has built up within the bay.[48] In addition to slowly driving off or reducing the numbers of fish, pollution is causing significant deterioration of offshore coral reefs and coastal mangrove habitats, especially in Southeast Asia, which are essential breeding areas for marine fish and wildlife.[49] A recent survey of coral reefs off the coast of the Philippines, for example, showed that over 95 percent were in deteriorating condition and judged nearly 40 percent to be seriously endangered.[50]

But fishing interests are also plagued by immediate pollution disasters that have made large-scale fish kills, particularly in inland waterways, an almost everyday occurrence in many rapidly developing countries. Malaysia, Thailand, and a number of other countries where inland riverine fisheries still employ large numbers of peasants and supply a high percentage of the protein in the average person's diet, have been especially hard hit by the rapid increases in fish kills from increased BOD and chemical poisoning.[51]

Similarly, although to a somewhat lesser extent, small-scale rural farmers in many developing countries have suffered significant economic losses as a result of polluted water and air. In Orissa, eastern India, hundreds of farmers were forced to leave their lands because of water pollution. Effluent containing chlorine from a nearby chemical plant was seeping into their irrigation waters and bleaching or killing paddy plants.[52] Also problematical for many rural farmers are industries which tend often to be located in rural areas (mineral processing, cement, fertilizer factories) and which emit air pollutants (sulfur dioxide, in particular) which severely burn vegetation.[53]

The consequences of these sectoral transfers of the costs of pollution may prove to be quite significant in a number of developing countries where most of the population still live in rural areas and earn their living in nonindustrial sectors. In spite of the rapid industrialization going on in many countries, there are few that could afford to further diminish productivity in rural areas or could find alternative employment quickly enough for vast numbers of already marginal farmers and fishermen deprived of their livelihood by pollution.

Another type of sectoral transfer—arguably less invidious from a human welfare standpoint, but potentially more harmful to a country's supply of all-important foreign exchange—is the impact that pollution has on tourism. Here we will not even raise the esthetic side of tourist attractions, but will instead look only at the practical side. Raw sewage from urban areas and clusters of resort hotels, as well as chemical pollution from industrial facilities, has significantly affected beaches in many rapidly growing areas. In Penang, water at the beaches of large resort areas has been found to contain $E. coli$ bacterial counts seven and a half times higher than levels permissible in Hawaii.[54] In Greece, tourists have been driven from some beaches by skin burns that result from high concentrations of untreated sewage in the water.[55]

Other tourist attractions may be significantly affected as well. The Taj Mahal, the Egyptian pyramids, and the Acropolis in Athens are all threatened by pollution—high concentrations of sulfur dioxide and other corrosive air pollutants have already begun to cause major deterioration.[56]

Public Health Problems

As yet, little long-term systematic data is available to demonstrate the extent to which public health in rapidly industrializing countries is adversely affected by growing air, water, and land pollution or to estimate the direct costs of health care and the indirect costs of lost productivity, etc. However, there are some tentative studies and circumstantial evidence from a few countries to show that the public health problems and economic costs associated with pollution may be increasing steeply.

One aspect of the problem is food supply. Where fish are not being driven away or killed by pollution, they may become major public health problems when brought to market. The Penang Consumers Union tested several different varieties of fish in three different markets recently, for example, and found fecal coliform counts (as a result of sewage in the water) up to 11,000 times the safety level set by the American Public Health Association.[57] Last year in North Jakarta, thirteen children died from mercury poisoning after eating fish caught in the waters of a Jakarta Bay tributary. Mercury levels in the water, polluted by chemical and heavy metal wastes from nearby factories, were found to be sixty-two times higher than international safety levels. The childrens' deaths may only be the most visible part of the public health problem, since 85 percent of the fish consumed in the capital city of Jakarta are caught in the bay and its tributaries.[58]

Soil contamination from water pollution also affects food supplies in many areas. In the São Paulo area, an epidemic of diarrhea, intestinal parasites, and other contagious diseases broke out after subterranean groundwater polluted by the city's untreated sewage was used to irrigate crops of vegetables.[59]

The problems of subterranean water pollution in São Paulo appear to have much more draconian implications. Local officials have estimated that about 650,000 cisterns, supplying water to three million people, have been contaminated by septic tanks and municipal wastes. Dependence by so many people on contaminated water is one of the main reasons cited by these officials for the fact that São Paulo's infant mortality rate is rising having increased by 45 percent to 95 per 1,000 births in the past eighteen years.[60] The infant mortality epidemic is twice as bad in Rio, where it now hovers at 200 per 1,000 births in the fourteen-city area around the Guanabara Bay—home of eight million people. This rate, more than ten times the rate in any industrialized nation, is directly traceable to rapid buildups of pollution in the Guanabara Bay, according to the state of Rio de Janeiro's Foundation for Environmental Engineering (FEEMA).[61]

High infant mortality rates in Cubatao are even more positively linked to the astounding levels of air pollution that prevail in that ultra-industrialized area. Called the "Valley of Death" by many Brazilians, 40 of every 1,000 babies are stillborn and forty more die within the first week—the majority being deformed.[62] Of course, the health consequences of living and working in a place like Cubatao extend throughout the life cycle. The city, with a population of 80,000, registered over 40,000 emergency medical calls in 1980, with more than 10,000 related to tuberculosis, pneumonia, bronchitis, emphysema, asthma, and related nose and throat ailments.[63] In the first six months of 1980, emergency calls for respiratory problems in one area of Cubatao rose by 50 percent after nearby fertilizer plants began to use sedimentary rocks whose dust was not easily captured by chimney filters.[64]

In Mexico, up to 30 percent of 100,000 residents living in proximity to three cement factories are thought to have contracted respiratory ailments and silicosis before the government forced the plants to shut down. Prior to their closing, these plants emitted about 300 tons of cement dust daily.[65]

Pollution and Politics

Obviously some of these numerous problems are likely to be addressed more quickly or with more conviction by developing country governments than are others. What helps determine which pollution problems will receive attention *and* some modicum of easement? We do not propose to discuss here the regulatory initiatives taken in developing countries to control pollution.[66] Suffice to say, a surprising number of governments have put a wide variety of pollution regulations on the books in the last decade, but these regulations are rarely enforced with systematic vigor.[67] Many overarching pollution problems are also being very slowly addressed through small programs with small budgetary allotments. The question we examine here is: What factors propel governments to take more urgent action to combat pollution?

The first point to emphasize is that the factors are generally localized. Crackdowns on polluters in one area do not seem to translate regularly into other areas or sectors unless the circumstances are the same. This being the case, it seems that three types of political pressures are most likely to push a government to redress localized pollution problems in the immediate term. One circumstance which induces governments to respond is when pollution is severe enough to threaten an entire sector of the economy on a local or regional basis and that sector is important to the national economy or the political needs of a government. By imposing marginal cleanup costs on private or public bodies in the industrial and urban sector—since it is generally true that the first 50 percent of pollution reduction is comparatively inexpensive—a government may reduce major political or economic disruptions in the three environment-dependent sectors discussed above, fisheries, agriculture, and tourism.

The clearest cases of intersectoral, economically motivated environmental politics found throughout the developing world in recent years have been those involving fishermen and farmers. In growing numbers of cases, the economic hardship caused by pollution of fishing grounds and fertile lands have become acute and widespread enough that governments must formulate some means of response. If the source of the pollution—a lone paper mill, for example—can be isolated, governments have sometimes opted simply to close down the plant. Villagers in the southern Indian state of Andhra Pradesh recently forced the closure of a paper mill which was polluting the water—their lifeblood for fish, irrigation, and domestic purposes.[68]

On other occasions, especially when the sources of pollution are many and deeply imbedded in regional or nationwide economic development, governments have tried to balance the costs to rural economic activities by forcing local industries and municipal governments to take piecemeal steps that alleviate the most severe consequences. A good example is found in the Malaysian government's response to pollution caused by the palm industry. Although the industry still is a heavy polluter, especially since it continues to grow in overall output, significant cutbacks have been made in the amount of pollution per unit in recent years and some of the most acute hardships imposed on farmers and fishermen have been eased.[69]

However, in a number of instances, governments have found the alleviation of pollution too costly or the damages too extreme and have resorted to compensation or relocation of those rural economic interests affected. In Inchon and Onsan Bays, for example, pollution became so bad that the government of South Korea agreed to pay local farmers and fishermen who protested that their livelihoods were ruined.[70]

Intersectoral environmental politics is especially notable in the rapidly industrializing nations of Southeast Asia.[71] This is probably because fish make up such an important part of the diet (generally about 75 percent of protein intake), because irrigated paddy agriculture is obviously most severely affected by polluted water, and because high population densities in rural areas make the clashes more dramatic and unavoidable.

Governments also seem to have a higher propensity to take steps to deal with pollution problems when strategic elites or political leaders either feel directly impinged upon by pollution or for various reasons view pollution as shameful and a reflection upon themselves or their nation.

Millions of poor Mexico City residents have long suffered the huge clouds of smoke and assorted chemicals that billow from outdoor burning at the city's municipal waste dump at Santa Cruz Meyehualco. But this only became an issue for serious political discussion after toxic gray clouds from the dump drifted for twenty miles into the richest suburbs of Mexico City in spring 1981. Suddenly, there was a major outcry about pollution from the dump among businessmen and government officials, and the government hastily began studying plans to move the dump and build a garbage processing plant.[72] As might be suspected, however, little more has been done in the year since the clouds receded from the wealthier quarters of the city.

Many Indian MPs argued recently in parliamentary debates that the government should take action to curb fly ash pollution from power stations in New Delhi. One major reason they cited was that it is a disgrace to India for the national capital to be covered with soot.[73] In Nigeria, action to alleviate the health problems caused by open sewers and poor sewage disposal has been catalyzed by middle- and upper-class citizens who are largely unaffected. They, too, see this as a reflection on them in the eyes of the outside world.[74] In Argentina, the military governor of one state has initiated steps to reduce pollution threatening coastal estuaries and marshlands, in large part because he grew up in the area and fondly remembers its rich fish and game and natural beauty.[75]

But political leaders, parties, and opposition organizations have also seen increased opportunities to mobilize supportive constituencies around their advocacy or delivery of antipollution measures. This is especially true for local politicians in highly urban areas. A recent newspaper article in Brazil noted:

Lately, public outcry has had a snowball effect as communities watch public demands give way to results. Those who once beat on the doors of City Hall for help are now surprised to find City Hall joining the protest.[76]

Thus, in response to growing public concern about pollution in the Jundai River, the mayor of Jundai, Brazil, organized the Jundai Front in order to lobby state and federal authorities to take action.[77] In Cordoba, Spain, the current mayor, a member of the Communist party, was elected several years ago in large part because he focused his campaign on pollution in the Guadalquivir River and capitalized on widespread antipollution sentiments among noncommunist voters.[78]

Pollution has even played a role in national politics and elections. The elevation of Socialist Andreas Papandreou from opposition leader to prime minister of Greece in 1981 is at least partly attributable to the Socialist's effective mobilization of antipollution sentiments in Athens, home of 30 percent of Greece's voters. Athens's Socialist mayor, Demetrios Beis, spearheaded a large grassroots protest movement in Athens which decried air and water pollution in the city and blamed the government of former Prime Minister George Rallis.[79]

But pollution has also become an issue around which antisystem opposition groups in some countries have sought to mobilize support for their own political program. In such cases, governments have sometimes found it advantageous to respond to pollution problems in order to defuse the issue. In the Basque region of Spain, for example, environmental protest has become an important way to express sentiments against the central government and in favor of regional autonomy. Industrial pollution, particularly in Bilbao, is viewed as a result and a symbol of external control over the Basque economy. Wall posters painted throughout the Basque region—supporting the terrorist separatist group, ETA, the more moderate separatist political party, Herri Batasuna, or other groups favoring some form of regional autonomy—often oppose nuclear power and decry pollution, singling out especially American-owned companies for criticism. Partly as a result of such a protest, the central government of Spain has initiated a campaign to clean up Bilbao.[80]

In Mexico, little organized public concern has yet been manifested about pollution in general, in spite of the fact that Mexico City is now widely regarded as one of the most polluted cities in the world. However, current officials in the administration of President Miguel de la Madrid, as well as political planners for the *Partido Revolucionario Institucional* (PRI) are increasingly worried that pollution may become a major political issue in the future.

One concern is that a prolonged temperature inversion in Mexico City during the dry (winter) season may cause a "killer smog" situation such as occurred in London, Tokyo, and Donora, Pennsylvania, and that the government will be ill prepared to respond in the short term to such a disaster.[81] Another fear, especially on the part of PRI political strategists, is that if the economy picks up, quality of life issues—pollution, clean water, traffic congestion, crime, etc.— may become important means by which Mexico's other political parties, especially the coalition of Left parties and the moderate Right party *Partido Accion Nacional* (PAN), seek to mobilize support.[82]

In fact, prior to the 1982 political campaign, PRI officials commissioned studies on the "Green Party" movement in Europe in an effort to assess the likelihood of such parties emerging in Mexico. During his election campaign in 1982, de la Madrid made an effort to make concern about pollution an important campaign issue.[83] In December 1982, shortly after taking office, President de la Madrid announced a governmental reorganization that centralized responsibility for conservation and environmental pollution control efforts in a new Secretariat of Urban Development and Ecology (SDUE). Since then, SDUE officials have sought to revise Mexican pollution control laws and to show for President de la Madrid's administration a record of success on at least the most urgent and visible pollution problems.[84]

SOME PUBLIC POLICY CHOICES

It is not likely that even large increases in the successful examples of the environmental political activism noted in the last section will collectively add up to anything like a solution to the pollution problems now plaguing most rapidly developing nations. As in most other issue areas, those with political power or who can find powerful patrons to advance their cause may find ways to insulate themselves from the costs of pollution or to distribute the costs more broadly. On an across-the-board basis, however, a legacy of weak or inadequate legislation, sporadic or nonexistent enforcement, and pitifully small penalties give little hope that a strict regulatory response to pollution problems will be formulated in the reasonable future—even where the adverse economic and public health consequences are marked.

At the same time, development planning processes and public policy choices have increasingly been influenced by consideration of pollution concerns, as it has grown clearer that many problems can be reduced or alleviated in advance by more attention to spatial and locational planning, the provision of infrastructure, and the choice and efficient use of raw materials in the production process. Some of the long-term public policy choices affected by pollution considerations are raised briefly below.

Location of Industry

One of the questions which virtually every rapidly growing country addresses is that of whether it should seek to disperse or concentrate its industries. Theoretically, there are advantages to both approaches from an environmental perspective. By creating so-called black holes—as, for example, Sweden has done—a country can concentrate its pollution control efforts and segregate major urban areas and desirable natural places from the worst industrial development. By contrast, the careful spreading of at least large-scale industrial development around the countryside may significantly reduce the problems related to the "multiplier" effects of pollution in many large urban areas.

In practice, few countries have such stark choices. Most already have a few areas that are not only overindustrialized and heavily polluted, but overurbanized in comparison to the rest of the country as well. Many rapidly industrializing countries—Mexico, Brazil, South Korea, Thailand, India, Spain, Colombia, to name just a few—are trying to move more industry away from the traditional areas of heavy industrialization and establish new, more manageable industrial growth poles.

Still, it remains true in most cases that industries deemed important enough by a government will be able to locate in even the most overpopulated, congested, and polluted areas if they push hard enough. Politicians, even if not planners, maintain what one Irish environmentalist describes as "mental pollution parks."[85] On the other hand, whether they disperse or concentrate industry on a regional basis, it is clear that concerns about pollution have been one factor prompting most rapidly industrializing countries to cluster industries in industrial estates where they can be segregated from other areas and take advantage of larger-scale cost savings in the provision of waste disposal and other infrastructure. This is an especially important step for reducing pollution problems in small- and medium-sized industries.

Industrial Specialization

Another public policy choice that may increasingly be influenced by pollution factors is the question of industrial specialization. Much of the recent progress by the world's rapidly industrializing countries has come as a result of expanded integration into the world industrial production system. In most instances, especially for small- and medium-sized countries in this category, countries have found particular manufacturing specializations to exploit as their comparative advantage—based on a combination of labor costs, geographical location, workforce skills, raw material availability, and other factors which determine what goods they can produce most competitively. In addition, transfers of technology from the developed countries—whether in the form of wholly owned subsidiaries of multinational corporations, joint venture projects, licensing agreements, or outright sale of equipment—have figured strategically in the industrial development of most of these countries.

The increasing number of countries competing to move up the industrial ladder by redefining their international comparative advantage and importing Western technologies heightens the possibility that environmental factors will affect a country's overall industrial development strategy. The choice of industries to build up and products to sell on the international market, for example, may be influenced by a country's willingness or unwillingness to accept technologies and productive processes that are heavily regulated in the advanced nations. Some countries may choose to compete for Western industries on this basis; others may refuse to accept industries which appear to be searching for a convenient haven from stringent environmental regulations. There appear to have been cases of both among rapidly industrializing countries in the 1970s.

However, it appears now that many rapidly industrializing countries are less willing than they were in the past to accept environmental side effects as the price for attracting new investments from multinational corporations. Early in the 1970s, governments and labor unions in industrialized countries expressed fear that many developing countries would try to attract foreign investment by offering multinational corporations "pollution havens" to escape the strict regulations the companies faced in their home nations. Some leaders in developing countries felt that lax pollution controls might help accelerate their nation's industrial development. Others, however, noted that competition among developing countries to attract investments on the basis of inadequate environmental regulations would result. Some observers pointed out that it would become difficult for a developing country, after it had attained a level of industrialization for which regulations would be considered desirable, to enact environmental standards. There would always be the fear of losing international investment to other countries still willing to accept any amount of pollution as the price for industrial development.[86]

Some types of production banned or stringently regulated in Europe and the United States now are tending to take place in rapidly industrializing countries. These include the production of asbestos, various dyes, and certain highly toxic chemicals. To date, however, there appears to have been no large-scale flight of industries to developing countries as a result of differences in pollution regulations.[87]

Several factors explain the absence of geographical shifts by multinational companies seeking to reduce pollution control expenditures. Such costs often are not very large when compared to the other factors that influence corporate siting decisions: labor costs, transportation costs, marketing considerations, political and economic stability, availability of infrastructure, trade barriers, and so on. Of equal importance, environmental constraints have emerged in many of the rapidly industrializing countries most attractive to multinational corporations. Many countries—such as Brazil and Venezuela in South America; South Korea, Singapore, and Taiwan in Asia; and Spain and Ireland on the periphery of Europe—have recently adopted much tighter pollution control and land use regulations.[88]

Some industrializing countries have the luxury of being more choosy than others. There appear to be few cases in which underindustrialized nations have spurned industries for environmental reasons if other alternatives were not readily available. Nevertheless, the number of countries willing to accept all comers, no matter how serious the threat of pollution or public health problems, clearly has shrunk in recent years. At the very least, most countries have become much better at negotiating with foreign companies about pollution control measures and at anticipating potential problems in advance of new plant construction.

Regulating and Bargaining with MNCs

A related question is whether it makes a difference from a pollution perspective if a country opts to solicit multinational corporations to build necessary industrial facilities or opts to rely on domestic industries, either parastatal or privately owned. The popular rhetoric, of course, is that MNCs are polluting and plundering in the third world with abandon. But, in reality, it may be far easier for an industrializing country to induce multinational corporations to take antipollution measures than domestically owned companies.

There clearly are examples in other parts of the world where U.S. firms have caused serious pollution problems. One recent report described, for example, how subsidiaries of American firms were creating serious problems in several countries: a Pennwalt affiliate in Nicaragua discharging mercury into a lake; a Johns Manville affiliate in India where workers observe no precautions around asbestos fibers; a Kaiser cement operation in Indonesia which has grossly polluted its surrounding area; a battery factory operated by Union Carbide in Indonesia where up to half of the workers have liver damage from mercury exposure.[89] Another report claimed that the United States was witnessing a "wholesale" exodus of "killer" industries to nonregulating export platforms in developing countries.[90] Yet, most of the documented examples are relegated to discrete categories: old industries set up a number of years ago and difficult to re-equip; low-technology operations such as mineral processing; industries which are declining in the advanced countries, not only in production but in product demand as well.[91]

For high-technology multinational producers building large integrated production plants, pollution control measures are routinely taken anywhere they locate. Most companies have the technology and the know-how to alleviate many of the most serious potential pollution problems and to operate modern efficient plants. In few cases will their investment decisions be influenced by the incremental additional costs of complying with reasonable pollution standards. This gives government officials an opportunity to ensure that incoming industries do not contribute substantially to existing pollution problems in the country.

Sometimes, in fact, MNCs have had a catalytic effect at the local level in developing countries. A Malaysian industrial sociologist, for example, says MNCs in Malaysia offered a sharp contrast to Malaysian firms that could not be overlooked:

Some of the multinationals, particularly the oil companies, were sensitive to their behavior abroad, and it just may have been easier to build their installations to the same standard everywhere. Whatever the reason, people began to become aware that something could be done to save the fish in the rivers.[92]

There is another reason why industrializing nations have a degree of latitude to drive a hard bargain on pollution control: most pollution control standards for industrial plants in industrializing nations are allocated on a case-by-case basis, according to the whim of local or national officials, the amount of public pressure, and some rough calculation of local "assimilative" capacity. Because of the ad hoc nature of this process, it appears that MNCs are being asked to abide by stricter standards in most countries than they would have to meet if they were locally owned or if the same regulations applied to all industry because of national standards.

In Spain, for example, the level of environmental concern among government officials and the general public is not very high. But, when it comes to multinational corporations, both the officials and the general public tend to have a markedly different attitude. Alfonso Ensenat, subdirector general for the industrial environment in the Ministry of Industry and Energy, explains one of the reasons why a double standard exists in everyone's mind even if not in the law itself:

There are two types of technology: pre-ecological ones and ecological ones. We have to be very careful to make sure that a foreign company will use the second type here, because if not, the public opinion will sooner or later turn against the company. Spaniards are very proud people. If we permit *our* industries to pollute *our* rivers, that is our business. But if a foreign company comes here and makes contamination, it is an insult to Spain.[93]

Mexican government officials are only at a very preliminary stage in attempting to deal with the country's pollution problems. National regulations governing the air emissions and water effluents of industry are still rudimentary, and even these are rarely enforced. The Mexican public, too, is notoriously apathetic about pollution problems, whether because of concern for persistent widespread poverty or the feeling that it is the responsibility of the government to find remedies.

Officials in Mexico openly admit that much new industrial development of recent years has not been carefully planned from an ecological standpoint and that one of the ways companies and the government have attempted to reduce initial capital costs is by minimizing outlays for pollution control devices.

Yet even in Mexico, there are limits to what companies, particularly foreign companies, can get away with. And these limits have been shrinking quickly. Mexican government officials recently initiated a system for evaluating new industrial proposals for potential ecological consequences and pollution problems. And they now require all new factories to receive a permit for air and water discharges from the Ministry of Health and Welfare.

In addition, industrial development planners in Mexico have become more concerned about pollution and health matters in judging which types of foreign firms Mexico should attract. Manuel Medellin Milan, former subdirector for the chemical industry in the Ministry of National Patrimony and Industrial Development, says there is increasing sentiment against the concept that Mexico can bear higher levels of contamination because it is a developing country. He says the ministry recently rejected a proposal from an American company to build a new plant to produce asbestos products in Mexico:

We did not accept the company's motives for wanting to come to Mexico. We think the problems of asbestos have been exaggerated in the United States, but we do not want to get involved with a company if it is running away from those problems. We are prepared to live with the risks associated with asbestos if it is for our own domestic needs, but we will not accept asbestos companies anymore if they want solely to produce for export.[94]

Allocation of Assimilative Capacity

Finally, since most rapidly industrializing nations will continue to rely for quite some time on the assimilative capacity of their waterways, the question of allocating that capacity is likely to become an increasingly politicized one in the future. Should priority go to municipalities or industry? That is, should the public or the private sector be the first to build water treatment facilities as assimilative capacities are severely strained and key waterways deteriorated?

In many rapidly industrializing countries, little or no long-term planning takes place to make such choices on a conscious basis. Rather, large industries—because of their employment-generating potential and their obvious need for a pollution repository—are often promised continued permission to dump raw effluents into rivers, bays, and coastal waters. Although these water bodies may be perfectly capable of cleansing themselves under existing levels of effluent, problems may arise later on when more industries cluster in the area or the urban population grows substantially.

As the self-cleansing capacity of a local water body is reached, the dilemma posed is whether to permit continued wanton pollution by all sources (often what occurs until a crisis arises); to require newcoming industries to make pollution control investments, forcing them to suffer a competitive disadvantage since older industries have assured pollution rights; to renege on agreements with existing industries and force all industries to make arrangements to treat their wastes; or to force the municipal governments to shoulder the burden by building new sewage treatment facilities. Careful advance planning can at least make these choices explicit, ensuring that a portion of the assimilative capacity is reserved for municipal growth and possibly leading to the planning of joint treatment facilities between public and private institutions.

Notes

1. Martin Melosi, ed., *Pollution and Reform in American Cities, 1870–1930* (Austin, Texas: University of Texas, 1980), p. 3.

2. Daniel M. Dworkin, ed., *Environment and Development*, Collected Papers, Summary Reports, and Recommendations SCOPE/UNEP Symposium on Environmental Sciences in Developing Countries, Nairobi, February 11–23, 1974 (Indianapolis, Ind.: SCOPE, 1974), pp. 400–401.

3. Karen Lowe, "São Paulo's Rivers Gag on the Filth," *Brazil Herald*, June 27, 1979.

4. United States Agency for International Development, *Environmental and Natural Resource Management in Developing Countries: A Report to Congress*, Vol. 1 (Washington, D.C. USAID, Department of State, February 1979), p. 109.

5. O. P. Dwivedi, "India: Pollution Control Policy and Programmes," *International Review of Administrative Sciences* 43, no. 2 (1977): p. 125.

6. Alaba Akinesete, "Some Pollution Problems in Nigeria," in *Pollution: Engineering and Scientific Solutions*, edited by Eral S. Barrekette (New York: Plenum Press, 1973), p. 648.

7. Peter H. Freeman, "The Environmental Impact of Rapid Urbanization: Guidelines for Policy and Planning," (Washington, D.C.: Smithsonian Institution, 1974), p. 68.

8. Rejeandran and Michael Reich, "The Double Burden of Health Problems: A Picture of the Situation in Malaysia." Undated mimeo, p. 9.

9. Sohabat Alan Malaysia, *State of the Malaysian Environment, 1980/81: Development Without Destruction?* (Penang, Malaysia: Sahabat Alam Malaysia, June 5, 1981), p. 11.

10. "Draft Environmental Report on Thailand." Prepared by the Science and Technology Division Library of Congress, for the United States Agency for International Development, p. 24.

11. Ralph A. Luken, "Economic Analysis of Effluent Standards." Regional Seminar on Environmental Aspects of Development (Bangkok, Thailand: UN Asian Development Institute, 1976), p. 5.

12. Lowe, "Rivers Gag on Filth."

13. This point is emphasized in *UNEP—Asia Report 1979* (Thailand: United Nations Regional Office for Asia and the Pacific, February 1980), p. 11.

14. Dwivedi, "India," p. 125.

15. Lowe, "Rivers Gag on Filth."

16. *UNEP—Asia Report 1979*, p. 24.

17. World Bank, "Indonesia: Appraisal of the Second Urban Development Project" (Washington, D.C., 1976), p. 5.

18. Institute of Environmental Research, "Pollution Problem of Heavy Metal in the Environment in Thailand" (Bangkok, Thailand: Chulalongkorn University, 1977), p. 4.

19. See, especially, USAID, *A Report to Congress*, p. 78.

20. Modhumita Mojumdar, "India: Poverty, Population and Pollution," *Christian Science Monitor*, November 12, 1981.

21. Dick Riley with Chris Kerrebrock, *Environment Latin America: Facing the Realities of Rapid Growth* (New York: World Environment Center, 1981), p. 19.

22. *UNEP—Asia Report 1979*.

23. Richard Cole, "Guanabara Bay Poses Health Threat," *Brazil Herald*, June 27, 1979.

24. USAID, *A Report to Congress*, p. 109.

25. Riley and Kerrebrock, *Realities of Rapid Growth* p. 27.

26. Richard Cole, "What Is Poisoning Rio's Air?" *Brazil Herald*, June 30–July 1, 1979.

27. Malaysia, *Malaysian Environment*, p. 16. The figure was for 1977. Sahabat Alam Malaysia estimates that the total air pollution had grown to 930,000 tons by 1981. Moreover, the number of automobiles in Malaysia is growing very fast, having expanded from 940,000 in 1973 to 1,800,000 in 1978 (almost 100 percent in five years)!

28. Richard Cole, "Rio is Poisoning Itself to Death," *Brazil Herald*, June 29, 1979.

29. See *Ibid.*, for the Rio figure. Mexico City's estimate comes from Riley and Kerrebrock, *Realities of Rapid Growth*, p. 26, which also reports that in an effort to speed up auto circulation in Mexico City some of the city's traffic circles are being dismantled.

30. Jyoti Parikh, "Environmental Problems in India and Their Possible Trends in the Future," *Environmental Conservation* 4, no. 3 (1977): p. 190.

31. Cole, "Poisoning Rio's Air?"; Rejeandran and Reich, "Double Burden," p. 8.

32. Cole, "Rio Poisoning Itself."

33. *World Environment Report*, November 15, 1981, p. 3.

34. USAID, *A Report to Congress*, p. 76.

35. Cole, "Poisoning Rio's Air."

36. *Ibid.*

37. USAID, *A Report to Congress* pp. 76–77, 80–81.

38. Cole, "Poisoning Rio's Air."

39. USAID, *A Report to Congress*, pp. 76–77, 80–81.

40. Mojumdar, "India."

41. USAID, *A Report to Congress*, p. 81.

42. Mojumdar, "India."

43. Cole, "Poisoning Rio's Air."

44. Consumer's Association of Penang, *The Malaysian Environment: Heading for Disaster* (Penang, Malaysia: CAP, 1980), p. 2.

45. USAID, *A Report to Congress*, pp. 79–80, 108–109.

46. Rejeandran and Reich, "Double Burden," p. 6. For a detailed study, see Persatuan Perlindungan Alam Sekitar Malaysia (EPSM), *Sampah Sarap-Rubbish* (Petaling Joya, Malaysia: EPSM, November 1979).

47. Christopher Dickey, "Burning Refuse Dump Chokes Mexico City, Arouses Ragpickers' Ire," *The Washington Post*, April 12, 1979.

48. Cole, "Guanabara Bay."

49. USAID, *A Report to Congress, p. 107.*

50. *World Environment Report,* November 30, 1981, p. 5.

51. See, for example, Rejeandran and Reich, "Double Burden," pp. 10–11.

52. *World Environment Report,* November 15, 1981, p. 5.

53. For example, a cement plant near Lagos, Nigeria, "burned out" vegetation on large areas of surrounding farmland, p. 649.

54. Akinesete, "Problems in Nigeria," p. 14.

55. "Greece: A Cloud Hangs Over the Fall Elections," *World Business Weekly,* June 1, 1981, p. 8.

56. Robert Frega, "Pollution is Destroying Egypt's Sphinx and Pyramids," *World Environment Report,* November 15, 1981, p. 5; Dr. Desh Bandhu, "Environmental Situation in India" (Stockholm: Swedish International Development Agency, March 1980) p. 6.

57. Rejeandran and Reich, "Double Burden," p. 5.

58. *World Environment Report,* October 30, 1981.

59. Cole, "Guanabara Bay."

60. Warren Hoge, "New Menace in Brazil's 'Valley of Death' Strikes Unborn," *The New York Times,* September 23, 1980.

61. Cole, "Guanabara Bay."

62. Hoge, "Valley of Death."

63. *Ibid.*

64. *Ibid.*

65. Riley and Kerrebrock, *Rapid Growth,* p. 27.

66. Two sources of information on the pollution control laws passed by particular countries are: Hope Johnson and Janice Marie Johnson, *Environmental Policies in Developing Countries* (Siegburg, West Germany: Erich Schmidt Verlag, 1977); and the more than thirty-five draft environmental reports on individual developing countries completed thus far for the USAID.

67. The problem of actually implementing laws passed is discussed in H. Jeffrey Leonard and David Morell, "The Emergence on Environmental Concern in Developing Countries: A Political Perspective," *Stanford Journal of International Law* 17, no. 2 (Summer 1981).

68. Mojumdar, "India."

69. Rejeandran and Reich, "Double Burden"; Malaysia, *Malaysian Environment.*

70. USAID, *A Report to Congress,* pp. 78–79. The government has agreed to pay $62 million in compensation to relocate 12,000 people living near the Onson International Complex, for example. *World Environment Report,* February 28, 1981, p. 5.

71. USAID, *A Report to Congress.*

72. Dickey, "Burning Refuse Dump."

73. Mojumdar, "India."

74. M. K. C. Scidhar, P. A. Oludwande, and A. O. Okubadejo, "Health Hazards and Pollution from Open Drains in a Nigerian City," *Ambio* 10, no. 1 (1981).

75. A colleague at The Conservation Foundation, Dr. John Clark, a world expert on coastal planning and management, was invited by the state government in 1980 to observe the area and suggest alternatives for the government.

76. Cole, "Poisoning Rio's Air?" and "Rio Poisoning Itself."

77. *Ibid*.

78. Personal interview with Julio Anquita, mayor of Cordoba, Spain, in Cordoba, July 1, 1980.

79. "Greece: A Cloud Hangs." Also, "Greek Census Reflects Appeal of Farms over Crowded, Dirty Cities," *The New York Times*, May 10, 1981.

80. The observation is based upon numerous interviews conducted in the Basque region of Spain during June 1980.

81. Interview with Juan Enriquez, coordinator, Subsecretariat for Regional Development, Secretariat for Programs and Budgets (SPP), May 7, 1983, in Mexico City.

82. Interview with Socrates Rizzo, director general of economic and social programs, SPP, July 15, 1982, in Mexico City.

83. See *Partido Revolucionario Institucional*, "Consulta Popular en Las Reuniones Nacionales: Media Ambiente y Calidad de Vida," proceedings of the meeting at Ciudad del Carmen, Campeche, on February 13, 1982.

84. Since fall 1982, shortly before the de la Madrid government took office, the Conservation Foundation has been providing advice and information to officials within the Mexican government who are attempting to revamp existing pollution regulations and reorganize governmental responsibility for addressing pollution problems.

85. Yvonne Scannell.

86. These points are discussed extensively in H. Jeffrey Leonard," "Environmental Regulations, Multinational Corporations and Industrial Development in the 1980s," *Habitat International* 6, no. 2 (1982); and Leonard and Morell, "Emergence of Concern."

87. H. Jeffrey Leonard, "Siting New Industry: An International Perspective," A Summary of the International Findings of the Conservation Foundation's Industrial Siting Project (Washington, D.C.: The Conservation Foundation, 1983).

88. Leonard and Morell, "Emergence of Concern."

89. Bob Wyrick, "Hazards for Export," a ten-part series in *Newsday* (Long Island, New York), December 13–22, 1981.

90. Barry Castleman, "How We Export Dangerous Industries," *Business and Society*, Fall 1978.

91. See footnote 86. Also, H. Jeffrey Leonard, "Pollution Plagues Industrial Firms in Growing Nations," *The Conservation Foundation Letter*, August 1982, and H. Jeffrey Leonard and Christopher J. Duerksen, "Environmental Regulations and the Location of Industry: An International Perspective," *Columbia Journal of World Business* 15, no. 2 (Summer 1980).

92. Pamela G. Hollie, "Malaysia Confronts Environment Issues," *The New York Times*, January 25, 1981.

93. Interview with Alfonso Ensenat in Madrid, June 11, 1980.

94. Interview with Manuel Medellin Milan in Mexico City, July 16, 1982.

ABOUT THE AUTHORS

Henry Bienen is William Stewart Tod Professor of Politics and International Affairs in the Woodrow Wilson School at Princeton University. Prof. Bienen is author of numerous books and articles on Africa and political development and is general editor of Holmes & Meier's series on the Political Economy of Income Distribution in Developing Countries.

George Ledec is currently working for the World Bank's Office of Environmental Affairs. Mr. Ledec is coauthor of *Environmental Management in Tropical Agriculture* and holds an MPA from the Woodrow Wilson School, Princeton University.

H. Jeffrey Leonard is a Senior Associate with the Conservation Foundation in Washington, D.C. Dr. Leonard is author of *Are Environmental Regulations Driving Industry Abroad?* and many articles and reports concerning environmental problems in developing countries.

David Morell is Special Assistant to the Regional Administrator (San Francisco) for the Environmental Protection Agency and coauthor of *Siting Hazardous Waste Facilities*. Previously Dr. Morell was Senior Political Scientist at the Center for Energy and Environmental Studies, Princeton University.

James T. Thomson is in the Washington Office of Associates in Rural Development and author of numerous articles on environmental management in the Sahel countries of Africa. Dr. Thomson was previously Assistant Profesor at Lafayette University.

Joanna Poznanski is an economist specializing in environmental affairs. Dr. Poznanski has published articles in Poland and the United States on environmental politics and environmental economics.

INDEX

Agricultural production: in ancient civilizations, 23–26, 41–42; environmental concerns and, 60–63; governmental interference with, 115–16; greenhouse effect and, 186; international support for, 8–9, 43–44; labor excesses in, 116–18; overspecialization in exports from, 65–66; relative access to land and, 105; in the Sahel, 228, 229–35, 239, 240–42, 249; shifting of, to other areas, 25–26, 29–30; slash-and-burn method of, 15, 187–95, 204–5; sustainability of, 7–8. *See also* Water management

Agroforestry, 194–95, 216

Air pollution, 148–50, 272–74; in Brazil, 110, 141, 143, 272, 273–74, 278; in India, 274, 280; in Malaysia, 273, 274; in Mexico, 272, 273, 278, 280, 281–82; in South Korea, 149, 273, 274

Aldridge, T. E., 148

Amazonia, 191–92, 193, 205, 206

Anderson, Perry, 28

Angola, 75

Aztec empire, 24

Bangladesh, 118–19

Baumol, William, 70

Becht, J. E., 42

Belzung, L. D., 42

Bilsky, Lester, 34–35

Birth rates, 63

Bolivia, 120

Boulding, Kenneth, 6

Brandt Commission, 4, 62

Braudel, Fernand, 27

Brazil, 152, 215; air pollution in, 110, 141, 143, 272, 273–74, 278; cattle raising in, 204, 205, 206, 212–13; emergence of environmental concern in, 139–40; industrial wood plantations in, 200–

201; nongovernmental organizations in, 214; planning for population growth in, 77; political issues of environmental policy in, 155; resettlement program of, 191–92; resource exploitation in, 123–24; water pollution in, 268–69, 270–72, 276, 278, 280–81

Brown, Lester, 42, 73–74

Brunei, 211

Bryan, William Jennings, 64–65

Building a Sustainable Society (Brown), 42

Burma, 195

Caiden, Naomi, 166

Capital, 52, 61

Carr, Claudia, 113

Carter, Jimmy, 100

Cattle raising: in Brazil, 204, 205, 206, 212–13; deforestation and, 204–8; in the Sahel, 228, 232, 235–37, 238, 239–40

Challenge/response theory, 30

China, 35, 61, 63, 75, 119; lack of environmental personnel in, 156; noise pollution studies in, 141

Citizen protests, 159–61; against deforestation, 214, 215; lack of, in the Sahel, 244–47, 252; against pollution, 280–82; relative importance of, 167–68; in rural areas, 163

Class: access to land resources and, 105–6, 107, 237–42, 250, 253; deforestation harm and, 16, 186–87; desertification and, 17; land management problems and, 12

Clausen, A. W., 140–41

Coal, 7, 53

Cohen, Nicholas, 73

Colombia, 184

Colonialism, in the Sahel, 244–47

DATE DUE

MY 6 '8B			
NO 13 '91			
MR 12 '92			
MR 12 '92			
AP 8 '92			
JUN 2 1 2007			

DEMCO 38-297